FROMMER'S

COMPREHENSIVE
TRAVEL GUIDE

Mexico City

1st Edition

by Marita Adair

D0112650

MACMILLAN • USA

ABOUT THE AUTHOR

Marita Adair's lifelong passion for Mexico's culture, people, and history began at age 11 on her first trip across the border to Nogales. An award-winning travel writer, she specializes in writing about Mexico and is the author of six Frommer guides to that country. Her freelance photographs and articles about Mexico have appeared in numerous newspapers and magazines, including the *Fort Worth Star-Telegram, Dallas Morning News, Houston Post, Chicago Tribune, USAir Magazine, Sunset,* and *Vacations.*

MACMILLAN TRAVEL

A Simon & Schuster Macmillan Company
15 Columbus Circle
New York, NY 10023

Copyright © 1995 by Simon & Schuster, Inc.

All rights reserved. No part of this book may be reproduced or transmitted in any form or by any means, electronic or mechanical, including photocopying, recording, or by any information storage and retrieval system, without permission in writing from the Publisher.

Macmillan is a registered trademark of Macmillan, Inc.

ISBN 0-02-860059-2
ISSN 1080-7020

Editor: Ian Wilker
Map Editor: Douglas Stallings
Editorial Assistant: Jim Moore
Design by Michele Laseau
Maps by Ortelius Design

SPECIAL SALES

Bulk purchases (10+ copies) of Frommer's Travel Guides are available to corporations at special discounts. The Special Sales Department can produce custom editions to be used as premiums and/or for sales promotion to suit individual needs. Existing editions can be produced with custom cover imprints such as corporate logos. For more information write to: Special Sales, Simon & Schuster, 1230 Avenue of the Americas, New York, NY 10020.

Manufactured in the United States of America

Contents

SPECIAL FEATURES

List of Maps

What the Symbols Mean

 FROMMER'S FAVORITES—Hotels, restaurants, attractions, and entertainments you should not miss

$ **SUPER-SPECIAL VALUES**—Really exceptional values

In Hotel & Other Listings

The following symbols refer to the standard amenities available in all rooms:

A/C   air conditioning
MINIBAR   refrigerator stocked with beverages and snacks
TEL   telephone
TV   television

Trip Planning with this Guide

Use the following features:

Calendar of Events   To plan for or avoid

Easy-to-Read Maps   Walking tours, city sights, hotel and restaurant locations—all referring to or keyed to the text

Fast Facts   All the essentials at a glance: climate, currency, embassies, emergencies, information, safety, taxes, tipping, and more

Suggested Itineraries   For seeing the city and environs

What Things Cost In   To help you plan your daily budget

What's Special About Checklist   A summary of the city's highlights

OTHER SPECIAL FROMMER FEATURES

Did You Know?   Offbeat, fun facts

Famous Capitalinos   The city's greats

Impressions   What others have said

An Invitation to the Reader

In researching this book, I discovered many wonderful places—hotels, restaurants, shops, and more. I'm sure you'll find others. Please tell us about them, so we can share the information with your fellow travelers in upcoming editions. If you were disappointed with a recommendation, we'd love to know that, too. Please write to:

Marita Adair
Mexico City, 1st Edition
Macmillan Travel
15 Columbus Circle
New York, NY 10023

An Additional Note

Please be advised that travel information is subject to change at any time—and this is especially true of prices. We therefore suggest that you write or call ahead for confirmation when making your travel plans. The authors, editors, and publisher cannot be held responsible for the experiences of readers while traveling. Your safety is important to us, however, so we encourage you to stay alert and be aware of your surroundings. Keep a close eye on cameras, purses, and wallets, all favorite targets of thieves and pickpockets.

Prices in Mexico

Please be aware that prices in this book were gathered before the December 1994 devaluation of the peso. They were converted into the dollar values you'll find in this book at a rate of 3.35 pesos to the dollar; by February 1995 the peso's value had declined to about 5.4 to the dollar. Since the exchange rate is still in flux, and inflation often occurs after a currency devaluation, it's impossible to predict what prices will be when you travel. Use the prices in this book as a guideline; depending on when you travel prices may be lower or higher than those quoted here. Finally, some hotels that quote rates to Americans in dollars have not lowered their rates, and some are offering travelers "discounts" rather than offer prices reflecting the devalued peso rate.

Mexico has a Value-Added Tax of 10% *(Impuesto de Valor Agregado,* or "IVA," pronounced "ee-bah") on almost everything, including hotel rooms, restaurant meals, bus tickets, tours, and souvenirs. This tax will not necessarily be included in prices quoted by a particular establishment. In addition, prices charged by hotels and restaurants have been deregulated; always ask to see a printed price sheet and ask if the tax is included. All prices given in this book already include the tax and are quoted in dollars.

Lastly, in 1993 Mexico introduced the New Peso, which knocks three zeros off the old currency, and in 1994 new, physically smaller bills began taking the place of the old paper notes. Old peso notes will be accepted until 1996; there's no announced time limit yet on coins.

1

Introducing Mexico City

No MATTER WHERE YOU BEGIN IN THIS AMAZING CITY, IT PRESENTS A jumble of first impressions—often startling, usually colorful, and always taking a while to sort through. Look out your plane's cabin window as you arrive and you'll see an immense, ugly, and congested city where squat buildings awash in monotones of gray spread without end to the horizon; the city sprawls across almost 1,000 square miles of the Valley of Mexico. Arrive at the bus or train stations and you'll be thrust immediately into the incredible, and at first intimidating, movement and jostle of life in the Western Hemisphere's largest city. How this city of more than 20 million people keeps traffic flowing daily should be counted among the wonders of the world. On your way to a city hotel, you'll gaze upon a passing scene revealing a country with one foot in the third world and the other in the information age, a capital city where 11th-century roots mingle with 21st-century plans.

Streetlife in the capital is such a fascinating introduction that no matter how weary you may find yourself once ensconced in your hotel, you might be eager to hit the streets again. Fire eaters, mimes, jugglers, windshield washers, and *chicle* (gum) sellers dart between cars, trying to make a quick peso as traffic stops. On street corners organ grinders churn out tunes on ancient German-made machines, pushcart vendors sell tacos, hot dogs, and ice cream. A string band of blind musicians plays foot-tappingly terrific tunes, while a block away a crowd gathers around Michoacán farmers skillfully playing horns, violins, and drums for tips. Repair shops along the streets announce their specialties the old-fashioned way—with bicycle, hubcap, stove, or muffler hanging above the entrance. Shop walls are adorned with gaily painted depictions of the inventory, be it plumbing or auto parts, food, pots and pans, or meat cuts. Exquisitely dressed Mexican men and women carry themselves with regal refinement while working their cellular phones. On the same sidewalk you may see newly arrived rural migrants still attired in the colorful handloomed dress of their region.

Every passing block shows decades and even centuries of radically variant architecture. Some of it is tall, some is short, small, and square—the ugly 1960s plaster-block style that swept Latin America. Numerous buildings are strikingly beautiful, hinting at the marvels to be found in nine centuries of architectural design. Foreign business signs mar the cityscape, but by announcing their presence they also reveal the country's rapid expansion into the global economy.

Passing through the fascinating Centro Historico, there's a refreshing air of renaissance, with hundreds of historic buildings undergoing renovation. Along the tree-lined Paseo de la Reforma and Avenida

IMPRESSIONS

Nowhere are Mexico's extremes as strong and as apparent as in the capital.
—Herbert Cerwin, *These Are the Mexicans* (1947)

What's Special About Mexico City & Environs

Museums

- In the capital, more than 50 sophisticated museums showcasing Mexico's heritage.
- Nearby Puebla's Museo del Arte Popular, with displays of regional costumes, household objects, and a tiled convent kitchen, and the Museo Amparo, with new finds form the pre-Hispanic past.
- Toluca's Centro Cultural Mexequense, Museo Taller Luis Nishezawa, and Museo de la Acuarela.
- The Museo de Artes y Tradiciones Populares in Tlaxcala features daily artist demonstrations and 3,000 examples of the area's crafts.
- The unique Museum of Puppets in Huamantla.

Architecture

- From pre-Hispanic temple remains to red tezontle stone colonial buildings, magnificent palaces, churches, mansions, and soaring skyscrapers, Mexico City has it all.
- Puebla's colorful tile building facades, church domes, and lavishly embellished Rosario Chapel.
- Toluca's renewed historic center.
- The elaborate Indian baroque interiors of the churches at Acatepec and Tonanzintla.
- Tlaxcala's colonial-era town center and baroque Basílica de Ocotlán; the ruins of Cacaxtla are nearby.

Performing Arts

- In theaters and on the streets, there's something to entertain everyone in the capital, from ballet to opera, mariachis to guitar trios, comedy to drama, organ grinders to accordian players.

Food

- Fine restaurants in the capital offer some of the country's best food and purvey a wide variety of the world's cuisines.
- Fine mole, rompope, and mixiote in Puebla.
- Toluca, known for its candy.
- The famous festival breads of Tlaxcala.

Shopping

- Mexico City's wonderful markets, crafts stores, department and antique stores, and boutiques.
- Numerous tile and pottery factories in Puebla.
- Toluca's fine baskets, rugs, pottery, and Friday market.

Insurgentes, expensive and sophisticated new hotels and ultramodern high-rises are springing up at an incredible rate.

Mexicans always refer to this city as "Mexico" rather than "Mexico City," and one does indeed find here a microcosm of all that is happening in the rest of the country. Deservedly or not, it's viewed as the city of hope throughout the country—for masses of rural migrants, going to the capital to live is synonymous with "making it." With the passage of NAFTA (the North American Free Trade Agreement) Mexico is becoming more and more a part of the modern global economy, and the capital is the stage on which this exciting new chapter in the country's history is being played out.

In the backdrop behind this drama are the ailments found throughout the country—growing poverty, governmental red tape, pollution, high cost of borrowing and living, and lack of health care, education, and sufficient land for the masses. But despite Mexico City's size and the inevitable problems that come with managing such a large city and population, the capital is stronger, more vital, and more alive than ever.

Though news from other areas of the country may be making more headlines now, the nation's leadership still starts in the capital. The streets, coffeehouses, and executive suites of Mexico City remain the places in which the nation's political and economic directions are set. And progress is being made: antipollution measures (restrictions on driving, factory closings, a new fleet of emission-controlled buses and taxis) have worked some noticeable wonders; and even before the passage of NAFTA in early 1994, foreign investment in the country had increased.

Despite its reputation as an undesirable pollution-wrapped metropolis, the capital city's hotels and restaurants are often filled with visitors. Not even air pollution (which can be avoided if your timing's on) deters foreign visitors from returning often to peel back more layers of the culture and history that are found here. Though immense, Mexico City is easily walkable and terrifically enjoyable on foot. The city is no less fascinating today than when it attracted William Cullen Bryant in 1872, Stephen Crane in 1895, and Katherine Anne Porter throughout her life. The taxi drivers are just as cantankerous as those described by Charles Flandrau in his account of his Mexico travels, *Viva Mexico,* published in 1905. A trip to Xochimilco can be the same colorful spectacle today that it was for Edward Weston, the famous American photographer, who took a white-knuckle taxi ride to it in the early 1920s.

Though large, Mexico City is not an impersonal place. It's easy to make eye contact and exchange pleasantries with perfect strangers. *Capitalinos,* as residents call themselves, usually take time to be helpful to tourists—they will go out of their way to help you with directions or tell you when your bus stop is approaching.

The Valley of Mexico and its environs (the geographic seat of Mexico City) has been the center of Mexican life since nearby Teotihuacán arose around 300 B.C. Signs abound of the march of history through the area: the pyramids of Teotihuacán are a short ride from downtown; the remains of the Aztec Templo Mayor are a block from the Zócalo; Xochimilco, a remnant of the Aztec gardens, is close by; the Spanish colonial Zócalo, with its cathedral and Palacio Nacional, is a classic example of that nation's method of colonial town planning; surrounding the Zócalo is the Centro Historico; the Castillo de Chapultepec (Chapultepec Castle) was designed by a Spanish viceroy; Maximilian of Hapsburg remodeled the castle and designed the magnificent Paseo de la Reforma; and the opulent Palacio de Bellas Artes and Correo were built during the Porfiriato. And throughout the city are fine buildings, thoroughfares, and monuments marking its long history.

Most of all, Mexico's history has been played out on the streets of the capital; in turn, these fascinating events have made the city what it is today.

1 The Land & Its People

The Valley of Mexico

Millions of years ago a vast ocean covered the area where Mexico City sits. Volcanic eruptions eventually created the mile-and-a-half-high (7,400 ft.) Valley of Anahuac, known today as the Valley of Mexico, the seat of contemporary Mexico City. Distant mountains encircle the valley, and on a clear day they can be seen, as can the volcanoes Popocatépetl and Ixtaccíhuatl, which lie to the east. South of the city, high up on the road to Mixquic, cones of other ancient dead volcanoes are visible from the valley, almost in a ring around the city. Though these mountains figure into the geography hemming in the valley, the city is flat. When leaving the city by land, there's only a gradual feeling of rising out of the valley.

Technically the basin where the city is located isn't a valley because there's no natural drainage—a requirement of valleys. It's a long, narrow basin, hemmed in by mountains, and is roughly 70 miles long by 50 miles wide. Water—both too much of it and too little—has often figured in the city's history. Early cultures, including the Aztecs, inhabited the area and founded their cities on islands in the middle of valley lakes (fed by rain and springs) and on the mainland boundaries. Spanish conquerors drained the lakes and built their capital on this soft lakebed, which today leaves the city vulnerable to earthquakes. (Prominent buildings in the old part of the capital are sinking due to the unstable underground.) Though human-made drainage has been created many times over the centuries, the lack of natural drainage plagues the city even today, when torrential rains flood some outlying areas. Rains can come at any time, but are most frequent between May and October, when daily showers are common. Though rain seems plentiful, the burgeoning population of the valley means that there are water shortages. Lakes and rivers hundreds of miles away are tapped to feed the water needs of the capital.

Urban sprawl has cluttered the area east of the city almost without end to Pachuca and Puebla, and north to Tepotzotlán. South of the city, in the mountains marching up toward Mixquic, Milpa Alta, and Chalco, city growth continues, but not as heavily. In that direction, the landscape is more pastoral—you'll see sheep and goats grazing and small plots of corn and beans.

The Mexican People

The population of Mexico is 85 million; 15% are ethnically European (most of Spanish descent), 60% are *mestizo* (mixed Spanish and Indian), and 25% are pure Indian (descendants of the Maya, Aztecs, Huastecs, Otomies, Totonacs, and other peoples). Added to this ethnic mix are Africans brought as slaves (this group has been so thoroughly assimilated that it is barely discernable); a French presence that lingers on from the time of Maximilian's abortive empire; and other Europeans. The people you see on the streets of the capital reflect this ethnic history.

Mexico's social complexity is nowhere more evident than in the capital. There's such a diversity of inhabitants from all walks of life and cultures that it's difficult to characterize the Mexican people as a whole, but there are some broad generalizations that can be drawn.

CLASS DIVISIONS

There are vast differences in the culture and values of Mexico City's various economic classes, and these gulfs have grown even wider over the last 10 years. The fabulously rich (and there are many such *Capitalinos*) drive expensive cars, wear the latest and most expensive fashions, live in sprawling walled estates, dine in the top restaurants, and go abroad often for vacations, shopping trips, and education. According to *Forbes* magazine, Mexico has the fourth-most billionaires in the world, with at least 24. Upper-class Mexicans are extremely well-educated and well-mannered; they are very culturally sophisticated and often speak several languages. Many of Mexico's recent presidents have been educated in the United States.

The Mexican middle class—merchants, small restaurant and souvenir-shop owners, taxi drivers, and tour guides, etc.—swelled from the 1950s through the 1980s but is struggling to stay afloat after a decade of incredible inflation. And yet these middle-class Mexicans are educating their children to higher standards—many young people now complete technical school or university. The middle-class standard of living includes trappings of life many take for granted in the States—maybe a phone in the home (a luxury that costs the equivalent of U.S. $1,000 to install), fancy tennis shoes for the children, occasional vacations, an economy car, and a tiny home or even smaller apartment in a modest neighborhood or highrise.

Mexico's poorer classes have expanded. Their hopes for a decent future are dim and the daily goal for many is simple survival. The desperately poor often resort to the whim of the street for their livelihood, selling trifles, performing for tips and begging.

Mostly the city teems with working people, many of whom are poor nonetheless—the maids, dishwashers, busboys, waiters, gas-station and parking-lot attendants, grocery clerks, newspaper and street vendors, and the like. Because of their neat attire, their basic, pleasant demeanor, powerful Mexican dignity, and almost inborn sense of courtesy, they usually blend in harmoniously. They don't look tattered or act hungry, though their clothes may be carefully patched, and their diet may consist mainly of simple, inexpensive staples: beans, rice, squash, and tortillas. Many live with the whole of an extended family in one small shack, without electricity, plumbing, or running water. They walk because they are often too poor to afford a bus ride. Despite all these hardships, some of the most genuinely kind, courteous, and generous people one meets in the capital are these working poor. The same can be said of the many newly arrived rural migrants, who set up shop on the streets selling whatever they've made or bought.

MANNERS & MORES

Capitalinos are more formal than residents of smaller Mexican cities, in dress as well as conversation. Many may form friendships slowly because they hold to traditional politeness and formality in business and personal dealings. To a foreigner the formality may seem stiff and somewhat standoffish. With time and familiarity, the stiffness eases gradually.

There is, to be sure, a certain breed of Capitalinos, sometimes referred to by non-Capitalinos as *chilangos* (a derogatory term), who've earned a reputation for being loud, bossy, pompous, aggressive, and rude. A "me first" attitude makes them feel entitled to push ahead in line, grab taxis out of turn, squeeze and dart ahead of you in traffic, and demand service anywhere—first. You'll probably see someone behaving like this, but it isn't pervasive. It seems you'll find people like this in all the world's large cities.

MACHISMO & MACHISMA

Sorting through the world of machismo and machisma in Mexico is fraught with subtleties better suited to sociological studies. Suffice it to say that in Mexico, and especially Mexico City, the roles of men and women are changing both slowly and rapidly. Both sexes cling to old sex roles—women in the home and men in the workplace—but they are relinquishing traditional ideas too. More women are being educated and working than ever before. And men are learning to work side by side with women of equal education and power.

Though women function in many professional positions, they encounter what they call the "adobe ceiling" (as opposed to the see-through "glass ceiling" in the United States): The male grip on upper-level positions in Mexico is so firm that women aren't able to even glimpse the top. Strong-willed women opt for setting up their own businesses as a result. Anyone used to a more liberated world may be frustrated by the extent to which Mexico is still a man's world—not uncommon are women who pander to old-fashioned negative stereotypes and flirtatious Mexican men who have difficulty sticking to business when dealing with a woman, even a serious businessperson who is dressed accordingly. Typically the Mexican man is charmingly polite, and affronted or embarrassed by the woman who won't permit him to open doors, seat her, and in every way put her on a respectful pedestal.

THE IMPORTANCE OF FAMILY

As a rule, Mexicans are very family-oriented. Family takes priority over work. Whole extended families routinely spend weekends and holidays together, filling parks and recreational spots until the last minute of the holiday. During those times men are often seen playing with, tending to, and enjoying the children as readily as women. In the home, girls are supervised closely until they are married. But the untethering of boys begins around age 15, when they are given more freedoms than their sisters. It's customary, however, for all children to remain in the home until they marry, although there are more young people breaking the mold nowadays.

Family roles among indigenous people are clearcut. Women tend the babies, the home, the hearth, and often the fields. Men do the heavy work, tilling the soil, but women often join them for planting and harvesting. Theirs is a joint life focused on survival. Though not so much an unbendable custom now among these cultures, it's common to see a woman walking behind her spouse, carrying a child on her back and heavy bundles on her shoulders. When these people reach Mexico City, these roles shift somewhat; for example, a husband and wife will take turns tending their street stall with a child sleeping in a box or playing nearby. But always she will prepare the food. A rural family may try to make it in Mexico City, but until the city gets a complete grip on them they may just as easily return to the country to help their extended families during the season of planting or harvesting corn.

Generally speaking children are coddled and loved and are very obedient. Misbehaving children are seldom rebuked in public, since Mexican parenting style seems to favor gentle prodding, comforting, or nurturing instead.

THE MEXICAN CHARACTER

Describing the Mexican character is at least as complex as trying to describe the differences between New Englanders and southerners in the United States. At the risk of offending some, I'll try to describe the values of the average Mexican. He or she is generous, honest, and loyal, and accepts acquaintances at face value. Visitors are far more likely to have something returned than to discover it stolen. But just as Mexicans are accepting, they can become unreasonably suspicious, and once doubt is planted nothing will divert them from suspecting ill will.

The fierce Mexican dignity doesn't allow for insult. An insulting shopper, for example, may discover that suddenly nothing in the store is for sale, or that the prices have become ridiculously high for the duration of the shopper's visit.

Longtime friendships can fall apart instantly over a real or imagined wrong. Once wronged, Mexicans seldom forgive and never forget. The expression of indifference and distrust a Mexican wears when wronged can appear to have been set in concrete. The more you try to right a wrong, or correct a wrong impression, the more entrenched it can become. This goes for personal friendships as well as dealings with the government.

Their long memories harbor the bad and the good. A Mexican will remember a kind deed or a fond, but brief, acquaintance, until death. They will never forget the number of times the United States has invaded Mexico, or the government massacre of peaceful demonstrators at Tlatelolco Square in the capital in 1968.

Mexicans seem to thrive on gossip. And it runs the gamut from what government is doing behind the public's back to neighborhood squabbles. It figures prominently in the breakdown of personal and business relationships as well as the lack of confidence the public has in the government. During Mexico's recent investigation of the assassinations of two prominent government leaders, newspapers published the intrigue and conspiracy the public believed caused both events, alongside different official government reports. Mexicans often express the belief that their president takes his orders from the U.S. president.

No matter how poor or opulent their lives may be, all Capitalinos love festivities, whether simple family affairs or the city-wide parades on Revolution and Independence days. Often this celebratory spirit is just as evident at lunch in a festive place such as the Fonda del Recuerdo, known for its lively music and jovial atmosphere. Capitalinos are great supporters of the arts, filling theaters and frequenting museums, and have a great awareness of, and pride in, their history.

When it comes to foreigners, Mexicans want visitors to know, love, and enjoy their country and will extend many thoughtful courtesies just to see pleasure spread across the face of a visitor. They'll invite them to share a table in a crowded restaurant, go out of their way to give directions, help with luggage and see stranded travelers safely on their way. An entire trip can be joyously colored by the many serendipitous encounters with the people of this nation, whose efficiency and concern will be as memorable as their warmth and good humor.

2 A Look at the Past

The history of the Mexico City area stretches back to around 13,000 B.C., when the first nomadic groups seem to have appeared in the Valley of Mexico. By 3000 B.C. signs of agriculture and domestication had appeared: baskets were woven; beans, squash, and tomatoes were grown; turkeys and dogs were kept for food, but the people

Dateline

■ **13,000–2300 B.C.**
Pre-Historic Period:
Nomadic tribes
enter Valley of
Mexico. Primitive
agriculture
established.

➤

Dateline

- **1500–300**
  Pre-Classic Period:
  The Gulf Coast
  Olmec culture
  (1200–800 B.C.)
  creates a jaguar deity
  symbol and serpent
  with crest on head,
  a forerunner of
  Quetzalcoatl.
  Farming
  communities are
  established in the
  Valley of Mexico.
- **600–200** Cholula
  is founded and
  becomes a huge
  ceremonial/civic
  center.
- **650 B.C.–1 A.D.**
  Cuicuilco culture
  (south of Mexico
  City) established
  and is destroyed by
  eruption of Xitle
  volcano; inhabi-
  tants migrate
  to Teotihuacán.
- **500 B.C.**
  Teotihuacán
  settlement started;
  coincident with the
  southern-Mexican
  Zapotecs' first work
  on the great
  mountaintop plaza
  of Monte Alban
  and beginning of
  disintegration of
  Olmec culture.
- **A.D. 100**
  Construction begins
  on Sun and Moon
  pyramids at
  Teotihuacán;
  Palenque dynasty
  emerges in
  Yucatán—
  Teotihuacán's
  influence is felt
  there in trade and
  architecture. ➤

were still nomadic. Life in these times was still very primitive. By 2400 B.C. the art of pot making had been developed—asignificant advance.

PRE-HISPANIC CIVILIZATIONS It was in the **Preclassic Period** (1500 B.C.–A.D. 300) that the area from the Valley of Mexico to Costa Rica known to archeologists as Mesoamerica began to show signs of an organized farming culture; one such pocket of progress was the highlands around Mexico City, where the first large towns developed. Shamans, the predecessors of the folk healers and nature priests, or *brujas,* still found in modern Mexico, began to proliferate.

The great ancient city just northeast of today's Mexico City, Teotihuacán, may have received an early boost when a volcanic eruption destroyed Cuicuilco, whose ruins are south of the University of Mexico, in A.D. 1; many of its citizens appear to have taken up residence in Teotihuacán. By around A.D. 500 Teotihuacán was a vast city of at least 100,000 inhabitants.

Tremendous artistic and cultural achievement came during the **Classic Period** (A.D. 300–900), when life centered in cities. Class distinctions arose between a new military and religious aristocracy, merchants and artisans, and once-independent farmers who now fell under a landlord's control. The cultural centers of the Classic Period were Teotihuacán (near present-day Mexico City), Yucatán and Guatemala (home of the Maya), the Mexican highlands at the Zapotec cities of Monte Alban and Mitla (near Oaxaca), and the cities of El Tajín and Zempoala on the Gulf Coast. These cultures all traded with each other.

Not much is known about Teotihuacán's (100 B.C.–A.D. 700) inhabitants, but at the city's height (around A.D. 600) it is thought to have had 100,000 or more inhabitants and to have sprawled across nine square miles—the greatest cultural center in Mexico, with influence as far southeast as Guatemala. Its layout has religious significance; the tops of its Pyramids of the Sun and Moon were the site of high priests' rituals, during which the general population would mass at the feet of the pyramids. As archeologists unearth more of the city's past, more is being learned of the culture's practice of human sacrifice and warmaking based on celestial movements. Replicas of some of the magnificent reliefs and frescoes that decorated the religious monuments can be seen in Mexico City's museums. Teotihuacán's influence can be seen in all contemporary Mexican cultures, especially in architecture and murals, and continues to provide archeologists with a seemingly endless supply of subject matter. Trade routes fanned out from Teotihuacán to the Yucatán, Puebla, Tehuacán, Tlaxcala, and Oaxaca in Mexico and into Guatemala in Central America.

In the **Postclassic Period** (A.D. 900–1500), warlike cultures developed impressive societies of their own, although they never surpassed those of the Classic peoples. Paintings and hieroglyphs of this period show war, migration, and disruption. Somehow the glue of society became unstuck, people wandered from their homes, and the religious hierarchy lost influence. As Teotihuacán declined, nomadic tribes were still roaming north of there, and it's possible some of those fleeing the great city may have joined them. Around 1000 they consolidated to form another culture—the Toltecs—at Tula, north of present-day Mexico City. Their architecture and warlike ways left a heavy mark on the Yucatán, but they lasted only a couple of centuries before being overcome by roaming tribes.

In the 1300s, the warlike Aztecs established an empire in the Valley of Mexico on Lake Texcoco (site of Mexico City), with the island city of Tenochtitlán as their capital. As legend has it, the wandering Aztecs were passing the lake when they saw a sign predicted by their prophets: An eagle perched on a cactus plant, with a snake in

Dateline

- **300–900** Classic Period; building boom at Monte Alban.
- **500** Teotihuacán is an immense city of 100,000 with a broad influence and trade into the rest of Mesoamerica.
- **650** Teotihuacán burns and is deserted by 700.
- **900–1500** Post-Classic Period: Toltec culture emerges at Tula and spreads to Chichén Itzá by 978.
- **1156 or 1168** After a fire, Toltecs abandon Tula. Aztecs trickle into the Valley of Mexico.
- **1325–45** Aztec capital Tenochtitlán founded. Aztecs dominate Mexico until 1521, when they are defeated by Spaniards.
- **1478** The Aztec Templo Mayor is constructed.
- **1519–21** Conquest of Mexico: Hernán Cortés and troops arrive near present-day Veracruz; Spanish gain final victory over Aztecs at Tlaltelolco near Tenochtitlán in 1521. Diseases brought by Spaniards begin to decimate native population.
- **1521–24** Cortés organizes Spanish

➤

Dateline

its mouth. They built their city there, and it became a huge and impressive capital of 300,000 people.

The Aztec empire included present-day Veracruz, Guerrero, Morelos, Puebla, and Oaxaca, although they were unable to conquer the neighboring Tlaxcaltecans of Tlaxcala and the Purepecha of present-day Michoacán. The high lords of the capital became fabulously rich in gold and stores of food, cotton, and perfumes; skilled artisans were prosperous; events of state were elaborately ceremonial. In numerous ceremonies built around battles, harvests, and celestial movements, they sacrificed thousands of victims (most often captives of war) on the altars atop the pyramids, cutting the victims' chests open with stone knives and ripping out their still-beating hearts to offer to the gods. Mythological gods were a central part of their belief system.

In terms of contemporary history, the god **Quetzalcoatl** turned out to be one of the most important. The tale of Quetzalcoatl, who began as a holy man who appeared to the Toltecs at Tula at the end of the Classic Period and grew to be a mythologic character of godlike abilities, is one of the most important tales in Mexican history and folklore, and contributed to the overthrow of the Aztec empire by the Spaniards. Quetzalcoatl means "feathered serpent." Learned beyond his years, he became the high priest and leader of the Toltecs, and put an end to human sacrifice. His influence completely changed the Toltecs from a group of warriors to peaceful and productive farmers and artisans. But his abolition of human sacrifice upset the old guard of the priesthood, who conspired against him. One night, the priests succeeded in getting Quetzalcoatl drunk, dressed in ridiculous garb, and in the horrific position of having broken his vow of chastity by sleeping with his sister. The next morning the shame of this night of debauchery drove him out of his own land and into the wilderness, where he lived for

20 years. He emerged in Coatzacoalcos, in the Isthmus of Tehuantepec, bade his few followers farewell, and sailed away, having promised to return in a future age. But evidence found at Chichén Itzá in the Yucatán suggests that in fact he landed there and successfully began his "ministry" again among the Maya, this time under the name Kukulkán. He died there, but the prophesy of his return in a future age remained.

THE CONQUEST OF MEXICO

When Hernán Cortés and his fellow conquistadors landed in 1519, in what would become Veracruz, the enormous Aztec empire was ruled by Moctezuma (a name often misspelled Montezuma) in great splendor. It was thought that these strange visitors might be Quetzalcoatl and his followers, returning at last. Moctezuma was not certain what course to pursue; if this was in fact the god returning, no resistance must be offered; on the other hand, if the leader was not Quetzalcoatl, he and his men might be a threat to his empire. Moctezuma tried to bribe them with gold to go away, but this only whetted the Spaniards' appetites. Along the way from Veracruz to Tenochtitlán, Cortés made allies of

Dateline

Casa de Moneda (the Mint), under leadership of Geronimo Antonio Gil.

- **1790** Turnip oil is used in the first street lights.
- **1810–21** Independence War: Miguel Hidalgo's *grito* starts independence movement; after a decade of war, Augustín Iturbide achieves compromise between monarchy and a republic. Mexico becomes independent nation.
- **1822–24** First Empire: Iturbide enjoys brief reign as emperor; is expelled; returns; and is executed by firing squad.

➤

IMPRESSIONS

When we [Cortés and Moctezuma] met I dismounted and stepped forward to embrace him, but the two lords who were with him stopped me with their hands so that I should not touch him. . . . When at last I came to speak to Mutezuma himself I took off a necklace of pearls and cut glass that I was wearing and placed it around his neck; after we had walked a little way up the street a servant of his came with two necklaces, wrapped in a cloth, made from red snails' shells, which they hold in great esteem; and from each necklace hung eight shrimps of refined gold almost a span in length.
—Hernán Cortés, *Letters from Mexico* (1519)

When they arrived at the treasure house called Teucalco, the riches of gold and feathers were brought out to them: ornaments made of quetzal feathers, richly worked shields, disks of gold, the necklaces of the idols, gold nose plugs, gold greaves and bracelets and crowns. . . . The Spaniards . . . gathered all the gold into a great mound and set fire to everything else. . . . Then they melted down the gold into ingots.
—*The Broken Spears: The Aztec Account of the Conquest of Mexico* (1528)

Dateline

- **1824–55** Federal Republic Period: Distrito Federale (Federal District) established. In 1824, Guadalupe Victoria elected first president of Mexico; 26 presidents and interim presidents follow during next three decades, among them Antonio Lopez de Santa Anna, who is president of Mexico off and on 11 times.
- **1835** Texas declares independence from Mexico.
- **1838** France invades Mexico at Veracruz.
- **1845** United States annexes Texas.
- **1846–48** War with United States concludes with U.S. paying Mexico $15 million for half of its national territory under terms of Treaty of Guadalupe Hidalgo.
- **1849** The first telegraph is in use in the capital.
- **1855–72** Era of Benito Juárez, literal or de facto president through Reform Wars and usurpation of Mexican leadership by foreign Emperor Maximilian. Juárez nationalizes church property and declares separation of church and state. Dies in Mexico City in 1872. ➤

Moctezuma's enemies, most notably the Tlaxcaltecans.

Though the Spaniards were outnumbered by the hundreds of thousands of Aztecs, they skillfully kept things under their control (with the help of their Tlaxcalan allies) until a revolt threatened Cortés's entire enterprise. He retreated to the countryside, made alliances with non-Aztec tribes, and finally marched on the empire when it was governed by the last Aztec emperor, Cuauhtémoc. Cuauhtémoc defended himself and his people valiantly for almost three months, but was finally captured, tortured, and ultimately executed.

What began as an adventure by Cortés and his men, unauthorized by the Spanish Crown or its governor in Cuba, turned out to be the undoing of a continent's worth of people and cultures. Soon Christianity was being spread through "New Spain." Guatemala and Honduras were explored and conquered, and by 1540 the territory of New Spain included Spanish possessions from Vancouver to Panama. In the two centuries that followed, Franciscan, Augustinian, and Dominican friars converted great numbers of Indians to Christianity, and the Spanish lords built up huge feudal estates on which the Indian farmers were little more than serfs. The silver and gold that Cortés had sought and found made Spain the richest country in Europe.

THE VICEREGAL ERA Hernán Cortés set about building a new city and the seat of government of New Spain upon the ruins of the old Aztec capital. Spain's influence was immediate. For indigenous peoples (excepting the Tlaxcaltecans, Cortés's Indian allies), heavy tributes once paid to the Aztecs were now rendered in forced labor to the Spanish. In many cases they were made to provide the materials for the building of New Spain as well. Diseases carried by the Spaniards, against which the Indian populations had no natural immunity, killed millions.

Over the three centuries of the Viceregal Period (1535–1821), Mexico was governed by 61 viceroys appointed by the king of Spain. From the beginning, more Spaniards arrived as overseers, merchants, artisans, architects, silversmiths, etc., and eventually negro slaves were brought in as well. Spain became rich from New World gold and silver, chiseled out by backbreaking Indian labor. The colonial elite built lavish homes both in Mexico City and in the countryside. They filled their homes with ornate furniture, had many servants, and adorned themselves in velvets, satins, and jewels imported from abroad. A new class system developed: the *gauchupines* (Spaniard born in Spain), considered themselves superior to the *criollos* (Spaniard born in Mexico). Those of other races, the *castas* or castes, the pure Indians and Negros, and mixtures of Spanish and Indian, Spanish and Negro, Indian and Negro, all took the last place in society.

It took great cunning to stay a step ahead of the money-hungry Spanish crown, which demanded increasingly higher taxes and contributions from its well-endowed faraway colony. Still, the wealthy prospered grandly enough to develop an extravagant society.

However, discontent with the mother country simmered for years over issues such as the Spanish-born citizen's advantages over a Mexican-born subject; taxes; the Spanish bureaucracy; and restrictions on commerce with Spain and other countries. Dissatisfaction with Spain boiled to the surface in 1808 when, under the weak leadership of King Charles IV, it was invaded by Napoleón Bonaparte of France, who placed his brother Joseph in the Spanish throne. To many in Mexico, allegiance to France was out of the question. Mexico seemed left without leadership. After nearly 300 years of restrictive Spanish rule, Mexican discontent with the mother country reached the level of revolution.

INDEPENDENCE   The independence movement began in 1810 when a priest,

Dateline

- **1872–84** Post-Reform Period: Only four presidents hold office but country is nearly bankrupt.
- **1880** Electric lights go on in Mexico City for the first time.
- **1876–1911** Porfiriato: With one four-year exception, Porfirio Díaz is president/dictator of Mexico for 35 years, leading country through rapid modernization.
- **1911** Mexican Revolution begins; Díaz resigns; Francisco Madero becomes president.
- **1913** Madero assassinated.
- **1914, 1916** United States invades Mexico.
- **1917–40** Reconstruction: Present constitution of Mexico signed in 1917. Land and education reforms are initiated and labor unions strengthened. Mexico expels U.S. oil companies and nationalizes all natural resources and railroads. Presidential term limited to one term of six years. Presidents Obregón and Carranza are assassinated as are Pancho Villa and Emiliano Zapata.
- **1940** President Lázaro Cárdenas

▶

Dateline

leaves office; Mexico enters period of political stability, tremendous economic progress, and rising quality of life that continues to this day, though not without many continuing problems.

- 1942 Mexico enters World War II when Germans sink two Mexican oil tankers in the Caribbean.
- 1946 10,000 year old "Tepexpan Man" is unearthed near Mexico City.
- 1955 Women given full voting rights.
- 1957 Major earthquake rocks the capital.
- 1960 Mexico nationalizes electrical industry.
- 1964 World-class Museo Nacional de Antropología opens.
- 1968 President Díaz Ordaz orders army to fire on protesters at Tlaltelolco Plaza meeting, killing hundreds of spectators and participants. Olympic games are held in the capital.
- 1969 Mexico City Metro opens.
- 1978 Excavation begins on the Templo Mayor archeological site. ➤

Father Miguel Hidalgo, gave the cry for independence from his pulpit in the town of Dolores, Guanajuato. The revolt soon became a revolution, and Hidalgo, Ignacio Allende, and another priest, José María Morelos, gathered an "army" of citizens and threatened Mexico City. Battle lines were drawn between those who sided with the Spanish crown and those who wanted Mexico to be a free and sovereign nation. Ultimately Hidalgo was executed, but he is honored as "the Father of Mexican Independence." Morelos kept the revolt alive until 1815, when he too was executed.

The nation endured a decade of upheaval (1810 until 1821), and then the warring factions finally agreed on a compromise, Augustín Iturbide's *Plan de Iguala*. It made three guarantees: Mexico would be a constitutional monarchy headed by a European prince; the Catholic church would have a monopoly on religion; and Mexican-born citizens would have the same rights as those born in Spain. He thoughtfully tagged on another proviso allowing for a Mexican emperor, should no European prince step forward to take the role of king. When the agreement was signed, Iturbide was positioned to take over. No suitable European monarch was located and the new Mexican congress named him emperor. His empire proved short-lived: the very next year his administration fell. The new nation became a republic, but endured a succession of presidents and military dictators, as well as invasions, a war, and devastating losses of territory to its neighbor to the north, the United States.

Characteristic of the Republic's turbulent history during the half-century following independence was the French Intervention, in which three old colonial powers—England, France, and Spain—

IMPRESSIONS

Without more chin than Maximilian ever had, one can be neither handsome nor a successful emperor.
—Charles Flandrau, *Viva Mexico* (1908)

and the United States demonstrated continued interest in meddling with Mexico's internal affairs, and found, in the fractured world of mid-19th-century Mexican politics, plenty of help in carrying out their intrigues. Before it was over, Mexico had seen troops from the three European powers occupy Veracruz (the English and Spanish withdrew before long, but the French remained and declared war on Mexico); had enjoyed a glorious, if hollow, victory over the French at Puebla (the event that birthed the nation's Cinco de Mayo celebrations); had watched the Mexican president, Benito Juárez, retreat to the countryside to bide his time while the French marched on Mexico City and, with the help of anti-Juárez factions, installed a naive young Austrian, Archduke Maximilian of Hapsburg, as king of Mexico; and finally had rolled its collective eyes at the three-year-long spectacle of Maximilian trying to "rule" a country effectively in the midst of civil war, only to be left in the lurch when the French troops that supported him withdrew at the behest of the United States and then summarily executed by Juárez upon his triumphant return. Juárez, who would be remembered as one of the nation's great heroes, did his best to strengthen and unify the country before dying of a heart attack in 1872.

THE PORFIRIATO & THE REVOLUTION From 1877 to 1911, a period now called the "Porfiriato," center stage in Mexico was occupied by Porfirio Díaz, a Juárez general who was president for 30 years and lived in the Castillo de (Castle of) Chapultepec in Mexico City. He was a terror to his enemies—that is, anyone

Dateline

- **1982** President Echeverria nationalizes the country's banks.
- **1985** Deadly earthquake crumbles buildings in the capital and takes thousands of lives.
- **1988** Mexico enters the General Agreement on Tariffs and Trade (GATT).
- **1992** Sale of *ejido* land (peasant communal property) to private citizens is allowed. Mexico and the Vatican establish diplomatic relations after an interruption of 100 years.
- **1993** Mexico deregulates hotel and restaurant prices; New Peso currency begins circulation.
- **1994** Mexico, Canada, and the United States sign the North American Free Trade Agreement. An Indian uprising in Chiapas sparks protests countrywide over land distribution, bank loans, health care,

➤

IMPRESSIONS

[Porfirio Díaz] looks what he is—a Man of Iron, the most forceful character in Mexico. Whatever was done in the sixteenth century was the work of Cortez ... who was responsible for everything but the climate. Whatever is effected in Mexico to-day is the work of Porfirio Díaz.
—Stanton Davis Kirkham, *Mexican Trails* (1909)

Dateline

who dared challenge his absolute power. Nevertheless, he is credited with bringing Mexico into the industrial age and for his patronage of architecture and the arts, the fruits of which are still enjoyed today. Public opinion forced him from office in 1911; he was succeeded by Francisco Madero.

After the fall of the Porfirist dictatorship, several factions split the country, including those led by "Pancho Villa" (whose real name was Doroteo Arango), Alvaro Obregón, Venustiano Carranza, and Emiliano Zapata. A famous photograph shows Zapata and Villa taking turns trying out Díaz's presidential chair in Mexico City. The decade that followed is referred to as the Mexican Revolution. Around two million Mexicans died for the cause. Drastic reforms occurred in this period, and the surge of vitality and progress from this exciting, if turbulent, time has inspired Mexicans to the present. Succeeding presidents have invoked the spirit of the Revolution, which lives in the hearts and minds of Mexicans as though it happened yesterday.

BEYOND THE REVOLUTION   The decades from the beginning of the revolution in 1911 to stabilization in the 1940s and 1950s were tumultuous. Great strides were made during these years in distributing land to the peasant populations, irrigation, development of mineral resources, and the establishment of education, health, and sanitation programs. However, the tremendous economic pressure Mexico faced from its own internal problems and the world depression of the 1930s did little for political stability. From 1911 to 1940, sixteen men were president of Mexico. Some stayed in power a year or less.

The longest-lasting (1934–40) and most significant leader of the period was Lázaro Cárdenas. He helped diminish the role of Mexico's military in national politics by dismantling the machine of Gen. Plutarco Calles and exiling him from the country. He is remembered fondly as a president who listened to and cared about commoners. He made good on a number of the revolution's promises, distributing nearly 50 million acres of land, primarily to *ejidos,* or communal farming groups; plowing money into education; encouraging organized labor. And in one of his most memorable and controversial decisions, he nationalized Mexico's oil industry in 1938, sending foreign oil companies packing. Although Mexicans still view this act with great pride—the government stood up for Mexican labor—it did considerable damage to Mexico's standing with the international business community. From the 1930s through the 1970s, socialism had a strong voice in Mexico; its impact was most marked in the state's attempts to run the country's businesses— not just oil, but railroads, mining, utilities, hotels, motion pictures, the telephone company, etc. With the world mired in the Great Depression and foreign investors increasingly shy of doing business in Mexico, the Cárdenas era ended in 1940 with the nation in dark economic circumstances.

Miguel Aleman, president from 1946 to 1958, helped stabilize things somewhat, building dams, improving highways and railways, encouraging trade, and building the Ciudad Universitario (University City) in Mexico City, home of Mexico's national university. Americans began to invest in Mexico again. Problems remained: the country's booming population created unemployment (neither ill has yet been successfully addressed), wages of the common people were appallingly low, and Aleman's administration was plagued by corruption and graft.

Two incidents from the last few decades remain at the forefront of the country's collective memory. One is the massacre of student protesters by government troops at the Plaza of Tlatelolco in downtown Mexico City on October 2, 1968, just before the Mexico City Olympics were to begin. It's likely that hundreds died on that tragic day. Popular confidence in the government has never been the same, and memories of the bloodbath surface at every use of police or military power against ordinary citizens.

Another blow to the people's faith in the government occurred on the morning of September 19, 1985, when a powerful earthquake rolled over the landscape from its origin near Ixtapa on the Pacific coast to Mexico City and on to Puebla. The capital suffered the worst devastation; the soft subsoil of the downtown area failed to support buildings. And in the aftermath of the disaster came the realization that the government had failed to enforce earthquake resistant construction codes for decades.

TOWARD THE FUTURE   From the time of the revolution to the present, political parties and their role have changed tremendously in Mexico. Although one political party, the **Partido Revolucionario Institucional** (PRI, called "el *pree*") has been in control under that name since 1946, opposition to it has become increasingly vocal and effective in recent years. In the beginning, the forerunner of the PRI, the Partido Revolucionario Mexicano, established by Lázaro Cárdenas, had four equal constituent groups—popular, agrarian, labor, and the military. At the risk of greatly oversimplifying a complex history and attendant issues, the widespread perception that the party is out of touch with the common Mexican, and its current problems retaining leadership, are the result of a change in focus away from those groups (with the exception of the military). The PRI today is heavily backed by, and in turn run by, business and industry leaders. Testament to the change in philosophy is the government's decision in the early 1990s to sell off all the state-owned businesses with the exception of oil.

The crisis in Chiapas has become a focal point for the nation's problems. Opposition parties such as the Partido Accion Nacional (PAN) have taken up the cause of the disenfranchised masses, but no one had spoken for or paid much attention to Mexico's millions of poor indigenous people for some time. And on New Year's Day in 1994, when militant Maya Indians attacked Chiapan towns, killing many, attention was drawn to the plight of neglected indigenous groups and others in the rural society, which the PRI-led government seemed to relegate to the bottom of the agenda. These groups are still clamoring for land they never received after the revolution. That population growth has outstripped the availability of distributable land, that Mexico needs large-scale, modern agribusiness to keep up with the country's food needs—these are realities not understood by the millions of rural Mexicans who depend on their small family field to feed the family. President Carlos Salinas de Gortari's bold, controversial decision in the early 1990s to allow sale of *ejido* land may reflect Mexico's 21st-century needs, but it is at odds with farm and land-use traditions born before the 16th-century Conquest. These issues of agrarian reform and lack of other basics of life (roads, electricity, running water, education, health care, etc.) are being raised in areas besides Chiapas, most notably Oaxaca, Chihuahua, Guerrero, and Michoacán; all told it is the gravest national issue since the revolution.

Free trade, expanding industries, and improved communications are changing the face of Mexico so fast now that it's impossible to keep up with it all. If Mexico can successfully solve its people problems, it's poised for unparalleled future growth.

3   Famous *Capitalinos*

Lola Alvarez Bravo (b. 1905) Photographer emeritus of Mexican life and times, she was friend and photographer of Mexico's greatest 20th-century artists—Rivera, Kahlo, Tamayo, Orozco—and teacher to others whose work she champions.

Raúl Anguiano Valdez (b. 1915) Born in Guadalajara, at 21 Anguiano had his first exhibition at the Palacio de Bellas Artes in Mexico City. One of his most famous paintings, *The Thorn,* depicts a young Indian removing a thorn from her foot with a knife. It hangs in the National Museum of Art in Mexico City.

Dr. Atl (Gerardo Murillo; 1875–1964) Possessing enormous energy as well as political and artistic passion, Gerardo Murillo (who, as a political statement, changed his name to Dr. Atl, a Nahuatl word meaning water) was a painter, writer, and not-too-successful politician. He is best known for his vast landscapes, usually including volcanoes, in which he produced an aerial feeling of the Mexican landscape.

Luis Barragán (1902–89) One of Mexico's most influential architects, he was from a wealthy Guadalajara family. Known primarily as an architect/designer of homes and for his use of bold Mexican colors and hacienda styles in modern buildings, he won the coveted Pritzker Award for architecture in 1980.

Miguel Cabrera (1695–1768) A Zapotec Indian, he is considered one of the leading artists of the 18th century. Works attributed to him are found in museums and churches throughout the republic, including the Museo Nacional de Arte in Mexico City.

Carlos Chávez (1899–1978). Considered Mexico's most renowned musician, his Mexican heritage inspired his highly acclaimed *Sinfonía India* and later *Xochibili-Macuilxochitl,* both of which were written for the use of pre-Hispanic musical instruments.

Juan Correa (1645?–1716) Correa began making his profoundly beautiful paintings at 21, and when he died at age 71 his skill and work were acclaimed both in Mexico and abroad. Collections of his paintings appear in the Metropolitan Cathedral, the Museo Nacional de Arte in Mexico City, and the Museo Nacional del Virreinato in Tepotzotlán.

Pedro Coronel (1923–85) Considered the most gifted of Rufino Tamayo's students, Coronel's development and use of color rivals that of his master. Among other places, his works are displayed in the Museo de Arte Moderno in Mexico City and the Pedro Coronel Museum in Zacatecas.

Hernán Cortés (1485–1547) Brash, bold, greedy, and a brilliant military leader, Hernán Cortés conquered Mexico in the name of Spain without the knowledge of that country's king. With only 550 men and 16 horses, he conquered a nation of 400,000 and a territory larger than his native country. Mexicans regard him as the destroyer of a nation and no monuments honor him. His remains are concealed in a marked vault in the Church of the Hospital of Jésus Nazareño in Mexico City, opposite the Museo de la Ciudad de Mexico.

Miguel Covarrubias (1904–57) His first caricature appeared in Mexican newspapers in 1920 when he was 16. By 1924 he was illustrating articles in *Vanity Fair* and two years later in the *New Yorker,* where his work continued to appear until 1950. A multitalented person, he contributed designs for silver produced by William Spratling, studied and taught ethnology and archeology at the University of Mexico, was twice awarded Guggenheim fellowships, and wrote seven books. His best-known painting, *The Bone,* hangs in Mexico City's National Museum of Art.

José Luis Cuevas (b. 1934) An outspoken, controversial artist and activist, Cuevas has had award-winning shows in Paris, Washington, D.C., Peru, Venezuela, Brazil, and Mexico City. He established the José Luis Cuevas Museum in Mexico City.

Cuauhtémoc (Late 1400s–1523?) Cousin of Moctezuma II, and last ruler of the Aztec Empire, Cuauhtémoc is revered for his valiant leadership. Though only in his twenties, he led his people nobly during the final Spanish siege, which lasted almost three months and brought an end to the Aztec Empire. Legend tells us that after the battle he was tortured to reveal the whereabouts of Aztec gold but would not give in. It is Cuauhtémoc, not Moctezuma, whom Mexicans hold up as an example of courage and strength and honor with a statue on Reforma Avenue in Mexico City.

Porfirio Díaz (1830–1915) Díaz was Mexico's dictator for 34 years, with one four-year interruption. His contributions were enormous: He moved the country from turmoil and bankruptcy into peace and stability through improvements in communication, railroads, agriculture, manufacturing, mining, port enlargement, oil exploration, and foreign investment. He built lavish public buildings throughout Mexico and sent promising art students to Europe on full scholarship. His love for all things French was legendary. He flouted the law and achieved his successes at the expense of the poor, Indians, and intellectuals who opposed his methods, all of which brought about his downfall in 1911 and the Mexican Revolution. He died in exile in Paris and is buried there in the Père Lachaise Cemetery.

Josefa Ortiz de Dominguez (1768–1829) Known as La Correguidora, wife of the Corriguidor (Mayor) of Quéretaro, she assured her place in history the night she sent a messenger to warn other conspirators, notably Miguel Hidalgo, that their plot to push for independence from Spain had been discovered by government officials. She was imprisoned several times in Mexico City between 1810 and 1817. She died impoverished and forgotten, but today she is much revered and is buried in the Cemetery of the Illustrious in Querétaro. She was the first woman to appear on a Mexican coin, the 5 centavo piece, minted from 1942–1946.

Carlos Fuentes (b. 1928) Fuentes is one of Mexico's most notable contemporary intellectuals. He gained international recognition at age 30 with his novel *Where the Air is Clear,* a classic in Mexican literature about the Mexican Revolution with an underlying anticapitalist theme. His *Old Gringo* was made a film in Zacatecas, starring Jane Fonda and Gregory Peck.

Francisco Goitia (1882–1960) The Zacatecas-born painter Goitia's reclusive, hermitlike lifestyle set him apart from some of his contemporaries. He chose Mexicans and the Mexican landscape as his themes and he lived humbly, like the people he painted. Peaceful Xochimilco was one of his favorite haunts for living and painting. His *Tata Jesus Cristo* depicts the contrasting figures of two people in mourning illuminated by a single candlelight and is acclaimed as one of the greatest paintings in Mexico.

Andrea Gómez (b. 1924) A renowned lithographer, many of her works are included in the collection of the Palacio de Bellas Artes in

Mexico City where she lives. Her linocut "Mother Against War" was included in the monumental show and catalog "Images of Mexico," in 1988.

Saturnino Herrán   (1887–1918) Born in Aguascalientes, Herrán painted only 15 years until his death at age 31, yet his impact on Mexican art was enormous. He was one of the first to paint the beauty of the common Mexican people. Among his most famous paintings are two works from 1914, *Man with a Rooster* and *Woman from Tehuantepec.*

Augustín Iturbide   (1783–1824) This man, born in Morelia, was crowned Emperor of Mexico, though he reigned only briefly, from 1822 to 1824. For years regarded as a usurper and self-interested politician, public sentiment has recognized his role in gaining Mexico's independence from Spain and his remains were interred more fittingly in Mexico City.

María Izquierdo   (1906–55) Born in San Juan de los Lagos, Jalisco, Izquierdo's career was a brief but important one. Contemporary with Frida Kahlo, her work, like Kahlo's, had a skilled but primitive edge to it. Her subjects were those of everyday Mexican life. Much of her work is in private collections, but good examples are at the Museo de Arte Moderno in Mexico City's Catedral Metropolitana.

Benito Juárez   (1806–1872) A full-blood Zapotec Indian from Guelatao, Oaxaca, he became president of Mexico first in 1858. His terms were interrupted once during the Reform Wars and again during the French intervention. Juárez cast the deciding vote favoring the execution of Maximilian. He died from a heart attack before completing his fourth term. Devoid of personal excesses, Juárez had a clear vision for Mexico that included honest leadership, separation of church and state, imposition of civilian rule, reduction of the military, and education reform. He's buried in the San Fernando Cemetery, Mexico City.

Frida Kahlo   (1907–54) Daughter of a German photographer and Mexican mother, she suffered childhood polio, and as a teenager was lamed further in a gory streetcar accident in Mexico City. She married Diego Rivera twice, and shared his political passions. As an artist she stayed in his shadow until after her death. Her surrealist paintings were mostly self-portraits depicting both her physical pain and the emotional torment she suffered as the wife of frequently unfaithful Rivera. A heavy presence of Kahlo is felt in her home and studio in Coyoacan, Mexico City now a museum left exactly as it was when she lived there.

Guadalupe Loaeza   (b. 1947) One of the capital's most widely read authors, Loaeza's specialty is satirizing the capital's elite. Her articles appear in the newspaper *Reforma* and the *Mira,* a weekly news magazine. Her books include "Las Ninas Bien" (The Chic Girls) and "Primero las Damas," (Ladies First).

Doña Marina (La Malinche)   (early 1500s) This young Indian girl became Hernán Cortés's translator and mistress, bearing him a son, Martin. Scorned as a traitor, to Mexicans her name Malinche (*malinchismo*) means traitor and a preference for foreign people and their customs. Her burial place is unknown.

Moctezuma II   (1468–1520) At age 52, after consolidating an empire that included all the territory surrounding his magnificent capital Tenochtitlán plus today's Veracruz, Chiapas, and Oaxaca, Moctezuma fell victim to a superstitious belief about the return of the white-skinned god Quetzalcoatl, a belief that cost him his life and his empire. Though so exalted that no one was allowed to look at him or sit in his presence, Moctezuma went out to meet Cortés when he arrived in Tenochtitlán, hosted him lavishly, and even toured the city with him. Eventually the Spaniards made Moctezuma a prisoner. During one confusing night, the Aztecs rebelled with every weapon in their arsenal, including stones. Somehow, by accident or on purpose, Moctezuma was hit by a stone and died three days later.

José Clemente Orozco   (1883–1949) Jalisco-born and one of the "Big Three" muralists, Orozco's gloomy, angry, but powerful works project his bitter view of politics. His years of struggle included a stint painting street signs and doll faces in the United States. On one trip north across the border U.S. customs destroyed his brothel series of paintings. His murals appear in the National Preparatory School and many of his easel works are in the Museo de Arte Moderno and the Museo de Arte Alvaro y Carrillo Gil in Mexico City.

Octavio Paz   (b. 1914) Poet, essayist, philosopher, intellectual, and critic, Paz's world-famous book *The Labyrinth of Solitude* appeared in 1950 when he was 36, and in 1990 at 76 he was awarded the Nobel Prize for Literature. His life has not been without controversy over his various positions on governmental policy. When Paz speaks, everybody listens.

José Guadalupe Posada   (1852–1913) His political cartoon characters are so frequently seen today, and his name so readily on the lips of Mexicans, it's amazing to discover he died so long ago. His career paralleled the muralists, but he discovered another vein of popular art—engraved illustrations that accompanied satirical poems. The Posada Museum in Aguascalientes and the Museo de la Estampa in Mexico City display his works.

Vasco de Quiroga   (1470–1565) Beloved "Tata" (daddy) Vasco, as the Tarascan Indians of Michoacán still call him, was nearly 70 when he became Bishop of Michoacán. There he took on the task of converting the Tarascans, who had been shamefully mistreated by ruling Spaniards. With love and tremendous energy he taught them trades in weaving, coppersmithing, pottery, and furniture making, all of which thrive in the region today.

Diego Rivera   (1886–1957) Considered the most outstanding of Mexico's famous "Big Three" muralists, his grand, often controversial murals present Mexico's history through the lense of his romantic Marxist vision. Some of his greatest murals are at the Palacio Nacional in Mexico City. His mural painted for New York City's Rockefeller Center was destroyed because Lenin appeared in it. He later recreated it in the Palacio de Bellas Artes in Mexico City. At his insistence the Mexican government gave communist leader Leon Trotsky refuge in Mexico City. He married, divorced, and remarried artist Frida Kahlo. Museums showing his work and pre-Hispanic art collections are in Mexico City and Guanajuato, the city of his birth. He's buried at the Dolores Cemetery, Chapultepec Park, Mexico City.

Antonio López de Santa Anna (1794–1876) One of the most scorned characters in Mexican history, he was president of Mexico 11 times between 1833 and 1855. Audacious, pompous, and self-absorbed, his outrageous exploits disgust and infuriate Mexicans even today, but none more than his role in losing half the territory of Mexico to the United States. Eventually Santa Anna was exiled, but returned two years before he died, poor, alone, and forgotten. He is buried in the Guadalupe Cemetery on the hill above the Basílica de Guadelupe in Mexico City.

David Alfaro Siquieros (1896–1974) Born in Chihuahua, and enrolled at age 15 in the San Carlos Academy, he became one of the "Big Three" Mexican muralists. Influenced early by communist thought, he spent a lifetime passionately fighting for his political ideals, even interrupting his painting career for five years from 1925–1930 to work for trade unionization, and again in 1937 when he fought in the Spanish Civil War. His criticism of the Mexican government landed him in prison for almost four years where he continued to paint. In 1966, two years after release, he received the government's prize for art.

Sor Juana Inés de la Cruz (1651–95) Known as colonial Mexico's greatest poetess, she was born in Nepantla, State of Mexico. She was openly critical of the subordinate role of women in society. Rather than marry, she became a nun, devoting herself to writing, scholarly studies, and theology. Eventually she was thought to be attracted to women, was accused as a heretic and shunned by other nuns, and died at age 43 during an epidemic in 1695. Remains believed to be hers are buried at the Ex-convent of San Jerónimo in Mexico City where she resided.

Rufino Tamayo (1899–1991) Born in Oaxaca and educated at the San Carlos Academy, he came into his own when he abandoned the muralist subjects of politics and history and developed his own design and use of color, for which he is famous. Acknowledged as the most daring of Mexican colorists (some scholars say the best in the modern world), his abstract easel paintings were most often themed around fruit and man-made objects, but seldom people. The Museo Rufino Tamayo in Mexico city holds his work and his personal art collection, while the Tamayo Museum in Oaxaca contains his collection of pre-Hispanic art.

Manuel Tolsa (1757–1816) Born in Spain and trained as a sculptor, he completed the Catedral Metropolitana, designed the Palacio Mineria, sculpted and cast in bronze the famous Caballito statue of Charles V on horseback, and designed the high altar and tabernacle of the cathedral in Puebla, as well as other works in the country. A portrait of him painted by Rafael Jimeno y Planes is in the Pinacoteca Virreinal de San Diego Museum in Mexico City. He is buried a block away from the museum in the atrium of the Church of Santa Veracruz, opposite the Alameda.

José María Velasco (1840–1912) Known as the father of Mexican landscape painting, Velasco's masterful eye turned toward the panoramic scenery around Mexico City for subject matter. He painted these grand scenes almost exclusively, except for a few resulting from a trip to Oaxaca. His work can be seen at the Museo Nacional de Arte in the capital and at the José María Velasco museum in Toluca.

Cristóbal de Villalpando (1645–1714) Born in the capital, Villalpando's skill and acclaim as a figure painter were equal to that of his contemporary Juan Correa, but his style has often been compared to Rubens. By the time he died at age 69, he left an enormous collection of work, examples of which are at the Catedral Metropolitana and in Xochimilco at the Convento de San Bernardino.

---

4 **A Very Public Splendor: Art & Architecture in the Capital**

ART

Fortunately for art and history lovers who visit the capital, the most abundant collection of the country's past and present art is represented here in museums and galleries, most notably the Museo Nacional del Arte, Museo de Arte Contemporaneo, Museo Rufino Tamayo, Museo Franz Mayer, Museo Nacional de Antropología, Museo Templo Mayor, and on the walls of public buildings throughout the capital.

Even before the arrival of the Spaniards, art, architecture, politics, and religion in Mexico were inextricably entertwined; this remained the case through the colonial period, although in a different way. In pre-Hispanic times art wasn't merely decorative or visual the way we think of it; instead, it expressed historic events and religious concepts in life-size murals, in fan-fold hand-painted books, on pottery, and as symbolism carved or painted on structures. It had primarily a nondecorative purpose.

The Toltecs used some of Teotihuacán's symbolism; the Aztecs, in turn, adopted ideas of both the Teotihuacán and Toltec cultures. For example, the *chac-mool,* a stone figure reclining backwards on knees and elbows with the stomach indented to hold the heart of a sacrificial victim, figured in these central Mexican cultures, and in southern Maya culture as well.

Pottery played an important role and different indigenous groups are distinguished by their use of color and style in pottery. The Cholulans had distinctive red clay pottery decorated in cream red and black; Teotihuacán was noted for its three-legged painted orangeware; Tenochtitlán for its use of brilliant blue and red. Besides regional museums, the best collection of all this work is in the Museo Nacional de Antropología in Mexico City.

When Spanish priests arrived, one way they tried to overcome the language barrier in reaching the natives was through graphic church adornment. The talents of native master stone and wood carvers were turned, under the direction of Spanish priests and architects, to Christian subjects. Biblical tales came to life in frescoes splashed across church walls, and Christian symbolism in stone supplanted that of pre-Hispanic times. Out went the eagle (sun symbol), feathered serpent (symbol of fertility, rain, earth and sky), and jaguar (power symbol); in came Christ on a cross, saintly statues, and Franciscan, Dominican, and Augustinian symbolism on church facades. It must have been a confusing time for the indigenous peoples, which accounts for the continued intermingling of Christian and pre-Hispanic ideas as they tried to make sense of it all by mixing pre-existing ideas with new ones.

Spanish colonists mingled the existing pottery-making tradition around Puebla with the Talavera pottery style from Toledo, Spain, and building facades and church domes countrywide began sporting colorfully painted tiles created from this new marriage of craft. Pottery dinnerware with these new designs began to appear on the tables of the elite; this style is still being made today in Puebla, Tlaxcala, and elsewhere.

After the Conquest, native artists were considered inferior to Spanish artists trained in Spain. However, the most famous 18th-century artist was a Zapotec Indian, Miguel Cabrera (1695–1768), who left an enormous legacy of secular and religious paintings. He captured the *castas* (see "The Viceregal Era" in "History & Politics," above) in a series of paintings, showing their colorful, varied manner of dress, which was often sassy and provocative.

Some 17th-century Mexican paintings feature the female servants of wealthy families, decked out in jewelry and colorful clothing. At the time, following the lead of the Spanish court, black was the only respectable color worn by the wealthy, who couldn't resist flaunting their wealth by draping it on their servants. Over the centuries, the upper crust posed before painters too, capturing themselves bedecked in silks and velvets from Europe and pearls from the Sea of Cortéz.

A curious trend seen in the portraits of many high-class women included the *chiqueador,* a dark circle, often a very large one, placed prominently on the temple. What eventually became used as a beauty mark actually began as a headache remedy. Circles of velvet, felt, or leather covered a mixture of herbs and were stuck to the temple. Later they evolved into beauty marks worn by elite women. The mark often appears on the female subjects of Cabrera's paintings. Even today women in Mexico's rural markets can sometimes be seen sporting the chiqueador.

Young women about to enter the convent also posed for paintings, a custom unique to Mexico. These paintings of *monjas coronadas* (crowned nuns), many of which were done by Cabrera, were evidently a keepsake for a nun's family. The women appeared with large, ornate crowns of flowers, wearing elaborate gowns and holding candles or other symbolic items in one hand and small religious figures in the other. On their chest were *escudos* (shields) made of tin or bronze that illustrated a religious subject. Those who led distinguished religious lives were often painted in death as well, wearing the elaborate crowns of flowers. Such paintings, by Cabrera and others, can be seen at the Museo Nacional de Arte and Museo Pinacoteca Virreinal de Santiago in Mexico City, and at the Museo Virreinato in Tepotzotlán, north of the city. Reproductions of some of Cabrera's *castas* paintings can be found in the exhibition catalog *Mexico Splendors of Thirty Centuries* (Metropolitan Museum of Art, New York, 1991).

The San Carlos Academy of Art was founded in Mexico City in 1785, taking after the renowned academies of Europe. Though the wider culture at the time was enthusiastic about a Europeanized Mexico, by the end of the 19th Century, the subject matter of easel artists at the San Carlos Academy and elsewhere in the country was becoming Mexican: Still lifes with Mexican fruit and pottery, clearly Mexican landscapes with cactus and volcanoes appeared, as did portraits, whose subjects wore Mexican regional clothing. José María Velasco (1840–1912), the father of Mexican landscape painting, emerged during this time. His work and others of this period are at the National Museum of Art in Mexico City and Velasco Museum in Toluca.

Mexican themes returned to the back burner during the Porfiriato. During his 30-year presidency Porfirio Díaz championed the arts and provided European scholarships to promising young artists. Though many of these artists later returned to Mexico to produce clearly Mexican subject paintings using techniques learned abroad, Díaz championed European—and particularly French—art and culture, and many of the artworks and buildings of the time are his legacy.

While the Mexican Revolution ripped the country apart between 1911 and 1917, it resulted in a new-found pride and appreciation of it by its citizens, which carried into the arts. Artists again turned to the Mexican landscape and culture for inspiration, and the public's tastes turned with them. In 1923, when Minister of Education José Vasconcelos invited Diego Rivera and several other budding artists to paint Mexican history on the walls of Mexico City's Ministry of Education building and National Preparatory School as a means of educating illiterate masses, he started the muralist movement. From then on, the "big three" muralists, David Siquieros, José Clemente Orozco, and Rivera, were joined by others in bringing Mexico's history to the walls of public buildings throughout the country as art for all to see and interpret. The years that followed eventually brought about a return to easel art, an exploration of Mexico's culture, and a new generation of artists and architects who today are free to invent and draw upon subjects and styles from around the world. Among the 20th-century greats are the big three muralists, as well as Rufino Tamayo, Gerardo Murillo, José Guadalupe Posada, Saturnino Herrán, Raúl Anguiano, Francisco Goitia, Frida Kahlo, José Maria Velasco, Pedro and Rafael Coronel, Miguel Covarrubias, Juan Soriano, Vicente Rojo, Alfredo Zalce, Roberto Montenegro, Cordelia Urueta, Olga Costa, and José Chávez Morado. Their works can be found in museums in the capital.

ARCHITECTURE

Regarding pre-Hispanic architecture, Mexico's pyramids are truncated platforms, not true pyramids, and come in many different shapes. Many sites, such as Cuicuilco south of the city, have circular buildings, usually called the observatory and dedicated to Ehécatl, god of the wind. Evidence of building one pyramidal structure on top of another, a method widely practiced by pre-Hispanic cultures, has been found throughout Mesoamerica. What's visible now of the Templo Mayor, in the capital's Centro Historico, is an example of an older temple once covered by several superimpositions. A characteristic of Teotihuacán architecture was the use of a sloping panel (tablud) alternating with a verticle panel (tablero) on building facades. Good examples of this are at Teotihuacán and the reconstructed portions of the pyramid at Cholula near Puebla.

Throughout Mexico, the pyramids were embellished with carved stone or mural art, not for the purpose of pure adornment, but for religious and historic reasons. Some of the fantastic painted murals are remarkably preserved at Cacaxtla near Tlaxcala. But at Teotihuacán and Cholula, only fragments remain.

With the arrival of the Spaniards a new form of architecture came to Mexico. Catholic churches, public buildings and palaces for conquerors and the king's bureaucrats appeared where once indigenous architecture had stood. Indian artisans, who formerly worked on pyramidal structures, were recruited (by forced labor) to give life to these structures, often guided by drawings of European buildings the Spanish architects tried to emulate. Frequently left on their own, the indigenous artisans sometimes implanted their symbolism on the buildings. They might sculpt a plaster angel swaddled in feathers reminiscent of the god Quetzalcoatl or the face of an fertility god surrounded by corn leaves (signifying life) or symbolic numbers of the thirteen steps to heaven or the nine levels of the underworld to determine how many flowerettes to carve around the church doorway. Good examples of native symbolism are at the Church of San Juan Tlaltentli and Convent of San Bernardino de Siena in Xochimilco near Mexico City, and Santa María Tonanzintla near Cholula and Puebla.

Baroque became even more baroque in Mexico and was dubbed *Churrigueresque.* Excellent Mexican baroque examples are the

Catedral Metropolitana and its neighbor El Sagrario in Mexico City. The term *Plateresque* was given to facade designs resembling silver design, but more planted on a structure than a part of it. The Vice-regal Museum in Tepotzotlán holds a wealth of artwork from Mexican churches during this period.

Public buildings modeled after those in European capitals were built. Talavera-style tile (see "Art," above) decorated public walls and church domes. Hacienda architecture—vast estates with massive, thick-walled, fortress-like structures built around a central patio—sprang up in the countryside. Remains of haciendas, some of them still operating, can be seen in almost all parts of Mexico.

Porfirio Díaz lavished a number of striking European-style public buildings, among them opera houses still used today, on the country. Among the country's important architects is Luis Barragán, who incorporated design elements from haciendas, and Mexican textiles, pottery, and furniture into sleek, marble-floored structures splashed with the vivid colors of Mexico. His ideas are used by architects all over Mexico today.

Over the centuries, the capital changed greatly from the original plan designed by the earliest Spaniards. Each decade and century demolished portions of the previous one and built upon the remains. When the present-day streets of Cinco de Mayo and Madero were widened to link the Zócalo to the Alameda, numerous historic buildings were sacrificed. Over the centuries many more magnificent structures disappeared, leaving us with remains of remains or nothing at all. Unfortunately, the most devastation of the past has occurred this century. The last 40 years have all too often produced uniform ugliness. But the capital is still deservingly called "The City of Palaces," for there remain numerous grand and historic buildings. The city's ongoing efforts to conserve and restore hundreds of historic structures in the *Centro Historico* (Historic Center) is strikingly evident not only in finished projects but in scaffolding around old structures of the area. With this renewed zeal for preservation, it's unlikely historic walls will come tumbling down as thoughtlessly as they have in the past.

5 By Word of Mouth or Stroke of Pen: Mexico's Storytelling Tradition

LITERATURE

By the time Cortés arrived in Mexico, the cultures of Mexico were already masters of literature, recording their poems and histories by painting in fanfold books (codices) made of deer skin and bark paper or carving on stone. To record history, gifted students were taught the art of book making, drawing, painting, reading and writing, abilities the general public didn't have.

After the Conquest the Spaniards deliberately destroyed native books. No authenticated Aztec painted books remain. However,

Aztec artist survivors of the Conquest painted some that were used to verify Aztec territories, tributes, property, etc., but that also contained Aztec history, ritual, and culture before the Conquest. Two revealing ones, the *Codex Telleriano-Remensis* and the *Codex Ixtlilxochitl*, are in the Bibliothèque Nationale in Paris. Alexander von Humboldt, the intrepid German naturalist who spent time in Mexico, rediscovered one in the 19th century and gave it the name *Telleriano-Remensis.*

During the Conquest Cortés wrote his now famous five letters to Charles V, which give us the first printed Conquest literature, but it was spare by contrast to the work of Bernal Díaz de Castillo. Enraged by an inaccurate account of the Conquest written by a flattering friend of Cortés, Bernal Diaz de Castillo, one of the conquerors, wrote (some 40 years after the the events) his lively and very readable version of the event, *True History of the Conquest of Mexico;* it's regarded as the most accurate.

The most important literary figure during the 16th century was Sor Juana Inez de la Cruz, a child prodigy and later poet-nun whose works are still treasured. The first Spanish novel written in Mexico was *Periquillo Sarniento* (Itching Parrot) by José Joaquín Fernández de Lizardi. It's a classic, satirical 19th-century tale about the wanton life a young man leads after his mother convinces him he is too aristocratic to work, though he has no means of support. Nineteenth-century writers produced a plethora of political fiction and nonfiction. Among the more explosive was *The Presidential Sucession of 1910* by Francisco Madero (who later became president), which contributed to the downfall of Porfirio Díaz; and *Regeneración,* a weekly anti-Díaz magazine published by the Flores Mignon brothers. Among 20th-century writers of note are Octavio Paz, author of *The Labyrinth of Solitude* and winner of the 1991 Nobel Prize for literature, and Carlos Fuentes, who wrote *Where the Air is Clear.* Books in Mexico are expensive and editions are not produced in great quantity. Newspapers and magazines proliferate, but comic book novels are the most visible form of literature.

LANGUAGE

Although Spanish is the official language, about 50 Indian languages are still spoken. Around Mexico City indigenous populations still speak Nahuatl, the language of the Aztecs. You can hear it readily in Valle de Bravo, west of the city, and to a lesser extent in Puebla and Tlaxcala, both of which are a short distance east.

RELIGION

Mexico is a predominantly Catholic country. Despite the preponderance of the Catholic faith, in many places it has pre-Hispanic overtones. One need only visit the *curandero* (folk medicine) section of a Mexican market, or attend a village festivity featuring pre-Hispanic dancers, to understand that supernatural beliefs often run parallel to Christian ones. The country's most sacred Catholic shrine is the Basílica de Guadalupe in Mexico City.

MYTH & FOLKLORE

Mexico's complicated mythological heritage from pre-Hispanic literature is jammed with images derived from nature—the wind, jaguars, eagles, snakes, flowers, and more, all intertwined with elaborate mythological stories to explain the universe, climate, seasons, and geography. So strong were the ancient beliefs in their mythological deities that Mexico's indigenous peoples built their cities according to the cardinal points, with each direction assigned a particular color (the colors might vary from group to group). The sun, moon, and stars took on godlike meaning, and religious, ceremonial, and secular calendars were arranged to show tribute to these omnipotent gods.

Most groups believed in an underworld (not a hell), usually of 9 levels, and a heaven of 13 levels, so the numbers 9 and 13 became mythologically significant. The solar calendar count of 365 days and the ceremonial calendar of 260 days are numerically significant. How one died determined where one wound up after death—in the underworld, heaven, or at one of the four cardinal points. Everyone had to first make the journey through the underworld.

Each of the ancient cultures had its set of gods and goddesses and while the names might not cross cultures, their characteristics or purpose often did. *Chac,* the hook-nosed rain god of the Maya, was *Tlaloc,* the mighty-figured rain god of the Aztecs; *Quetzalcoatl,* the plumed serpent god/man of the Toltecs, became *Kukulkán* of the Maya. The tales of the powers and creation of these deified personages makes up Mexico's rich mythology. Sorting out the pre-Hispanic pantheon and mythological beliefs in ancient Mexico can become an all-consuming study, so below is a list of some of the most important Aztec and Aztec-related gods:

Coatlíque Huitzilopochtli's mother; the name means "she of serpent skirt," goddess of death and earth.

Coyolxauhqui Daughter of Coatlíaue and goddess of the moon and night.

Ehécatl Wind god whose temple is usually round; another aspect of Quetzalcoatl.

Huitzilopochtli War god and primary Aztec god; sun god and son of Coatlique. Appeasing Huitzilopochtli required great quantities of human blood, mostly from those taken captive in war.

Kukulkán Quetzalcoatl's name in the Yucatán.

Mayahuel Goddess of pulque.

Ometeotl God/goddess, all-powerful creator of the universe; ruler of heaven, earth, and underworld.

Quetzalcoatl A mortal who took on legendary characteristics as a god (or visa versa). He is also symbolized as Venus, the morning star, and Ehécatl, the wind god. Said to have introduced Mexico to cacao and taught the people how to grow, ferment, roast, and grind it into chocolate.

Tezcaltipoca Aztec sun god known as "Smoking Mirror," god of vengeance, of the night, and of magic.

Tlaloc   Aztec rain god responsible for abundant crops.
Tonantzin   Aztec motherhood goddess.
Tótec   Nature god and god of jewelry makers.
Xochipilli   Aztec god of dance, flowers, and music.
Xochiquetzal   Flower and love goddess.

6 Mariachi Serenades & More: Mexico's Music & Dance

One has only to walk down almost any street or attend any festival to understand that Mexico's vast musical tradition is inborn; it predates the Conquest. Musical instruments were made from almost anything that could be made to rattle, produce a rhythm, or a sound—conch-shell trumpets; high sounding antler horns; rattles from seashells and rattlesnakes; drums of turtle shell, as well as upright leather-covered wood (*tlalpanhuéhuetl*) and horizontal hollowed logs (*teponaztli*); bells of gold and copper; wind instruments of hollow reeds or fired clay; and soundmakers from leather-topped armadillo shells and gourds. Many were elaborately carved or decorated to befit the important ceremonies they accompanied. So important was music that one of Moctezuma's palaces, the Mixcoacalli, was devoted to the care and housing of musical instruments, which were guarded around the clock. The dead were buried with musical instruments for the journey into the afterlife. In Aztec times, music, dance, and religion were tied together with literature. Music was usually intended to accompany poems, which were written for religious ceremonies.

Music and dance in Mexico today is divided into three kinds, pre- and post-Hispanic and secular. Besides local village fiestas, two of the best places to see pre-Hispanic dancing are the Ballet Folklorico de Mexico and the Ballet Folklorico Nacional Aztlán both in Mexico City. Among pre-Hispanic dances still performed there or elsewhere in Mexico are "The Flying Pole Dance," "Dance of the Quetzales," "Deer Dance," and dances of the Huicholes and Coras of Jalisco and Nayarit. Post-Hispanic music and dance evolved first in order to teach the native inhabitants about Christianity with such dances as "Los Santiagos" (featuring St. James battling heathens), and "Los Moros" (Moors battling Christians). Others, like "Los Jardineros," were spoofs on pretentious Spanish life. Secular dances are variations of Spanish dances, performed by both men and women and characterized by lots of foot-tapping, skirt-swishing, and flirtatious gestures. No "Mexican fiesta night" would be complete without the "Jarabe Tapatío," the national folk dance of Mexico. The "Huapango," accompanied by violins and guitars, is a native dance of Veracruz, Tamaulipas, and San Luis Potosí. "Jaranas" are folk dances of the Yucatán, danced to the lively beat of a ukelele-like instrument and drums.

Besides the native music and dances, there are regional, state, and national orchestras. On weekends state bands often perform free in central plazas such as that of Tlaxcala. You'll find national as well as international groups touring most of the year.

7 More Than Margaritas and Tortillas: Mexico City's Dining Scene

Some of the best restaurants in Mexico are in the capital, and in many ways it's possible to savor more authentic Mexican food here, in all its regional variations, than anywhere else in the country.

Mexican food served in the United States or almost anywhere else in the world is almost never truly Mexican. The farther you get from the source the more the authenticity is lost in translation. True Mexican food usually isn't fiery hot, for example; hot spices are added from sauces and garnishes at the table.

While there are certain staples like tortillas and beans that appear almost universally around the country, Mexican food and drink varies considerably from region to region; even the beans and tortillas will sidestep the usual in different locales.

MEALS & RESTAURANTS Á LA MEXICANA

BREAKFAST Traditionally, businesspeople in Mexico may start their day with a cup of coffee or *atole* and a piece of sweet bread just before heading for work around 8am; they won't sit down for a real breakfast until around 10 or 11am, when restaurants fill with men (usually) eating hearty breakfasts that may look more like lunch with steak, eggs, beans, and tortillas. Things are slowly changing as some executives are beginning to favor an earlier breakfast hour, beginning between 7 and 8am, during which business and the morning meal are combined.

Foreigners searching for an early breakfast will often find that nothing gets going in restaurants until around 9am; however, markets are bustling by 7am (they are a great place to get an early breakfast) and the capital's hotel restaurants often open as early as 7am to accommodate business travelers and those leaving on early flights. If you like to stoke the fires first thing, you might also bring your own portable coffee pot and coffee and buy bakery goodies the night before and make breakfast yourself.

LUNCH The main meal of the day, lunch, has traditionally been a two- to three-hour break, occurring between 1 and 5pm. But in the capital, at least, an abbreviated lunch is beginning to take hold. Short or long, the typical Mexican lunch begins with soup, then rice, then a main course with beans and tortillas and a bit of vegetable, and lastly dessert and coffee. But here too you'll see one-plate meals and fast food beginning to encroach on the multicourse meal. Workers return to their jobs until 7 or 8pm.

DINNER The evening meal is taken late, usually around 9 or 10pm. Although you may see many Mexicans eating in restaurants at night, big evening meals aren't traditional; a typical meal at home would be a light one with leftovers from breakfast or lunch, perhaps soup or tortillas and jam, or a little meat and rice.

RESTAURANT TIPS & ETIQUETTE   Some of the foreigner's greatest frustrations in Mexico occur in restaurants, when they need to hail and retain the waiter or get their check. To summon the waiter, waive or raise your hand, but don't motion with your index finger, a demeaning gesture that may even cause the waiter to ignore you. To gesture someone to them, Mexicans will stand up, extend an arm straight out at shoulder level, and make a straight-armed, downward, diving motion with their hand cupped. A more discreet version, good to use when seated, has the elbow bent and perpendicular to the shoulder; with hand cupped, make a quick, diving motion out a bit from the armpit. (Both of these motions may make you feel silly until you practice. The latter one looks rather like the motion Americans make to signify "be still" or "shut up.")

If the waiter arrives to take your order before you are ready, you may have trouble getting him again. Once an order is in, however, the food usually arrives in steady sequence. Frequently, just before you've finished, when your plate is nearly empty, the waiter appears out of nowhere to whisk it away—unwary diners have seen their plates disappear mid-bite.

Finding your waiter when you're ready for the check can also be difficult. While waiters may hover too much while you're dining, they tend to disappear entirely by meal's end. It's considered rude for the waiter to bring the check before it's requested, so you have to ask for it, sometimes more than once. (To find a missing waiter, get up as if to leave and scrape the chairs loudly; if that fails, you'll probably find him chatting in the kitchen.) If you want the check and the waiter is simply across the room, a smile and a scribbling motion into the palm of your hand will send the message. In many budget restaurants, waiters don't clear the table of finished plates or soft drink bottles because they use them to figure the tab. Always double-check the addition.

FOOD IN THE CAPITAL CITY

You won't have to confine yourself to Mexican food during a visit to Mexico City—you'll find restaurants that prepare world-class French, Italian, Swiss, German, and other international cuisines. But there's also no better city to delve into the variety of Mexico's traditional foods, which derive from pre-Hispanic, Spanish, and French cuisines. At its best Mexican food is among the most delicious in the world. Often, however, traditional food preparations are only mediocre, though several traditional restaurants in the capital do a stellar job. Visitors can fairly easily find hearty, filling meals on a budget, but finding truly delicious food is not so easy. One positive is that some of the capital's best Mexican food is found in small inexpensive restaurants where regional specialties are made to please discerning locals. Explanations of specific dishes are found in the appendix.

Recipes such as mole poblano—developed by nuns during colonial times to please priests and visiting dignitaries—have become part of the national patrimony, but the basics of Mexico's cuisine have endured since pre-Hispanic times. Corn, considered holy, was the foundation staple food of pre-Hispanic peoples. These people used corn leaves to bake and wrap food and ground corn to make the *atole* drink in many flavors (bitter, picante, or sweet) as well as tortillas and tamales (stuffed with meat).

When the Spanish arrived they found a bounty of edibles never seen in the Old World, including turkey, chocolate, tomatoes, squash, beans, avocados, peanuts, and vanilla (in addition to corn). All of these ingredients were integral parts of pre-Hispanic foods, and remain at the heart of today's Mexican cooking. Also central to the Indian peoples' cuisines were chiles, nopal cactus, amaranth, eggs of ants, turtles and iguanas, corn and maguey worms, bee and fly larvae, flowers of the maguey and squash, grasshoppers, jumiles (similar to stinkbugs), armadillos, rattlesnake, hairless dogs, deer, squirrels, monkeys, rats, frogs, ducks, parrots, quail, shrimp, fish, crabs, and crawfish. Exotic fruits such as sapodilla, guava, mamey, chirimoya, and pitahuayas rounded out the diet. Some of these are mainstream foods today, and others are considered delicacies and may be seen on specialty menus.

But much of what we consider Mexican food wouldn't exist without the contributions of the Spanish. They introduced sugar cane, cattle, sheep, wheat, grapes, barley, and rice. The French influence is best seen in the extensive variety of baked goods available in the capital.

MEXICO'S REGIONAL CUISINES Tamales are a traditional food all around Mexico, but there are many regional differences. In Mexico City you can often find the traditional Oaxaca tamales, which are steamed in a banana leaf. The zacahuil of coastal Veracruz is the size of a pig's leg (and that's what's in the center) and is pit-baked in a banana leaf; it can be sampled from street vendors on Sunday at the Lagunilla market.

Tortillas, another Mexican basic, are also not made or used equally. In Northern Mexico flour tortillas are served more often than corn tortillas. Blue corn tortillas, once a market food, have found their way to gourmet tables throughout the country. Tortillas are fried and used as a garnish in tortilla and Tarascan soup. Filled with meat they become, of course, tacos. A tortilla stuffed, rolled, or covered in a sauce and garnished results in an enchilada. A tortilla filled with cheese and lightly fried is a quesadilla. Rolled into a narrow tube stuffed with chicken, then deep fried, they become a flauta. Leftover tortillas cut in wedges and crispy fried are called totopos and used to scoop beans and guacamole salad. Yesterday's tortillas mixed with eggs, chicken, peppers, and other spices are called chilaquiles. Small fried corn tortillas are delicious with ceviche, or when topped with fresh lettuce, tomatoes, sauce, onions, and chicken they become tostadas. Each region has a variation of these tortilla-based dishes and most can be found in Mexico City.

Since a variety of Mexico's cuisines appear on menus in the capital, its useful to know some of the best to try.

Puebla is known for the many dishes created by colonial-era nuns, among them traditional *mole poblano* (a rich sauce with more than 20 ingredients served over turkey), the eggnoglike rompope, and bunuelos (a kind of puff pastry dipped in sugar). Puebla is also known for its Mexican-style barbeque, lamb *mixiotes* (cooked in spicy sauce and wrapped in maguey paper), and tinga (a delicious beef stew). And *chiles enogada,* the national dish of Mexico, was created in Puebla in honor of Emperor Agustin Iturbide. The national colors of red, white, and green appear in this dish, in which large green poblano peppers are stuffed with spicy beef, topped with white almond sauce, and sprinkled with red pomegranate seeds. It's served around Independence Day in September.

Tamales wrapped in banana leaves and a number of different mole sauces are hallmarks of **Oaxacan** cuisine.

The **Yucatán** is noted for its rich (but not *picante*) sauces and pit-baked meat. Mild but flavorful achiote-based paste is one of the main flavorings for Yucatecan sauces.

The states of **Guerrero, Nayarit,** and **Jalisco** produce *pozole,* a soup of hominy and chicken or pork made in a clear broth or one from tomatoes or green chiles (depending on the state), and topped with a variety of garnishes.

Michoacán comes forth with a triangular-shaped tamal called *corunda,* and *uchepo,* a rectangular tamal that is either sweet or has meat inside. The state is also known for its soups, among them the delicious *Tarascan* soup, made with a bean-broth base.

And **Veracruz,** of course, is famous for seafood dishes, especially red snapper Veracruz-style, smothered in tomatoes, onions, garlic, and olives.

DRINK

Though Mexico grows flavorful **coffee** in Chiapas, Veracruz, and Oaxaca, a jar of instant coffee is often all that's offered, especially in budget restaurants. Decaffeinated coffee appears on some menus, but often it's the instant variety, even in the best restaurants.

Specialty drinks are almost as varied as the food in Mexico. **Tequila** comes from the blue agave grown near Guadalajara and it's the intoxicating ingredient in the famed Margarita. Hot *ponche* (punch) is found often at festivals and is usually made with fresh fruit and spiked with tequila or rum.

Domestic wine and beer are excellent choices in Mexico, and in the past have been cheaper than any imported variety. However, NAFTA has lowered trade barriers against U.S.-made alcoholic drinks, and prices for them are becoming lower as well.

Baja California and the region around Querétaro is prime grape growing land for Mexico's **wine** production. Excellent **beer** is produced in Monterrey, the Yucatán and Veracruz. The best *pulque,* a pre-Hispanic drink derived from the juice of the maguey plant, supposedly comes from Hidalgo state. Mexicans prefer freshly fermented pulque and generally avoid the canned variety, saying it's just not the real thing. Visitors to the capital can sample it at restaurants around Garibaldi square. Delicious **fruit-flavored waters** appear on tables countrywide; they are made from hibiscus flowers, ground rice and melon seeds, watermelon, and other fresh fruits. Be sure to ask if they are made with purified water. **Sangria** is a spicy tomato-, orange juice-, and pepper-based chaser for tequila shots.

Though the rich, eggnoglike *rompope* was invented in Puebla, now other regions such as San Juan de los Lagos, Jalisco, produce it. It's sold in liquor and grocery stores countrywide.

8 Recommended Books, Films & Recordings

BOOKS

There are countless books and periodicals dealing with the history, culture, and archeology of Mexico. I have listed those that are especially relevant to Mexico City, and the country as it involves the capital.

General History

The True History of the Conquest of New Spain (Shoe String, 1988), by Bernal Díaz del Castillo, a lieutenant of Cortés, is considered the most reliable first-person account of the Mexican Conquest. The Conqueror himself wrote six letters to the King of Spain telling about the Conquest and the wonders of this new land. Five letters exist and are published in *Letters from Mexico* (Grossman Publishers, 1971). Aztec victims of the Conquest give their gripping version of the events in *The Broken Spears,* edited by Miguel Leon-Portilla (Beacon Press, 1962). *Ancient Mexico: An Overview* (University of New Mexico, 1985), by Jaime Litvak, is a short, very readable history of pre-Hispanic Mexico. W. H. Prescott's *The Conquest of Mexico* (1843), long the standard-setting scholarly account of the Spanish Conquest of Mexico, is remarkable for its detail and readability, though an abridged version is more pleasurable. *Conquest: Montezuma, Cortes and the Fall of Old Mexico,* by Hugh Thomas (Simon & Schuster, 1994), with illustrations, goes beyond the Prescott classic with a fresh look at the Conquest, giving versions from Aztecs, conquerors, and Spanish authorities, and details of Cortés's trial in Spain after the Conquest.

Scholar Charles Gibson unlocks the unique relationship between the Spanish conquerors and their Tlaxcalan allies in *Tlaxcala in the Sixteenth Century* (Stanford University 1952). By chronicling 200 years of one hacienda in *A Jesuit Hacienda in Colonial Mexico, Santa Lucia, 1576–1767* (Stanford, 1980), Herman W. Konrad brings readers inside the fascinating history of the rise of haciendas in Mexico (Santa Lucia was just north of Mexico City), and their political and economic relation to the rest of Mexico, especially the capital.

A Short History of Mexico (Doubleday, 1962), by J. Patrick McHenry, is a concise historical account. A remarkably readable and thorough college textbook is *The Course of Mexican History* (Oxford

University Press, 1987) by Michael C. Meyer and William L. Sherman.

Don't miss the chance to devour Jonathan Kandell's assiduously researched, yet wonderfully readable *La Capital, Biography of Mexico City* (Random House, 1988).

The Crown of Mexico (Holt Rinehart & Winston, 1971) by Joan Haslip, a biography of Maximilian and Carlotta, reads like a novel. *The Wind that Swept Mexico* (University of Texas Press, 1971), by Anita Brenner, is a classic illustrated account of the Mexican Revolution.

Most people can't put down Gary Jennings's *Aztec* (Avon, 1981), a superbly researched and colorfully written fictionalized account of Aztec life before and after the Conquest. Equally revealing is *The Luck of Huemac,* by Daniel Peters (Random House, 1981), a compelling novel about four generations of an Aztec family between the years 1428 and 1520.

Artes de Mexico produced special illustrated issues on Xochimilco and its history (Number 20, Summer 1993), and on Templo Mayor Art (Number 7, Spring 1990).

Culture

In *Everyday Life of the Aztecs* (Dorset Press, 1968), Warwick Bray outlines the three phases of Aztec history and shows how the Aztecs burned their history books to create a more lofty version of their rise to power. *Mexican and Central American Mythology* (Peter Bedrick Books, 1983), by Irene Nicholson, is a concise illustrated book that simplifies this complex subject.

The classic *Life in Mexico: Letters of Fanny Calderón de la Barca* (Doubleday, 1966), is as lively and entertaining today as when it first appeared in 1843. But the illustrated and annotated update by Howard T. Fisher and Marion Hall Fisher makes it even more contemporary. Scottish born Fanny lived in Mexico City and was married to the Spanish Ambassador assigned there. The letters are written to her relatives with the accounts of her experiences in the capital and countryside, flecked with her colorful and descriptive observations of Mexican culture, politics, and religion. Early this century Charles Flandrau wrote *Viva Mexico: A Traveller's Account of Life In Mexico* (Eland Books, 1985), a blunt and humorous description of Mexico.

Five Families (Basic Books, 1959), and *Children of Sanchez* (Random House, 1979), by Oscar Lewis, are memorable, tremendously insightful, and very readable sociological studies written in the late 1950s and early 1960s about labor class Mexican families in and around Mexico City.

Several contemporary writers have written lively accounts of their pursuit of the Conquest route of Cortés, which contain history interwoven with customs of rural and city life of this century. Two of these are *Trailing Cortés Through Mexico* by Harry A. Franck (Frederick A. Stokes, 1935), and *Reconquest of Mexico* by Mathew J. Bruccoli (Vanguard Press, 1974).

A good but controversial all-around introduction to contemporary Mexico and its people is *Distant Neighbors: A Portrait of the Mexicans,* (Random House, 1984), by Alan Riding. Another such book is Patrick Oster's *The Mexicans: A Personal Portrait of the Mexican People* (Harper & Row, 1989), a reporter's insightful account of ordinary citizens of the capital. Another book with valuable insights into the Mexican character is *The Labyrinth of Solitude,* (Grove Press, 1985), by Octavio Paz. The best book for understanding how Mexico works from the inside is *Mexico, A Country Guide* (The Inter-Hemispheric Education Resource Center, 1992), edited by Tom Barry and written by 10 journalist contributors. With thoroughly reported topics such as economics, politics, culture, the military, human rights, foreign policy, society, environment and more, it's essential reading. *Entrepreneurs and Politics in Twentieth Century Mexico* (Oxford, 1988), by Roderic A. Camp, delves into the relationship between business and government and the importance of families and contacts in successful business. Large wealthy families, conglomerates, and their holdings are mentioned by name. *Mexico Insight,* published by Excelsior in Mexico City, Bucarelli No. 1, 5 Piso, Mexico, D. F. Mexico 06600, is a twice-monthly hard-hitting news magazine in English. It's the best way to keep on top of what's happening from economics, to politics, to day-to-day issues on such recent topics as police, Mexico City's earthquake warning system, border agents, developers, business, free trade, the Chiapas uprising, etc.

Selden Rodman's *Mexican Journal* (Devin-Adair, 1958), offers wonderful impressions of, and conversations with, prominent artists and intellectuals living in and around the capital, including Rivera, Orozco, Covarrubias, Siquieros, Barragán, Alma Reed, Juan O'Gorman, Carlos Fuentes, Octavio Paz, and others.

The best single source of information on Mexican music, dance, festivals, customs, and mythology is Frances Toor's *A Treasury of Mexican Folkways* (Crown, 1967).

Two good contemporary cookbooks with cultural historical background on Mexico's cuisines are Diana Kennedy's *Mexican Regional Cooking* (Harper & Row, 1984), and *The Taste of Mexico* (Stewart, Tabori & Chang, 1986), by Patricia Quintana.

Art, Archeology & Architecture

The Mexican Codices and Their Extraordinary History (Ediciones Lara, 1985) by María Sten, tells the story of the Indian's "painted books." *Mexico Splendors of Thirty Centuries* (Metropolitan Museum of Art, 1990), the catalog of the 1991 traveling exhibition, is a wonderful resource on Mexico's art from 1500 B.C. through the 1950s. Another superb catalog, *Images of Mexico: The Contribution of Mexico to 20th Century Art* (Dallas Museum of Art, 1987), is a fabulously illustrated and detailed account of Mexican art gathered from collections around the world. *Art and Time in Mexico: From the Conquest to the Revolution* (Harper & Row, 1985), by Elizabeth Wilder Weismann, illustrated with 351 photographs and covers Mexican religious, public and private architecture with excellent photos and text.

The beautifully illustrated *Teotihuacán Art from the City of the Gods* (Thames and Hudson, 1993), by Kathleen Berrin and Esther Pasztory, is an excellent introduction to the remains of this mysterious ancient culture so near to Mexico City. The July–December 1991 issue of *ArqueologiA,* the scholarly magazine of the Instituto Nacional de Antropologia y Historia (INAH), is devoted to recent discoveries at Teotihuacán and Tlaltelolco. The October–November 1994 issue of *Arqueología Mexicana,* another INAH co-sponsored publication sold on newsstands, showcases Tenochtitlán (Mexico City's name before the Conquest), Quetzalcóatl, and the Aztec books. (These serial publications mentioned above continue to be sold on newsstands even when a new one appears.) Archeologist John Carlson's observations of the cult of Venus on Teotihuacán is featured in the November–December 1993 issue of *Archaeology,* published by the Archaeological Institute of America.

Written in Spanish, the two-volume *La Ciudad de los Palacios: Crónica de un Patrimonio Perdido* (The City of Palaces: Chronicle of a Lost Patrimony), by Guillermo Tovar de Teresa, Mexico City's official historian, is a brilliantly illustrated, colorfully written, and respected work of monumental value. Besides the detail of the city's incredible history through it's historic architecture, maps show the positioning of historic buildings before partial or complete demolition over the centuries. *Official Guide to Downtown Mexico City,* (INAH-SALVAT, 1991) written by Mexican archeologists, and translated into several languages, divides the historic center into 12 walking tours. With color photographs, *Centro Historico de la Ciudad de Mexico* (Enlace, 1994), chronicles the historic buildings that have been restored in the Centro Historico between 1988 and 1995.

Casa Mexicana (Stewart, Tabori & Chang, 1989), by Tim Street-Porter takes readers through the interiors of some of Mexico's finest private homes, homes-turned-museum or public-building using color photographs. *Mexican Interiors* (Architectural Book Publishing Co., 1962) by Verna Cook Shipway and Warren Shipway uses black and white photographs to highlight architectural details from homes all over Mexico.

Folk Art

Excellent reading before visiting the ethnographic section of the Museum of Anthropology would be Chloè Sayer's *Costumes of Mexico* (University of Texas Press, 1985), a beautifully illustrated and written work. *Mexican Masks* (University of Texas Press, 1980), by Donald Cordry remains a definitive work on Mexican masks based on the author's collection and travels. Cordry's *Mexican Indian Costumes* (University of Texas Press, 1968) is another classic on the subject. Carlos Espejel wrote both *Mexican Folk Ceramics* and *Mexican Folk Crafts* (Editorial Blume 1975 and 1978), two comprehensive books that explore crafts state-by-state. *Folk Treasures of Mexico* (Harry N. Abrams, 1990) by Marion Oettinger, Curator of Folk Art and Latin American Art at the San Antonio Museum of Art, is the fascinating illustrated story behind the 3,000-piece Mexican folk art collection amassed by Nelson Rockefeller over a 50-year period, as well as much information about individual folk artists.

Nature

Peterson Field Guides Mexican Birds (Houghton Mifflin, 1973), by Roger Tory Peterson and Edward L. Chalif, is an excellent guide to the country's birds. *A Guide to Mexican Mammals & Reptiles* (Minutiae Mexicana, 1989), by Norman Pelham Wright and Dr. Bernardo Villa Ramírez, is a small, but useful guide to some of the country's wildlife.

FILMS

Classic films and directors from the golden age of Mexican cinema are *Alla en el Rancho Grande* (Out on the Big Ranch) and *Vamonos Con Pancho Villa* (Let's Go with Pancho Villa), both by Fernando de Fuentes; *Campeón sin Corona* (Champion without a Crown) a true-life boxing drama by Alejandro Galindo; *La Perla* (The Pearl), by Emilio Fernández based on John Steinbeck's novel; *Yanco*, by Servando Gonzalez about a poor, young boy of Xochimilco who learned to play a violin, and the tear-jerking tale of *María Candelaria,* also set in Xochimilco, a Fernández film starring Dolores del Río. Comedian Cantinflas starred in many Mexican films, and became known in the United States for his role in *Around the World in Eighty Days.* If the salad days of Mexican movies didn't last long, Mexico continues to be a popular subject location. The Durango mountains have become the film backdrop capital of Mexico. *The Night of the Iguana* was filmed in Puerto Vallarta, putting that seaside village on the map. *The Old Gringo* was filmed in Zacatecas, and *Viva Zapata* and *Under the Volcano* were both set in Cuernavaca. The most recent well-known film produced in Mexico is *Like Water for Chocolate,* which is both a novel (Doubleday, 1992) and a wonderfully done movie. Lusty and intimate, the story intertwines the secrets of traditional Mexican food preparation with a magical and surrealistic, yet believable account of Mexican hacienda family life along the Río Grande/Río Bravo at the turn of the century.

RECORDINGS

Mexicans take their music very seriously—just notice tapes for sale almost everywhere, nearly ceaseless music in the streets, organ grinders all over the capital, and bus driver's collections of tapes to entertain passengers by. For the collector there are numerous choices, from contemporary rock to ballads from the revolution, ranchero, salsa, sones, and romantic trios. For trio music, some of the best is by Los Tres Diamantes, Los Tres Reyes, and Trio Los Soberanos. If you're requesting songs of a trio, good ones to ask for are "Sin Ti," "Usted," "Adios Mi Chaparita," "Amor de la Calle," and "Cielito Lindo." Traditional Ranchero music to request, which can be sung by soloists or trios, are "Tu Solo Tu," "No Volveré," and "Adios Mi Chaparita." From the Yucatán are the Trio Los Soberanos and Dueto Yucalpeten. Typical Yucatecan songs that are played all over the country are "Las Golondrinas Yucatecas," "Peregrina" (a love song written for the American journalist, Alma Reed), "Ella," "El Pajaro Azul," and "Ojos Tristes." Heartthrob soloists from years past include Pedro Vargas, Pedro Infante, Hector Cabrera, Lucho Gatica, Pepe Jara, and Alberto Vazquez. Marimba music is popular in Veracruz, Chiapas and the Yucatán, but may be heard anywhere in the republic. Peña Ríos makes excellent marimba recordings. Though marimba musicians seldom ask for requests, some typical renditions would include "Huapango de Moncayo" and "El Bolero de Ravel." Mariachi music is played and sold all over Mexico. In Mexico City, Garibaldi Square is the place to hear mariachis. Among the top recording artists is Mariachi Vargas. No mariachi performance is complete without "Guadalajara," "Las Mañanitas," and "Jarabe Tapatío." *Kiauitzin, Canciones Mexicanas en Nahuatl,* is a tape of Mexican songs such as "Mexico Lindo" and "La Malagueña" sung in the language of the Aztecs. One of the best recordings of recent times is the Royal Philharmonic Orchestra's rendition of classic Mexican music entitled *Mexicano,* conducted by Luis Cobos—it's one purchase you must make.

2

Planning a Trip to Mexico City

FACED WITH THE CHALLENGE OF TRAVELING TO AN UNFAMILIAR CITY OR country, most people have two fundamental questions: How do I get there? and What will it cost? This chapter should answer these questions as well as address other important touchstones of a well-planned trip. When is the best time to visit Mexico City? What are the pros and cons of travel packages? What pretrip health precautions should you take? What insurance coverage might you want? Where can you obtain additional information on topics beyond this book's coverage? Read on for answers to these questions and more.

1 Information, Entry Requirements & Money

Sources of Information

Turn to the **Mexico Hotline** (☎ 800/44-MEXICO in the U.S.) for answers to most commonly asked questions and very general informational brochures on the country. (Once in Mexico, travelers needing information can call toll free **91-800/9-0392** to a Secretary of Tourism office [SECTUR] in Mexico.)

For information on driving your car into Mexico call toll free **800/446-8277** in the U.S. (See also the "By Car" section under "Getting There" later in this chapter.)

In the United States and Canada information about Mexico can be obtained from the following **Mexican Government Tourism Offices** (MGTO): **Chicago** (70 E. Lake St., Suite 1413, Chicago, IL 60601; ☎ **312/565-2778**); **Houston** (2702 N. Loop W., Suite 450, Houston, TX 77008; ☎ **713/880-5153**); **Los Angeles** (10100 Santa Monica Blvd., Suite 224, Los Angeles, CA 90067; ☎ **310/203-8191**); **Florida** (233 Ponce de Leon Blvd., Suite 710, Coral Gables, FL 33134; ☎ **305/443-9160**); **New York** (405 Park Ave., Suite 1401, New York, NY 10022; ☎ **212/755-7261**); **Washington, D.C.** (1911 Pennsylvania Ave. NW, Washington, DC 20006; ☎ **202/728-1750**); **Montreal** (One Place Ville-Marie, Suite 1526, Montréal, PQ H3B 2B5 Canada; ☎ **514/871-1052**); and **Toronto** (2 Bloor St. W., Suite 1801, Toronto, ON M4W 3E2 Canada; ☎ **416/925-0704**).

In Europe and Asia Mexican Government Tourism offices are in the following cities: **Frankfurt** (Weisenhüttenplatz 26, 6000 Frankfurt-am-Main 1, Germany; ☎ **4969/25-3413**); **London** (60-61 Trafalgar Sq., London WC2N 5DS, UK; ☎ **071/734-1058**); **Madrid** (Calle de Velázquez 126, Madrid 28006, Spain; ☎ **341/261-1827**); **Paris** (4 rue Notre-Dame-des-Victoires, 75002 Paris, France; ☎ **331/40-20-07-34**); **Rome** (via Barberini 3, 00187 Roma, Italy; ☎ **396/482-7160**); and **Tokyo** (2.15.1 Nagata-Cho, Chiyoda-Ku, Tokyo 100, Japan; ☎ **813/580-2962**).

Entry Requirements

DOCUMENTS

All travelers to Mexico are required to present **proof of citizenship,** such as an original birth certificate *with a raised seal,* a valid passport, or naturalization papers. This proof of citizenship may also be requested when you reenter either the U.S. or Mexico. **Note:** Photocopies are not acceptable. Also, if you use proof of citizenship without a photograph, such as a birth certificate, you may be required to present a photo identification such as a driver's license.

You must also carry a **Mexican Tourist Permit,** issued free of charge at one of the following places: border stations, Mexican consulates, any of the Mexican tourist offices listed above, travel agents, or your airline at check-in time. The tourist permit is more important than a passport in Mexico, so guard it carefully. If you lose it, permission to leave the country may be withheld until you get a replacement—a bureaucratic hassle that takes several days at least, and can take upwards of a week.

A tourist permit can be issued for up to 180 days, and although your stay south of the border may be less than that, you should get the card for the maximum time, just in case. Sometimes the officials will just stamp a time limit without asking—be sure to say "180 days," or at least twice as long as you think you'll be in the country. If you do stay longer than planned, you'll eliminate hassle by not needing to renew your papers. This is especially important for people who take a car into Mexico. *Additional documentation is required for driving a personal vehicle into Mexico (see "By Car" in "Getting There," below).*

Visitors on business in Mexico must also have a **Business Permit,** available from Mexican Consulates in the United States. Contracts signed while traveling on a Tourist Permit are not valid.

Note that **children under age 18** traveling without parents, or with only one parent, must have a notarized letter from the absent parent or parents authorizing the travel.

Lost Documents

To replace a passport lost while in Mexico, contact your embassy or the nearest consular agent (listed in "Fast Facts: Mexico City" in Chapter 3). You must establish a record of your citizenship, and fill out a form requesting another Mexican Tourist Permit if it too is lost. You can't leave the country without turning in the tourist permit, and without an affidavit regarding your passport and citizenship, you may have hassles at Customs when you get home. And you'll need them to get a new passport later. So you must get it all cleared up *before* trying to leave.

CUSTOMS

When you enter Mexico, Customs (*Aduana* in Spanish) officials are tolerant as long as you have no illegal drugs or firearms. You're allowed to bring 2 cartons of cigarettes, or 50 cigars, plus a kilogram (2.2 lb.) of smoking tobacco; the liquor allowance is 2 bottles of either wine or hard liquor.

When you're reentering the United States, federal law allows, duty free, up to $400 in purchases outside the country every 30 days. After $400, the first $1000 is taxed at 10%. You may bring in a carton of cigarettes, or 50 cigars, or 2 kg (total 4.4 lb.) of smoking tobacco, plus 1 liter of alcoholic beverage (wine, beer, or spirits). In addition, you can't surpass the quotas set by the state in which you reenter the U.S.—which may be different (less) than Federal limits.

Canadian Citizens are allowed $20 in purchases after a 24-hour absence from the country or $100 after 48 hours or more.

Money

THE CURRENCY

In 1993 the Mexican government dropped three zeroes from its currency. The new currency is called the *Nuevo Peso,* or New Peso. The change was made to simplify accounting; all those zeroes were becoming too difficult to manage. Old Peso notes will be valid until 1996; no date for last use of old coins has been announced. Paper currency comes in denominations of 2, 5, 10, 20, 50 and 100 New Pesos, and in large (old) and small (new) sized bills. Coins come in denominations of 1, 2, 5, and 10 pesos, and 20 and 50 centavos (100 centavos make 1 New Peso). The coins are somewhat confusing because different denominations have a similar appearance. New Peso prices appear written with an *N* or *NP* beside them; for a while the Old Peso prices will appear as well.

Note: Mexico also uses the dollar sign [$] to indicate pesos. To avoid confusion, I will use the dollar sign in this book *only* to denote U.S. currency. In addition, for the first time, in years, everyone must become accustomed to making small change and seeing it on restaurant bills and credit cards. On restaurant bills that you pay in cash, for example, the change will be rounded up or down to the nearest five-centavo multiple. But credit-card bills will show the exact amount and will have *N* written before the amount to denote that the bill is in New Pesos. Be sure to double-check any credit-card vouchers to be sure the *N* or *NP* appears on the total line.

Many establishments dealing with tourists quote prices in dollars as well as in New Pesos. To clarify prices, they use the abbreviations "Dlls." for dollars, and "m.n." ("moneda nacional," meaning national currency) for pesos, so "$5 m.n." means 5 pesos.

Shopkeepers everywhere seem always to be out of change and small bills; that's doubly true in a market. So start collecting small change as soon as you cross the border and continue as you travel.

To be on the safe side, always enter a weekend or a Mexican holiday with enough pesos to get you through it, since banks are closed, and traveler's checks and sometimes credit cards may be hard to use then. This is doubly true if your travel plans include stops away from major population centers. See also "Wire Funds" below.

In December 1994, the Mexican Government devalued the peso, which had been artificially bolstered for several years. At presstime the peso was worth around 5.4 to the dollar as opposed to 3.4 pesos to the dollar prior devaluation. In the past, travelers have benefitted most from devaluations at the beginning: rapid inflation usually ensues and boosts prices up again. Prior to devaluation Mexico's annual inflation had been reduced from 200% in 1989 to 8% - 10% by 1994. Experts are predicting another period of upward inflation after this devaluation. Its impossible to say what the situation will be when you travel, but it is likely that it will take a year or more for prices to reach predevaluation highs. some luxury hotels with published dollar prices did not lower rates. Every effort is made to provide the most accurate and up-to-date information in this book, but price changes are inevitable.

EXCHANGING MONEY

Cash can sometimes be difficult to exchange because counterfeit U.S. dollars have been circulating in Mexico; merchants and banks are wary, and many such establishments—especially in small towns—refuse to accept dollars in cash.

Banks in Mexico often give a rate of exchange below the official daily rate, and hotels usually exchange below the banks' daily rate. You can usually get a cash advance on your credit card but there may be a wait of 20 minutes to two hours. Canadian dollars seem to be most easily exchanged for pesos at branches of Banamex and Bancomer.

In Mexico, **banks** are open Monday through Friday from 9am to 1:30pm; a few banks in large cities offer extended afternoon hours. You'll save time at the bank or the *casa de cambio* (currency-exchange booth) by arriving no earlier than 10am. Generally they don't receive the official rate for that day until shortly before then and they won't exchange your money until they have the daily rate.

Currency exchange booths are located in most heavily touristed cities and at major airports. They keep longer hours than do banks, often doing business Monday through Saturday from 9am to 8pm. Currency exchange booths pay more for cash than for traveler's checks.

TRAVELER'S CHECKS

Mexican banks pay more for traveler's checks than for dollars in cash. Some banks, but not all, charge a service fee as high as 5% to cash either dollars or traveler's checks. Banks do not always post the service charge amount so you can see it—it pays to ask first and shop around for a bank without a fee.

PERSONAL CHECKS

Personal checks written from banks outside Mexico are generally not accepted anywhere in the country. Even if you do succeed in getting a Mexican bank to accept one, the bank will wait for it to clear before giving you your money and you may face a delay of weeks.

CREDIT CARDS

You'll be able to charge to a credit card *some* hotel and restaurant bills, almost all airline tickets, and many store purchases. You can get cash advances of several hundred dollars on your card. However, you can't charge gasoline purchases in Mexico. And even though you'll often find credit-card stickers on the entry doors or windows of budget-level inns and restaurants, don't count on them actually accepting credit cards. Even in a quality restaurant or hotel, you should ask the cashier if credit cards are accepted before assuming that they are.

VISA ("Bancomer" in Mexico), MasterCard ("Carnet" in Mexico), and (less widely) American Express are the most accepted cards. Mexico's Bancomer, with branches throughout the country, has inaugurated a system of Automatic Teller Machines linked to VISA International's network. If you are a VISA customer, you may be able to get peso cash from one of these Bancomer ATMs.

BRIBES & SCAMS

Bribes

Called the *propina* (tip), *mordida* (bite), or worse, the custom of soliciting bribes or kickbacks for services is probably almost as old as humankind. Bribes exist in every country, but in Third World countries the amounts tend to be smaller and collected more often. You may meet with bribery, so you should know how to deal with it.

With the administration of President Salinas de Gortari, border officials became more courteous, less bureaucratic, and less inclined to ask/hint for a bribe. I'm still wary, however, so to be prepared here are a few hints based on the past.

Some border officials will do what they're supposed to do (stamp your passport or birth certificate and inspect your luggage) and then wave you on through. If you're charged for it, ask for a receipt. If you get no receipt, you've paid a bribe.

Officials don't ask for bribes from everybody. Travelers dressed in a formal suit and tie, with pitch-black sunglasses and a scowl on their face, are rarely asked to pay a bribe. Those who are dressed for vacation fun or seem good-natured and accommodating may feel the sting. You may not want the bother of dressing up for border crossings, but you should at least act formal—rather cold, dignified, and businesslike—as if preoccupied with "important affairs." Wear those dark sunglasses. Scowl. Ignore any requests for money. Even if you understand every word, pretend that you don't, and don't speak Spanish. But whatever you do, avoid impoliteness, and absolutely never insult a Latin American official! When an official's sense of machismo is roused, he can and will throw the book at you, and you may be in trouble. Stand your ground—politely.

Scams

The **shoeshine scam** is an old trick that seems to happen most often in Mexico City. Here's how it works. A tourist agrees to a shine for, say, 3 pesos. When the work is complete the vendor says, "that'll be 30," and insists the shocked tourist misunderstood. A big brouhaha ensues involving bystanders who side with the shoeshine vendor. The object is to get the bewildered tourist to succumb to the howling crowd and embarrassing scene and fork over the money. A variation of the scam has the vendor saying the price quoted is per shoe. To avoid this scam, ask around about the price of a shine, and when the vendor quotes his price, write it down and show it to him *before* the shine.

Another con game is the **"your hotel is closed/dirty/overpriced" scam.** This one can happen almost anywhere and usually involves the taxi driver who has picked you up at the airport, bus, or train station. You state your hotel destination and the driver says "Don't you know, that hotel is closed." Or he places doubt: "That hotel is really run down now or overpriced," or "it has new owners who are dishonest." Then he goes in for the kill. "How much do you want to pay?" He of course has a hotel in mind, but naturally he doesn't tell you about the commission arrangement he has for bringing in clients. Go ahead with your original plans and you can always move if you don't like your hotel.

And speaking of taxi drivers there's the **"you didn't pay enough" scam,** which has happened to me several times in Mexico City. You buy a ticket at the official taxi ticket booth at the airport or bus station based on the rate for your destination zone; that's all the trip

What Things Cost in Mexico City	U.S. $
Taxi from airport to Zona Rosa	14.00
Bus from Zócalo to Chapultepec Park	.50
Metro ticket	.25
Local telephone call from public street booth	.50
Local telephone call from hotel	.50–1.50
Double room at the Hotel Four Seasons (very expensive)	250.00–500.00
Double room at Hotel Metropol (moderate)	71.00
Double room at Hotel Regente (moderate)	55.00
Double room at Gran Hotel Texas (budget)	30.00
Lunch for one at Angus (expensive)	20.00
Lunch for one at Chalet Suizo (moderate)	15.00
Lunch for one at Restaurant Mariane (budget)	5.00
Dinner for one at Les Moustaches (expensive)	25.00
Dinner for one at Hostería Santo Domingo (moderate)	15.00
Dinner for one at Cafe La Blanca (budget)	6.00
Margarita	3.00–4.50
Coca-Cola	.75–1.00
Cup of coffee	.75–1.00
Admission to Museo de Antropología	5.50
Ticket to Bellas Artes Ballet Folklorico	30.00–42.00

legally costs. You're on your way when the driver looks at the ticket stub and says "this charge isn't enough for your zone," then he names a higher price, or says "the price is per person," so that you owe whatever the price would be per passenger traveling in your party. The truth is, if four (and sometimes five) people traveling together as a group wish to share a taxi, the price is the same as for one person. Strangers not traveling together who share a taxi each pay the individual price. When the driver says you didn't pay enough for the zone, tell him to take it up with the ticket seller. They can, however, legitimately charge extra for excess luggage.

While I'm still on the subject of Mexico City taxi drivers I'll mention the **"accelerated-meter" scam.** You won't know it's happening until you've taken a taxi to and from the same destination and have a feel for charges. A racing meter is another clue. Taxi meters in Mexico City start out at 2 pesos and increase in slow, regular increments of centavos, not leaps of whole pesos. If you think you've been overcharged by a driver with a trick meter, when you reach your destination, get out with all your possessions. Then hand the driver what you think the ride should have cost. Take into consideration whether or not traffic was heavy, and therefore slow, which *does* increase the cost. This idea is from a friend who lives in the city. It's only backfired once, she told me, when she didn't get out of the taxi first—the driver took her back to her starting point.

Because hotel desk clerks are usually so helpful, I hesitate to mention the **"lost objects" scam** for fear of tainting them all. But here's how it works. You "lose" your wallet after cashing money at the desk, or you leave something valuable such as a purse or camera in the lobby. You report it. The clerk has it, but instead of telling you that he does, he says he will see what he can do; meanwhile, he suggests that you offer a high reward. This one has all kinds of variations. In one story a reader wrote about, a desk clerk was in cahoots with a bystander who lifted her wallet in the elevator.

Another scam readers have written about might be called the **"infraction" scam.** Officials, or men passing themselves off as officials (such as police), demand money for some supposed infraction. Never get into a car with them. And never hand over your driver's license—hold it firmly so it can be read. Some people recommend asking the policeman how much it would cost to pay a fine right there. The official names a price, usually a high one. They bargain for a lower price, often finally amounting to only a few dollars. Others recommend telling the policeman they'd prefer going to the police station to settle it rather than pay a fine for an infraction they didn't commit. A policeman on the take won't want to do that, and will find some reason to save face and permit the driver to continue with the trip without paying a fine. And some people pay the fine rather than waste time arguing about it. It's also useful not to speak Spanish in these situations or even let on that you understand a word of what's said.

My own tactic, which has worked so far, is to respond to everything the officer says with a smile and perplexed-but-innocent expression, and say *graaaaacias, graaaaacias* (thank you, thank you) dragging the word out in my absolute worst Spanish accent. He thinks that I regard him as a benevolent cop helping a tourist. To make me fearful of him would take knowledge of English (which most police don't seem to have), and more time than he has. So, in exasperation he gives up. Mexico City has a particularly annoying **cargidor law** (hauling for hire), which tourists can run afoul of if they've visibly filled a car with purchases or luggage. The law requires drivers to have a special permit for hauling, but it doesn't apply to tourists. Still, that doesn't keep streetcorner policemen from trying to apply it. I just say *graaaacias*, as many times as possible, no matter what he says. I never act like I understand. Then I smile, wave, and move on with the traffic.

Legal and necessary car searches by military personnel looking for drugs happen occasionally. But every now and then there are **police-controlled yet illegal roadblocks** where motorists are allowed to continue after paying a small amount, often to support some strike or other local cause.

The advice offered here is to help you be aware of potential hazards and how to deal with them. I log thousands of miles and many months in Mexico each year without serious incident, and I feel safer there than at home. (See also "Emergencies" and "Safety" in "Fast Facts" in Chapter 3.)

2 When to Go—Climate, Holidays & Events

Climate

Most of the year the capital has springlike weather, often with temperatures in the fifties (Fahrenheit) in the evening warming up to the seventies by mid-day. During April, May, and June daytime temperatures in the eighties aren't uncommon. The rainy season from May through October brings daily showers that can also create a chill. Toluca is nearly 1,300 feet higher than Mexico City, and it's cooler there overall than Mexico City. Puebla and Tlaxcala are at about the same elevation as the capital, but both cities are slightly drier.

Most hotels don't have heat of any kind, but generally it's not cold enough to require it. Pricier hotels will have air conditioning. Nighttime temperatures can be 10°F to 15°F cooler than the average daytime temperatures mentioned below. And daytime temperatures can be 10°F higher, especially in April, May, and June.

Mexico City's Average Daytime Temperature

	Jan	Feb	Mar	Apr	May	June	July	Aug	Sept	Oct	Nov	Dec
Temp (°F)	64	66	69	70	71	69	68	68	68	66	66	64
Temp (°C)	19	21	24	25	26	24	23	23	23	21	21	19

Holidays

In Mexico public holidays include New Year's Day, Constitution day (February 5), Benito Juárez's birthday (March 21), Good Friday, Labor Day (May 1), Cinco de Mayo (May 5), President's message day (Sept 1), Independence Day (September 15–16), Columbus Day (October 12), All Saints' and All Souls' Days (November 1–2), Mexican Revolution Anniversary (November 20), Day of the Virgin of Guadalupe (December 12), and Christmas Eve and Christmas Day (December 24–25). Banks, stores, and businesses are closed on these national holidays, hotels fill up quickly, and transportation is crowded. Stores may be closed on Three Kings Day (January 6).

Mexico City Calendar of Events

January

- **Worshipping the Niñopa** In Xochimilco, the Niñopa, a figure of the Christ child said to produce miracles for its worshipers, is revered on this day with a procession through village streets. January 6.
- **Feast of San Antonio Abad** Blessing of the Animals at the Santiago Tlatelolco Church on the Plaza of Three Cultures, at San Juan Bautista Church in Coyoacán, and at the Church of San Fernando, two blocks north of the intersection of Juárez and Reforma. January 17.

May

- **Corpus Christi** Children dressed as Indians and their parents gather before the Catedral Metropolitana on the Zócalo, carrying decorated baskets of fruit for the priest's blessing. Painted, hand-made "Mulitas" (mules) made with dried corn husks and often featuring a cornhusk rider sometimes accompanied by pairs of cornhusk dolls, are traditionally sold there on that day. Moveable date 66 days after Easter.

August

- **Fall of Tenochtitlán** The last battle of the Conquest took place at Tlatelolco, the ruins that are now a part of the Plaza of Three Cultures. Wreathlaying ceremonies there and at the Cuauhtémoc monument on Reforma commemorate an event during which thousands lost their lives and the last Aztec king, Cuauhtémoc, surrendered to Hernán Cortés. August 13.

September

⭐ Independence Day

The President of Mexico gives the famous independence *grito* (shout) from the central balcony of the National Palace in Mexico City before at least half a million people crowded into the Zócalo, and to the rest of the country via television. Tall buildings downtown are draped in the national colors of red, green, and white and the Zócalo is ablaze with lights; it's popular to drive downtown at night to see the lights—truly spectacular. **Where:** Be at the Zòcalo at 11pm for the grito; the next day the enormous military parade on September 16 starts at the Zócalo and ends at the Independence Monument on Reforma. **When:** September 15 for the grito; September 16 for the parade.

November

★ Days of the Dead

What's commonly called the Day of the Dead is actually two days. All Saints' Day, honoring saints and deceased children and All Souls' Day, honoring deceased adults. Relatives gather at cemeteries countrywide, carrying candles and food, often spending the night beside graves of loved ones. Bakers produce bread formed in the shape of mummies or round loaves decorated with bones shaped in bread. Decorated sugar skulls emblazoned with glitter names are sold everywhere. Many days beforehand, homes and churches erect special altars laden with Day of the Dead bread, fruit, flowers, candles, and favorite foods and photographs of saints and of the deceased. On the two nights of the Day of the Dead, children dress in costumes and masks, often carrying mock coffins through the streets and pumpkin lanterns into which they expect money will be dropped. **Where:** Mixquic (pronounced *meesh-kee*), a village south of Mexico City and east of Xochimilco, has an elaborate street fair with extensive food booths and a number of *papel picado* (cut paper) makers designing cutouts with skeleton themes. The village cemetery in the center of town is ablaze with candles and full of families paying respect to the deceased. Many people light fires on the sidewalk or curb outside their homes. The Merced Market in Mexico City has elaborate flower displays during this time. Toluca's main plaza is full of vendors selling special Day of the Dead sugar skulls. **When:** November 1–2.

- **Revolution Day**   Commemorates the start of the Mexican Revolution in 1910, with parades, speeches, rodeos, and patriotic events. In Mexico City the elaborate downtown parade lasts for hours and features marching bands, mariachis, jugglers, the military, and more. November 20.

December

★ Day of Guadalupe

Throughout Mexico, the patroness of Mexico is honored with religious processions, street fairs, dancing, fireworks, and mass. The Virgin of Guadalupe appeared to a man named Juan Diego in December 1531 on a hill near Mexico City, telling him that a church should be built where she stood. She left an image of herself emblazoned on Juan Diego's cloak, which was the proof that finally convinced the local bishop of the authenticity of Diego's story. It's customary for children to dress up as Juan Diego, wearing mustaches and red bandannas. The most famous and elaborate celebration takes place at the Basílica of Guadalupe, north of Mexico City, where the virgin appeared. Penitents will walk for days from distant homes to the basílica, approaching on their knees, and Indian dancers perform outside the church. The solemn celebration is almost ruined by vendors of food and religious objects, who line the roadways around the basílica, and pickpockets come in droves.

If you can't make it to the Basílica of Guadalupe, almost every Mexican village celebrates this day, often with processions of children carrying banners of the virgin, and with charreadas, bicycle races, dancing, and fireworks. December 12.
Where: Basílica of Guadalupe, Mexico City. **When:** December 12 and the week before. **How:** Public transportation will be packed, so your best bet is a taxi, which will let you off several blocks from the basílica.

- **Christmas**   The capital decks itself out for the holidays with Christmas lights in the downtown section and gardens of poinsettias along the Alameda. It all culminates on the Zócalo, which blazes with bannered lights declaring *Feliz Navidad y Prospero Nuevo Año.*

3 Health & Insurance

Health

The very best ways to avoid illness during travel or to mitigate its effects are to take to the road in top health and make sure you don't overdo it. Travel in general tends to sap your energy more than would a normal working day, and missed meals mean that you get less nutrition than you need. Make sure you have three good, wholesome meals a day, get more rest than you normally do, and don't push yourself if you're not feeling in top form. Keep in mind that Mexico City's altitude causes shortness of breath and slows digestion. Most hotels maintain a list of doctors on call, many of which will speak English.

COMMON AILMENTS

Turista

Turista, Moctezuma's revenge, the Aztec two-step—all are names given to the pervasive diarrhea, often accompanied by fever, nausea, and vomiting, that attacks so many travelers to Mexico. Doctors, who call it traveler's diarrhea, say no one "bug" or factor is responsible for this indignation; the blame lies with a combination of different food and water, upset schedules, overtiring, and the stresses that accompany travel. Being tired and careless about food and drink is a sure ticket to turista. A good high-potency (or "therapeutic") vitamin supplement, and even extra vitamin C, is a help. Yogurt is good for healthy digestion, but it is not available everywhere in Mexico.

PREVENTING TURISTA The U.S. Public Health Service recommends the following measures for prevention of traveler's diarrhea:

- *Drink only purified water.* This means tea, coffee, and other beverages made with boiled water; canned or bottled carbonated beverages, including carbonated water; or water that you yourself have brought to a rolling boil or otherwise purified. Avoid ice, which may be made with untreated water.
- *Choose food carefully.* In general, avoid salads, uncooked vegetables, and unpasteurized milk or milk products (including cheese). Choose food that is freshly cooked and still hot. Peel fruit yourself. Don't eat undercooked meat, fish, or shellfish.

The Public Health Service does not recommend that you take any medicines as preventatives. All the applicable medicines can have nasty side effects if taken for several weeks.

HOW TO GET WELL If you get sick, there are lots of medicines available in Mexico which can harm more than help. You should ask your doctor before you leave home what medicine he or she recommends for traveler's diarrhea, and follow that advice.

Public Health Service guidelines are these: If there are three or more loose stools in an eight-hour period, especially with other symptoms such as nausea, vomiting, abdominal cramps and fever, it's time to go to a doctor.

The first thing to do is go to bed and don't move until it runs its course. Traveling makes it last longer. Drink lots of liquids: tea without milk or sugar, or the Mexican *té de manzanilla* (chamomile tea), is best. Eat only *pan tostada* (dry toast). Keep to this diet for at least 24 hours, and you'll be well over the worst of it. If you fool yourself into thinking that a plate of enchiladas can't hurt, or that beer or liquor will kill the germs, you'll likely have a total relapse.

The Public Health Service advises that you be especially careful to replace fluids and electrolytes (potassium, sodium, etc.) during a bout of diarrhea. Do this by drinking glasses of fruit juice (high in potassium) with honey and a pinch of salt added; and also a glass of pure water with $\frac{1}{4}$ teaspoon of sodium bicarbonate (baking soda) added.

Altitude Sickness

At high altitudes it takes about 10 days or so to acquire the extra red blood corpuscles you need to adjust to the scarcity of oxygen. Symptoms include shortness of breath, fatigue, headache, and even nausea. At very high-altitude places such as Ixta-Popo Park outside Mexico City (13,000 feet), you may not even sleep well at night.

Avoid altitude sickness by taking it easy for the first few days after you arrive at high altitude. Drink extra fluids, *but avoid alcoholic beverages,* which not only tend to dehydrate you, but also are more potent in a low-oxygen environment. If you have heart or lung problems, talk to your doctor before going above 8,000 feet.

Bugs & Bites

Mosquitoes and gnats are prevalent along the coasts and in the Yucatán lowlands. Insect repellent (*rapellante contra insectos*) is a must, and it's not always available in Mexico. If you're sensitive to bites, pick up some antihistamine cream from a drugstore at home. Rubbed on a fresh mosquito bite, the cream keeps down the swelling and reduces the itch.

Most readers won't ever see a scorpion, but if you're stung, it's best to go to a doctor.

More Serious Diseases

You don't have to worry about tropical diseases too much if you stay on the normal tourist routes (that is, if you don't head out into the boondocks to camp with the locals for a week).

You can also protect yourself by taking some simple precautions. Besides being careful about what you eat and drink, do not go swimming in polluted waters. This includes any stagnant water such as ponds and slow-moving rivers. Avoid mosquitoes because they carry malaria, dengue fever, and other serious illnesses.

To prevent malaria if you go to a malarial area, you must get a prescription for antimalarial drugs, and begin taking them before you enter the area. You must also continue to take them for a certain amount of time after you leave the malarial area. Talk to your doctor about this. It's a good idea to be inoculated against tetanus, typhoid, and diphtheria, but doing so is not a guarantee against contracting these diseases.

The following list of diseases are rare among tourists:

- **Cholera** comes from water contaminated with sewage and is transmitted when the contaminated water is used for drinking, cooking, or washing food. Raw fish and raw or lightly cooked vegetables are good candidates for transmitting the disease. Outbreaks of cholera in Mexico have been isolated and contained immediately, and have not occurred in any major touristic area. Symptoms are extreme—diarrhea, vomiting, abdominal pain, and rapid dehydration and incapacitation. Dehydration can be quick and deadly, so no matter how difficult to keep them down, keep drinking liquids and get to a hospital immediately. The disease is curable if looked after quickly.

- **Dysentery** is caused by contaminated food or water, either amoebic or bacillary in form, and is somewhat like traveler's diarrhea, only more severe. Risk for tourists is low.
- **Typhoid Fever** can be prevented by having a typhoid vaccination (or booster, as needed), but protection is not total; you can still get this very serious disease from contaminated food and water. Symptoms are similar to those for traveler's diarrhea, but much worse. If you get typhoid fever, you'll need close attention by a doctor, perhaps hospitalization for a short period.
- **Viral Hepatitis** is spread through contaminated food and water (often in rural areas), and through intimate contact with infected persons. Risk for tourists is normally low.

Emergency Evacuation

For extreme medical emergencies there's a service from the United States that will fly people to American hospitals: **Air-Evac,** 24-hour air ambulance (☎ toll free **800/854-2569** in the U.S. or collect **713/880-9767** in Houston, **619/278-3822** in San Diego or **305/772-0003** in Miami).

Insurance

Before purchasing additional insurance, check your home-owner and medical insurance policies. Also check the membership contracts for travel clubs and credit-card companies. Foreign car insurance, however, is not valid in Mexico and rental car insurance covered by your credit card isn't advisable (see the "By Car" section in "Getting There," below). For additional coverage you may want to consider policies from the following companies: **Health Care Abroad** 107 W. Federal St. (P.O. Box 480), Middleburg, VA 22117 (☎ **703/687-3166,** or toll free **800/237-6615**), and **Access America,** 6600 W. Broad St., Richmond, VA 23230 (☎ **804/285-3300,** or toll free **800/628-3300**); **Mutual of Omaha** (Tele-Trip), Mutual of Omaha Plaza, Omaha, NE 68175 (☎ toll free **800/228-9792**); **Travel Guard International,** 1145 Clark St., Stevens Point, WI 54481 (☎ toll free **800/826-1300**); and **Travel Insurance PAK,** Travelers Insurance Co., 1 Tower Sq., Hartford, CT 06183-5040 (☎ toll free **800/243-3174**). **Note:** In all cases always ask to see the policy first, and read the fine print to see that you're getting the coverage you want.

FOR BRITISH TRAVELERS

Most big travel agents offer their own insurance, and will probably try to sell you their package when you book a holiday. Think before you sign. Britain's Consumers' Association recommends that you insist on seeing the policy and reading the fine print before buying travel insurance.

You should also shop around for better deals. Try **Columbus Travel Insurance Ltd.** (☎ 071/375-0011) or, for students, **Campus Travel** (☎ 071/730-3402). If you're unsure about who can give you the best deal, contact the **Association of British Insurers,** 51 Gresham St., London EC2V 7HQ (☎ 071/600-333).

LOST POSSESSIONS

One way to minimize the woes of having lost your wallet, your passport, your airline ticket, or your tourist permit is not to leave home without a photocopy of these documents in your luggage. Replacing them will be easier if you have copies. If you do lose official documents, you'll need to contact both Mexican and U.S. officials in Mexico before you leave the country. (See Chapter 3 "Embassies and Consulates" under "Fast Facts.")

If while in Mexico you lose a possession you've taken insurance on, you'll need to report the loss to the Mexican police and get a written report. Once you return, insurance companies will want a record of such before they reimburse you for the insured item. If you don't speak Spanish, take along someone who does.

---

4   What to Pack

CLOTHING

In winter, if you're in Mexico City or another high-elevation city such as Toluca, you'll require a warm jacket or a heavy sweater. In summer, it gets warm during the day and cool—or even cold—at night. Generally speaking, it rains throughout Mexico almost every afternoon or evening between May and October—so take rain gear. An easily packable rain poncho is most handy, since it fits in a purse or backpack and is ready for use in an instant.

Capitalinos dress conservatively. Casual slacks and shirts are fine for daytime touring, but shorts are very out of place in any city. A blazer with coordinated skirt or pants is acceptable in most places. When in doubt, you can't go wrong by wearing your best dress or suit, since upper class Mexicans are extremely well dressed. When dining out in a nice restaurant in conservative and sophisticated Mexico City, a jacket and tie for men and nice dress or suit for women is appropriate. Most fine restaurants in the capital actually require that men wear a coat and tie.

GADGETS

Bring your own washcloth, or better yet a sponge (which dries quickly). Washcloths are always provided in deluxe hotels, but moderate- and budget-priced hotels rarely have them. A bathtub plug (one of those big round ones for all sizes) is a help since fitted plugs are frequently missing, or don't work even in quality hotels. A plastic bag stuffed in the drain works too. Collapsible hangers and a stretch clothesline are handy. A luggage cart saves much effort and tip money, and is especially useful in small towns where there are no porters at bus stations. Buy a sturdy one with wheels at least four inches in diameter that can take the beating of cobblestone streets, stairs, and curbs. A heat immersion coil, plastic cup, and spoon are handy for preparing coffee, tea, and instant soup. For power failures a small flashlight is a help. A combo pocket knife (for peeling fruit), with screw driver (for fixing cameras and eyeglasses), bottle opener, and corkscrew, is a must. See also Chapter 3, "Electricity" in "Fast Facts" in Chapter 3, "Getting to Know Mexico City," for info regarding the usefulness of a two-pronged plug adapter and electrical surge protector.

5 Tips for the Disabled, Seniors, Singles, Families, Students & Business Travelers

For the Disabled

Travelers in wheelchairs or on crutches discover quickly that Mexico is one giant obstacle course. At the airport, elevators or escalators can be hard to find—some parts of the airport don't have them at all—and you may encounter steep stairs. Airlines will often arrange wheelchair assistance to the baggage area for passengers. Ramps used by luggage handlers *may* also be convenient for wheelchairs. Porters are generally available to help with luggage at airports once you've cleared baggage claim and at large bus stations.

Escalators (and there aren't many in the country) are often out of order. Or they'll be one-way—up, but not down. Few handicap-equipped restrooms exist; when one is available, access to it may be via a narrow passage that won't accommodate a wheelchair or someone on crutches. Many deluxe hotels (the most expensive) now have rooms with handicapped bathrooms and handicap access to the hotel. As a general rule, stick with one-story hotels, or those with elevators. Even so there will probably still be step obstacles somewhere. Stairs without handrails abound in Mexico. Intracity bus drivers generally don't bother with the courtesy step upon boarding or disembarking. On city buses the distance between the street and the bus can require considerable force to board. Generally speaking, no matter where you are, someone will lend a hand, although you may have to ask for it.

Before you go, there are several agencies to check with about information for the disabled. **Travel Information Service,** MossRehab, 1200 W. Tabor Rd., Philadelphia, PA 19141-3099 (☎ **215/456-9600**), provides names of accessible hotels, restaurants, and attractions. There's a small fee for information packets, which include reports from disabled travelers. Tours for travelers with disabilities are available from the **Society for the Advancement of Travel for the Handicapped,** 347 Fifth Ave., Suite 610, New York, NY 10016 (☎ **212/447-7284**); send a self-addressed stamped envelope. Annual membership costs $45 ($25 for senior citizens and students) and includes information sources and a quarterly newsletter. **The Federation of the Handicapped,** 211 W. 14th St., New York, NY 10011 (☎ **212/727-4200**), offers tours and information about them costs $14 annually. Blind travelers may find useful information through the **American Foundation for the Blind,** 15 W. 16th St., New York, NY 10011 (☎ **212/620-2000,** or toll free **800/232-5463**).

For Seniors

"Travel Tips for Older Americans" (publication #8970), is available for $1 from the **U.S. Government Printing Office,** Washington, DC 20402 (☎ **202/512-2164**). "101 Tips for the Mature Traveler" is a free booklet available from **Grand Circle Travel,** 347 Congress St., Suite 3A, Boston, MA 02210 (☎ **617/350-7500,** or toll free **800/221-2610**).

Bus tours organized in the U.S. are beginning to travel in Mexico again. One source for this kind of travel as well as other group travel would be the **American Association of Retired Persons,** 601 E St. NW, Washington, DC 20049 (☎ **202/434-AARP**). Membership costs $8 annually and members are offered discounts on car rentals, hotels, and airfares. Land tours and cruises are also available.

World Learning Inc., The U.S. Experiment in International Living, Kipling Road, P.O. Box 676, Brattleboro, VT 05302-0676 (☎ **802/257-7751;** fax 802/252-3248), offers a wide range of options for international experiences ranging from accredited programs to homestays and Elderhostel affiliation.

RETIREMENT

Mexico is a popular country for retirees, although money doesn't go nearly as far as it once did. How much it costs to live depends on your lifestyle and where you choose to live. Car upkeep and insurance, clothing, and health costs are important variables to consider. Successful transplants do several things before venturing south permanently:

- Stay for several weeks in any place under consideration.
- Rent before buying.
- Check on the availability and quality of health care, banking, transportation, and rental costs.

The Mexican government requires foreign residents to prove a specific amount of income before permanent residence is granted, but you can visit for six months on a tourist visa and renew it every six months without committing to a "legal" status.

Mexican health care is surprisingly inexpensive. You can save money by living on the local economy—buying food at the local market instead of purchasing imported items from specialty stores; using local transportation and saving the car for long-distance trips.

The following newsletters are written to inform the prospective retiree about Mexico: *AIM,* Apdo. Postal 31-70, Guadalajara 45050, Jal. Mexico, is a well-written, plain-talking, very informative newsletter on retirement in Mexico. Recent issues reported on retirement background and considerations for Lake Chapala, Aguascalientes, Alamos, Zacatecas, West Coast beaches, Acapulco, and San Miguel de Allende. Subscriptions cost $16 in the U.S. and $19 in Canada. You can get three back issues for $5. *Retiring in Mexico,* Apdo. Postal 5-409, Guadalajara, Jal. (☎ **36/21-2348** or **47-9924**), appears three times a year—a large January edition and smaller spring and fall supplements—all for $12. Each newsletter is packed with useful information about retiring in Guadalajara. It's written by Fran and Judy Furton, who also sell other packets of information as well as host an open house in their home every Tuesday for $12. And **Sanborn Tours,** 1007 Main Street, Bastrop, TX 78602 (☎ toll free **800/531-5440** in the U.S.) offers a "Retire in Mexico" Guadalajara orientation tour.

For Singles

Mexico may be a land known for romantic honeymoons, but it's also a great place to travel on your own without really being or feeling alone. Although it's a given that deluxe hotels will offer rooms at one rate regardless of single and double occupancy, most of the moderately priced and budget hotels mentioned in this book offer rooms at single occupancy for lower rates.

There's so much to see and do in and around the capital that a single person needn't become bored or lonely. Mexicans are very friendly, and it's easy to strike up a conversation. It's also not unusual or difficult to meet other foreigners and take up with them for a day or two or a meal along the way if you desire.

If you don't like the idea of traveling alone then you might try **Travel Companion Exchange,** P.O. Box 833, Amityville, NY 11701 (☎ **516/454-0880;** fax 516/454-0170), an organization that brings prospective travelers together. Members complete a profile, then place an anonymous listing of their travel interests in the newsletter. Prospective traveling companions then make contact through the exchange. Membership costs $36 to $66 for six months.

FOR WOMEN

As a female who travels frequently in Mexico, most of the time alone, I can tell you first hand that I feel safer in Mexico than in the United States. And no, traveling alone here is not scary. That answers the first two questions most people ask me. Mexicans are a very warm and welcoming people and I'm not afraid to be friendly wherever I go. But I take the same common sense precautions I would traveling anywhere else in the world. I stay alert, keeping tabs on what's going on around me; for example, at night in Mexico City, I always use door-to-door taxi service, rather than walking alone on the streets.

In general, Mexicans—the men in particular—are nosy about single travelers, especially women. They want to know with whom you're traveling, whether you're married or have a boyfriend, and how many children you have. My advice to anyone exchanging these details with taxi drivers or other people whose paths you'll never cross again or with whom you don't want to become friendly is to make up a set of answers regardless of the truth: "I'm married, I'm traveling with friends, and I have three children." Men told that a woman is divorced may get the wrong message about the woman's availability or degree of loneliness. Drunks are a particular nuisance to the lone female traveler; even when they can hardly walk they still muster up a "staggering" amount of machismo to speak, stumble along with you, or otherwise become a pest. Don't try to be polite; just leave or duck into a public place.

Although women alone will generally feel comfortable going to a hotel lobby bar, *pulquerias* (a bar selling pulque, a fermented cactus drink) and cantinas can be rough places in Mexico City. And in restaurants, as a general rule, single women are offered the worst table and service. You'll have to be vocal about your preference and insist on service. Service *may* be better if you dine at off-peak hours. Tip well if you plan to return. Don't tip at all if service is bad.

And finally: remember, Mexican men learn charm early. The chase is as important as the conquest (maybe more so). Despite whatever charms *you* may possess, think twice before taking personally or seriously all the adoring, admiring words you'll hear.

FOR MEN

I'm not sure why, but non-Spanish-speaking foreign men seem to be special targets for scam artists and pickpockets. If you fit this description, regardless of whether you're traveling alone or with others, exercise special vigilance. Pickpockets are adept at retrieving a wallet even from a front pocket.

For Families

Mexicans travel extensively with their families, so your child will feel very welcome. Hotels will often arrange for a babysitter. Some of the pricier hotels in Mexico City have small playgrounds for children and hire caretakers on weekends to oversee them and the children's pool so the parents can relax. Few budget hotels offer these amenities. High chairs in restaurants are just now being offered in Mexico, and are not widely available. They are not available at all in exclusive restaurants, which usually prefer that patrons not bring small children.

Before leaving for Mexico, you should check with your doctor and get advice on medicines to combat diarrhea and other ailments. Bring a supply of medicines, just to be sure. Disposable diapers are made and sold in Mexico (one popular brand is Kleen Bebé). The price is about the same as at home, but the quality is lower. Also, Gerber's baby foods are sold in many stores. Dry cereals, powdered formulas, baby bottles, and purified water are all readily available in mid-size to large cities.

Finding a crib can be a problem. Except for the largest and most luxurious hotels, few Mexican hotels provide cribs.

For Students

Students traveling on a budget may want to contact the student headquarters in the various cities that can supply information on student hostels. For a list, write to **SETEJ,** Hamburgo 305, México, D.F. (☎ 5/211-0743). A source of information on inexpensive youth hostel tours is the **Agencia Nacional de Turismo Juvenil,** Glorieta del Metro Insurgentes, Local C-11, México 6, D.F. (☎ 5/211-6636). It's at the Insurgentes Metro plaza, in case you are in the area and want to stop in. Keep in mind that Mexican hostels are very basic—help and information as you travel will be minimal, and everything will be in Spanish.

Another excellent source is **Council Travel** (a subsidiary of the Council on International Educational Exchange), America's largest student, youth, and budget travel group with more than 60 offices worldwide. The main office is at 205 E. 42nd St., New York, NY 10017 (☎ 212/661-1414). For a fee, bona fide students can receive an International Student Identity Card, and eligibility for discounts on airlines, trains, hotels, etc. They also sell several travel handbooks on volunteering, work, and study.

The **National Registration Center for Studies Abroad (NRCSA),** 823 N. 2nd St., Milwaukee, WI 53203 (☎ 414/278-0631), has a catalog ($5) of schools in Mexico. They will register you at the school of your choice, arrange for room and board with a Mexican family, and make your airline reservations. Charge for their service is reflected in an additional fee that's included in the price quoted to you for the course you select. Contact them and ask for a free copy of their newsletter.

For Business Travelers

Taking into account a few customs, conveniences, and time constraints peculiar to Mexico City can help travelers on business in the capital make the most of their time.

SOURCES OF INFORMATION

A good resource to consult before you go is the *Mexico Business Monthly,* 52 Maple Avenue, Maplewood, NJ 07040. It reports on a wide range of Mexican industries, covers environmental news, and lists conventions and business meetings on a full range of business topics relating to Mexico and the United States. Included in each issue is a useful directory of individual government and private enterprise contacts in the United States and Mexico.

The **U.S. Department of Commerce** has representatives at the U.S. Embassy in Mexico City and in Guadalajara and Monterrey. The department maintains an extensive library at the embassy and works to bring U.S. and Mexican businesses together. They produce an invaluable assortment of statistics, extensive studies, and literature on the Mexican business climate for potential U.S. investors. They also maintain lists of Mexican businesses looking for U.S. partners and vice versa. In the United States, contact Director, Commercial Programs, Office of Mexico, Western Hemisphere, International Trade Administration, Department of Commerce, Washington, DC 20230 (☎ 202/377-4464).

The **American Chamber of Commerce,** Lucerna 78, Col. Juárez, Del. Cuauhtémoc 06600 México, D.F. (☎ **5/705-0995;** fax 5/535-3166), mailing address Apdo. Postal 82 bis, Centro Del. Cuauhtémoc, 06000 México, D.F., is another resource with a business library and client-pairing program.

The **U.S. Mexico Chamber of Commerce,** 1900 L St. NW, Suite 612, Washington DC 20036 (☎ **202/296-5198;** fax 202/785-4905), is yet another important contact, with offices in Mexico City, Los Angeles, Dallas, and New York.

For useful information on doing business in Mexico, the **Mexican Investment Board,** 1500 Broadway, 25th Floor, New York, NY 10036 (☎ toll free **800/MIB-2434**), with offices in Mexico City as well, may be helpful.

GETTING SITUATED

Make sure you choose a hotel that meets your needs. The capital's deluxe hotels all have executive centers where business travelers can send and receive faxes, rent a cellular phone, use a computer and copier, reserve a conference room, have documents translated and secure secretarial assistance. Most have direct-dial phones, allowing you to access an ATT operator directly. Many, but not all, have voice mail. If a particular service is essential, be sure to verify that the hotel you've chosen has it. Upon arrival, inspect these facilities to see if they meet your needs. Rooms in most of the deluxe hotels usually have a connection for fax and computer, and three-pronged plug (*trifacico*) outlets. (Older and more moderately priced hotels don't have three-pronged outlets; for more essential information on Mexico's electricity see "Fast Facts" in Chapter 3, "Getting to Know Mexico City.")

Once in the capital, two invaluable people to cultivate at the outset are a dependable English-speaking taxi driver, and a bilingual secretary. Secretaries are available for hire in the better hotels; they can set up your appointments by phone, reconfirm them in writing by fax, type out a list of appointments with names, times, addresses, and telephone numbers, reserve conference rooms, and reconfirm your flight home. The taxi driver, hired for the day, will map out the fastest route to your appointments, wait for you, and whisk you to the next one efficiently. A savvy driver will be willing to call ahead to your next appointment and reconfirm your arrival there. And a multitalented driver can double as the secretary, doing everything except writing and faxing the confirming appointment letter. Naturally you'll pay for the transportation, waiting time, and tip graciously for other services, but the reduction in hassles will make it worth the price (see my recommendation for a dependable taxi driver at the beginning of Chapter 6, "What to See & Do in Mexico City").

CONDUCTING BUSINESS IN THE CAPITAL

Plan no more than three, or at the most four, appointments in a day. Besides office hour time limitations, you'll have to deal with traffic between destinations, over-long meetings, and waiting, all of which eat up enormous amounts of time. Plan at least an hour and a half between meetings, if the locations are far apart. Though office hours start around 9am, it's not a good idea to count on an appointment that early. Arrange office appointments between 10am and 1pm and from 5 to 7 or 8pm. The sacred lunch break happens between 1:30 and 5pm. Lunch and dinner with a prospective client will serve to increase familiarity, but business is generally not discussed. However, working breakfast meetings, between 7:30 and 10am, are becoming popular in the capital's business community.

Generally speaking, cultivating a business associate in Mexico is a time-consuming process. The American habit of getting down to business quickly may not go over well; you'll want to take your cues from people you're doing business with. Usually there's a time of courtship, so to speak, where the Mexican uses social situations to get to know the foreigner better and sizes up his or her integrity, knowledge, and intentions. During this time there may be no discussion about business whatsoever. If a deal seems to be coming together too rapidly, exercise a bit of caution. Never sign a binding contract without consulting a U.S. lawyer who is also an expert in Mexican law. And remember too that a contract signed while traveling on a Tourist Permit rather than a Business Permit is not valid. Business Permits are available from Mexican Consulates in the United States.

The capital's business executives may take pride in personal efficiency and promptness, but they are hampered by secretarial inefficiency, burdensome governmental bureaucracy, and horrible phone systems, both external and internal. Good interoffice phone systems are almost nonexistent, so you'll often notice five or more phones lined up on a secretary's or executive's desk (all with different numbers), rather than one phone with a number of incoming lines. Mexican executives' habit of taking dozens of phone and secretarial interruptions can be exasperating when you're trying to do business. *"Permitame tantito"* ("give me a tiny minute"), the executive says politely, holding the thumb and index finger close as a measure of how little time the phone call will take—interruption after interruption … and on and on.

Just as there are inconsistencies in business, you never know whether a governmental bureaucrat or private-industry office worker will be infuriatingly indifferent or shower you with helpfulness and information. Shop clerks often seem bored beyond belief. In the capital's top shops, haughty clerks can be off-putting. Pushing a sale seems to be reserved for market and street vendors.

Office employees often work six and a half days a week with a long work day—often from 7am to 8pm with a lunch break from 2 or 3pm to 5pm or so. Then without concern for business, they take lengthy advantage of every holiday, often with extensions way beyond the official days. Sundays are sacred family days, when parks, and holiday resorts fill with extended families taking a break. Families, in fact, take precedence over work, not a bad trait, of course, until it's carried to what seems like an extreme. Family calls, no matter how trivial, may be permitted to interrupt business. This family priority is a given and so, without an apology of any kind, regular employees and even top management will miss important business deadlines in favor of their own or a relative's birthday or other "important" event such as mother's day which falls mid-week. It's a given that Easter week and two weeks or more at Christmas and New Years' is holiday time for many employees. But *any* holiday is an excuse for mass exodus from the job, regardless of pending obligations. These, of course are generalized quirks that *may* be apparent to visitors from more regimented societies.

6 Getting There

By Plane

The best advice on finding an economical airfare to Mexico City is to shop around. Prices can vary dramatically between airlines and during different travel seasons. Make your reservations as soon as possible after your plans are firm, since a limited number of seats are sold at reduced fares and those sell before others. Unlike the country's coastal resorts, for example, Mexico City does not have a high or low season; there are few seasonal variations in air fares to the capital. However, you may find the occasional unadvertised special during the summer and early fall, and possibly on weekends, if flights aren't booked. There may be also be slumps in travel after Easter and just after the New Year, during which airlines may offer some promotions. Call the airlines to find out when or if this is about to happen. A travel agent that books a lot of Mexico business will have a feel for these pricing variations. Because of increased international business travel, weekday flights from outside the country to the capital may be heavily booked, and Friday flights out of the capital may be full. Thursday or Friday flights to Mexico City have better availability from outside the country.

   Important Note: Tour operators often book whole sections of seats and keep them blocked for some time. If a flight is booked when you first call, try again later—it's highly likely that there will be some cancellations. Another way to get around this obstacle is by booking a package that includes air and hotel through a travel agent.

MAJOR AIRLINES

The main airlines operating direct or nonstop flights from the United States to points in Mexico include: **Aero California** (☎ **800/237-6225**), **Aeromexico** (☎ **800/237-6639**), **Air France** (☎ **800/237-2747**), **Alaska Airlines** (☎ **800/426-0333**), **American** (☎ **800/433-7300**), **Continental** (☎ **800/231-0856**), **Delta** (☎ **800/221-1212**), **Lacsa** (☎ **800/225-2272**), **Lufthansa** (☎ **800/645-3880**), **Mexicana** (☎ **800/531-7921**), and **Northwest** (**800/225-2525**). **Southwest Airlines** (☎ **800/435-9727**) serves the U.S. border. The main international airline departure points in North America for flights to Mexico City are Chicago, Dallas/Fort Worth, Denver, Houston, Los Angeles, Miami, New Orleans, New York, Orlando, Philadelphia, Raleigh/Durham, San Antonio, San Francisco, Seattle, Toronto, Tucson, and Washington, D.C.

TRAVEL PACKAGES

Package plans that include airfare, accommodations, and some sightseeing excursions may reduce costs somewhat. The cheapest package rates will be those in hotels in the lower range, always without the luxury amenities or beautiful rooms found in more costly hotels. A good travel agent specializing in Mexico will be able to give you all the latest schedules, details, and prices for airfare alone or various package deals. In addition, travel clubs such as AAA, Sanborn's, and those affiliated with credit cards, automobile clubs, and the American Association of Retired Persons (AARP) may have special discounts. To determine the best deal, you'll want to compare their specials against any the airlines or hotels are offering directly. Packages, however, often include transportation transfers to and from the airport and hotel, a convenience that's worth the added cost, especially for novice travelers to Mexico.

CHARTER FLIGHTS

Charter flights are usually reserved months in advance to and from certain cities for a specific time period and for a limited number of passengers. Charter flights to Mexico are common during winter months from major U.S. cities to resort areas, usually bypassing the capital. European travelers have a good chance of finding a charter flight to Mexico's cultural centers such as Mexico City during their country's most popular vacation months. Information about these flights appears as advertisements in travel sections in local newspapers. Travel agents specializing in Mexico will more readily have this information than a general interest agent.

FOR BRITISH TRAVELERS

Many airlines can arrange connecting flights to Mexico City, often with the Mexican carriers Aeromexico and Mexicana, but only British Airways flies direct from London to Mexico City. Discuss your options with your travel agent or call the Air Travel Advisory Bureau for advice (☎ **071/636-5000** in London; **061/832-2000** in Manchester). The flight from London to Mexico City takes approximately ten hours.

By Train

For information on getting to the border by train, call **AMTRAK** (☎ toll free in the U.S. **800/872-7245**) for fares, information, and reservations. From the border to the capital, there are several trains, but none of them are first class, and all are slow. Usually they don't have sleeping cars and may have no dining cars. (You'll want to bring your own water, food, and toilet paper). Border or near-border cities with trains to the capital include Nuevo Laredo, Piedras Negras, Monterrey, and Saltillo. For tickets and the latest information on train amenities (or lack thereof), contact **Mexico by Train** (not to be confused with Mexico by Rail), P.O. Box 2782, Laredo, Texas 78044 (☎ toll free **800/321-1699;** fax 210/725-3659). Given 15 days notice they will prepurchase your train tickets to anywhere in Mexico, and mail them to you. For holiday travel, make plans at least 30 days ahead of your proposed trip.

By Bus

Greyhound-Trailways or their affiliates offer service from the U.S. to the border, where passengers disembark, cross the border, and buy a ticket for travel into the interior of Mexico. At many border crossings there are scheduled buses from the U.S. bus station to the Mexican bus station.

By Car

Driving is certainly not the cheapest way to get to Mexico, but it is the best way to see the country. Even if this is your priority, you may think twice about driving your own car south of the border once you've pondered Mexico's many bureaucratic requirements for doing so (see below). Other considerations for driving include the high cost of gasoline, toll roads, and Mexican auto insurance. Unleaded gas (*Magna Sin*) costs around $1.60 a gallon, and regular gas (*Nova*) only slightly less. According to Sanborn's Insurance, cars using toll roads in Mexico pay between 22¢ and 52¢ U.S. per mile. This, according to the World Bank, means that driving on Mexican toll roads costs five to ten times what it would to travel an equivalent distance on a U.S. toll road. Recreational vehicles and cars pulling trailers pay more, and the price varies with the individual ticket seller. There are always non-toll alternatives to toll roads, but there may be no signs directing drivers to them. Traffic on them is usually heavier than traffic on toll roads—the trip will take longer, although the roadbeds are usually in fairly good condition. If you're driving from the Texas border, some hotels in Monterrey and Saltillo are offering to pay the highway toll for guests. From Nogales tourists *may* be offered a toll road discount card, which (if they are still offering it when you travel) is given at the 21-kilometer checkpoint. Insurance costs are high (see below). Parking is a problem in the cities.

If you want to drive to the Mexican border, but not into Mexico, border area chambers of commerce or convention and visitor's bureaus can supply names of secured parking lots. You can leave your car there while you see the country by rail, bus or plane.

For a full list of **driving rules, restricted days of car use** in Mexico City, **car rental information,** and information on **purchasing gasoline** and **making repairs** see "Getting Around By Car" in Chapter 3, "Getting to Know Mexico City."

In 1994, Mexico's Ministry of Tourism published its own *Official Guide: Traveling to Mexico by Car.* Don't depend on it—its information can be inconsistent, unclear, or inaccurate. Of possible use, however, is the list it includes of the hours that government officials are on duty at border crossings to review your car documents and issue Temporary Car Importation Permits. To get a copy, call the Mexican Vehicle Import Information line (☎ toll free **800/446-8277** in the U.S.).

It's wise to check and double-check all the requirements before setting out for a driving tour of Mexico. Read through the rest of this section, and then address any additional questions you have or confirm the current rules by calling your nearest Mexican consulate, Mexican Government Tourist Office, AAA, Sanborn's, (☎ **210-686-3601**), or the above-mentioned Mexican Vehicle Information line. At the latter, the person who answered the phone when I called seemed to have accurate information.

CAR DOCUMENTS

To drive a personal car into Mexico, you'll need a Temporary Car Importation Permit with a window decal, granted upon satisfaction of a strictly required list of documents (see below). The permit can be obtained through *Banco del Ejército (Banjercito)* officials, who have a desk, booth, or office at the Mexican Customs (*Aduana*) building immediately upon crossing the border into Mexico, or, before you travel, through Sanborn's Insurance and the American Automobile Association (AAA), each of which maintains border state offices in Texas, New Mexico, Arizona, and California. These companies may charge a fee for this service, but it will be worth it if it improves the uncertain prospects of traveling all the way to the border without proper documents for crossing. But even if you go through Sanborn's or AAA, your credentials will be reviewed by Mexican officials at the border—you must have them all with you—and will still be subject to questions of validity.

At presstime, you must have the following documents (originals where noted, copies otherwise) to bring your car into Mexico:

- *A valid, original driver's license,* issued outside of Mexico.
- *Current, original car registration and a copy of the original car title.* If the registration or title is in more than one name, and not all the named people are traveling with you, then a notarized letter from the absent person(s) authorizing use of the vehicle for the trip may be required—have it ready just in case. The car registration and credit card (see below) must be in the same name.
- *An original notarized letter from the lien holder,* if your registration shows a lien, giving you permission to take the vehicle into Mexico.
- *A valid international major credit card.* Using only your credit card, you are required to pay a $12 car-importation fee. The credit card used must be in the same name as the registration for the car.

    Note: Those without credit cards are required to post a **cash bond** based on the value of the car. Cost of the bond varies wildly from border entry to border entry. Sanborn's may be allowed to issue bonds, so check with them first. Those posting bonds must also present an *original and two copies* of their Resident Card or Passport, Social Security card and foreign (not Mexican) driver's license. If you don't have a credit card and don't post a bond, then you must make a *cash deposit* of the exact amount of the car's value, which is returned when you cross back into the United States. Both bond and deposit travelers must therefore come and go through the same border entry.

• A *signed declaration* promising to return to your country of origin with the vehicle. This form is provided by AAA or Sanborn's before you go, or by Banjercito officials at the border.

After completing all documentation requirements, an official decal will be affixed to the windshield and you're ready to go.

You must carry your Temporary Car Importation Permit, Tourist Permit, and, if you purchased it, your proof of Mexican car insurance in the car at all times. **Important reminder:** Someone else may drive the car, but the person (or relative of the person) whose name appears on the Car Importation Permit must *always* be in the car at the same time. (If stopped by police, a nonregistered family member driving without the registered driver must therefore be prepared to prove familial relationship to the registered driver.) Violation of this rule makes the car subject to impoundment and the nonregistered driver may be jailed and fined.

Only under certain circumstances will the driver of the car be allowed to leave the country without the car. If it's undriveable, you can leave it at a mechanic's shop if you get a letter to that effect from the mechanic and present it to the Secretaría de Hacienda y Credito Publico (treasury department) for further documentation, which you then present to a Banjercito official upon leaving the country. Then you must return personally to retrieve the car. If the driver of the car must leave the country without the car due to an emergency, the car must be put under Customs seal at the airport and the driver's Tourist Permit must be stamped to that effect. There may be storage fees. If it's wrecked or stolen, your insurance adjuster will provide the necessary paperwork, which you must present to Hacienda officials.

It's a good idea to make *two copies* of all your documents, including your driver's license, before you leave home. One copy of everything is for you, and the other is required by the Mexicans. This may save you some time and money at the border (if you decide to obtain your permit there); border officials will otherwise make copies of everything and charge you for them.

The Temporary Car Importation Permit papers will be issued for six months and the Tourist Permit is usually issued for 180 days—but they might stamp it for half that, so check. It's a good idea also to overestimate the time you'll spend in Mexico when applying for your permit, so that if something unforeseen happens and you have to (or want to) stay longer, you'll have avoided the long hassle of getting your papers renewed. **Important Note:** Whatever you do, don't overstay either permit. Doing so invites heavy fines and/or confiscation of your vehicle, which will not be returned. Remember also that six months does not necessarily work out to 180 days—be sure that you return before whichever expiration date comes first.

Other documentation is required for an individual's permit to enter the country (see "Entry Requirements," above):

PREPARING YOUR CAR

Check the condition of your car before you cross the border. Parts made in Mexico may be inferior, but service generally is quite good and relatively inexpensive. Carry a spare radiator hose, and belts for the engine fan and air-conditioner. Be sure your car is in tune to handle Mexican gasoline and that your tires can last a few thousand miles on Mexican roads.

Take simple tools along, also a flashlight or spotlight, a cloth to wipe the windshield, and a tire gauge. Mexican filling stations may have air to fill tires, but no gauge to check the pressure. You'll save time if you find a tire repair shop (*llanteria*—pronounced yahn-teh-*reeah*) to get your tires aired and checked. Mechanics will do it for a tip of a few pesos. A combination tire gauge/air compressor sold at U.S. automotive stores is an invaluable gadget to carry along. It plugs into the car cigarette lighter, making it a simple procedure to check the tires every morning and pump them up at the same time.

Not that many Mexican cars comply, but Mexican law requires that every car have **seat belts** and **a fire extinguisher.** Be prepared.

CROSSING INTO MEXICO WITH YOUR CAR

After you cross the border into Mexico from the United States (where you obtained your Temporary Car Importation Permit and Tourist Permit—see above), you'll come to a Mexican Aduana post somewhere between 12 and 16 miles down the road. In the past, every motorist had to stop for inspection. Now a light regulates inspection by stopping motorists mechanically chosen at random. If the light is green go on through. If it's red, stop for inspection. This means that all motorists must still stop to present their car and tourist papers, but only those with a red light undergo an inspection of the car and its contents. In the Baja Peninsula the procedures may differ slightly—first you get your tourist permit, then on down the road you may or may not be stopped again.

RETURNING TO THE U.S. WITH YOUR CAR

The car papers obtained when you entered Mexico *must* be returned when you cross back with your car—or within the time limit of 180 days. (You can cross as many times as you wish within the 180 days.) If the documents aren't returned, heavy fines are imposed ($250 for each 15 days late), and your car may be impounded and confiscated if you ever re-cross in the same car again. You can only return them to a Banjercito official, on duty at the Mexican Customs (Aduana) building immediately before you cross back into the United States.

Important note: At presstime Mexican authorities were only scolding people who failed to turn in car documents, but the mechanism was in place to begin charging fines and it could happen at any time. Some Mexican border cities have Banjercito officials on duty 24 hours, others are open fewer hours, and some don't have Sunday hours. Call the Vehicle Import Information office (see above) for current hours at each entry point. On the U.S. side customs agents may or may not inspect your car from stem to stern.

MEXICAN AUTO INSURANCE

Although auto insurance is not legally required in Mexico, anyone who drives without it is foolish. U.S. car insurance is invalid in Mexico. To be insured there, you must purchase Mexican insurance. Any party involved in an accident who has no insurance is automatically sent to jail and the car is impounded until all claims are settled. This is true even if you just drive across the border to spend the day—and it may be true even if you're injured. Those with insurance are assumed to be good for claims and may be released earlier.

Agencies selling Mexican auto insurance will show you a full table of current rates and will recommend the coverage it thinks adequate. The policies are written along lines similar to those north of the border, with this exception: the contents of your vehicle aren't covered. It's no longer necessary to overestimate the amount of time you plan to be in Mexico, because it's now possible to get your policy term lengthened by fax from the insurer (be sure to get their fax number). However, if you are staying longer than 48 days, it's more economical to buy a nonrefundable annual policy. For example, from Sanborn's Insurance a car (registered to an individual, not a business) with a value of $10,000 costs $133.45 to insure for two weeks, or $72.25 for one week. An annual policy for a car valued between $10,000 and $15,000 would be $397. Be sure the policy you buy from any company will pay for repairs in either the United States or Mexico and that it will pay out in dollars, not pesos.

One of the best insurance companies for south of the border travel is **Sanborn's Mexico Insurance,** with offices at all of the border crossings in the U.S. I never drive across the border without Sanborn's insurance. It costs the same as the competition, and you get a **travelog** that's almost like a mile-by-mile guide along your proposed route. For the most part it's like having a knowledgeable friend in the car telling you how to get in and out of town, where to buy gas (and which stations to avoid), highway conditions, and scams. It's especially helpful in remote places. They also have a travel club that offers discounts at many Mexican hotels. That alone is worth the cost

IMPRESSIONS

Bedlam, with cars rushing at you from every direction, without any apparent order, in spite of many red-and-green traffic lights and traffic policemen, is the first impression of driving into Mexico City.
—Harry A. Franck, *Trailing Cortez through Mexico* (1935)

of club membership. Most of Sanborn's border offices are open Monday through Friday, and a few are staffed on Saturday and Sunday. You can purchase your auto liability and collision coverage by phone in advance and have it waiting at a 24-hour location if you are crossing when their office is closed. For information contact Sanborn's Mexico Insurance, P.O. Box 310, Dept. FR, 2009 South 10th, McAllen, TX 78502 (☎ **210/686-0711;** fax 210/686-0732). AAA auto club also sells insurance.

3

Getting to Know Mexico City

THE ENORMITY OF MEXICO CITY IS LIKELY TO OVERWHELM YOU IN YOUR FIRST
minutes at street level, no matter which way you you choose to get
here or how intently you try to brace yourself. The traffic is chaotic
and intense; it usually moves rapidly along the vaguely marked
multilane highways and streets. When jams form drivers figure a way
around the snarls, muttering and shaking their fists all the while.
Signage reveals foreign business influence, restaurants, small grocery
stores, and banks galore.

All this kinetic complexity could be daunting, but this exciting
and historic city is relatively easy to learn. Transportation is readily
available, and most of the sightseeing highlights are in easily reachable clusters. The historic Alameda and Centro Historico areas are
within walking distance of each other. The Zona Rosa is near both
of these, while the Chapultepec and Polanco areas are a short jaunt
from the Zona Rosa. A 30-minute ride south of the Zona Rosa brings
you to San Angel, the university area, and Coyoacán. Xochimilco is
20 minutes beyond Coyoacán.

The following information will help even the first-time visitor glide
along manageably through the city.

1 Orientation

Arriving

BY PLANE

Mexico City's **Benito Juárez International Airport** is something
of a small city—you can grab a bite; buy a wardrobe, books, gifts,
and insurance; and exchange money or arrange a hotel.

Near gate "A" there's a guarded **baggage storage area.** The Mexico
City Hotel and Motel Association maintains a **hotel reservation service booth** here for their member hotels. If you miss their booth
before you leave the baggage claim area there's another one near gate
"A" on the concourse. Use this book to select a hotel. They'll call the
hotel and make your reservation according to your specifications for
location and price. If they book the hotel for you, they require one
night's advance payment and give you a voucher showing payment,
which you present at the hotel. Ask about hotels with specials (*tarifa
promocional,* pronounced tah-*ree*-fah pro-*moh*-sea-oh-nahl), which
may substantially reduce the rate. Special **long distance telephones**
(Ladatel) are strategically placed all along the public concourse (for
instructions on how to use them see the Appendix). **Bookstores**

IMPRESSIONS

*The effect of the city on strangers is as unaccountable as an
uninitiate's reaction to a bullfight. Some go into an ecstasy; others
speak mainly of the defects and mention bowel trouble. But whatever
its glories, its fakes, its fascinations, not to see Mexico [City] would
greatly discredit your travels.*
—Hudson Strode, *Now in Mexico* (1947)

Greater Mexico City

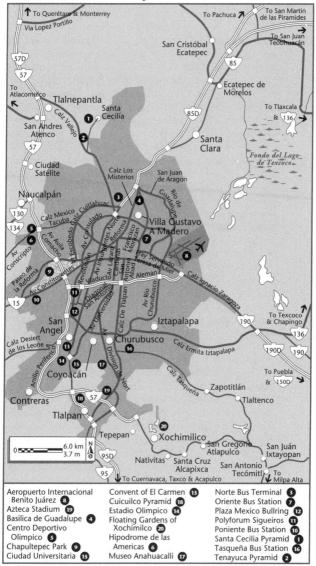

Aeropuerto Internacional Benito Juárez **8**	Convent of El Carmen **13**	Norte Bus Terminal **3**
Azteca Stadium **19**	Cuicuilco Pyramid **18**	Oriente Bus Station **7**
Basilica de Guadalupe **4**	Estadio Olimpico **14**	Plaza Mexico Bullring **12**
Centro Deportivo Olimpico **5**	Floating Gardens of Xochimilco **20**	Polyforum Siguleros **11**
Chapultepec Park **9**	Hipodrome de las Americas **6**	Poniente Bus Station **10**
Ciudad Universitaria **15**	Museo Anahuacalli **17**	Santa Cecilia Pyramid **1**
		Tasqueña Bus Station **16**
		Tenayuca Pyramid **2**

include one operated near Gate "A" by the Instituto Nacional de Antropologia (INAH) which has a large selection of historic, artistic, scholarly, and sometimes travel-related books. Another bookstore, this one privately owned, is near gate "D" and has a larger, more eclectic selection that includes novels and Mexican cookbooks. A map store occupies a tiny location near gate "C."

Getting into the City

The trip into the city from the airport takes between 20 and 45 minutes depending on the time of day. The **authorized airport taxis** provide good, fast service. They are relatively expensive but are generally the most reliable. Here's how to use them: After exiting the baggage claim area and entering the public concourse, you'll see yellow booths marked "Taxi." These authorized taxi booths are staffed by personnel wearing bright yellow jackets or bibs emblazoned with "Taxi Autorizado" (authorized taxi). Tell the ticket-seller your hotel or destination, as price is based on a zone system. Expect to pay around $14 for a ticket to the Zona Rosa. Count your change! A yellow-shirted escort will then show you to an available taxi in front, or to the end of a line if there is one. An authorized cab has familiar markings: yellow car, white taxi light on the roof, "Transportación Terrestre" painted on the doors. Present your ticket to the driver. Avoid turning your luggage over to an unauthorized taxi "assistant" who does nothing but take your luggage a few steps or lift it into the waiting taxi—naturally he will want a nice tip. Putting your luggage in the taxi is the driver's job and these "assistants" seem to whiz in out of nowhere to do the job and then brazenly insist on a tip.

As you exit the baggage area dozens of men will be shouting at you "Taxi, Taxi"; once you've managed to get past them, others may approach you on the concourse. These are usually **unlicensed and unauthorized taxi drivers.** Most are just regular people trying to make a buck with their private cars, but you are taking a needless chance to use them. Your savings over an authorized taxi will be minimal or nil, so I suggest that you ignore them.

Though the authorized cabs maintain a monopoly on the airport business, you can try to beat the system without using the unauthorized cabs. First, at the taxi booth at the terminal find out how much it costs to your destination, so you'll have a basis for comparison. Then walk left out the front door to the Terminal Area Metro station (see below), at the intersection of the busy Bulevar Aeropuerto and the airport entrance. When you see a yellow VW Beetle or little yellow Datsun cab, flag it down. You may save at least 25%, perhaps even 50%, by doing so.

To make sure you get a proper, trustworthy cab, be sure to read the information on taxis in "Getting Around," below.

When you're ready to return to the airport, the Metro or a taxi is your only option, since there's no other scheduled service.

If you have only a small bag, Mexico City's modern subway system, the **Metro** is cheaper and faster than a taxi. Large bags or multiple pieces of luggage are forbidden on the Metro. A smallish backpack or large shoulder purse will be all right. (Locals get on with large plastic shopping bags, filled with groceries.) As you come from your plane into the arrivals hall, turn left, walk all the way through the long terminal, out the doors, and along a covered sidewalk. Soon you'll see the distinctive Metro logo that identifies the Terminal Area station, down a flight of stairs. The station is on Metro Línea 5.

Follow the signs for trains to Pantitlán. At Pantitlán, change for Línea 1 ("Observatorio"), which will take you to stations that are just a few blocks south of the Zócalo and the Alameda Central: Pino Suarez, Isabel la Catolica, Salto del Agua, Balderas. The ride costs around 25¢. Do remember that the most crowded times to try the Metro are weekdays between 6:30 and 9am and 5 and 8pm. If you find that you can get on the Metro with a heavy bag, don't plan to take a Metro route that requires changing trains at La Raza station. The walk between lines there is a good 10 minutes, and it's difficult carrying anything heavy.

BY TRAIN

The Buenavista railroad station (**547-1097** or **547-1084**), three blocks north of the Revolución Metro station along Insurgentes, is called officially the **Terminal de Ferrocarriles Nacionales de Mexico.** You can get away with **Estacion Buenavista.**

If you know exactly when you want to leave the city by train, buy your ticket when you arrive, or as early as possible before your date of departure. If you want information on train schedules from here, there's usually someone staffing an information booth in the lobby, but you have to be a wizard to extract information from that person, who seldom has printed train schedules. Schedule boards are on the wall at one end of the lobby and have the times of departures and arrivals from Mexico City, but nothing about connections elsewhere. Ticket sellers are inside the terminal against the front wall, and, if there isn't a line, they may be willing to answer questions about schedules, dining cars, pullmans, etc. For a printed schedule go to the office which is in the middle of the same wall as the ticket sellers. The door is unmarked. It's usually closed from 2 to 5pm.

To get your bearings for the city from here, walk out the right-hand set of front doors in the terminal. You're facing south. The big boulevard on the right is **Avenida Insurgentes,** the city's main north-south axis. You can catch an "Indios Verdes-Tlalpan" bus south along Insurgentes to get to the Plaza de la República, Paseo de la Reforma, and the Zona Rosa; catch one north to get to the Terminal Norte (the main bus station). Straight ahead of you about 12 blocks away, the dome of the Monumento a la Revolución floats on the skyline from its site in the Plaza de la República. A distance left of it, the spire of the Torre Latino America (Latin American Tower) juts skyward from the intersection of Avenida Juárez and Avenida Lázaro Cárdenas.

If you're going to the center of town, it's better to take a taxi, since buses are often jammed. Taxis meet every train arrival and usually gather at the far right end of the terminal. There's no regulated system, so just bargain for the fare.

IMPRESSIONS

Mexicans may have no sense of time, but you will be given more of it to get off a bus in our own hurried land.
—Harry A. Franck, *Trailing Cortez through Mexico* (1935)

BY BUS

Mexico City has a bus terminal for each of the four points of the compass: north, east, south, and west. You can't necessarily tell which terminal serves which area of the country by looking at a map, however. Some destinations are served from more than one terminal. For bus rider's terms and translations, see "Bus Terms" in the Appendix.

All stations have restaurants, book and magazine stands, money exchange booths or banks, a post office, long-distance telephone booths, and fax capability. Each station has a taxi system based on set-price tickets to various zones within the city, operated from a booth or kiosk in or near the entry foyer of the terminal. Locate your destination on a zone map, or tell the seller where you want to go, buy a ticket (boleto), and present it to the driver out front.

Words you'll encounter are: *taquilla* (ticket window), *recibo de equipajes*—or simply *equipajes*—(baggage claim), *llegadas* (gates), *sanitarios* (toilets), and *sala espera* (waiting room).

Terminal Central de Autobuses del Norte

Called by shorter names such as "Camiones Norte," "Terminal Norte," or "Central del Norte," or even just "C.N.," this is Mexico's largest bus station, on Avenida de los 100 (or "Cien") Metros, in the northern part of the city. It handles most buses coming from the U.S./ Mexican border. All buses from the Pacific Coast as far south as Puerto Vallarta and Manzanillo, from the Gulf Coast as far south as Tampico and Veracruz, and such cities as Guadalajara, San Luis Potosí, Durango, Zacatecas, and Colima arrive and depart from here. You can get out to the pyramids of San Juan Teotihuacán and Tula from here.

A **tourist information booth** is set up at the center of the terminal's crescent-shaped facade, and nearby there's a **hotel reservations booth.**

To get downtown from the Terminal Norte, you have a choice of modes. The **Metro** has a station (Estacion Terminal de Autobuses del Norte, or T.A.N.) right here, so it's easy to hop a train and connect for all points. But only a small bag can be carried on the Metro. Walk to the center of the terminal, go out the front door, straight ahead, down the steps, and to the **Metro station.** This is Línea 5. Follow the signs that say "Dirección Pantitlán." For downtown, you can change trains at either "La Raza" or "Consulado" (see the Metro map in this book). Be aware that if you change at "La Raza," you will have to walk for about 15 minutes, and you'll encounter stairs. The walk is through a nice marble-lined underground corridor, but it's still long if you have heavy luggage.

Another way to get downtown is by trolleybus. The stop is on **Avenida de los Cien Metros,** in front of the terminal. The trolleybus runs right down Avenida Lázaro Cárdenas, the "Eje Central" (Central Artery). Or the "Central Camionera del Norte-Villa Olimpica" bus goes all the way down Insurgentes, past the university.

Finally, there's a taxi system based on set-price tickets to various zones within the city, operated from a kiosk in the terminal. Locate your destination on the zone map, buy a ticket (boleto) for that zone, and present it to the taxi driver out front.

Terminal de Autobuses de Pasajeros de Oriente ["TAPO"]

Buses from the east (Puebla, Cholula, Tlaxcala, Oaxaca, Amecameca, the Yucatán Peninsula, Veracruz, San Cristóbal de las Casas, etc.) begin and end at TAPO. Though Oaxaca is in the southern part of the country buses to that city begin here, pass through Puebla (which is east of Mexico City), and then go on to Oaxaca.

Taxi tickets to anywhere in the city are sold inside on the main concourse near exit doors. They are priced by zone. Count your change!

Terminal Central de Autobuses del Sur

Mexico City's southern bus terminal is right next to the **Taxqueña** Metro stop, last stop on that line. The Central del Sur handles buses from Cuernavaca, Taxco, Acapulco, Zihuatanejo, and intermediate points. The easiest way to get to or from the Central del Sur is on the Metro, all the way to Taxqueña (or Tasqueña, as it's also spelled). Or take a trolleybus down Avenida Lázaro Cárdenas.

To get downtown by taxi, buy your ticket in the terminal before you exit, then get in the taxi line out front (if it's busy) or hand it to a waiting driver.

Terminal Poniente de Autobuses

The western bus terminal is conveniently located right next to the Observatorio Metro station, at Sur 122 and Río Tacubaya. This is the station you'll be on if you're coming from Acapulco, Cuernavaca, Toluca, Ixtapan de la Sal, Valle de Bravo, Ixtapa, Taxco, or Zihuatanejo.

BY CAR

If you are brave enough to drive in Mexico City here are a few tips. Arrive and depart before dawn, when there is very little traffic. This way you can arrive at your destination without the added distraction of a zillion cars all coming at you from as many directions. Then park the car in a guarded lot and don't drive it again until you are ready to leave the city—at dawn. Driving in this city is best left to those who know it.

Tourist Information

For basic information on the city try the **Infotur** offices, the most convenient of which is in the Zona Rosa at Amberes 54, at the corner of Londres (☎ **525-9380** to **525-9384**). Others are at the bus terminals, airport, and railroad station. They're open daily 9am to 9pm except holidays when the office is closed. Very little information is on display, so you have to ask and be specific about what you want. Then they may pull it out from behind the desk. They can usually provide maps of the city.

The **Secretaría de Turismo** (SECTUR), Av. Presidente Masaryk 172 (☎ **250-0151** or **250-0585**), north of Chapultepec Park in the district known as Polanco, is a bit out of the way, but either phone

Downtown Mexico City

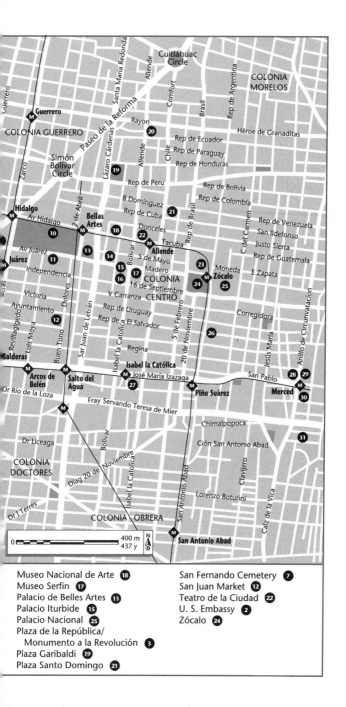

Museo Nacional de Arte ⓲
Museo Serfin ⓱
Palacio de Belles Artes ⓭
Palacio Iturbide ⓯
Palacio Nacional ㉕
Plaza de la República/
  Monumento a la Revolución ❸
Plaza Garibaldi ⓲
Plaza Santo Domingo ㉑

San Fernando Cemetery ❼
San Juan Market ⓬
Teatro de la Ciudad ㉒
U. S. Embassy ❷
Zócalo ㉔

number will serve to get you information or emergency help. They'll speak English and staff the phones 24 hours.

The **Camara Nacional de Comercio de la Ciudad de Mexico (Mexico City Chamber of Commerce, ☎ 566-0457)** maintains an information office with a very friendly, helpful staff who can provide you with a detailed map of the city (or country) and answer some of your questions and provide numerous brochures. It's conveniently located at Reforma 42, and is open from 9am to 2pm and 3 to 6pm Monday through Thursday, or until 5:30pm on Friday.

City Layout

MAIN ARTERIES, STREETS & A LANDMARK

The **Paseo de la Reforma** goes northeast to the Basílica of Guadalupe and west crossing Insurgentes, through Chapultepec Park eventually leading to Toluca. **Insurgentes Norte** (north) a major north-south artery, goes from Reforma north to the Pyramids of Teotihuacán. To the south it crosses Reforma and becomes **Insurgentes Sur** (south). This is the artery that leads to San Angel, the Ciudad Universitario (University City), the Pedregal, and Coyoacán, and farther south it becomes Highway 95 to Taxco and Cuernavaca. Another main north-south artery starts just south of the historic city center at Servando Teresa de Mier and is called **Calzada San Antonio Abad** until it crosses Miguel Aleman and becomes **Calzada Tlalpan** and continues south terminating in the suburb of Tlalpan. The **Periférico** (Highway 57) is a loop around the city which is also named Camacho as it heads north. It leads north to Tula, Querétaro, and San Miguel de Allende. As it goes south, it crosses Reforma, passes through Chapultepec Park, crosses Constituyentes and heads south to San Angel before turning east south of the Ciudad Universitario, crosses Highway 95 to Taxco and continues past Xochimilco and eventually loops back again to the city center.

In the downtown area the main east-west arteries are **Juárez** which runs from the Plaza de la República past the south side of the Alameda, and becomes **Madero** which ends at the Zócalo. **5 de Mayo** runs between the Alameda and the Zócalo. **Hidalgo** runs along the north side of the Alameda, becomes **Calzada Tacuba** and passes in back of the Catedral Metropolitana (Metropolitan Cathedral).

Streets change names frequently, as you probably noted.

FINDING AN ADDRESS

Despite its size, Mexico City is not outrageously hard to understand. The city is divided into 350 *colonias,* or neighborhoods. But unless you are venturing out of the Colonia Centro (city center), you'll rarely need to know the colonia names. However, when you're trying to find an obscure address, such as a shop or a restaurant that may be unfamiliar to a taxi driver, it may be helpful to have these handy. A few to know are Colonia Polanco, a fashionable neighborhood immediately north of Chapultepec park, and all the Lomas—Lomas de Chapultepec, Lomas Tecamachalco etc.—which are very exclusive neighborhoods west of Chapultepec Park, the "in" addresses so to speak. In addresses the word is abbreviated *Col.*; the full colonia name is vital in addressing correspondence.

Taxi drivers are notoriously ignorant of the city, including the major tourist sights and popular restaurants. Before getting in the taxi always give them, in addition to a street address and colonia, cross streets as a reference and locate your destination on a map that you carry with you.

A LANDMARK

Probably the most frequently used and noticed landmark in Mexico City is the Monumento a la Independencia, often referred to as the Angel of Independence Monument, at the intersection of Reforma, Florencia, and Río Tiber. Set upon a tall marble shaft, the golden angel is an important and easily discerned guidepost for travelers. A creation of Antonio Rivas Mercado, the 22-foot-high gold-plated bronze angel—cast in Florence, Italy—was completed in 1906 at a cost of $2.5 million. With its base of marble and Italian granite, the monument's total height is 150 feet.

NEIGHBORHOODS IN BRIEF

Centro   Centro refers to the heart of Mexico City, its business, banking, and historic center, including the areas in and around the Parque Alameda Central and Zócalo.

Chapultepec   A huge area west of the city center, it mainly includes Chapultepec park—with its numerous museums—and its immediate environs.

Coyoacán   Thirteen miles from the city center, south of San Angel and east of the Ciudad Universitario, Coyoacán is another colonial-era suburb noted for its beautiful town square, cobblestone streets lined with fine old mansions, and several of the city's most interesting museums.

Polanco   A district immediately north of Chapultepec Park, Polanco is one of the city's trendiest neighborhoods. It's dotted with glitzy boutiques, luxury hotels, interesting antique shops, and some of the city's best restaurants. President Mazaryk is the main artery running through it.

San Angel   Nine miles south of the city center, San Angel was once a distinct village but is now surrounded by the city. Yet the neighborhood remains a beautiful suburb of cobbled streets and beautiful colonial-era homes.

Xochimilco   Fifteen miles south of town center, Xochimilco is noted for its famed canals and "floating gardens," which date from pre-Hispanic times.

Zona Rosa   West of the Centro, the "Pink Zone" is a trendy area noted for its pedestrian-only streets, shops, restaurants, and hotels.

STREET MAPS

Should you want more detailed maps of Mexico City than the ones included in this guide, you can obtain them easily. Most bookstores (including Sanborn's), and many newsstands carry a local map-guide entitled *Mexico City Trillas Tourist Guide,* a softcover book of gorgeous block-by-block pictorial maps covering most areas of the city that are of interest to visitors. The text, which includes interesting facts and statistics on Mexico City and its sights, is in English. Fully detailed street plans of the entire city are published by **Guía Amarilla** and **Guía Roji.** These are probably more detailed than you need or want, unless you have business to conduct in the city. They're available in bookstores and at newsstands.

The **American Automobile Association** publishes a motorist's map of Mexico and Central America, which includes a very handsome map of downtown Mexico City. The map is available for free to AAA members at any AAA office in the United States; it's not available in Mexico.

2 Getting Around

By Public Transportation

Mexico City has a highly developed and remarkably cheap public transportation system, and there are plenty of private transportation options as well. The Metro, minibuses, colectivo vans, and yellow VW taxis will take you anywhere you want to go for very little money. The city has no system of advance bus tickets, and no printed schedules.

BY METRO

The subway system in Mexico City offers a smooth ride for around 25¢. Once you've paid the initial price of a ticket, you can transfer as many times as you need to get to your final destination. Nine lines are completed in the sprawling system, with one more under construction.

As you enter the station, buy a *boleto* (ticket) at the glass *caja* (ticket booth). Insert your ticket into the slot at the turnstile and pass through; inside you'll see two large signs showing the line's destination (for example, for Línea 1, it's "Observatorio" and "Pantitlán"). Follow the signs in the direction you want, and *know where you're going,* since there is usually only one map of the routes, at the entrance to the station. There are, however, two signs you'll see everywhere: *Salida,* which means "exit"; and *Andenes,* which means "platforms." Once inside the train, you'll see above each door a map of the station stops for that line, with symbols and names.

Transfer of lines is indicated by *Correspondencias.* The ride is smooth, fast, and efficient (although hot and crowded during rush hours). The stations are clean and beautifully designed, and have the added attraction of several archeological ruins unearthed during construction. There is also a subterranean passage that goes between the "Pino Suárez" and "Zócalo" stations so you can avoid the crowds (and rain) along the Pino Suárez. The "Zócalo" station has dioramas and large photographs of the different periods in the history of the

Valley of Mexico, and at "Pino Suárez" there is the foundation of a pyramid from the Aztec empire.

Important Notes: The Metro system runs between 6am and 1am Monday through Friday, and 7am to midnight Saturday and Sunday. Bulky, large baggage is not allowed into the system and signs are duly posted. In practice this means that bulky suitcases or backpacks sometimes make you *persona non grata,* but a large shoulder-bag such as I use is not classed as luggage; nor is an attache case, or even a case that's slightly bigger. The reason is that Mexico City's Metro on an average day handles over five million riders, leaving precious little room for bags! But, in effect, if no one stops you as you enter, you're in.

Metro travel is crowded during daylight hours on weekdays, and consequently pretty hot and muggy in summer. In fact, you may find that between 4 and 7pm on weekdays the Metro downtown is virtually unusable because of sardine-can conditions. At some stations there are even separate lanes roped off for women and children. Buses, colectivos, and taxis are all heavily used during these hours. On weekends and holidays, the Metro is a joy to ride.

BY BUS

Moving millions of people through this sprawling urban mass is a gargantuan task, but the city officials do a pretty good job of it. (They do tend to change bus numbers and routes frequently.) The municipal bus system is run on an enormous grid plan. Odd-numbered buses run roughly north-south, even-numbered buses go east-west, and a special express service runs along the main routes downtown. Maps of the entire system are impossible to find.

The large buses that ran on the major tourist routes (Reforma and Insurgentes) tended to become suffocatingly packed and have been phased out in favor of small buses, and more of them. Thus, crowding is uncommon except perhaps during peak hours. The cost is usually the U.S. equivalent in pesos of around 17¢ to 25¢. Although the driver usually has change, try to have the exact fare when you board. Bus stops on the major tourist streets usually have a map with the full route description.

One of the most important bus routes is the one that runs between the Zócalo and the Auditorio Nacional (the National Auditorium, in Chapultepec Park) or the "Observatorio" Metro station. The route is via Avenida Madero or 5 de Mayo, Avenida Juárez, or Paseo de la Reforma; maps of the route are posted at each bus stop. Buses marked "Zócalo" run this route.

Another important route is "Indios Verdes-Tlalpan," which runs along Avenida Insurgentes connecting the northern bus terminal (Terminal Norte), Buenavista railroad station, Reforma, the Zona Rosa, and—far to the south—San Angel and the Ciudad Universitario (University City).

By Taxi

Mexico City is pretty easy to negotiate by Metro and bus, and these methods bring you few hassles. Taxis are another matter, but there are times when nothing else will do. Cabs operate under several distinct sets of rules established in early 1991 that sometimes make using one less of a combat zone situation than in the past.

Don't use a car that is not an official taxi. All official taxis (except those expensive "Turismo" cabs) are painted yellow or green and gray. Except the "Turismo" cabs, they have white plastic roof signs bearing the word "Taxi" and they have "Taxi" or "Sitio" painted on the doors and they have meters. Look for all of these indications, not just one or two of them.

There is no need to tip any taxi driver in Mexico, unless the driver has performed a special service, such as carrying your luggage inside a hotel.

METERED TAXIS Yellow and white, or green and gray Volkswagen Beetle and "sitio" (radio-operated) Datsun cabs are your best bet for low cost and good service. Though you will often encounter a gouging driver ("Ah, the meter just broke yesterday; I'll have it fixed tomorrow!"), or one who advances the meter (yes, I've seen it), or drives farther than necessary to run up the tab, most of the service will be quick and adequate. As of early 1991, these taxis began operating strictly by the meter, which starts at 2 pesos. If the driver says his meter isn't working, or starts with a reading higher than 2 pesos, find another taxi. Also don't get in a taxi that doesn't have the driver's taxi permit prominently displayed. It's a laminated license about 5 by 7 inches and it's often above the rear-view mirror or attached to a string near the glove box. It's illegal for a taxi to operate without the license in view. A taxi operating without it usually means the person driving the taxi is not a registered driver. These drivers are most often the ones that will try to cheat the passenger and you have no recourse if something goes wrong with the service.

"TURISMO" TAXIS These are unmarked, have special license plates, bags covering their meters, are usually well-kept big cars, and are assigned to specific hotels. The drivers negotiate rates with individual passengers for sightseeing and the like but rates to and from the airport are established, although higher than the Datsun or VW taxis. Ask the bell captain what the airport rate should be and establish the rate before taking off. These drivers are often English-speaking licensed guides and can provide exceptional service.

By Colectivo

Also called *peseros,* these are sedans or minibuses, usually green and gray, that run along major arteries. They pick up and discharge passengers along the route, charge established fares, and provide more comfort and speed than the bus. Routes are displayed on cards in the windshield; often a Metro station will be the destination. One of the most useful routes for tourists is runs from the Zócalo along Avenida Juárez, along Reforma to Chapultepec, and back again. Get a colectivo with a sign saying "Zócalo," not "Villa." A "Villa" bus or pesero goes to the Basílica de Guadalupe.

Note that some of the minibuses on this route have automatic sliding doors—you don't have to shut them, a motor does.

As the driver approaches a stop, he may put his hand out the window and hold up one or more fingers. This is the number of passengers he's willing to take on (vacant seats are difficult to see if you're outside the car).

By Car

Generally speaking, touring around the world's largest city in a car will be extremely frustrating, and I don't recommend it. Besides the usual one-way streets, there are numerous traffic circles, streets change names constantly, and drivers do not heed signs. If you want to spend a few days touring by car outside the capital, don't hesitate to rent one, but time your exit and reentry to the city (to return the car) carefully. The traffic is horrendous and it requires one person to drive and another to navigate. If you rent a car at the airport, ask one of the rental car employees to drive you and the car to your hotel (pay his taxi fare back to the airport), park the car overnight in protected parking, then leave the city before dawn the next morning when there is almost no traffic. Avoid heavy traffic between 7 and 10am and 5 to 9pm.

To control pollution in the capital, regulations for car use according to day of the week, tag number, and color are in force as follows in the chart below:

Prohibited Driving Days

Day	Mon.	Tues.	Wed.	Thurs.	Fri.
Tag color	Yellow	Pink	Red	Green	Blue
Tag ends in	5 or 6	7 or 8	3 or 4	1 or 2	9 or 0

This means that if your car tag is yellow and ends in a 5 or 6 you are prohibited from driving on Monday in Mexico City, but you can drive any other day of the week. **Note:** This applies to rental cars and to tourist cars, but it is not in effect on Saturday or Sunday. There's a large fine for violating this regulation. And be aware also that during severe pollution alerts an extra day of nondriving is often added. To know what rules apply when you are there, before entering the city, call the tourist help line (☎ 5/250-0151 or 250-0598).

For important information on **toll roads,** see "Getting There: By Car" in Chapter 2, "Planning a Trip to Mexico City."

CAR RENTALS

I don't recommend renting a car in Mexico City for touring the city or any other reason. Besides an amazing amount of traffic, the crazy traffic circles, one way streets and lack of parking will have you craving the hospital mental ward in no time. It may be useful for a day excursion to small towns outside the city. But it's important to remember that street parking in Mexico City, Toluca, Puebla, Cuernavaca, and Taxco is very difficult. Otherwise, cars are a good option, especially if you have enough people to fill one and can share the cost.

Car-rental rules change often in Mexico, so double check those mentioned here. The best prices are obtained by reserving your car a week in advance from the United States. Mexico City and most other large Mexican cities have several rental offices representing the various big firms and some smaller ones. You'll find rental desks at the airports, at all major hotels, and at many travel agencies. The large firms like Avis, Hertz, National, and Budget have rental offices on main streets as well. Cars are easy to rent if you have a credit card (American Express, VISA, or MasterCard), are 25 or over, and have a valid driver's license and passport with you. Without a credit card you must leave a cash deposit, usually a big one. One-way rentals, where you pick up the car in one place and leave it in another, are usually simple to make, but are very costly.

Costs

Don't underestimate the cost of renting a car. The best prices are obtained by reserving your car a week in advance from your home country. But shop for the best rate before settling on one since the cost of renting can vary enormously from company to company. The least expensive car to rent is the VW Beetle with standard shift and without air conditioning, which is made in Puebla, Mexico. Daily charges are much higher than the daily rate if you keep the car a week (and arrange for the weekly rate in advance). Besides varying from company to company, rates can vary greatly from city to city and during certain times of year. I recommend taking the mileage-included option rather than mileage-added—the latter can run up the cost of using a car considerably. Rental agents don't volunteer information about the cost of insurance or the added tax, so be sure to include that information in your calculations.

A VW Beetle with manual shift and unlimited mileage, rented for one day through Avis at the Mexico City airport, would cost:

Basic daily rental	$47.00
Insurance	15.50
10% IVA tax	6.20
Total	$68.70

At Avis, weekly cost of a VW Beetle in Mexico City is:

Weekly rate	$276.00
Insurance @ $15 per day	108.00
10% IVA tax	38.40
Total	$425.40

Rental Confirmation

Make your reservation directly with the car-rental company using their toll-free number. Write down your confirmation number and request that a copy of the confirmation be mailed to you (rent at least a week in advance so the confirmation has time to reach you). Present that confirmation slip when you appear to collect your car. If you're dealing with a U.S. company, the confirmation must be honored, even if they have to upgrade you to a better class of car—don't allow them to send you to another agency. The rental confirmation also has the agreed-on price, which prevents you from being charged more in case there is a price change before you arrive. Insist on the rate printed on the confirmation.

Deductibles

Be careful: Deductibles vary greatly; some are as high as $2,500, which comes out of your pocket immediately in case of car damage. Rental agents don't volunteer this information, so don't fail to ask about the deductibles.

Insurance

Many credit-card companies offer their cardholders free rental-car insurance. *Don't use it in Mexico,* for several reasons. Even though rental-car insurance is supposedly optional in Mexico, there may be major consequences if you don't have it: First, if you buy insurance, and you have an accident, you pay only the deductible, which limits your expense. If you are hauled to jail and found guilty, you have an insurance agent on your side to vouch that you are good for the damages. Second, if you don't have insurance and you have an accident, or the car is vandalized or stolen, you'll have to pay for everything before you can leave the rental-car office. This includes full value of the car if it is unrepairable—a determination resting solely with the rental-car company. While your credit card may eventually pay your costs, you will have to lay out the money in the meantime. Third, if an accident occurs, everyone may wind up in jail until guilt is determined. If you are the guilty party, you may not be released from jail until all restitution is paid to the rental-car owners and to injured persons—made doubly difficult if you have no rental-car insurance. Insurance is offered in two parts: **Collision and damage insurance** covers your car and others if the accident is your fault, and **personal accident** insurance covers you and anyone in your car. I always take both.

Damage

Always inspect your car carefully before renting it, using this checklist:

- Hubcaps
- Windshield (for nicks and cracks)
- Body (for dents, nicks, rust, etc.)
- Fenders (for dents, etc.)
- Muffler (is it smashed?)
- Trim (loose, damaged, or missing?)
- Head and tail lights
- Fire extinguisher (it should be under the driver's seat, required by law)

- Spare tire and tools (in the trunk)
- Seat belts (required by law)
- Gas cap
- Outside mirror
- Floor mats

Note in writing on the rental agreement *every* damaged or missing area, no matter how minute, or you will be charged for all missing or damaged parts, including missing car tags, should the police confiscate your tags for a parking infraction (very costly). I can't stress enough how important it is to check your car carefully. Car companies have attempted to rent me cars with bald tires and tires with bulges, a car with a license that would expire before I returned the car, as well as cars with missing trim, floor mats, fire extinguisher, etc.

Fine Print

Read the fine print on the back of your rental agreement and note that insurance is invalid if you have an accident while driving on an unpaved road.

Trouble Number

One last recommendation. Before starting out with a rental car, be sure you know their trouble number. The large firms have toll-free numbers, which may not be well staffed on weekends.

Problems, Perils, & Deals

At present, I find the best prices are through Avis and that's the company I use; generally I am a satisfied customer, though I sometimes have to dig in my heels and insist on proper service. I have had more difficult problems with other agencies. In the past several years I have encountered certain kinds of situations that could occur with any company: An attempt to push me off to a no-name company rather than upgrade me to a more expensive car when a VW Beetle wasn't available; poorly staffed offices with no extra cars, parts, or mechanics in case of a breakdown; a demand from Hertz that I sign a credit-card voucher for 75% of the value of the car in case of an accident even though I had purchased insurance (I always refuse to do this and still rent the car). Since potential problems are varied, I'd rather deal with a company based in the States, so that at least I have recourse when these obstacles arise.

Signing the Rental Agreement

Once you've agreed on everything, the rental clerk will tally the bill before you leave and you will sign an open credit-card voucher that will be filled in when you return the car. Read the agreement and double-check all the addition. The time to catch mistakes is before you leave, not when you return. Hertz also requires car renters to sign an additional rental agreement form, written in Spanish, that appears to relieve them of a lot of responsibility, and the renter of none. To decipher for sure what it says legally would take ten graduating classes of Harvard lawyers. If Hertz is the only choice in town, you have no alternative but to sign it if you want a car, even though you may have no idea what the form says.

Picking Up/Returning the Car

When you rent the car, you agree to pick it up at a certain time and return it at a certain time. If you're late in picking it up or cancel the reservation, there are usually penalties—ask what they are when you make the reservation. If you return the car more than an hour late, an expensive hourly rate kicks in. Also, you must return the car with the same amount of gas in the tank that it had when you drove out. If you don't, the charge added to your bill for the difference is much more than for gas bought at a public station.

GASOLINE

Throughout the country gasoline is sold only through government-owned Pemex (Petroleras Mexicanas). Each station has a franchise owner who buys everything from Pemex. There are two types of gas in Mexico—Nova (leaded gas), and Magna Sin (unleaded gas). Magna Sin is sold from bright green pumps and costs around $1.60 a gallon. Nova costs almost the same. In Mexico, fuel and oil are sold by the liter, which is slightly more than a quart (40 liters equals about $10^1/_2$ gallons). Nova is readily available. Magna Sin is available in most areas of Mexico, along major highways, and in the larger cities. Even in areas where it should be available, you may have to hunt around. The typical station may be out of Magna Sin for a couple of days—weekends and holidays especially. Or you may be told that none is available in the area, just to get your business. Plan ahead: Fill up every chance you get; keep your tank topped off. Pemex publishes a helpful *Atlas de Carreteras* (road atlas), which includes a list of filling stations with Magna Sin gas, although there are some inaccuracies in the list. No credit cards are accepted for gas purchases.

It's best to pay close attention when you have to fuel up in Mexico: Drive up to the pump, close enough so that you will be able to watch the pump run as your tank is being filled. Check that the pump is turned back to zero, go to your fuel filler cap and unlock it yourself, and watch the pump and the attendant as the gas goes in. Though many service station attendants are honest, many are not. It's good to ask for a specific peso amount rather than saying "full," (*lleno,* pronounced "yea no"). This is because the attendants tend to over-fill, splashing gas on the car and anything within range.

When there are lines at the gas pumps, attendants often finish fueling one vehicle, turn the pump back quickly (or don't turn it back at all), and start on another vehicle. You've got to be looking at the pump when the fueling is finished, because it may show the amount you owe for only a few seconds. This "quick draw" from car to car is another good reason to ask for a specific peso amount of gas. If you've asked for N.P. $20 worth, the attendant can't charge you N.P. $22 for it.

Once the fueling is complete, let the attendant check the oil, or radiator, or put air in the tires. Do only one thing at a time, be with him as he does it, and don't let him rush you. Get into these habits, or it'll cost you. If you get oil, make sure that the can that is tipped into your engine is a full one. If in doubt, have the attendant check the dipstick again after the oil has supposedly been put in. Check your change, and again, don't let them rush you. Check that your locking gas cap is back in place.

DRIVING RULES

If you park illegally or commit some other infraction and you are not around to discuss it, police are authorized to remove your license plates (*placas*). You must then trundle over to the police station and pay a fine to get them back. Mexican car rental agencies have begun to weld the license tag to the tag frame; you may want to devise a method of your own to make the tags difficult to remove. Theoretically, this will encourage the policeman to move on in search of another set of plates easier to confiscate. On the other hand, he could get his hackles up and decide to have your car towed. To weld or not to weld is up to you.

Be attentive to road signs. A drawing of a row of little bumps means that there are speed bumps (*topes*) across the road to warn you to reduce your speed while driving through towns or villages. Slow down when coming to a village whether you see the sign or not—sometimes they install the bumps but not the sign!

Kilometer markers on main highways register the distance from local population centers. There is always a shortage of directional signs, so check quite frequently that you are on the right road. Other common road signs include:

Camino en Reparación	Road Repairs
Circulación	Direction traffic flows
Conserva Su Derecha	Keep Right
Cuidado con el Ganado, el Tren	Watch Out for Cattle, Trains
Curva Peligrosa	Dangerous Curve
Derrumbes	Falling Rocks
Deslave	Caved-in Roadbed
Despacio	Slow
Desviación	Detour
Disminuya Su Velocidad	Slow Down
Entronque	Highway Junction
Escuela	School (Zone)
Grava Suelta	Loose Gravel
Hombres Trabajando	Men Working
No Hay Paso	Road Closed
Peligro	Danger
Puente Angosto	Narrow Bridge
Raya Continua	Continuous (Solid) White Line
Tramo en Reparación	Road Under Construction

| Un Solo Carril | One-lane Road or Bridge |
| Zona Escolar | School Zone |

BREAKDOWNS

Your best guide to repair shops is the Yellow Pages. For specific makes and shops that repair them, look under "Automoviles y Camiones: Talleres de Reparación y Servicio;" auto-parts stores are listed under "Refacciones y Accesorios para Automoviles." On the road often the sign of a mechanic simply says Taller Mecánico. Junkyards (and there are few of them in Mexico) are called a *huesero* (boneyard). Tire repair shops are called *llantería*.

I've found that the Ford and Volkswagen dealerships in Mexico give prompt, courteous attention to my car problems, and prices for repairs are, in general, much lower than in the United States or Canada. I suspect that other big-name dealerships—General Motors, Chrysler, etc.—give similar, very satisfactory service. Often they will take your car right away and make repairs in just a few hours, sometimes minutes. Hondas are now being manufactured in Guadalajara; in time, dealerships, service departments, and parts should be available.

If your car breaks down on the road, help might already be on the way. Green, radio-equipped repair trucks driven by uniformed, English-speaking officers patrol the major highways during daylight hours to aid motorists in trouble. These **"Green Angels"** will perform minor repairs and adjustments free, but you pay for parts and materials.

ACCIDENTS

When the car is driveable, many Mexicans drive away from accidents to avoid hassles with police. Even people who have damages but are not at fault leave the scene. And they leave the scene even if there are injuries. If the police arrive while the involved persons are still there, everyone may be locked in jail until blame is assessed. Whoever is deemed to be at fault must settle up immediately, which may take days of red tape, or be an even bigger hassle if people are hospitalized with serious injuries. Foreigners without fluent Spanish are at a distinct disadvantage when trying to explain their side of the event. Three steps may help the foreigner who doesn't wish to do as the Mexicans do: If you have damage to your own car, notify your Mexican insurance company, whose job it is to intervene on your behalf. Your U.S. car insurance is invalid in Mexico (see "Getting There: By Car" in Chapter 2, "Planning a Trip to Mexico City"). If you're in a rental car, notify the rental company immediately and ask how to contact the nearest adjuster (you did buy insurance with the rental—right?). Finally, if all else fails, ask to contact the nearest Green Angels, who may be able to explain to officials that you are covered by Mexican insurance.

PARKING

You hear more about car break-ins than any other kind of crime in Mexico. When you park your car on the street, lock up and leave nothing within view inside (day or night). I use guarded, gate-locked parking lots to avoid vandalism and break-ins, especially at night. This way you also avoid parking violations. During the day, when pay lots are not available, dozens of small boys will surround you as you stop, wanting to "watch your car for you." Pick the leader of the group, let him know you want him to guard it, and give him a peso or two when you leave. Kids may be very curious about the car and may look in, crawl underneath, or even climb on top, but they rarely do any damage.

By RV

Touring Mexico by recreational vehicle is a popular way of seeing the country. Many hotels have hookups. RV parks, while not as plentiful as in the United States, are available throughout the country. Many RV organizations join together to caravan as a group through Mexico, following a scheduled itinerary. Mexico's Green Angels (see "Breakdowns" above), often send along a representative to smooth the way and help lead the group. Many cities that have no RV parks will set aside a place for the caravan and welcome the foreigners with special festivities.

Fast Facts: Mexico City

Airport   See "Orientation" earlier in this chapter.

Altitude   At an altitude of 7,240 feet—almost a mile and a half in the sky—there's a lot less oxygen in the air here than you may be accustomed to. If you run for a bus and feel dizzy when you sit down, blame the altitude; if you think you're in shape, but puff and puff getting up Chapultepec hill, blame the altitude. It takes about 10 days or so to adjust to the scarcity of oxygen. Go easy on food and alcohol during your first few days in the city.

American Express   The Mexico City office is at Reforma 234 (☎ 5/533-0380), in the Zona Rosa. It's open for banking, for mail pick-up (American Express clients only), and for travel advice from 9am to 6pm Monday through Friday and also 9am to 1pm on Saturday.

Area Code   The area code for Mexico City is 5. The country code for Mexico is 52.

Babysitters   Better hotels can often recommend a babysitter.

Bookstores   In Mexico City, Sanborn's always has books in English, as well as magazines and newspapers. So does the American Bookstore, Madero 25 near Bolívar (☎ 512-7284). It's open from 9:30am to 7pm Monday through Saturday. About the most convenient foreign-and-Spanish-language bookstore in Mexico City, with a good selection of guides and books on Mexico, is Central de Publicaciones—Librería Mizrachi, Juárez 4, near Avenida Lázaro Cárdenas (☎ **510-4231**), right across from the Palacio de Bellas Artes. Another shop, nearby, is the Librería Britanica, Madero 30-1, in the Hotel Ritz building (☎ **521-0180**). For a full selection of books in French try Librarie Francoise, Genova 2 between Reforma and Hamburgo (☎ **525-1213**). The Museo Nacional de Antropologia in Chapultepec Park (☎ **553-6266**) also has an excellent shop with a good selection of books on Mexico, particularly special-interest guides (birds, flowers, geology, minerology, archeology, cuisine and folk art, and so forth).

Business Hours Banks are usually open Monday through Friday from 9am to 1:30pm. Banamex is open Monday through Friday from 9am to 5:50pm. Bank branches at the airport are open whenever the airport is busy, including weekends. Business offices are generally open from 10am to 7pm Monday through Friday and until noon on Saturday. Most are closed on Sunday. Mexico City stores are open Monday through Friday usually between 10am and 8pm and on Saturday until 5 or 6pm. Bars are open around 11am until 2 to 3am. Discos open between 9 and 10:30pm and thrive until 2 to 5am or so.

Car Rentals See "Getting Around" in this chapter.

Climate "When to Go" in Chapter 2.

Crime See "Safety" below.

Currency See "Information, Entry Requirements, and Money" in Chapter 2 and "Currency Exchange" below.

Currency Exchange The alternative to a bank is a currency-exchange booth, or *casa de cambio*. There are currency-exchange booths in many parts of the city where foreigners circulate; they are often open Monday through Friday from 8:30am to 5:30pm, and on Saturday from 8:30am to 2:30pm as well. Many stay open until 6pm. The exchange rates offered by casas de cambio are sometimes better than and sometimes worse than those offered by the banks. Usually, the rates are much better than the rates offered by most hotels.

Doctors Embassies maintain a reputable list of doctors. Better hotels usually have a doctor on call 24 hours.

Documents Required See "Information, Entry Requirements, and Money" in Chapter 2.

Drugstores Sanborn's drug departments stay open late. Check the phone directory for the location nearest you. For after hours hotels can usually contact the drug store "de turno," (on call).

Electricity The electrical system in Mexico runs at 110 volts, 60 cycles, as in the United States and Canada. However, in reality it may cycle more slowly and overheat your appliances. To compensate, select a medium or low speed for your hairdryer, though it may still overheat. Older hotels still have electrical outlets for flat two-pronged plugs; you'll need an adapter for using any modern electrical apparatus which has an enlarged end on one prong, or which as three prongs to insert. Many first-class and deluxe hotels have the three-holed outlets (*trifacico* in Spanish). Those that don't may loan adapters, but to be sure, it's always better to carry your own. Just be sure it has two even prongs. Adapters with one prong larger than the other won't fit into Mexico's two-pronged outlets.

Important Note: Electric current fluctuates radically in Mexico, so bring your own surge protector if you are using a personal computer.

Embassies and Consulates Embassies and consulates provide valuable lists of doctors and lawyers, as well as regulations concerning marriages in Mexico, and they'll act as facilitators in bringing business concerns together. Contrary to popular belief, your embassy cannot get you out of a Mexican jail, provide postal or banking services, or fly you home when you run out of money. Most countries have a representative embassy in Mexico City and many have consular offices or representatives in the provinces. Hours vary but most are open only weekdays from 8 or 9am to 1 or 2pm. The U.S. Embassy is open until 5pm. Most embassies close on legal holidays of their home country and of Mexico. On holidays and weekends, there's usually an officer on duty for emergencies.

The Embassy of **Australia** is at Jaime Balmes 11, Plaza Polanco, Torre B. (☎ 5/395-9988 or 566-3053).

The Embassy of **Canada** is at Schiller 529, in Polanco (☎ 5/724-7900).

The Embassy of **New Zealand** is at Homero 229, 8th floor (☎ 5/250-5999).

The Embassy of the **United Kingdom** is at Lerma 71, at Río Sena (☎ 5/207-2569 or 207-2593).

The Embassy of the **United States** is next to the Hotel María Isabel Sheraton at Paseo de la Reforma 305, at the corner of Río Danubio (☎ 5/211-0042).

Emergencies Locatel (☎ 658-1111) is a government-operated service most often associated with finding missing persons anywhere in the country. With a good description of car and occupants they'll look for motorists who must be in an emergency. SECTUR (Secretaría de Turismo) staffs telephones 24 hours (☎ 250-0123 or 250 0150) to help tourists in difficulty.

Eyeglasses For repairs or prescription try Santosoy, Hamburgo 99, in the Zona Rosa. Open Monday through Saturday 10am to 8pm.

Hairdressers/Barbers Ask at your hotel. The average cost of a haircut is $10 to $15; a hairdo costs between $12 and $50.

Holidays See "When to Go" in Chapter 2.

Hospitals The American-British Cowdray (A.B.C.) Hospital caters to foreigners and is located at Calle Sur 132 No. 136, corner of Avenida Observatorio, Colonia Las Americas (☎ **277-5000** or **277-6211** or for emergencies **515-8359** or **516-8077**). Take the Metro (Línea 1) to "Observatorio"; the hospital is a short taxi ride from there.

Hotlines If you think you've been ripped off in a purchase, call the consumer protection office (Procuraduría Nacional del Consumidor; ☎ **761-3811** or **761-3801**). Since there's often no one staffing those phones you're better off calling the SECTUR tourist assistance numbers (☎ **250-0123, 250-0150, 250-0493,** or **250-0027**).

Information See "Tourist Information" in this chapter.

Laundry/Dry Cleaning Your hotel can take care of this for you, but you'll save money, and perhaps time, if you take it to a branch of Lavandería Jiffy (pronounced "hee-fee," not "jiffy"). There are branches at the corner of Río Tiber and Río Lerma (near the Monumento a la Independencia) and at the corner of Revillagigedo and Victoria (south of the Alameda Central). Another laundry, north of the Plaza de la República, is the Lavandería Automatica, Calle Edison 91, between Iglesias and Arriaga. Hours are Monday through Friday from 9am to 7pm and on Saturday from 9am to 8pm.

Legal Assistance If you need legal help call SECTUR (☎ **250-0123** or **250-0493** or **250-0151**). International Legal Defense Counsel, 111 S. 15th St., Packard Building, 24th Floor, Philadelphia, PA 19102 (☎ **215/977-9982**), is a law firm specializing in legal difficulties of Americans abroad. See also "Embassies and Consulates" and "Emergencies," above.

Libraries Mexico City has several libraries of English-language books connected with the city's diplomatic missions. Check out the Benjamin Franklin (American) Library, on Niza between Londres and Liverpool. The U.S. Embassy (☎ **211-0042**) has a full reference library and numerous U.S. Department of Commerce publications relating to doing business in Mexico. Make arrangements to use it prior to arriving in Mexico. The Canadian Embassy Library (Canadian books and periodicals in French and English) is at Schiller 529, in Polanco (☎ **724-7900**), open Monday through Friday from 9am to 12:30pm. The American Chamber of Commerce (☎ **724-3800**) has a complete commercial library.

Lost Property See "Health & Insurance" in Chapter 2.

Luggage Storage/Lockers There are *guarda equipaje* rooms at the airport and bus stations. Most hotels have a key-locked storage area for guests who want to leave possessions for a few days.

Mail Mail service is slow and unreliable in Mexico. However, international postal service companies such as Federal Express, UPS, and DHL have rapid service into and out of Mexico. Mail receipt services such as Mail Boxes Etc. also have branches in major Mexican cities and where there are large concentrations of foreigners. If you use the Mexican mail service, mail your cards and letters early in your trip to improve chances they'll get home before you do.

The city's main post office is a block north of the Palacio de Bellas Artes on Avenida Lázaro Cárdenas, corner of Tacuba. Ask for the Correo Mayor. Although I don't recommend mailing a package in Mexico—it may never get to its intended destination—if you must mail one in Mexico City, here's what to do. Take it to the special post office called Correo Internacional no. 2, Calle Dr. Andrade and Río de la Loza (Metro: Balderas or Salto del Agua), open Monday through Friday from 8am to noon. Don't wrap up your package securely until an inspector examines it.

Newspapers/Magazines The *Mexico City News* is the city's English language daily. See also "Bookstores" above.

Photographic Needs Try the Foto Regis, Juárez 80, near the Alameda.

Photography All archeological sites and many museums have restrictions on the use of personal cameras. At archeological sites visitors using their own video cameras are charged $8.50. A similar charge is permitted at all sites for still cameras; however, not all sites charge it. It's courteous to ask permission before photographing anyone.

Police See "Emergencies" above.

Pollution September and October seem to be light months for pollution, while mid- to late November, as well as December and January, are months noted for heavy pollution. Schools are often closed because of it during January; restrictions on driving may be imposed on weekends as well (usually on weekdays). (See "Getting Around: By Car," above.) Be careful if you have respiratory problems; being at an altitude of 7,240 feet makes things even worse. Just before your planned visit, call the Mexican Government Tourist Office nearest you (see Chapter 2, "Planning a Trip to Mexico," for the numbers), and ask for the latest information on pollution in the capital. Minimize your exposure to the fumes by refraining from walking busy streets during rush hour. Make Sunday, when many factories are closed and many cars escape the city, your prime sightseeing day.

Radio and TV Radio VIP (☎ **595-1122;** 88.1 FM), a CBS affiliate, has partial English-language broadcasts and news. For jazz, dial EXPRESS Radio 590 AM (☎ **662-0590**). All top hotels and many moderately priced hotels receive U.S. cable and sometimes network television stations.

Religious Services Most major religions have services in English in Mexico City. Check the current telephone directory or the Saturday and Sunday edition of the English-language newspaper *Mexico City News* for time and place.

Restrooms   There are few public restrooms so take advantage of those in the larger hotels, in cafés and restaurants, and in museums. Always carry your own toilet paper and hand soap—neither are in great supply in Mexican restrooms. No matter where you are, even if the toilet flushes with paper, there'll be a waste basket for paper disposal. Many people come from homes without plumbing and are not accustomed to toilets that will take paper, and will throw paper on the floor rather than put it in the toilet; other people know that water pressure is often not sufficient to carry paper away and they won't put paper in the toilet either. Thus, you'll see the basket, no matter what quality of place you are in. There's often a sign that says "do" or "don't" flush paper.

Safety   In the capital (as elsewhere in Mexico), please remember *pedestrians do not have the right of way—vehicles do.* In many crossings in the city, there are "walk, don't walk" signals, but even then vehicles don't give much importance to pedestrians' "rights." And traffic lights are short, so you have to move quickly when you have the chance, all the while looking all around you to be sure you're out of the way of turning and oncoming traffic.

Crime is more of a problem in Mexico than it used to be although muggings and blatant thievery are not pervasive. There have been a few carjackings in the capital, but again, it's not the problem here that it is in the States; carjackers find it impossible to make a quick getaway in the city's congested traffic. In general, though you'll feel physically safer in Mexico City than in comparable big cities in the United States, you should take some basic, sensible precautions.

First, remember that you're a tourist, and an obvious target for crime. Beware of pickpockets on crowded buses, the Metro, museums, in markets and at crowded festivals. Stay alert. Be aware of your immediate surroundings. Wear a moneybelt and don't sling your camera or purse over your shoulder; wear the strap diagonally across your body and keep your purse closed. This will minimize the possibility of your becoming a victim of crime. Guard your possessions very carefully at all times; don't let packs or bags out of sight even for a second. The big first-class bus lines will store your bag in the luggage compartment under the bus, and that's generally all right, but keep your things with you on village and second-class buses on country routes. At airport ticket check in, while you're distracted with making boarding arrangements, keep your carry-on luggage between your feet. When you send your carry-on items through the security X-ray machines, get to the other side immediately to retrieve your items, since theft at this vulnerable point has been known to happen.

In hotels, don't open your door to anyone purporting to represent the hotel until you've checked with the front desk that the person is authorized.

Be careful when walking alone, night or day. Busy streets are no problem, but empty streets (even if empty just for afternoon siesta) are lonely places. As a sensible precaution, take a taxi to and from your hotel door at night.

If you have a car, park it in an enclosed or guarded lot at night. Vans are a special mark. Don't depend on "major downtown streets" to protect your car—park it in a private lot with a guard, or at least a fence.

Important Warning: Agreeing to carry a package back to the States for an acquaintance or a stranger may mean you've involved yourself in a smuggling scheme—it could land you in jail for years and cost a lot of money to get you out. Never do it, no matter how friendly, honest, or sincere the request may seem. Perpetrators of this illegal activity prey on innocent-looking single travelers and especially senior citizens. Also, don't purchase pre-Hispanic artifacts. This is against the law and furthermore there are rewards for those who help authorities stop the removal of pre-Hispanic artifacts from the country—the person who sold it to you may very well turn you in for a reward. The same scam works in illegal drug purchases. See also "Bribes and Scams" in Chapter 2.

Shoe Repairs   Ask the bell captain or desk clerk at your hotel.

Taxes   Mexico's 10% tax may be included in posted prices *or* added to a posted price. It's wise to ask *¿Más IVA?* (plus tax) or *¿Con IVA?* (with tax). There are also airport taxes for domestic and international flights. (See "Getting Around" in Chapter 2).

Taxis   See "Getting Around" earlier in this chapter.

Telephone and Fax   Generally speaking Mexico City's telephone system is in terrible shape. A number you reached five seconds ago may not be reachable again for days. As in the rest of the country, the telephone company may change telephone numbers without telling the owner of the telephone and without informing the information operator of the new number. Changes of telephone numbers are ongoing in the capital, thus numbers that were correct at the time this edition was updated may be changed by the time you visit. The local number for information is 04, and you are allowed to request three numbers with each information call. However, reaching the information operator can be difficult, so make every call count. Very few of the old coin-operated public telephones remain. Most have been replaced by Ladatel phones, which are sometimes coin operated, sometimes card operated, and sometimes accept both cards and coins. Of those that use coins, only the old 100 peso coins will operate them, since phones have not been adapted for New Pesos. More often than not, however, phones are card operated, using a Ladatel card usually available for purchase at pharmacies and newsstands near public phones. They come in denominations of 10, 30, 50, and 100 New Pesos. If you expect to do much calling, buy at least a 30-peso card—the 10-peso card lasts for about 10 minutes' worth of talking. Long-distance calls within Mexico and to foreign points are surprisingly expensive. Read "Telephones and Mail" in the Appendix on how to use phones. Hotels are beginning to charge for local calls, but budget-priced hotels are less likely to charge because they lack the equipment to track calls from individual rooms.

Fax machines are often turned off when offices are closed. And many fax numbers are also regular telephone numbers; for these you have to ask for the fax tone "por favor dar me el tono por fax." Then you wait for the tone and send your fax. Telephone etiquette in Mexico does not require the answerer to suggest taking a message or having someone return the call; you'll have to suggest it. Although many businesses do, phone etiquette doesn't necessarily require answering with the business name; you have to ask if you have the right place.

Television   "Cablevision" provides CBS, ABC, and NBC, as well as Arts and Entertainment, Movie Channel, and Sports Channel, from 6am to 2am. Many first-class and several budget-category hotels receive these channels.

Time   Central standard time prevails in the capital and throughout most of Mexico. *Beginning in the spring of 1995, Mexico will adopt daylight saving time to save on energy costs.* (This decision has been made twice in the past and rescinded, so don't count on it.)

Transit Info   See "Getting Around" in this chapter.

Water   Most budget and moderately priced hotels in the capital don't have purified tap water. A few of the deluxe hotels don't either. Most, however, provide free purified bottled water in each guest room. Even deluxe hotels with purified water systems will usually provide bottled water also, because they know foreigners have been told "Don't drink the water." Purified water in hotels that have a purification system may flow through regular taps or special taps marked *Agua Purificada.* In most cases, however, hotels that have purified water don't place a sign in the room announcing it. You'll have to call the receptionist to find out for sure. Virtually any hotel, restaurant, or bar will bring you purified water if you specifically request it, but you may be charged for it.

Wire Funds   If you need cash in a hurry *Dineros en Minutos* (Money in Minutes) is affiliated with Western Union and makes wire cash transactions at Electrika furniture and electronics stores in Mexico. Your contact on the other end presents cash to Western Union, which is credited by Electrika, and presented (in pesos) to you. The service only recently began in Mexico but 500 outlets are planned.

4

Mexico City Accommodations

Luxury hotels in Mexico City can be every bit as plush and expensive as first-class hotels in the world's other great cities. But you can also stay here in perfectly adequate and comfortable hotels for far less. When you consider that for $30 to $70 you can find a double room—complete with bath and often such extras as air conditioning, TV with U.S. channels, tour desk, bar, and restaurant—within steps of choice neighborhoods like the Zócalo, Alameda, or Revolución Monument areas, you'll agree that the city can be a great bargain for travelers on a budget.

Most hotels built in the city during the last decade are of the luxury variety. They may feature central air conditioning; elevators; concierge; several restaurants; sophisticated phone systems that boast voice mail; in-room computer and fax outlets or even the machines themselves; cellular phone rentals; executive business centers; and the like.

Less expensive hotels tend to be older; they are usually well kept but come without all the extras that inflate prices. Several of these older standbys have completely remodeled their facilities in the last several years without substantially increasing their rates.

In apartment hotels (most of which are in or near the Zona Rosa), you can rent a fully furnished studio or one-bedroom apartment with a kitchen by the week or month, at rates similar to or lower than those at a standard hotel. If you're traveling with a small group or if you're staying for a week or more, apartment hotels may offer you both savings and more space than would a conventional hotel.

The recommendations below are grouped by neighborhood or landmark; these are places that are well known to every city-dweller and should be easily located by first-time visitors. Although you'll pay more to stay in the Zona Rosa, Chapultepec, or Polanco areas, doing so will put you right in the thick of the city's best shopping and dining districts. The Chapultepec area, with all its hotels and museums, borders Polanco's fashionable dining and shopping. The Zona Rosa and its plethora of shops and restaurants is near both Chapultepec and Polanco as well as the Alameda area. Hotels near the Alameda and Zócalo will have you well positioned for sightseeing on foot, with plenty of good restaurant selections.

RATES

Prices at hotels classified below as "Very Expensive" begin at about $170 for a single or double room. "Expensive" hotels begin at around $130 for a single or double room. "Moderate" hotels range from about $50 to $125. "Budget" hotels range from $20 to $45 for one or two people.

Corporate rates for qualified businesses and corporations reduce costs considerably. Hotel rates, which are no longer government regulated, are required to be visibly posted at the front desk.

RESERVATIONS

Most hotels in the Very Expensive and Expensive categories have U.S. toll-free telephone numbers (included in the hotel listings) and will accept credit cards when booking reservations. Rates quoted on these numbers usually do not include the 10% hotel tax. Policies regarding cancellations and the subsequent return of your deposit vary among hotels. Hotels in the Moderate and Budget categories will usually accept an international money order or a cashier's check to reserve a room for the first night. Ask which they prefer, inquire about their cancellation policy, and take the name of the person you spoke with. You'll find that telephoning is more efficient than writing when looking into reservations and cancellation policies at the latter two categories of hotels. In budget hotels the person answering the phone probably won't speak English, however, so if you don't speak Spanish, find someone who does to make the call for you. Reply letters and faxes cost a lot in Mexico and hotels with slim profit margins won't use these for a reply. Hotels in the Moderate category may be booked during the week as well, since these are more popular with Mexicans on business than with foreigners. Hotels in the low range of moderate and budget priced hotels can usually be booked on arrival.

Many hotels have their own garages where guests can park free, while other hotels are beginning to charge for parking.

OTHER INFORMATION

See also "Electricity," "Water," and "Telephone" in the "Fast Facts" section of Chapter 3 for information pertinent to staying in a Mexico City hotel. Guest rooms in all of the luxury hotels and many of the moderately priced hotels have cable TV with U.S. as well as Mexican channels. Budget priced hotels that offer television in the room usually have only Mexican channels. Minibars in Mexico are called *servibars.*

---

1   Chapultepec Park & Polanco

Very Expensive

Hotel Camino Real, Mariano Escobedo 700, México, D.F. 11590.
   ☎ 5/203-2121 or 203-3113 or toll free 800/722-6466 in the U.S. and Canada. Fax 5/250-6935 or 250-6897. 710 rms. A/C MINIBAR TEL TV **Metro:** "Chapultepec."
   Rates: $210–$225 single or double; $250 Executive Club rooms.

Long one of the capital's leading hotels, the Camino Real continues to be so popular that often every room is booked. Designed by famous Mexican architect Ricardo Legorreta, its standout features include the Rufino Tamayo mural "Man Facing Eternity," which greets visitors as they enter the front doors, and a mural by José Luis Covarrubias that graces the hotel's La Huerta restaurant. No expense is spared as the Camino Real vies to remain one of the capital's hot spots for business and social entertaining. The spacious rooms, all with pastel-colored modern furnishings and a sitting and desk area, come with armoires concealing the television and minibar, in-room safety boxes, hairdryers, remote-control TVs, electronic card door locks, fax connections, and direct-dial phones with voice mail. There are only 30 rooms for nonsmokers, however; other rooms are afflicted with the lingering, powerful odor of tobacco smoke, so book early if it's important to you to avoid this. Two rooms are handicap equipped. Executive Club rooms come with bathrobes, continental breakfast and evening cocktail hour, and daily newspaper.

Dining/Entertainment: Fouquet's de Paris is the hotel's best restaurant and one of the capital's top dining establishments. Each month features an international specialty, often from Mexico's cuisines. Popular for business breakfasts, it's open Monday through Saturday from 7 to 11am and for dinner from 6:30pm to midnight. Azulejos Restaurant, featuring Mexican and international specialties, is open for all three meals. La Huerta is the informal ground floor restaurant, open daily from 7am to midnight.

Services: Laundry and dry cleaning, car rental, travel agency, barber and beauty shop, concierge, boutiques, book and gift shop, jewelry store.

Facilities: Full service business center, private conference rooms, complete gym, massage, sauna, steam room, four tennis courts, pool.

Hotel Four Seasons—Regent, Reforma 500, Col. Juárez, México, D.F. 06600. ☎ **5/230-1818,** or toll free **800/332-3442** in the U.S., **800/268-6282** in Canada. Fax 5/230-1817. 248 rms and suites. A/C MINIBAR TEL TV **Metro:** "Sevilla."
Rates: $220–$1,075.

This hotel, built in the style of an elegant Mexican hacienda with four sides surrounding a beautiful interior courtyard, is a veritable sanctuary in this busy city. Though you're only steps from the busy Paseo de la Reforma, the grounds inside the eight-story hotel seem more like the quiet countryside around a gracious manor house. On one side of the large and inviting outdoor courtyard there's umbrella-covered al fresco dining with colonnaded walkways all around; other dining rooms and bars face this pleasant scene. Gracious manners are the hallmark of the staff here; rather than point you to an elevator or restaurant, someone will escort you. The light, airy, huge rooms have high ceilings and are sumptuous to the ultimate degree. Each has plush, thick bedspreads, pastel walls, beautiful talavera pottery lamps and talavera-coordinated bathroom accessories, Indonesian tapestries, and rich dark wood furnishings. All rooms have twice-daily maid service (with ice refills), hairdryer, remote-control TV, safety deposit box, fax outlet, separate shower and tub, robes, and illuminated makeup mirrors. Most rooms face the interior courtyard, two deluxe suites have patios facing the courtyard, and most Executive Suites (with one or two separate bedrooms) overlook Reforma. Thirty rooms are reserved for nonsmokers and there are two handicap-equipped rooms. The Four Seasons—Regent is located at the western end of the Zona Rosa, near Chapultepec Park and Polanco and opposite the Hotel Marquis Reforma.

Dining/Entertainment: El Restaurante is the fine-dining spot here and features international specialties and low-key live entertainment. It's open daily from 6pm to midnight. A more informal

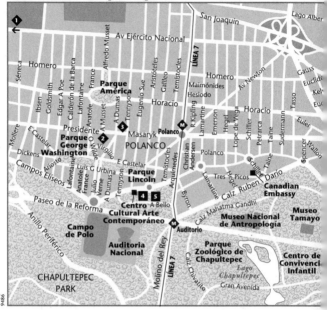

dining option is the delightful El Café, with excellent service and an international menu; it's open for all three meals. El Salón, a cozy bar with dark wood and comfortable chairs, faces the courtyard and has outdoor tables as well. The Lobby Lounge, open from 4pm to midnight, is like a series of gracious living rooms with comfortable couch-and-chair groupings and an excellent atmosphere for conversation. Offerings include coffee specialties, ports and sherries, cocktails, pastries, and light finger sandwiches.

Services: Laundry, dry cleaning, room service, private specialist-led tours to the capital's museums, concierge, boutiques, beauty and barber shop.

Facilities: Spa with completely equipped gym, sauna, massage, whirlpool, swimming pool, complete business center with private meeting rooms.

Hotel Marquis Reforma, Reforma 465, Col. Cuauhtémoc, México, D.F. 06500. ☎ **5/211-3600, 211-0577** or toll free 800/525-7800 in the U.S. Fax 5/211-5561. 116 rms, 84 suites. MINIBAR TEL TV Metro: "Sevilla."

Rates: $180 single or double; $280–$340 suites single or double.

With an art deco exterior and elegant combinations of glass, marble, and rich dark mahogany within, the Marquis Reforma opened in 1991 as one of the city's state-of-the-art luxury hotels. For its quality it's also a member of Small Luxury Hotels of the World. Excellently located, it's at the eastern end of Chapultepec Park opposite

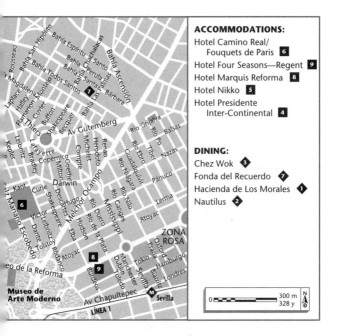

ACCOMMODATIONS:

Hotel Camino Real/
    Fouquets de Paris **6**
Hotel Four Seasons—Regent **9**
Hotel Marquis Reforma **8**
Hotel Nikko **5**
Hotel Presidente
    Inter-Continental **4**

DINING:

Chez Wok **3**
Fonda del Recuerdo **7**
Hacienda de Los Morales **1**
Nautilus **2**

the Four Seasons—Regent and western end of the Zona Rosa, and it's almost equidistant between the U.S. Embassy and the Chapultepec/Polanco area. Among the standard amenities in each luxuriously furnished room are full-length mirrors, lighted makeup mirror, bathrobe, fax outlet, remote-control TV with U.S. channels, and an in-room safe large enough for a camera, laptop computer, and more. Rooms are quite varied in shape and size. Some have terraces; some have separate living, dining, and bedrooms; some have an attached meeting room; and standard double rooms have a king-size bed and small sitting area. The Suite Reforma has a view of the Castillo de Chaputepec. The fourth floor is for nonsmokers and there's one handicap-equipped room. Guests staying in first or second floor Diamond floor rooms have separate check-in and check-out and receive complimentary continental breakfast as well as late afternoon cocktails and appetizers. When I checked, the hotel reserved Diamond floor rooms directly, rather than through its toll-free number.

Dining/Entertainment: The street-side Café Royal offers an international menu for all three meals daily, and there's a no-smoking section. The gourmet restaurant La Jolla (pronounced "la *hoy*-a"), on the second floor, serves northern Italian food and is open Monday through Saturday from 2pm to midnight. An elegant musical quartet entertains nightly in the lobby Caviar Bar where tea, drinks, and light meals are served.

Services: Laundry and room service, hair salon, newsstand with small drug section, concierge, car rental, travel agency, bookstore, florist, video recorders, computers and fax machines for rent, electric adapters and converters on request. Golf privileges at a local course.

Facilities: Complete business center, fitness center with workout equipment, massage service, three whirlpools and sauna and steam rooms, parking adjacent to hotel.

Hotel Nikko, Campos Elíseos 204, Col. Polanco, México, D.F. 11560. ☎ **5/280-1111** or toll free **800/NIKKO-US** in the U.S. Fax 5/280-8965 or 280-9191. 750 rms. A/C MINIBAR TEL TV **Metro:** "Auditorio."

Rates: Deluxe $195 single or double; Executive floors $225 single or double; suites $450–$1,030.

One of the best hotels in the city, with 38 floors and plushly decorated rooms, the Nikko is located opposite Chapultepec Park and the Auditorio Nacional, near all the Chapultepec Park museums. It blends modern comfort and convenience with traditional Asian decorating styles, making for a world-class hotel with a hint of the Far East. Rooms, which are quiet and spacious, are accessed with electronic keys. When I visited, some amenities standard in other hotels of this class were lacking—in-room security boxes, voice mail, purified tap water. (Security boxes and remote control for the television are available at the front desk, and electric plug adapters are found at the concierge.) These deficiencies may all disappear during the life of this book, since the Nikko is a top hotel. Nonsmokers have two floors reserved for them. Handicapped clients will find four specially equipped rooms. Two floors are "Nikko Floors," with special check-in and check-out, concierge service, and a lounge for continental breakfast and evening cocktails.

Dining/Entertainment: Benkay serves up the traditional specialties of Japan. It's open daily from 7 to 10:30am, 1:30 to 5pm, and 7:30 to 11pm. The Teppan Grill serves teppanyaki (Japanese griddle-fried steak, chicken, and seafood) as well as other meals, and is open Monday through Friday from 8am to noon, 1:30 to 5pm, and 7:30 to 11pm. Le Célébrités is an elegant restaurant specializing in French cuisine; it's open Monday through Saturday from 7:30 to 11pm. El Jardín, the coffee shop, is open for all meals beginning at 6:30am. Shelty Bar, with an English theme, often features live music and is open daily from noon to 1am. The Lobby Bar is open long hours. The disco, Dynasty Club, is open Monday through Thursday from 9pm to 1am and Friday and Saturday from 9pm to 3am.

Services: Laundry and dry cleaning, room service, beauty and barber shop, boutiques, art gallery, jewelry shop, car rental, and travel agency.

Facilities: Indoor glass-topped pool, three tennis courts, practice court, fitness center, steam and sauna, whirlpool, massage, jogging track.

Hotel Presidente Inter-Continental, Campos Elíseos 218, Col. Polanco, México, D.F. 11560. ☎ **5/327-7700** or toll free **800/327-0200** in the U.S. and Canada. Fax 5/327-7737. 635 rms, 34 suites. A/C MINIBAR TEL TV **Metro:** "Auditorio."
Rates: $325–$845 single or double.

Opposite Chapultepec Park, next to the Nikko Hotel, this 42-story hotel was the first luxury hotel in the area and has been admirably kept up. The enormous lobby, with its sitting areas and off-lobby bars and restaurants, holds some of the capital's most popular meeting places. Rooms at this distinguished hotel are spacious, quiet, and nicely furnished, with many talavera pottery accents. All have remote control televisions, magnified and lighted makeup mirrors, hairdryers, and purified tap water. One of the best perks of staying here is the complimentary coffee or tea that arrives at the door just after a wake-up call (if you request it in advance). All suites have fax machines. Three-pronged and European electrical outlets were being added. Safety deposit boxes are at the front desk. Phones have direct access to international operators, but there's no voice mail. Rooms on the 28th and 29th floors are reserved for nonsmokers and 24 rooms on the 14th floor are equipped for the handicapped. Parking is available but costs $20 daily.

Dining/Entertainment: Maxim's de Paris, an elegant French restaurant, is open Monday through Friday from 1pm to 1am and Saturday from 7pm to 1am. Off the lobby is Balmoral Tearoom, an elegant and tranquil spot for pastries, coffees, and classical music; it's open Monday through Friday from 8am to 10pm and Saturday from 9am to 10pm. El Arrecife, open from 1pm to 1am daily, features seafood. Frutas y Floras is the 24-hour coffee shop. La Chimenea Grill Room and Bar, open from 7am to 1am, is a popular meeting place for breakfast and other meals and specializes in grilled steaks. El Café features international food and has an outdoor section. It's open from 7am to 1am. On Sunday the El Café buffet is served between 1 and 5pm.

Services: Laundry, dry cleaning, beauty and barber shops, boutiques, bookstore, gift shop, art gallery, florist, travel agency, car rental.

Facilities: Full service business center with meeting rooms on the 12th floor, complete gym on the 10th floor.

2 The Zona Rosa

Very Expensive

Hotel María Isabel Sheraton, Reforma 325, at Río Tiber, México, D.F. 06500. ☎ **5/207-3933,** or toll free **800/325-3535** in the U.S. Fax 5/207-0684. 750 rms, 64 suites. A/C MINIBAR TEL TV **Metro:** "Insurgentes."
Rates: $150–$240 single or double; $175–$195 single or double Tower suites.

The María Isabel Sheraton set the original standard for luxury hotels in Mexico City, and it continues to hold its own against newer competition. Its location in front of the Monumento a la Independencia is ideal, next to the U.S. Embassy and across Reforma from the heart of the Zona Rosa. The plush marble lobby hums with the comings and goings of foreign guests and the efficient activity of hotel personnel. In all its rooms the hotel offers amenities such as hairdryers and magnified makeup mirrors, purified tap water, three-pronged electrical outlets, and telephone voice mail. Three floors are reserved for nonsmokers, and seven rooms are outfitted for handicapped guests. Tower suites, the most deluxe in the hotel, occupy the fourth floor and have private check-in, butler service, continental breakfast and evening canapés, remote control TV, and robes.

Dining/Entertainment: The Cafe Pavillión on the first floor, with both a hotel and a street side entrance, is open from 6:30am to 1am. Breakfast and lunch buffets are served as well as à la carte service. The Restaurant Cardinale serves Italian food in an elegant black-and-white themed setting; at lunch from Monday through Friday you'll find in addition to the regular menu a fixed price special that includes antipasto, main course, coffee, and wine. Sunday there's a kosher buffet between 2 and 6pm. The restaurant is open Monday through Friday from 1 to 11pm, Saturday 6 to 11pm and Sunday 2 to 6pm. The Veranda, the hotel's fine-dining restaurant, features an international menu and live guitar music each evening. It's housed along several split levels, and there are some good spots for intimate dining. Breakfast is served from 7 to 11:30am, lunch from 1:30 to 5pm, and dinner from 7 to 11pm. There's a Fiesta Mexicana Monday through Friday from 7 to 10pm. The Jorongo Bar, open noon to 1am, is just off the lobby and offers live entertainment nightly. (See Chapter 9, Mexico City Nights for more on the Jorongo.)

Services: Laundry, dry cleaning, room service, travel agency, beauty and barber shop, concierge, boutiques, art galleries, jewelry stores, first-floor business center.

Facilities: Complete business center with computers, workout facilities, two tennis courts, pool.

Expensive

Hotel Krystal, Liverpool 155, México, D.F. 06600. ☎ **5/228-9928,** or toll free **800/231-9860** in the U.S. Fax 5/511-3480. 288 rms, 14 suites. A/C MINIBAR TEL TV **Metro:** "Insurgentes."

Rates: Deluxe, $160 single or double; junior suite, $260 single or double; Krystal Club, $180 single or double.

Foreigners have tended to overlook the stylish Krystal among the Zona Rosa's numerous posh accommodations. There's really no good reason—located in the heart of the Zona Rosa at the corner of Liverpool and Amberes, the Krystal belongs to one of the best Mexican-owned chains, with a reputation for quality and service. In the enormous yet cozy lobby, a lake of white marble floors is

Accommodations in the
Zona Rosa/Sullivan Park Area

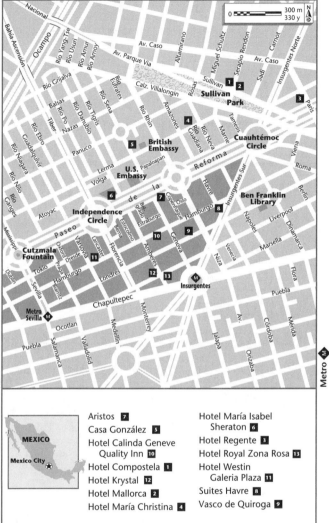

Aristos **7**
Casa González **5**
Hotel Calinda Geneve
   Quality Inn **10**
Hotel Compostela **1**
Hotel Krystal **12**
Hotel Mallorca **2**
Hotel María Christina **4**

Hotel María Isabel
   Sheraton **6**
Hotel Regente **3**
Hotel Royal Zona Rosa **13**
Hotel Westin
   Galeria Plaza **11**
Suites Havre **8**
Vasco de Quiroga **9**

covered with oriental carpets and potted plant groupings, which help
separate the comfortable seating areas. Rooms, which are large and
bright, have neutral-colored wood furniture and pastel fabrics on beds
and drapes. All rooms come with direct-dial phones, voice mail,
purified tap water, electronic card door lock, and in-room safety box.
Electrical adapters are available from the concierge. Floors 5 and 16

are no-smoking floors, and there's one handicap-equipped room. Rooms in the three floors of the Krystal Club have separate check-in and checkout, hairdryers, robes and magnified makeup mirrors, complimentary daily newspaper, continental breakfast and afternoon canapés and cocktails.

Dining/Entertainment: The hotel's finest restaurant is Kamakura, featuring the best foods of Japan (see listing in Chapter 5, "Mexico City Dining" for a full description). It's open Monday through Saturday from 1 to 11:30pm. The Café Martinique is a more informal restaurant, open daily from 7am to midnight. Maquiavelo, the hotel's entertainment club, is open from 1pm to 5pm with taped music, and from 5pm to midnight for live jazz entertainment.

Services: Laundry and dry cleaning, room service, ice machines on each floor, travel agency, car rental, boutiques.

Facilities: First-floor business center, heated swimming pool.

Hotel Royal Zona Rosa, Amberes 78, México, D.F. 06600.
☎ **5/525-4850,** or toll free **800/972-2162** in the U.S.
Fax 5/514-3330. 162 rms. A/C MINIBAR TEL TV **Metro:** "Insurgentes" (2 blocks away); the hotel is near the corner of Liverpool.

Rates: $145 single; $180 double.

The Royal was about to complete a total renovation when I checked. No vestige of the past remains in the rooms (which are large); they now feature neutral-toned carpets along with stylish pastel bedspreads and drapes, with natural-toned wood accents throughout. All rooms have remote-control cable TV and most have a sofa bed. Though the Royal is now more stylish and its location is outstanding, I don't think it will command the rates quoted here—double-check them when you travel. The Royal's owners also run the Casa Blanca and Regente hotels.

Dining/Entertainment: La Moralesa serves Spanish cuisine daily from 1pm to 1am. The informal Lancelot is open from 7am to 1am.
Services: Laundry, room service, newsstand, gift shop.
Facilities: Roof-top sun deck, pool.

Hotel Westin Galeria Plaza, Hamburgo 195, Col. Juárez, México, D.F. 06600. ☎ **5/211-0014,** or toll free **800/228-3000** in the U.S. Fax 5/208-0334. 415 rms, 19 suites. A/C MINIBAR TV **Metro:** "Insurgentes."

Rates: Standard, $160 single or double; Executive Club, $195 single or double; Premier Suite, $245 single or double; one-bedroom suite, $300 single or double.

This Westin-operated hotel is excellent for its location and top-quality amenities. The lobby bar is one of the capital's most popular meeting places. Standard rooms and suites are stylishly furnished in soft pastels and natural wood. All rooms have electronic key cards, remote control TV, illuminated magnified makeup mirror, hairdryer, purified tap water, and in-room safety deposit box. Premier Suites are equipped with a computer, laser printer, and fax machine.

Executive Club rooms on the 10th and 11th floors have 24-hour concierge service, robes, hairdryers, continental breakfast, coffee, tea, and cookies all day, and late-afternoon drinks and hot refreshments. On the 5th floor, 42 rooms have been reserved for nonsmokers. Two rooms are reserved for handicapped guests. It's two blocks from the Monumento a la Independencia near the corner of Florencia. Parking is available for $8.50 daily.

Dining/Entertainment: The Plaza is open for breakfast from 6am to 1pm. The Ile de France, a more exclusive restaurant featuring French and Mexican food, is open for breakfast and lunch Monday through Friday from 7 to 10am and from 1 to 5pm. Cava Baja, a more casual eating and drinking establishment with a street-side entrance, is open Monday through Friday from 1pm to midnight and on Saturday from 5pm to midnight. The Lobby Bar is open from noon to midnight and has live music.

Services: Laundry and dry cleaning, room service, business center, voice mail, boutiques, beauty and barber shop, bookstore, flower and gift shop, car rental, cellular phone rental, travel agency, 24-hour money exchange.

Facilities: First-floor full business center; 13th-floor pool with fully equipped gym, sauna, and whirlpool; golf privileges at nearby country club.

Moderate

Aristos, Reforma 276, Col. Juárez, México, D.F. 06600.
☎ **5/211-0112,** or toll free **800/223-0888** in the U.S.
Fax 5/514-8005. 326 rms. A/C MINIBAR TEL TV **Metro:**
"Insurgentes."
Rates: $110 single or double.

You're paying for location here: the Aristos is situated in the heart of the Zona Rosa, opposite the American Embassy. While weekday rates are high for the quality of rooms, weekend rates may be slashed more than in half and can make the hotel a bargain address. Rooms are well-kept, but the decor is dated; they have a 1970s look, with Formica furniture and matching bedspreads and drapes that I recognize from other eras and other Aristos hotels elsewhere in the country. Though you aren't buying luxury, there are some modern perks such as electronic key locks, magnified and lighted makeup mirrors, and hairdryers. The eighth floor is reserved for nonsmokers. Adjacent parking is available.

Chez'ar, the Aristos' fine-dining restaurant, is open Monday through Saturday from 7pm to 1am with music for dancing. Restaurant Colorines is open 24 hours; Lipstick, the hotel's disco, is open Thursday, Friday, and Saturday nights from 8pm to 2:30am.

The hotel's services and facilities include laundry and dry cleaning, room service, travel agency, cellular phone rental, secretarial services, copier and fax in the lobby reception area, a pool, and a workout room.

Hotel Calinda Geneve Quality Inn, Londres 130, México, D.F. 06600. ☎ **5/211-0071,** or toll free **800/228-5151** in the U.S. 337 rms. A/C MINIBAR TEL TV **Metro:** "Insurgentes."

Rates: $80–$105 single or double.

Probably one of the capital's most popular hotels, the Geneve has been receiving guests for more than 50 years. The lobby is always teeming with travelers who've chosen it for its comfort and convenience—the location is top-notch. It's just steps from all the Zona Rosa restaurants and shops. Rooms are fresh and modern with colonial-style furniture, though you may want to request one on the upper floors; lobby noise has a way of traveling in this hotel. Problems with the new phones installed a few years ago haven't been ironed out; the old interior system continues to cross lines and the like, and you can't count on your phone working. There's a casual restaurant to the left of the lobby after you enter, but the hot spot here is El Jardín, a restaurant/bar. Guests have basked in the glow of its gorgeous stained-glass walls for years while drinking, enjoying buffet breakfasts, relaxing, and listening to music. The hotel is at the corner of Londres and Genova.

Vasco de Quiroga, Londres 15, México, D.F. 06600. ☎ **5/546-2614.** Fax 5/535-2257. 48 rms, 8 suites. TEL **Metro:** "Insurgentes."

Rates: $52 single; $60 double; $114–$160 suites.

On a shady street at the eastern end of the Zona Rosa, this aging four-story standby is a monument to the 1930s. The elevator is ancient and off the lobby is a fine living room with an enormously high ceiling, fireplace, elegant wallpaper, game table, a grand piano, and cozy sitting areas. The pristinely kept furnishings in each room make for a confusion of decorator motifs from the 1930s all the way to the 1970s, but somehow it's appealing. Although Vasco de Quiroga is somewhat overpriced in terms of overall quality, it's a good choice for location, and you'll be especially glad to know about it if other hotels are full. Some rooms come with two twin beds, but most have one or two double beds. Rooms 116 and 115 share a small terrace, room 107 has its own private terrace, and room 305 has a small kitchen, living room, and terrace.

3 Fringes of the Zona Rosa

Moderate

Hotel María Cristina, Río Lerma 31, México, D.F. 06500. ☎ **5/546-9880.** Fax 566-9194. 150 rms. TEL TV

Rates: $55 single; $60 double.

The colonial-style Hotel María Cristina is situated in a quiet residential section within three blocks of Sullivan Park, and five from the heart of the Zona Rosa. The lobby is richly done up with blue-and-white tiles, dark wood, and wrought iron. A garden to the left of the entrance is a nice place for relaxing and reading. When the María Cristina offered delightful comfort at budget prices, one could overlook the surly and indifferent receptionists. Now that it's overpriced, former lovers of this hotel may want to consider if it's worth facing the unwelcoming front desk. If these prices don't sell, they'll probably reduce them, so give it a try if it's one of your old favorites. Rooms offer basic comfort but can be stuffy, and there's no air-conditioning or ceiling fans. The hotel is at Río Guadiana between Río Amazonas and Río Napoles. Adjacent parking is available.

★ **Hotel Regente**, Paris 9, México, D.F. 06030. ☎ **5/566-8933.** Fax 5/593-5794. 132 rms. TEL TV **Metro:** "Revolución" or "Insurgentes"; the hotel is in the triangle formed by Insurgentes Centro, Antonio Caso, and Reforma.
Rates: $43 single; $47 double.

Location and quality rooms are advantages at this recently remodeled hotel. It's within walking distance of Sullivan Park, the Alameda, and the Zona Rosa. Once a frumpy hotel with mismatched furnishings and a horrible phone system, today the Regente is state-of-the-art. Rooms have matching bedspreads and drapes, carpeted floors patterned in pastel green, gray, and blue, over-bed reading lights, full-length mirrors, and new tile bathrooms. The hotel's excellent Restaurant Corinto, open daily from 7am to 11pm, is off the lobby. Free parking is available.

Budget

Casa González, Río Sena 69, México, D.F. 06500. ☎ **5/514-3302.** 22 rms (all with bath). **Metro:** "Insurgentes" (4 blocks); the hotel is between Río Lerma and Río Panuco.
Rates: $22–$25 single; $30 double; $49 suite for four.

Casa González is a two-story hostelry made up of two mansions that have been converted to hold the guest rooms, each of which is unique. The houses, with little grassy patios out back and a huge shade tree, make a pleasant and quiet oasis in the middle of the city. Meals (optional) are taken in a dining room bright with stained glass. The price for a single is low, but there are only two. Some mattresses sag like a hammock, but they are being replaced one by one. There's limited parking in the driveway. The Casa González is especially good for women traveling alone.

4   Sullivan Park

Budget

Hotel Compostela, Sullivan 35, México, D.F. 06470. ☎ **5/566-0733.** Fax 5/566-2677. 78 rms. TEL TV **Metro:** "Revolución."
Rates: $30 single; $35 double.

Tucked in on a quiet corner opposite Sullivan Park, this older five-story hotel (it does have an elevator) is a little off the main tourist track but is worth considering. Each clean, freshly painted room is furnished with Formica furniture, matching bedspreads and drapes, and good over-bed lights. Halls are brightly lit. Rooms facing inside (with windows on an air shaft) may be quieter but are more stuffy than those with windows on Sullivan or Rendón. While its shiny marble lobby and the rest of the hotel are well maintained, the Compostela is not in the heart of the tourist zone—you might for this reason be able to get a discount. It's at the corner of Sullivan and Rendón.

⭐ **Hotel Mallorca,** Serapio Rendón 119, México, D.F. 06470. ☎ **5/566-4833.** Fax 5/566-1789. 150 rms. TEL TV **Metro:** "Revolución."
Rates: $28 single; $35–$38 double.

Almost catercorner from the Hotel Compostela and opposite the western end of the Jardín del Arte, the nine-story (with elevator) Mallorca is an excellent budget choice. Rooms are freshly painted and bedspreads coordinate with the drapes. Single rooms with a twin or double bed are small, however. The hotel is at the corner of Sullivan and Rendón. Free parking is available.

5 Near the Monumento a la Revolución/Plaza de la República

Expensive

Hotel Fiesta Americana Reforma, Reforma 80, México D.F., 06600. ☎ **5/705-1515** or toll free **800/223-2332** in the U.S. Fax 5/705-1313. 628 rms. A/C MINIBAR TEL TV
Rates: $140 single or double; $150–$460 Executive Suites floor.

The Fiesta America Reforma is one of the city's premier hotels, and you can always be assured of a comfortable stay here. Its location between the Alameda and the Zona Rosa is a good one, and the hotel caters to both vacationers and business travelers, with 25 floors of stylish, sizeable rooms that overlook Columbus Circle on Reforma and one of the most efficient telephone systems in town. All rooms come equipped with remote-control TV, robes, electronic card locks, voice mail, and purified tap water. Security boxes are at the front desk. The 20th floor is a no-smoking floor; there's a handicap-equipped room on this floor as well. The three floors of Executive Suites have a private, express, key-operated elevator, and rooms on these floors have hairdryers and magnified makeup mirrors; the price for these suites includes continental breakfast, afternoon canapés, and 24-hour concierge.

Dining/Entertainment: Maximilians, one of the city's finer international restaurants, is open Monday through Friday from 8am to 11:30pm and Saturday and Sunday from 1 to 11:30pm. La Fiesta

Accommodations & Dining
near the **Monumento a la Revolución**

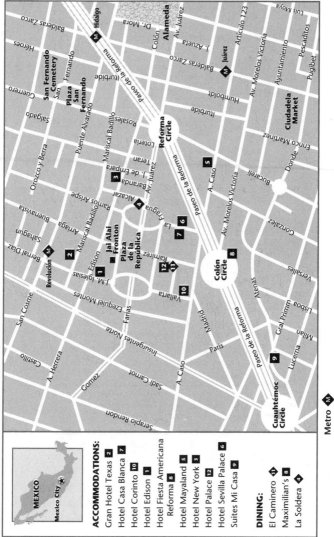

Metro Ⓜ

MEXICO

Mexico City

ACCOMMODATIONS:

Gran Hotel Texas **2**
Hotel Casa Blanca **7**
Hotel Corinto **10**
Hotel Edison **1**
Hotel Fiesta Americana Reforma **8**
Hotel Mayaland **5**
Hotel New York **3**
Hotel Palace **12**
Hotel Sevilla Palace **6**
Suites Mi Casa **9**

DINING:

El Caminero ◆
Maximilian's **8**
La Soldera ◆

is the informal restaurant open from 6am to 12:30am. La Hacienda Steak House and Bar features grilled steaks, pork, seafood, and excellent Mexican food. It's open from 7am to 11:30pm. The Lobby Bar offers jazz and other live entertainment daily from 11am to 1am. The hotel has three nightclubs: Caballo Negro, Barbarela, and Las Sillas (see Chapter 9, "Mexico City Nights" for details).

Services: Laundry and dry cleaning, room service, beauty and barber shop, travel agency, car rental, babysitting, florist.

Facilities: Business center and gym on the fourth floor. Gym has a sauna, massage, and beauty shop.

Hotel Sevilla Palace, Reforma 105, México, D.F. 06030.
☎ **5/566-8877** or toll free **800/732-9488** in the U.S.
Fax 5/703-1521. 413 rms and suites. A/C MINIBAR TEL TV
Rates: $132 single or double; $222–$590 suite.

Although the Sevilla Palace is top quality in every way, it's another of those hotels overlooked by foreigners that deserves more attention. Its soaring lobby is embellished with teak-stained wood and burgundy marble and has four glass elevators whizzing up and down. Rooms are large, handsomely furnished, and all have remote-control TV, direct dial phones with voice mail, in-room safety boxes, electronic card locks, and hairdryers. Most rooms have large showers and a couch with a sitting/table area. Three-prong electrical adapters are available at the reception desk. The 21st floor is reserved for non-smokers. The toll-free number listed above answers in Mexico and *may* only be answered Monday through Friday from 9am to 6pm. Free parking is available.

Dining/Entertainment: The fine dining restaurant, El Lepanto, is open Monday through Friday from 6pm to midnight. Los Naranjos is open from 7am to 11pm. El Atrio is the lobby bar with piano entertainment from 6 to 11pm.

Services: Laundry and room service, ice machine on each floor, travel agency, beauty and barber shop, gift shop, newsstand.

Facilities: Business center on the first floor, rooftop workout room with enclosed swimming pool and whirlpool.

Moderate

Hotel Casa Blanca, Lafragua 7, México, D.F. 06030.
☎ **5/566-3211,** or toll free **800/972-2162** in the U.S.
Fax 5/705-4197. 248 rms, 22 suites. A/C TEL TV **Metro:** "Revolución" or "Hidalgo" (5 long blocks away); the hotel is between Antonio Caso and Plaza de la República.
Rates: $80–$98 single; $94–$136 double.

Just a few steps off the Plaza de la República, Hotel Casa Blanca is located on a quiet street only a block or so from Reforma and Avenida Juárez. It's been a dependably comfortable, friendly, and efficient place to stay for many years. Amenities found in much more expensive hotels are found here at a fraction of the price. Renovation of the guest rooms in 1993 and 1994 gave them a light and airy feel with pastel walls and furnishings. All rooms have purified tap water, full-length mirrors, in-room safety deposit boxes, over-bed reading lights with bedside switches, remote-control TV (with U.S. channels), and direct-dial phones. Several rooms are equipped for the handicapped and several are reserved for nonsmokers. Single rooms, with one double or one twin-size bed, are small, but other rooms are substantially larger. Several suites have saunas and separate living/ conference rooms. The small kidney-shaped swimming pool and sun deck on the hotel's top floor goes undiscovered by most guests, making it a wonderfully quiet—almost private—getaway. Free parking is available.

The Casa Blanca's Restaurant/Bar Seibal, on the second floor, is open from 7am to 1am daily. There's a pianist or trio in the lobby bar starting at 6pm. The Restaurant Brittanica, on the first floor, is open Monday through Saturday from 7pm to 1am. Adjacent to it is the Brittanica Bar with a singer Monday through Saturday from 8pm to 1am for a cover charge of $7.

The hotel offers laundry and dry cleaning, room service, concierge, car rental, travel agency, beauty and barber shop, ice machines on each floor, babysitting. There's a rooftop pool. Hotel office fax and copier are available to guests.

Budget

$ **Gran Hotel Texas,** Ignacio Mariscal 129, México, D.F. 06030. ☎ **5/546-4626** or **546-4627.** 52 rms (all with bath). TEL TV **Metro:** "Revolución"; hotel is between Arriega and Iglesias.
Rates: $23 single; $27 double.

This small, modest hotel, a five-story walk-up on a quiet street, gets high marks for effort. There's nothing fancy here, but notice the smiles that greet you and the tidiness of the premises. The comfortable lobby, with its tile floor and sofas, has a wall of windows facing Mariscal. The carpeted rooms are small—there's barely enough room to walk around, especially with luggage taking up space. The small tiled bathrooms all have showers. Ask for a discount, especially if your room is on an upper floor.

Hotel Corinto, Vallarta 24, México, D.F. 06030. ☎ **5/566-6555** or **566-9711.** Fax 5/546-6888. 155 rms. TEL TV **Metro:** "Revolución" (5 blocks away); the hotel is near the corner of Gómez Farías opposite the Monumento a la Revolución.
Rates: $40 single; $43 double.

The chief virtue of the modern nine-story Hotel Corinto, located just a few steps north of Antonio Caso, is value. It caters to both tourists and Mexican clients and has clean rooms, coordinated furnishings, tiled showers, piped-in music, and special taps for purified water. Just off the lobby is a restaurant, and on the ninth floor is a small swimming pool, sunning area, patch of grass, and a bar. Most rooms have either twin single beds or one double bed.

Hotel Edison, Edison 106, México, D.F. 06030. ☎ **5/566-0933.** 45 rms. TEL TV **Metro:** "Revolución" (2 blocks away); the hotel is at Edison and Iglesias.
Rates: $23 single; $26–$30 double.

The Hotel Edison, a block from the Monumento a la Revolución, has an odd three-story construction, around a narrow court with grass and trees. But it gives a sense of sanctuary from the city's noise and bustle. The well-kept furniture dates from the 1950s and the carpeted rooms are done in pale pink and rose. Some rooms are built in tiers overlooking the court, and even larger ones are hidden away down hallways. These latter rooms tend to be dark but are big and comfortable. Many rooms, however, are bright and have good cross ventilation. Bedspreads match the drapes and the small tile bathrooms have a tub/shower combination. There's a bakery across the street. A refrigerator in the lobby is stocked with soft drinks available to guests for a small charge.

Hotel Mayaland, Antonio Caso 23, México, D.F. 06030.
☎ **5/566-6066.** Fax 5/535-1273. 91 rms. TEL TV **Metro:** "Juárez" (3¹/₂ blocks away); the hotel is between González and Bucareli.
Rates: $39 single; $43–$48 double.

The conveniently located six-story Mayaland features coordinated drapes and spreads in its pleasant rooms. Bathrooms have an additional faucet for purified water. You can't miss the Maya mural on one wall of the lobby; another stained glass wall separates the lobby from the hotel's small restaurant.

Hotel New York, Edison 45, México, D.F. 06030.
☎ and fax **5/566-9700.** 45 rms. TEL TV **Metro:** "Revolución" (5 blocks away); the hotel is between Emparan and Baranda.
Rates: $25 single; $30–$34 double. **Parking:** Free.

The Hotel New York, two short blocks from the jai-alai fronton, is a large four-story building that's a cubist's dream of mosaic tile, grass-green paneling, and glass. The carpeted rooms have Formica furniture, wood paneling on one wall, and hanging glass lamps. The hotel's small restaurant is open daily from 7am to 10pm.

Hotel Palace, Ignacio Ramírez 7, México, D.F. 06030.
☎ **5/566-2400.** Fax 5/535-7520. 200 rms. A/C TEL TV **Metro:** "Revolución" (5 blocks away); the hotel is between Reforma and Plaza de la República.
Rates: $40 single; $43 double.

A few decades ago one of Mexico's outstanding luxury hotels, today the nine-story Hotel Palace retains its comfort, experienced staff, and well-kept rooms. The bustle of a large hotel surrounds you here, with tobacco kiosk and travel desk in the lobby, bag-bearing bellboys scurrying here and there, and the occasional busload of tourists.

6   Near the Alameda Central

Moderate

 Hotel Metropol, Luis Moya 39, México, D.F. 06050.
☎ **5/521-4901** or **510-8660.** Fax 5/512-1273. 165 rms. A/C TEL TV **Metro:** "Juárez" (2 blocks away); the hotel is between Articulo 123 and Independencia.
Rates: $54 single; $62 double.

Accommodations & Dining
near the Alameda

ACCOMMODATIONS:
Hotel Capitol **11**
Hotel Conde **15**
Hotel El Salvador **13**
Hotel Estoril **16**
Hotel Fleming **2**
Hotel Metropol **4**

DINING:
Fonda Santa Anita ❶
La Opera Bar ❻
Pastelería Ideal ❽
El Prendes ❾
Restaurant Danubio ⓬
Restaurante Continental ❸

Restaurant los Faroles ❺
Salón la Luz ❿
Salón Victoria ⓮
Sanborn's Casa
de Azulejos ❼

With a recent total facelift the Hotel Metropol shed its 1960s image and emerged looking more like a small luxury hotel. Each room is beautifully furnished and carpeted and has an in-room safety deposit box, color TV with U.S. channels, and purified water from a special tap. If it's the essence of luxury you want at relatively low prices, this is the place. The location is choice—within walking distance of both the Zócalo and Alameda. Parking is available but costs $1.50 an hour.

Budget

Hotel Capitol, Uruguay 12, México, D.F. 06050. ☎ **5/518-1750.**
Fax 5/521-1149. 75 rms. TEL TV **Metro:** "Bellas Artes" or "Salto de Agua" (5 blocks away); the hotel is between Cárdenas and Bolívar.
Rates: $30 single; $34–$42 double.

The four-story Hotel Capitol opened in late 1989 with rooms opening onto the lobby atrium. The rooms are carpeted and have good over-bed reading lights. Double rooms are furnished with either a king-size bed or two doubles. Rooms and bathrooms are large except for the three "suites," which are tiny but have an enormous whirlpool bathtub big enough for two. Rooms along the front have a small balcony opening to Uruguay, while other rooms have interior windows opening to the lobby atrium. The hotel's restaurant is in the far back of the lobby. This is a good buy within walking distance of the Alameda, Palacio de Bellas Artes, and historic Zócalo.

Hotel Conde, Pescaditos 15, México, D.F. 06070. ☎ **5/521-1084.**
80 rms. TEL TV **Metro:** "Balderas" or "Juárez"; hotel is at the corner of Revillagigedo.
Rates: $23 single or double.

The Hotel Conde, just five blocks off Juárez and equally far from Reforma, offers some of the best rooms for the price in this area. The hotel's entrance is at Pescaditos 15, but the building is on the corner of Revillagigedo, and would be numbered about Revillagigedo 56. It's fairly new with a small marbled lobby; rooms have clean bathrooms, wall-to-wall carpet, and radios. Free parking is available.

⭐ **Hotel El Salvador,** República del Salvador 16, México, D.F. 06000. ☎ **and fax 5/521-1247 or 521-2160.** 94 rms. TEL TV **Metro:** "Salto de Agua" (6 blocks away); the hotel is between Cárdenas and Bolívar.
Rates: $25 single; $30 double.

The five-story Hotel El Salvador, half a block off Lázaro Cárdenas, completed a total remodeling in 1994. The impressive new lobby, aswirl in beige marble, is up a wide staircase from the sidewalk. Rooms have nice natural-colored pine furniture, fresh stucco and paint, carpeting, over-bed reading lights, and pastel coordinated drapes and spreads. Bathrooms are small, but luggage storage areas (found either in the closet or a built-in luggage bench) are sizeable. Halls are narrow and dark with only a few hall lights on during the day. A small restaurant is adjacent. Rates may rise once news of the renovation spreads, but for now it's a very nice and convenient place to stay at budget prices. Free parking.

Hotel Estoril, Luis Moya 93, México D.F. 06070.
☎ **and fax 5/521-9762.** 125 rooms. TEL TV **Metro:** "Juárez."
Rates: $41 single; $48 double.

The recently renovated Estoril has an accommodating staff and clean, quiet rooms, most with one or two double beds; fifth-floor rooms all have king-size beds. The decorator had a field day—walls, carpets, drapes, bedspreads and linens, even bathroom floors and tile are different colors. There's a restaurant off the lobby. The hotel is six blocks south of the Alameda Park, near Calle Sterling.

⭐ **Hotel Fleming,** Revillagigedo 35, México, D.F. 06050.
☎ **5/510-4530.** 75 rms. TEL TV **Metro:** "Juárez"; the hotel is between Articulo 123 and Victoria.
Rates: $30–$39 single; $39–$50 double; $51 room with whirlpool tub.

In 1992, the Fleming's mismatched ancient furnishings gave way to soft cool colors, coordinated carpeting and textiles, mirrored closet doors, and updated bathrooms—even some with whirlpool tubs. Rooms come with either a king-size bed, two doubles, or two twin-size beds. The hotel's clean, dependable restaurant is off the lobby. It's excellently located near the Alameda and within walking distance of the Zócalo. Free parking.

7   Near the Zócalo

Moderate

Hotel Best Western Majestic, Madero 73, México, D.F. 06000.
☎ **5/521-8600** or toll free **800/528-1234** in the U.S. 85 rms. A/C TEL TV **Metro:** "Zócalo."
Rates: $61 single or double. Ask about discounted rates.

The Majestic is one of the city's most popular hotels because of its location overlooking the Zócalo. The lobby, with its stone arches, beautiful tiles, and stone fountain, is one of the loveliest in the city. On other floors, each doorway has a border of blue-and-white tiles. Some rooms look onto the massive city center that is the Zócalo, others overlook Avenida Madero, and still others have an interior view of the hotel's own inner court. Furnishings are somewhat dated but are comfortable, and all rooms have tile bathrooms with tubs. On the lower floors, noise from the street may be a problem in rooms facing Avenida Madero—and you might not like the quieter rooms that look out onto the interior court either (because people look in on you!)—but on the upper floors and in rooms that front the Zócalo you needn't worry about voyeurs. On the other hand, occupants of rooms facing the Zócalo will receive the unexpected jolt of the 6am flag-raising ceremony on the Zócalo, complete with marching feet, drums, and bugle. The finishing touch to the Majestic is a popular rooftop cafe-restaurant with umbrella shaded tables for all three meals.

Budget

Hotel Canada, 5 de Mayo No. 47, México, D.F. 06000.
☎ **5/518-2106.** Fax 5/512-9310. 85 rms. TEL TV **Metro:** "Zócalo" (1¹/₂ blocks away); the hotel is between Isabel la Católica and Palma.
Rates: $30 single; $34–$38 double.

The Hotel Canada opened in 1984 with up-to-date decor, white Formica furnishings, piped-in music, one or two double beds, and showers. It's comfortable and so distinguishes itself from the rest of the downtown hotels, which tend to be older and somewhat worn.

★ **Hotel Catedral,** Donceles 95, México, D.F. 06010.
☎ **5/518-5232.** Fax 512-4343. 116 rms. TEL TV **Metro:** "Zócalo"; the hotel is between Brasil and Argentina.
Rates: $34 single; $44 double.

The six-story Hotel Catedral is set back from Calle Donceles by a shopping arcade (one block north of Tacuba, Donceles is noted for its bookstores, stationery stores, and gunsmith shops). Only half a block from the Templo Mayor, the hotel is very popular with Mexico's middle class. In front of the big cool lobby is the hotel's restaurant-bar, bustling with white-jacketed waiters. The Catedral is remodeling and rooms are well kept. Some rooms have tub/shower combinations. Bonuses include a bar, free parking in a garage next door, elevator, good housekeeping standards, and rooms on the upper floors with views of Mexico City's mammoth cathedral.

★ **Hotel Gillow,** Isabel la Católica 17, México, D.F. 06000.
☎ **5/518-1440.** Fax 5/512-2078. 110 rms (all with bath). TEL TV **Metro:** "Allende"; the hotel is between 5 de Mayo and Madero.
Rates: $33 single; $39 double.

From the lobby, the six-story Hotel Gillow appears to belong to the older and dignified if simple class of downtown Mexico City hotels. But take one of the two elevators up to the guest rooms, and you'll discover behind the old-fashioned facade a modern hotel with rooms grouped in five stories around a long, rectangular, glass-canopied central courtyard with a nice colonial fountain. The clean, contemporary rooms have new tile-and-marble bathrooms and a feeling of cheery comfort. Interior windows open to an air shaft. There's a restaurant on the first floor. It's at the corner of 5 de Mayo.

💲 **Hotel Montecarlo,** Uruguay 69, México, D.F. 06000.
☎ **5/518-1418** or 521-2559. 60 rms (40 with bath). TEL **Metro:** "Zócalo" or "Isabel la Católica"; the hotel is between 5 de Febrero and Isabel la Católica, next to the Biblioteca Nacional.
Rates: $15–$20 single; $16–$26 double. **Parking:** Free.

The Hotel Montecarlo has a fascinating history. Built about 1772 as an Augustinian monastery, it later became the residence of D. H. Lawrence for a time. Recently renovated, the rooms come in various sizes, with modern baths, new furniture, rugs, and beds. Rooms in the original monastery section, plus the added third story, tend to carry lobby and hallway noise. Rooms in the newer section in back are quieter. Note that some rooms have windows looking onto hallways and courtyards, not to the streets outside. Rooms without private bathrooms are priced lower and share communal bathrooms (separated for men and women) down the hall. It's a good idea to call ahead to reserve a room—the Montecarlo is often full. Parking for six or seven cars is reached by driving *through* the lobby.

Accommodations & Dining near the Zócalo

ACCOMMODATIONS:
Hotel Best Western Majestic **11**
Hotel Canada **9**
Hotel Catedral **4**
Hotel Gillow **6**
Hotel Montecarlo **13**

DINING:
Café Cinco de Mayo **10**
Café de Tacuba **3**
Café el Popular **8**
Café la Blanca **5**
Cicero Centenario **2**
La Ciudad de los Espejos **14**
Fonda Don Chon **15**
Hostería de Santo Domingo **1**
Pastelería Madrid **12**
Restaurante Vegetariano y Dietetico **7**

---

8   Near the Buenavista Railroad Station

Budget

Hotel Pontevedra, Insurgentes Norte 226, México, D.F. 06400.
☎ **5/541-3160** or **547-0146.** 140 rms (all with bath). TEL TV
Metro: "Revolución."

Rates: $23 single; $39 double.

If you're looking for a hotel close to the railroad station, you can't do much better than this one. Rooms are plain but comfortable, and a delight after a long train trip. There's a restaurant on the ground floor. To find it from the train station, take the yellow stairs at the side of the terminal up and over the street traffic on Insurgentes.

9 Near the Airport

With the exception of the Hotel Aeropuerto and Riazor, airport hotels are expensive. However, by the time you consider that the cost of a round-trip taxi to a Zócalo area hotel for example would run around $10, then add the cost of the hotel and getting up 45 minutes early to return back to the airport, an airport hotel may be appealing.

Very Expensive

Hotel Continental Plaza Aeropuerto, opposite the airport.
☎ **5/762-0199,** or toll free **800/342-6446.** Fax 5/785-1034.
480 rms. A/C MINIBAR TEL TV **Metro:** "Terminal."
Rates: $195 single or double.

This luxury hotel (formerly the Fiesta Americana), directly opposite the airport terminal, is the closest hotel to the airport. It may be useful to know about, especially if less expensive hotels in the area are full, and you've gone your last vacation inch before taking an early flight the next day. Even if you aren't a guest, the pleasant public areas and excellent restaurants area a welcome respite from the airport frenzy. The hotel's elevator is near exit "A." It takes you to the pedestrian walkway over the terminal auto traffic to the hotel. There's usually an attendant there to help with bags.

Expensive

Ramada Inn Aeropuerto, Blv. Aeropuerto 502, México, D.F. 15620. ☎ **5/785-8522,** or toll free **800/228-9898.** Fax 5/762-9934.
324 rms. A/C MINIBAR TEL TV **Transportation:** Wait for the courtesy van under the white Ramada Inn shelter in front of the airport.
Rates: $147–$157 single or double.

This Ramada Inn is close to the airport; to get there, call from the Holiday Inn phone in the airport terminal and the courtesy van will take you on a circuitous block-long ride to the hotel. Recently revamped, the hotel has taken great steps toward improving its sagging image. The staff is attentive and the rooms are fashionably furnished, each with color TV with U.S. channels and purified water from the tap. You'll find several restaurants, a bar, a disco, and a pool and workout facilities. The hotel also provides a courtesy van to the airport, but those with early flights should leave in plenty of time since the demand for transportation may be greater than the vans can handle.

Moderate

Hotel Aeropuerto, Blv. Aeropuerto 380, México, D.F. 15530.
☎ 5/785-6928. Fax 5/784-1329. 52 rms. A/C TEL TV **Metro:**
"Terminal."

Rates: $43 single; $51 double. **Parking:** Free; guarded.

Don't let the thick glass around the front desk put you off. The Hotel
Aeropuerto is actually an excellent choice, and is just across the street
from the airport. The brown on brown decor, with nice natural pine
accents, is comfortable if not particularly cheerful. Rooms are clean
with new mattresses, large bathrooms, and powerful showers. However, you'll have to make peace with the sound of jets roaring over-
head. The coffee shop, which is reasonably priced, has very good
coffee. The hotel is next to the more visible and much more expensive JM Hotel Aeropuerto. Taxis are easy to flag down in front of
the hotel. It's possible to walk to the terminal, though you must climb
the steep stairway to the overpass over the main road into the
airport—a difficult feat with luggage.

Hotel Riazor, Viaducto Miguel Aleman 297, México, D.F. 08310.
☎ 5/726-9998. Fax 5/654-3840. 175 rms. TEL TV **Metro:**
"Aeropuerto," then take a taxi.

Rates: $45 single; $49 double.

The six-story Hotel Riazor is only a short cab ride from the airport.
You can take shelter in any one of their modern, comfy rooms complete with king-size bed, shower, and perhaps even a view of the city.
There's a pool, restaurant, and bar. The hotel fills up by nightfall,
but if you arrive early in the day there's a good chance to get a room.

10   Long-Term Stays

Apartment hotels, often called suites ("soo-*wee*-tess"), are found in
several city districts, but mostly in and near the Zona Rosa. Who
stays here? Families, businesspeople, and consultants on extended
stays; people waiting to find houses or permanent apartments; students; tourists staying a week or more. Some apartment hotels rent
by the day, but preferential rates really come into play with stops of
a week or more.

If you're planning a truly lengthy stay, the first place to look is in
the classified ads section of the *Mexico City News.* This will give you
an idea of the choice neighborhoods and the going rates. To save
money, you might then dust off your Spanish and look at the similar sections in the Spanish-language dailies. Since landlords advertising in the *News* will obviously be catering to the foreigners, their
rents may well be higher than the norm.

Suites Havre, Havre 74, México, D.F. 06010. ☎ 5/533-5670.
56 suites. **Metro:** "Insurgentes"; the hotel is between Hamburgo and
Reforma.

Rates: $255 per week; $680 per month.

On the fringes of the Zona Rosa, the Suites Havre at Hamburgo are popular with students of all ages looking for economical lodgings. All suites (really just small apartments) have a two-burner stove, small refrigerator, table and chairs, and two twin beds. Rooms are narrow and some have a window view of an air shaft. The ones overlooking this quiet section of Havre are cheerier and recommended for lengthy stays. The apartments don't rent by the day. An elevator makes all seven floors accessible.

Suites Mi Casa, Gral. Prim 106, México, D.F. 06600. ☎ **5/566-6711** or 566-6947. Fax 5/566-6010. 26 suites. TEL TV

Rates: $49 single; $92 double. Discounts for a week or more if paid in cash.

Suites Mi Casa's location is ideal for exploring the touristic areas of the central city—it's a 10-minute walk in opposite directions both to the Zona Rosa and Alameda. Each of the well-kept suites has a small, fully equipped stainless steel kitchen with sink, refrigerator, gas stove, and dishes for four people. Each comes with red carpeted floors and white leatherette furniture. Bedrooms have one double or two single beds. Built in dividers allow you to separate the living room and dining area from the bedroom and other folding doors shut off the kitchen area. It's between Milan and Viena one block off Reforma and directly behind the Hotel Emporio.

5

Mexico City Dining

THE CAPITAL OF MEXICO IS ALSO THE DINING CAPITAL OF THE COUNTRY. SOME of the country's top restaurants are here, among them Fouquets de Paris, Honfleur, Passy, Hacienda de los Morales, and Chez Wok. The cuisines of the world are here—Japanese, Chinese, German, French, pre-Hispanic—you name it and there's a lineup of several to choose from in this grand city. And some of the country's best traditional Mexican restaurants—Danubio, Café de Tacuba, El Prendes, Fonda Don Chon, Fonda del Recuerdo—almost always have a crowd of faithful followers. Cantinas, until not so long ago the privilege of men only, offer some of the best food and colorful local atmosphere. The best cantinas are mentioned in this chapter. Other cantinas may be too local for tourist taste—women may get hassled and men cajoled to fight.

Everybody eats out in Mexico, so it's easy to find restaurants of every type, size, and price. Mexicans take their food and dining seriously too, so wherever you see a full house that's generally recommendation enough. Those same places may be entirely empty if you arrive early. This section includes the tried-and-true establishments, those that give the best food for the best price in various price categories.

I have not specifically described American-type chains and franchises such as Houlahan's, McDonalds, Subway Sandwiches, Burger King, Burger Boy, Pizza Hut, Vip's, Denny's, and Lyni's—but you'll see them frequently. The latter three (with branches all over the city), have standard, familiar fare at reasonable prices, which will cure a bout of homesickness with apple pie a la mode, hash brown potatoes, hot fudge sundaes, fresh salads, good service, and free coffee refills.

SOME DINING NOTES

Prices in the categories vary dramatically. One person can expect to pay $55 to $125 for a meal without drinks or tip at restaurants in the "Very Expensive" category. In "Expensive" restaurants one person can expect to pay $35 to $55 for a three course meal without drinks or tip. Those classified "Moderate" will offer a three-course meal for between $10 and $35. And in the inexpensive restaurants a full meal costs between $4 and $10 or so, but you can often get by for much less. If you're hunting for value, stalk the *comida corrida* at lunch; the best deals include dessert and drink. Generally in Mexico the tip is not included in the bill, however, in places serving many Europeans (who are accustomed to having the tip included), a tip of 10 to 15% may be added to the bill when you receive it. Restaurants are busiest between 2 and 5pm and 9pm to midnight. You'll get better service and have a more leisurely dining experience if you arrive before the crowds. Many of the city's best restaurants are closed on Sunday and the best of those that are open are often crowded.

1 | Chapultepec & Polanco

Very Expensive

Chez Wok, Tennyson 117 at Mazaryk. ☎ **281-3410** or **281-2921.**

    Cuisine: HAUTE CHINESE. **Reservations:** Recommended. **Metro:** "Polanco."

    Prices: Appetizers $7–$30; main courses $17–$55.

    Open: Mon–Sat 1:45–4:45pm and 7:45–11:45pm.

Opened in the fashionable Polanco area in 1992 with five chefs from Hong Kong and their incredible recipes, Chez Wok immediately became *the* place to feast on Chinese food. It's packed at every open hour; the high prices seem not to deter anyone, perhaps because most dishes serve two or three people. The second-floor dining area, with large and small sections, has a combination of booths and tables with an elegant but simple decor of yellow, black, and beige. Lettuce handrolls come stuffed with minced quail and vegetables, and authentic shark fin soup at $55 a bowl is the most expensive item on the menu. Main courses include steamed red snapper with white wine sauce, chicken in a shrimp paste with sesame and crab sauce, and the house specialty of Peking duck. To beat the crowd, plan to be there when it opens, before the later dining locals. Jacket and tie are required for dinner.

★ **Fouquets de Paris,** in the Hotel Camino Real, Mariano Escobedo 700. ☎ **5/203-2121,** ext. 8500.

    Cuisine: INTERNATIONAL. **Reservations:** Recommended for dinner. **Metro:** "Chapultepec."

    Prices: Appetizers $5.50–$17: main courses $18.50–$26.50.

    Open: Daily 7–10:30am for breakfast; 2–4:30pm for lunch; 7–11:30pm for dinner.

Dining at Fouquets de Paris is a culinary experience of the first order, made all the better by the elegant atmosphere and refined service. Government ministers, senators and visiting dignitaries often dine here. And this is a popular place for those trendy power breakfasts; the morning menu mixes creative combinations of Mexican and international cuisines—for example, crêpes with machaca(dried beef) and eggs, huitlacoche omelettes, or omelettes with morel mushrooms and artichokes—with traditional breakfast fare such as hotcakes. For other meals you might consider lobster bisque, asparagus and crawfish in a puff pastry, rack of lamb, beef tenderloin, or veal in morel mushrooms. For men, a jacket and tie is required. Highly recommended.

Hacienda de Los Morales, Vazquez de Mella 525. ☎ **540-3225** or **202-1973.**

    Cuisine: MEXICAN/AMERICAN/CONTINENTAL. **Reservations:** Required.

    Prices: Appetizers $6–$21.50; main courses $17–$64.

    Open: Mon–Sat 1pm–midnight.

The Hacienda de los Morales, which resides in a great Spanish colonial house not far from Chapultepec Park, has been a favorite of visitors and locals for years. Within the house are a cocktail lounge with entertainment, numerous richly decorated dining rooms, and a plant-filled inner courtyard. The service is polished, the food delicious. In the evenings men are required to wear jackets and ties. The restaurant is northwest of Chapultepec Park at the corner of Avenida Ejercito Nacional.

Expensive

 Fonda del Recuerdo, Bahía de las Palmas 39. ☎ **545-7260.**

Cuisine: MEXICAN/SEAFOOD. **Reservations:** Not accepted.
Metro: "Sevilla."
Prices: Main courses $8.50–$25.50.
Open: Mon–Sat 1pm–midnight.

For an all-out good time, no other restaurant in the city compares to this one. Diners at Fonda del Recuerdo enjoy their platters of Mexican food amid a glorious din created by *jarocho* musicians from Veracruz (there will be several groups roving around the restaurant at once). Come here if you want to immerse yourself in Mexico and join people eating, drinking, and singing, having the time of their lives. The menu is authentically Mexican, with an emphasis on seafood; specials match the culinary traditions of whichever Mexican holiday is closest on the calendar. Arrive before 1:30pm for lunch or you'll have to wait in a long line—which will nonetheless be worth it if you have all afternoon for lunch. At night it's just as festive, but try to make it before 9pm, when it begins to get crowded.

Moderate

Nautilus, Mazaryk 160. ☎ **280-2283.**

Cuisine: SEAFOOD/INTERNATIONAL. **Reservations:** Not required.
Prices: Main courses $8.50–$21.25.
Open: Mon–Sat noon–11pm, Sun Noon–7pm.

An outdoor restaurant on Polanco's main drag, Nautilus is a popular place to grab an umbrella-shaded sidewalk table and feast while watching the passing scene. The menu choices feature seafood, pasta, and steak. The Filet Oaxaca comes breaded with Oaxaca cheese and cream sauce. The Filet Moctezuma is accompanied with huitlacoche and flor de calabaza (squash flower). There's also a full line-up of special tacos. The restaurant is between Oscar Wilde and Muset.

2 Zona Rosa

Very Expensive

 Cicero Centenario, Londres 195. ☎ **533-3800.**

Cuisine: INTERNATIONAL/NOUVELLE MEXICAN. **Reservations:** Recommended. **Metro:** "Insurgentes."

Dining in the Zona Rosa

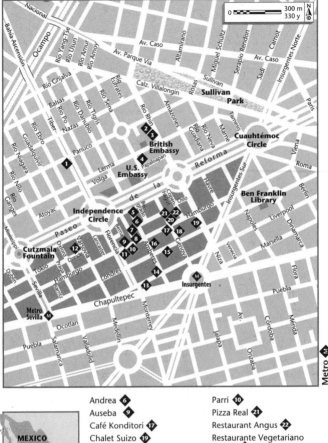

Andrea	6	Parri	10
Auseba	9	Pizza Real	21
Café Konditori	17	Restaurant Angus	22
Chalet Suizo	19	Restaurante Vegetariano	
Cicero Centenario	8	Yug	12
Focolare	20	Restaurant Marianne	3
Fonda el Refugio	13	Restaurant Passy	5
Las Fuentes	1	Restaurant Tokyo	16
Honfleur	7	Restaurant y Cafeteria	
Kamakura Japanese Restaurant		del Rhin	2
and Sushi Bar	14	Salón de Thé Duca d'Este	11
Montserrat Belle Cuisine	15	Yuppies Sports Bar	18
Les Moustaches	4		

MEXICO

Mexico City

Prices: Appetizers $6–$30; main courses $18–$42.50.
Open: Mon–Sat 7pm–2am.

Cicero Centenario is the epitome of the capital's elegant café society. Tables in the intimate nooks of the restaurant's leafy salons look out on a dim backdrop of stained glass and flickering candlelight. There are two menus here: among the heights of the main menu are a delectable cream-of-morel-mushroom soup, an excellent Caesar salad, and main dishes like chicken in a rich almond sauce and red snapper in green sauce. The second and smaller menu features recipes developed for the restaurant by noted chef and author Patricia Quintana. The restaurant is between Florencia and Amberes.

⭐ **Honfleur,** Amberes 14-A. ☎ **533-2115** or **533-1181.**
Cuisine: FRENCH. **Reservations:** Recommended. **Metro:** "Insurgentes."
Prices: Appetizers $8.50–$59.50; main courses $17–$64.
Open: Mon–Sat 1pm–1am.

Honfleur's European-style sophistication makes it one of the city's top restaurants; it's known both for its food and elegant French country decor. The mirror-lined bar is on the first floor; stairs lead to the second-floor dining room, where pastel cloth-covered tables are set with fresh flowers and sparkling china and cutlery. The efficient service has a refined touch. Honfleur's top price tag goes to pheasant in morel sauce, a house specialty; other less costly specialties include fresh-grilled salmon, dinner or dessert souffles, and dessert crêpes. Come well-dressed (jacket and tie are required evenings) and ready to dine, not snack; the high prices are part of the experience. It's between Reforma and Estrasburgo.

Restaurant Angus, Copenhague 21, near the corner of Hamburgo. ☎ **207-3747** or **522-8633.**
Cuisine: STEAKS. **Metro:** "Insurgentes." **Reservations:** Recommended.
Prices: Appetizers $4–$8.50; main courses $16–$23; steaks $8.50–$25.50.
Open: Daily 1pm–12:45am.

Restaurant Angus is the place to go in the D.F. when you want nothing so much as a good, juicy steak. The refined interior features lots of dark wood and brass, there's outdoor dining under a green awning with brass rails on cafe-lined Copenhague. The clientele is a mix of business types clad in suits and others dressed a bit more casually. All variety of steaks are served here, and there's prime rib and fajitas as well. A few shrimp selections may satisfy those who don't want beef.

Expensive

Andrea, Amberes 12. ☎ **208-7617** or **208-7436.**
Cuisine: ITALIAN/MEXICAN. **Reservations:** Recommended. **Metro:** "Insurgentes."

IMPRESSIONS

"There is mole to-day, señor," the boy announced. . . . It was brought, and proved to be some sort of meat floating in a sauce of pure pepper. The hottest dish that was ever concocted, it gives you a distinct shock, as it you were swallowing flame.
—Stanton Davis Kirkham, *Mexican Trails* (1909)

Prices: Appetizers $6–$21.50; main courses $7.50–$34.
Open: Mon–Sat 2–11pm.

Andrea opened in 1992 on a street that's becoming known for its fine-dining restaurants housed in stately old mansions—Honfleur and Restaurant Passy are just a few doors away. You may have a hard time deciding between the temptations on the the intriguing menu. Among the appetizers I suggest cream of olive soup or shrimp on nopales cactus in a secret Oaxaca sauce. Daily specials might include crab in achiote (a delectable Yucatecan seasoning) or rabbit baked in herbs. From the standard daily menu there's fish in a pesto and hollandaise sauce, or lasagna with huitlacoche, onions, and garlic. Early evening is a good time to beat the crowd, but you may be all alone until 9:30 or 10pm.

Kamakura Japanese Restaurant and Sushi Bar, at the Hotel Krystal, Liverpool 155, corner of Amberes. ☎ **511-8308.**
Cuisine: JAPANESE. **Reservations:** Recommended for dinner. **Metro:** "Insurgentes."
Prices: Appetizers $5–$13.50; main courses $7–$30.
Open: Daily 1–11:30pm.

This streetside restaurant of the Hotel Krystal's garden is a serene retreat any time of day. Select your Japanese favorite—teppanyaki, shabu shabu, sushi, and others are offered—then watch the meal as it's prepared. If you aren't familiar with all a Japanese meal offers, the menu has full descriptions in Spanish and English.

⭐ **Montserrat Belle Cuisine,** Londres 104 at Genova.
☎ **511-5518** or **511-7105.**
Cuisine: FRENCH/NOUVELLE MEXICAN. **Reservations:** Not required.
Metro: "Insurgentes."
Prices: Appetizers $9–$46; main courses $13.50–$30.
Open: Mon–Sat 1pm–1am.

You'll find this restaurant by the black and pink umbrella-covered tables set out in the short passage off Londres near Genova. Montserrat Margalef Fisher, the young chef/owner of this inviting bistro, earns your repeat business with a refreshing menu that combines her love and knowledge of both French and Mexican food. She grew up in Mexico but honed her culinary skills at the La Varenne School in Paris. Upon her return to Mexico, it didn't take long for her culinary expertise to gain recognition, and she was invited on a number of occasions to prepare food for the president of Mexico's social gatherings. She personally shops for all the food daily to ensure its freshness. The perfectly seasoned beef carpaccio makes an excellent light appetizer. One tasty main course is huachinango (red snapper) in parsley sauce; another, duck in a light green pepper sauce, is wonderfully smooth. Don't leave without tempting yourself with the exquisite pastries that Montserrat prepares fresh daily. The mango mousse is excellent but you may want to try one of the specialty dessert souffles. In fact this is a great place to stop in for dessert and coffee as a respite from Zona Rosa shopping, or to top off your evening with a full meal or dessert.

⭐ **Restaurant Passy,** Amberes 10, between Reforma and Hamburgo. ☎ 511-0257.

Cuisine: INTERNATIONAL. **Reservations:** Recommended. **Metro:** "Insurgentes."
Prices: Appetizers $4.50–$7; main courses $8.50–$17.
Open: Mon–Sat 1–11pm.

The Restaurant Passy, just off Reforma, is an elegant old favorite of locals and tourists alike. With low lights, antiques, linens, and candles, the decor is attractive, classic, and restrained. The service is polished and polite, and the menu is traditional in the French way: oysters Rockefeller, onion or oyster soup, chicken Cordon Bleu, canard (duck) a l'orange, and coq au vin are among the continental favorites. There's also a good selection of fish. The dessert menu is highlighted by rich pastries. It's next to Honfleur and opposite Champs Elysees.

Moderate

Café Konditori, Genova 61, between Hamburgo and Londres.
☎ 511-1589.

Cuisine: DANISH. **Reservations:** Not required. **Metro:** "Insurgentes."
Prices: Appetizers $4–$7; main courses $8.50–$13; coffee and dessert $4–$6.
Open: Daily 7am–midnight.

Cafe Konditori advertises itself as a Danish restaurant, bar, and coffee shop. Though it's not what you'd call aggressively Danish, it does have a very pleasant sidewalk cafe section. There are 11 different coffees to choose from; the cappuccino is the perfect accompaniment for one of the Konditori's luscious cakes or tarts. You should pick out your choice from the dessert display before you sit down.

⭐ **Chalet Suizo,** Niza 37, between Hamburgo and Londres.
☎ 511-7529.

Cuisine: INTERNATIONAL. **Reservations:** Not required. **Metro:** "Insurgentes."
Prices: Appetizers $3–$7; main courses $7–$22.
Open: Daily 12:30pm–midnight.

One of the most dependable and cozy restaurants around, Chalet Suizo's decor is Swiss, of course, with checked tablecloths, enormous wooden horns, and alpine landscapes. The menu features hearty French onion soup and a wide range of interesting main courses, some of which are changed daily. Among these are veal with morel mushrooms, smoked pork chops, German-style beef pot roast, chicken tarragon, veal goulash, sauerbraten, and excellent fondue. One caveat: the bread and butter placed on your table is not included with the price of the meal and costs extra. The food is delicious, portions are large, and the service is friendly and quick.

⭐ **Focolare,** Hamburgo 87, between Niza and Copenhague.
☎ 525-1487 or 511-2679.

Cuisine: REGIONAL MEXICAN. **Reservations:** Recommended. **Metro:** "Insurgentes."

Prices: Appetizers $3.50–$9; main courses $9–$15.50; Sat–Sun breakfast buffet $18; Fri–Sat night Mexican Fiesta à la carte.
Open: Mon–Fri 7:30am–11:30pm, Sat–Sun 9am–12:30am; Sat and Sun breakfast buffet 9am–12:30pm; Fri and Sat night Mexican Fiesta 9–11pm.

Focolare calls itself a restaurant with three souls—Yucatecan, Oaxacan, and Veracruzano. I call it a tribute to three of Mexico's best regional cuisines. As you enter, piano music drifts from both left and right from the Bar Pirinola and Cantina Trompo. In the dining area, with its tiled fountain and ceiling of baskets, a trio sings Mexican ballads. Upon taking in this scene you'll be primed for a thoroughly Mexican dining experience. For starters you might try the Yucatecan salbutes, a tortilla stuffed with roast suckling pig, or the sierra mixteca soup, made with fresh wild Oaxacan mushrooms. A sure hit among the main courses is pok chuk, a flavorful pork specialty from the Yucatán. If you want a tasty but not too filling dish, try the sopa tortilla. In addition, every day there's a different Oaxacan mole sauce. Don't pass up one of the delicious fruit drinks made from zapote, guanabana, or the spicy-but-smooth horchata blend. Friday and Saturday nights you can reserve space for the lively Mexican Fiesta with music and performing dancers. Dining is a la carte.

⭐ **Fonda El Refugio,** Liverpool 166, between Florencia and Amberes. ☎ 207-2732 or 525-8128.
Cuisine: MEXICAN. **Reservations:** Recommended for dinner. **Metro:** "Insurgentes."
Prices: Appetizers $3.50–$8.50; main courses $10–$13.50.
Open: Mon–Sat 1pm–midnight.

The Fonda El Refugio, with its traditions of more than 40 years, is a very special place to dine *a la mexicana.* Although small, it's unusually congenial, with a large fireplace decorated with gleaming copper pots and pans, and rows and rows of culinary awards and citations behind the desk. It manages the almost impossible task of being elegant and informal at the same time. The menu is one that runs the gamut of Mexican cuisine—arroz con platanos (rice with fried bananas), tamales de elote con pollo (fresh corn tamales with chicken), chalupas poblanas (tortillas topped with chicken, onions, cheese, lettuce, and green chile sauce), or perhaps enchiladas con mole poblano, topped with the rich, thick, spicy chocolate sauce of Puebla. Each day of the week there's a specialty—Tuesdays, for example, feature manchamanteles (tablecloth stainer); Saturdays offer albondigas en chile chipotle (meatballs in a chipotle sauce). The Fonda El Refugio is very popular, especially on a Saturday night, so get there early—remember, it's small.

Restaurant Tokyo, Hamburgo 134, corner of Amberes. ☎ 525-3775.
Cuisine: JAPANESE. **Reservations:** Not required. **Metro:** "Insurgentes."
Prices: Appetizers $3–$10; specialties $8–$13; combination plates $11–$13.
Open: Daily noon–11pm.

One of Mexico City's several Japanese restaurants, Tokyo is both good and centrally located. A flight of stairs with a Japanese flair brings you to the second-story restaurant, done in simple Japanese style. This is not a formal place, so moderately presentable dress will do fine. Folks in business attire often shed their jackets here. The menu is in English, Spanish, and Japanese. There's a wide selection of Japanese fare including sukiyaki and shabu-shabu (fresh vegetables and beef in broth) both cooked at your table. The tempura is another good choice, as is the delicious sashimi (strips of raw fish). The combination plates offer a good deal if you're not sure what to order since they come scaled for different appetites and budgets.

Yuppies Sports Bar, Genova 34. ☎ **533-0919** or **208-2267.**
> **Cuisine:** AMERICAN/ASIAN. **Reservations:** Not required. **Metro:** "Insurgentes."
> **Prices:** Appetizers $5.50–$7.50; salads $6–$10.50; main courses $10.50–$34.
> **Open:** Daily 1pm–1am.

Trendy and popular, you'll get the feel of this place immediately. Its tile floors, stained glass and brass, sports memorabilia, and menu are all familiar to visitors from the U.S. and Canada, but are unusual for Mexico. Here you'll find clam chowder; chicken wings and fingers; egg rolls; Reuben sandwiches; pastrami, turkey, and BLT sandwiches; fettuccini; blackened rib-eye steaks; cajun red fish; ribs; and shrimp tempura—just to mention a few of the specialties. Owners of the Angus restaurant have a hand in this restaurant too.

Inexpensive

Parri, Hamburgo 154-A, between Florencia and Amberes. ☎ **207-0757.**
> **Cuisine:** MEXICAN. **Metro:** "Insurgentes."
> **Prices:** Appetizers $2.50–$5; main courses $5–$14.50.
> **Open:** Sun–Thurs 11am–1am, Fri–Sat noon–3am.

For tasty, authentic Mexican food at very reasonable prices in the Zona Rosa, search out the Parri. The decor is ranch and big windows look onto the busy sidewalk. Meats are marinated and grilled Sonoran-style and the whole cooking operation is on view from the street or inside tables. You might try a filling tortilla soup, burritas norteñas (which come with refried beans, guacamole, and cheese), enchiladas, or quesadillas, and either crispy buñuelos or creamy flan for dessert. There are also more expensive grilled dishes such as carne asada a la Tampiquena (grilled beef, Tampico-style) or chicken brochettes.

Pizza Real, Genova 28, between Reforma and Hamburgo.
☎ **511-8834.**
> **Cuisine:** ITALIAN/PIZZA. **Metro:** "Insurgentes."
> **Prices:** Breakfast $1.50–$4.50; pizza $5.50–$21.50; pizza slice 30¢–$1.50.
> **Open:** Daily 8am–11:30pm.

Pizza Real boasts that it serves 50 different varieties of pizza, depending on size and toppings. The "Infante" size is enough for one person, the "Princesa" for two people and the "Real" for three to four people. A "rabanada" is a slice. Although it is billed as a pizza joint, Pizza Real is half pizza parlor and half Italian restaurant, with a concise menu of salads, sandwiches, pastas, and traditional Italian favorites. Though there's indoor dining, most people prefer the covered outdoor area where Zona Rosa people-watching can be part of the experience.

$ Restaurante Vegetariano Yug, Varsovia 3 Reforma, between Reforma and Hamburgo. ☎ 533-3296.

Cuisine: VEGETARIAN. **Metro:** "Sevilla" (6 blocks away).
Prices: Breakfast $1.50–$4; à la carte main courses $2.25–$6; salad buffet $2.00; fixed-price lunch or dinner $4–$6.
Open: Mon–Fri 7am–8:30pm, Sat–8:30am–7pm, Sun 1–8:30pm; buffet served Sun–Fri 1–5pm.

Mexicans are fond of vegetarian and health-food restaurants. The most convenient one in the Zona Rosa is the Restaurante Vegetariano Yug. This upbeat, modern place offers several set-price breakfasts, a dozen fantastic salads (the "Africa" features spinach and nuts), plus crêpes, spinach lasagne, and soya "meat" Mexican-style. Portions are huge and prices are low.

3 Fringes of the Zona Rosa

Very Expensive

★ Les Moustaches, Sena 88, one block north of Reforma between Río Papaloapan and Río Usumacinta. ☎ 533-3390 or 525-1265.

Cuisine: FRENCH/INTERNATIONAL. **Reservations:** Recommended.
Prices: Appetizers $8.50–$15.50; main courses $13.50–$34.
Open: Daily 1pm–midnight.

Housed in one of the city's 19th-century mansions, this well-established restaurant is one of the most popular in town. As you might expect from the name "the mustaches," the waiters all have them in addition to a polished attire of stiff white shirts, black suits, vests, and ties. Service is quiet, smooth, and sophisticated. Diners are seated in the covered and plant-filled patio and in small surrounding rooms on two levels. The menu starts with cold and hot appetizers, among them abalone with chipotle sauce and noodles in pesto sauce. Main courses include beef Wellington, and shrimp in gruyere sauce. Daily specials might include chiles enogada in season, or cream of snail soup. For men a coat and tie are required. To find the restaurant use the Aristos Hotel at Reforma and Genova as a landmark and cross Reforma there. Once across Reforma the street becomes Río Sena and the restaurant is 1¹/₂ blocks ahead on the right.

Inexpensive

⭐ **Las Fuentes,** Río Panuco 127. ☎ **514-8187.**
Cuisine: VEGETARIAN.
Prices: Breakfast $5; lunch, appetizers $3–$5; main courses $4.50;
comida corrida $8–$10.
Open: Daily 8am–6pm (comida corrida noon–6pm).

A spotless place, Las Fuentes is like an upscale, inviting coffee shop,
with shiny marble floors, well-kept booths, Formica-topped tables,
and greenery all around. Best of all it's popular for good nutritious
food, which you select from a pictorial menu. Huge portions are the
rule, and you may enjoy lentil soup, carrot-and-potato-filled tacos
with apple salad, a side order of peas or beans, then coffee or tea and
whole-wheat-and-honey cookies. It takes up a big chunk of the corner at Río Tiber and Río Panuco, three blocks north of Reforma and
the Independence Circle.

⭐ **Restaurant Marianne,** Río Rhin 63, two blocks north of
Reforma between Río Lerma and Río Panuco. ☎ **207-8831.**
$ **Cuisine:** CONTINENTAL. **Metro:** "Insurgentes."
Prices: Breakfast $3; comida corrida $4.50–$5; pastries 50¢;
cappuccino $2.
Open: Mon–Fri 8am–7pm.

Tucked away one block from the British Embassy is the little Restaurant Marianne, where the atmosphere is European-coffeehouse
and the specialty is pastries and cappuccino and an excellent
three-course lunch. No children under 12 are accepted.

Restaurant y Cafeteria del Rhin, Río Rhin 49, ☎ 571-9452.
Cuisine: MEXICAN. **Directions:** Walk 3 blocks north of Reforma
between Río Lerma and Río Panuco.
Prices: Main courses $4–$7; comida corrida $4.50–$5; enchiladas
suizas $4.
Open: Mon–Sat 8:00am–8pm.

The Restaurant y Cafetería del Rhin, (up the block from Restaurant
Marianne), is one of those terrific little neighborhood restaurants
every travel writer dreams of discovering. Mirrors, tan-colored
plastic booths, and waiters in natty black-and-white uniforms make
it efficient and inviting. The enchiladas suizas are a little triumph of
tortillas in a creamy sauce stuffed with Swiss cheese. There are plenty
of other Mexican plates — lots of tacos — as well as such comforts
as soup and filet mignon.

IMPRESSIONS

*A coatless waiter approaches, bearing a soup tureen. He disappears in
a twinkling, leaving me without a spoon. Your true Mexican garçon
always arrives circumspectly and with deliberation, but he departs
with celerity, and once out of the room there is no telling when he may
return. When you get your eye on him, you must hypnotise him
forthwith.*
—Stanton Davis Kirkham, *Mexican Trails* (1909)

4 Near the Monumento a la Revolución

Besides the restaurants mentioned below, there's a **Vip's** next to El Caminero and a block away a branch of **Houlihan's** on La Fragua faces the Hotel Casa Blanca.

Very Expensive

★ **Maximilians,** Hotel Fiesta Americana Reforma, Reforma 80.
☎ 705-1515.
Cuisine: INTERNATIONAL. **Reservations:** Recommended.
Prices: Main courses $17–$51.
Open: Mon–Fri 8–11am, 1–11:30pm; Sat 7:30–11:30pm.

Taking in Maximilians from the street, you'll notice the distinctive accordion sheers covering a wall of windows. Inside the small serene restaurant, tables are situated in intimate groupings on several minilevels. Muted lighting and a pianist's soft tickling of the ivory contributes to the atmosphere. A large selection of starters, including a pannequete of smoked salmon and deliciously fresh spinach salad, will pique appetites. Fish, chicken, and beef main courses include such stand-bys as fillet of sole and (most days) roast duckling. For dessert it's worth the wait to try pears with toffee, an artistic creation of pastry and pears swimming in a delicious yellow and red sauce.

Moderate

La Soldera, La Republica 157, at the corner of Ramírez and Revolución, opposite the monument. ☎ 535-7929.
Cuisine: MEXICAN TRADITIONAL. **Reservations:** Recommended for lunch. **Metro:** "Revolución."
Prices: Appetizers $5–$21.50; main courses $11–$13.50.
Open: Mon–Sat 2–11pm.

Taking their cue from their new restaurant's location in the shadow of the Monumento a la Revolución, the creators of La Soldera (which opened in 1994) chose a name in honor of Mexican women's contributions to the Revolution. (Although there were no female soldiers, women did tend to and cook for the soldiers.) Hostesses attired in abbreviated revolutionary attire—bullet belts crossed at the chest, tall boots, and short-shorts—greet and seat guests. The atmosphere inside is created by a muted scheme of the national colors (green, red, and white), an aural background of revolutionary music, and photos of—what else—the Revolution. The regional Mexican food includes sopas de tinga de pollo from Puebla, ant eggs and maguey worms (seasonal), cream of cilantro soup, campesina soup with nopal cactus, chiles and beans, mole, pollo en achiote from the Yucatán, snapper stuffed with huitlacoche, barbeque in pulque sauce, lamb mixiotes, and a variety of other dishes using beef, pork, and lamb. If it all sounds too authentic, there are also recognizably tame choices too.

Inexpensive

El Caminero, Ramirez 17. ☎ **566-3981.**

> **Cuisine:** TACOS. **Metro:** "Revolución."
> **Prices:** Tacos $3–$6; soft drinks $1; beer $1.50.
> **Open:** Mon–Fri 10am–midnight, Sat 1pm–1am, Sun 1pm–11pm.

This branch of El Caminero is between the Monumento a la Revolución and the Colón monument, which is on Reforma. Take a stool at one of the tall tables and scrutinize the wall menu for a taco combination that piques your interest— steak, pork, sausage, cheese, onions, bacon, etc. Some come with three tacos to the order, others have eight tacos. Side orders to taste include grilled onions, beans, and quesadillas.

5 Near the Alameda

Very Expensive

El Prendes, 16 de Septiembre No. 10, between Lázaro Cárdenas and Gante. ☎ **521-5404** or **512-3611.**

> **Cuisine:** MEXICAN TRADITIONAL. **Reservations:** Recommended for Sunday lunch. **Metro:** "Bellas Artes" (4$^1/2$ blocks away).
> **Prices:** Appetizers $2–$30; main courses $13–$21.50.
> **Open:** Daily 1–6:30pm.

Though this restaurant has been through several locations and even closed for a while in 1988, dining at El Prendes has been a tradition since 1892. On Sundays the dining room is filled with large middle- and upper-class Mexican families, who linger over their meals for hours. Even if you don't come for a full meal, be sure to step in for a drink or snack to see the wonderful murals of the social elites, Mexican and otherwise, who've dined at El Prendes. Among the more than 100 famous personalities fixed in paint are Walt Disney, Gary Cooper, Leon Trotsky, Frida Kahlo, Diego Rivera, Dr. Atl (Gerardo Murillo), Pancho Villa, Porfirio Díaz, and José Clemente Orozco. This artistic tribute to a bygone Mexico covers several long walls and was painted by Eduardo Castellanos between 1960 and 1962 and Teresa Moran in 1992. Although the Sunday special is paella, it's overrated and is not worth the high price. Other chef's specialities include bean stuffed ravioli in a huitlacoche sauce.

Moderate

⭐ **Restaurant Danubio,** Uruguay 3. ☎ **512-0912.**

> **Cuisine:** INTERNATIONAL. **Reservations:** Not required. **Metro:** "Bellas Artes" or "Salto de Agua."
> **Prices:** Appetizers $2.50–$10; main courses $8.50–$25.50; comida corrida $8.
> **Open:** Daily 1pm–midnight; comida corrida 1–4pm.

Danubio's gigantic fixed-price lunch—it's plenty for two—is practically an institution; you'll have to elbow your way in past crowds to sample it. A typical comida corrida consists of a shrimp or oyster cocktail, perhaps Valencia soup or tomato consomme, boiled lentils, a choice of a hot or cold fish dish, a choice of three main courses, custard or fruit, and coffee or tea. The à la carte menu is extensive, but you get better service during the busy time if you stick to the fixed-price meal. They serve cocktails, wine, and beer. You may find more breathing space aloft in an upstairs room that accommodates the lunchtime overflow—many people don't know about it. The house specialty is langostinos (baby crayfish); they're well worth the splurge! The restaurant is south of the Alameda, at the corner of Cárdenas and Uruguay.

Sanborn's Casa de Azulejos, Madero 4. ☎ 512-9820.

Cuisine: MEXICAN/AMERICAN. **Reservations:** Not required. **Metro:** "Bellas Artes."

Prices: Appetizers $3–$6; main courses $5–$11; dessert and coffee $2.50–$5.

Open: Daily 7:30am–11pm.

Sooner or later everybody winds up at Sanborn's. There are many other branches, but this is the most famous. Casa de Azulejos means "house of tiles," and this gorgeous antique building was once the palace of the counts of the Valley of Orizaba. For many years now it has been a landmark of the Sanborn's restaurant and variety-store chain. Dining tables are set in an elaborate courtyard complete with carved pillars, tiles, and peacock frescoes. Waitresses wear long starched dresses and scurry about giving the most efficient service. It's a dependable place for a respite and the menu features both Mexican and American food. Also part of this Sanborn's (as at other branches) are stores adjacent to the restaurant filled with gifts, magazines, books, jewelry, appliances, and even a pharmacy—all of which makes Sanborn's one very popular stop. The restaurant is on the corner of Correo, the alleyway that runs along the main post office. For more details on the building's history see "Walking Tour 2— The Alameda" in Chapter 7, "Strolling Around Mexico City."

Inexpensive

Fonda Santa Anita, Humboldt 48, between Juárez and Donato Guerra. ☎ 518-4609.

Cuisine: MEXICAN. **Metro:** "Juárez."

Prices: Appetizers $2.50–$5; main courses $4–$8.50; fixed-price meal $6.50.

Open: Mon–Fri noon–10pm, Sat–Sun 1:30–9pm.

Situated in the little half-block south of Avenida Juárez near the Hotel Ambassador, Fonda Santa Anita doesn't look like much from the outside. But inside it's festooned in colorful banners and gaily painted walls, and it's one of the city's longest-established places with moderate prices and speedy service. There's an English-language menu from which you can order peppers stuffed with cheese, or black-bean soup with tortilla strips and epazote, pork loin in red sauce, or breakfast food at any hour. You might order the set-price menu *solidaridad,* a four-course meal including a Mexican combination plate.

Restaurante Continental, Independencia 72 C, one block south of the Alameda, at the corner of Revillagigedo. ☎ 521-1913.

> **Cuisine:** MEXICAN. **Metro:** "Juárez."
> **Prices:** Breakfast $1.50–$5; main courses $5–$9.50; pizza $4–$15; comida corrida $4–$5.
> **Open:** Daily 8am–1am.

The Restaurante Continental is one of several good, inexpensive restaurants located south of Avenida Juárez. It's open long hours and has an extensive menu filled with inexpensive fare. You'll find lots of soups and sandwiches, including a hamburguesa Americana con queso (burger with cheese); Mexican traditional favorites such as enchiladas and quesadillas; substantial restaurant meals based on beef, pork, and chicken; and a full range of pizzas. The daily fixed-price meal has three courses. Monday through Friday from 5 to 10pm you can have your fortune told in your Turkish coffee cup. If the bright yellow-and-red streetside dining room of booths, tables, and lunch counter is full, make your way upstairs to another one.

Restaurant Los Faroles, Luis Moya 41. ☎ 521-7634.

> **Cuisine:** MEXICAN. **Metro:** "Juárez."
> **Prices:** Breakfast $2.50–$4; appetizers $1.50–$4; comida corrida $4–$4.50.
> **Open:** Daily 8am–7pm.

Through the brick arches of Los Faroles you'll see a firepit filled with *cazuelas,* or big earthenware cooking pots, and a bevy of white-aproned señoras preparing some of the city's cheapest and most authentic Mexican food. Tacos, enchiladas, caldos (stews), and other truly Mexican dishes are the forte here, and low prices are the rule. Los Faroles is darkish and is not air-conditioned (no surprise at these prices), but it is good, and it's open every day of the year. The restaurant is one block south of the Alameda, between Articulo 123 and Independencia, next to the Hotel Metropol.

6 Near the Zócalo

Very Expensive

Cicero Centenario, Cuba 79. ☎ 521-2934 or 521-7866.

> **Cuisine:** INTERNATIONAL/NOUVELLE MEXICAN. **Reservations:** Recommended 2 days in advance Mon–Wed; 5 days in advance Thurs–Sat. **Metro:** "Zócalo."
> **Prices:** Appetizers $6–$30; main courses $14.50–$25.50.
> **Open:** Mon–Sat 1pm–1am.

Tucked in the Centro Historico in an elegant two-story, 19th-century mansion, this sibling of the Zona Rosa restaurant is also one of the most popular eating establishments in the city. At any meal all the tables have reservation cards by name of client. If you come early for either lunch or dinner, say between 1 and 2pm for lunch or between 6 and 8pm for dinner, there's a chance you could get in without a reservation—capitalinos habitually take their afternoon meal between

3 and 5pm and dinner between 8:30 or 9pm and midnight. The menu is essentially the same as the Cicero's in the Zona Rosa—fish, beef, and chicken served with great sauces and seasonings. Each day there's a different special—whitefish from Pátzcuaro are offered on Fridays, and Saturdays feature manchamantales; both are gourmet delights. Seasonal specialties include chiles enogada (June through September) and gusanos de maguey (April and May). The restaurant is five blocks northeast of the Alameda, between República de Chile and Palma not far from the Santo Domingo Plaza and Church.

Moderate

⭐ **Café de Tacuba,** Tacuba 28, between República de Chile and Bolivar. ☎ **512-8482.**

Cuisine: MEXICAN. **Reservations:** Not required. **Metro:** "Allende." **Prices:** Appetizers $3–$5.50; main courses $5.50–$13; comida corrida $14.50–$21.50.
Open: Daily 8am–11:30pm.

Although the Café de Tacuba has that handsome colonial-era look, it dates from 1912. The orange, blue, and white wainscoting in the two long dining rooms, the brass lamps, dark and brooding oil paintings, and a large mural of several nuns working in a kitchen come together to create a stately ambience. Soups here are excellent. The customary fixed-price meal offers a selection of daily lunch plates served with soup. In the front window and nearby pastry case is a tempting selection of homemade cakes and pies and candied fruit. Thursday through Sunday from 6pm until closing, entertainment includes a wonderful group of singers in medieval costumes. The sound is something like the melodious *estudiantina* groups of Guanajuato accompanied by mandolins and guitars.

Fonda Don Chon, Regina 159. ☎ **522-2170.**

Cuisine: PRE-HISPANIC/MEXICAN. **Reservations:** Not required. **Metro:** "Piño Suarez."
Prices: Appetizers $2–$3; main courses $6–$24.50.
Open: Daily 11am–7pm.

If you're intrigued by Mexico's "exotic" foods, then you'll want to try Fonda Don Chon. Billing itself as "the cathedral of pre-Hispanic cooking," it has been pleasing locals and winning acclaim from New York to New Zealand for more than 40 years. The decor is Formica and concrete, but this Mexican food isn't run of the mill even by Mexican standards. You can dine on rib-eye or T-bone steaks, liver and onions, or mole poblano, but the fame of the place arises in its pre-Hispanic food. Try rabbit in chile sauce, armadillo en chimole or dried and shredded, accompanied by baked beans, salad, and guacamole. Savor a little grilled American buffalo, a heap of wood worms (gusano de madera), toasted grasshoppers (chapulines), deer several ways, Guerrero-style iguana in mole verde, chrysanthemums stuffed with tuna, or ant eggs (escamoles) in a guanabana sauce. It's worth a trip here just to read the menu, see the framed articles that have been written about the place, and read the accolades from patrons that decorate walls. Or you can just linger looking at the old prints of Mexico City and the surrounding area. It's between Jesús María and Topacio. To find it from the Palacio Nacional (beginning at the corner of Corregidora and Pino Suarez), a walk 4 long blocks south on Suarez from the Palace. Turn left on Regina and walk 7¹/₂ blocks. It's on the right just after crossing Jesús María, sandwiched among dozens of stores selling sewing necessities.

Hostería de Santo Domingo, Dominguez 72, between República de Brazil and República de Chile. ☎ 510-1434.

> **Cuisine:** MEXICAN. **Reservations:** Not required. **Metro:** "Allende."
> **Prices:** Breakfast $3.50–$4.50; appetizers $3–$5.50; main courses $5–$11; daily specials $5.50–$12.
> **Open:** Daily 9am–11pm.

Established in 1860, the Hostería de Santo Domingo is said to be the oldest restaurant in the city still in operation. In commemoration of its name, a mural on one end of the main dining room shows the Plaza Domingo during colonial times. The player piano will fool you into thinking a pianist is playing nonstop. The food is excellent, with large portions. Generally the restaurant is packed at lunch time, so come early. Try the stuffed peppers with cheese, pork loin, or the unusual bread soup. **Note:** The bread placed on your table costs extra.

Inexpensive

Café Cinco de Mayo, 5 de Mayo No. 57, between Palma and Monte de Piedad. ☎ 510-1995.

> **Cuisine:** MEXICAN. **Metro:** "Zócalo."
> **Prices:** Appetizers $1.50–$2.50; main courses $2.50–$6; comida corrida $6.50.
> **Open:** Daily 7am–11pm.

A real money-saver near the Zócalo, the Cafe Cinco de Mayo is the very picture of a Mexican lunchroom. Less than a block west of the Catedral Metropolitana, on the south side of the street, you'll find it bright with fluorescent lights and loud with conversation, with walls of fake stone and mirrors and a long lunch counter lined with regulars. Waiters scurry here and there bearing enormous glasses of fresh orange juice, cups of hot coffee, baskets of pan dulce, sandwiches, pork chops—just about anything you can imagine. If you order cafe con leche, a waiter will approach with a big copper coffee pot, pour an inch of thick, bitter coffee into the bottom of your glass, then fill it up with hot milk.

 Café El Popular, 5 de Mayo, between Isabel La Católica and the Zócalo. ☎ 518-6081.

> **$** **Cuisine:** MEXICAN. **Metro:** "Zócalo."
> **Prices:** Breakfast $1.50–$4; main courses $2.50–$7; comida corrida $3–$5.50; Oaxaca tamal $1.50.
> **Open:** Daily 24 hours.

Located on the same side of the street as the Café La Blanca (see below), Cafe El Popular is popular not only for its prices but also because it has the charm La Blanca lacks. It looks like a cozy French cafe with inviting streetside windows filled with pastries. Go on in—it only looks expensive. You'll find one of the best-priced menus downtown. If the lower level is full, take the narrow stairs up to the loft level. Either way, expect your waitress to greet you with a heaping basket of pastries (they charge you for what you eat). Breakfast or merienda (tea time) specials include a Oaxaca tamal, beans, a cup of atole (sweet thick corn drink), or coffee.

Café La Blanca, 5 de Mayo No. 40, between Motolinia and Isabel La Católica. ☎ **510-0399.**
   Cuisine: MEXICAN/INTERNATIONAL. **Metro:** "Allende."
   Prices: Appetizers $1.50–$3.50; main courses $2.50–$7.
   Open: Daily 7am–11:30pm.

Café La Blanca, on the north side of the street, is a large cafeteria-style place with two levels. There is no decor to speak of, but the fare is good, as is indicated by the enormous business the place does. They serve only à la carte items but with daily specials such as huachinango (red snapper) or jumbo shrimp, you can't go wrong eating here.

⭐ **Restaurante Vegetariano y Dietetico,** Madero 56.
   ☎ **521-6880** or **585-4191.**
💲 **Cuisine:** VEGETARIAN. **Metro:** "Zócalo."
   Prices: Breakfast $3; main courses and comida corrida $5.50–$6; soups and salads $1.50–$5.50.
   Open: Mon–Sat 9am–7pm.

I can't say enough good things about the food at the Restaurante Vegetariano y Dietetico. There's only a small brass plaque with the restaurant's name next to the doorway on Madero between Isabel La Católica and Palma, so look for a stairway marked "Penella" or the menu posted outside on the entrance; walk one flight up and you'll enter the restaurant. The decor is nothing special—the restaurant was founded in 1942 and probably never redecorated—but the food is fantastic. As the name implies, they serve no meat, but you can easily eat your fill from the huge salad starters, superb soups, choice of two main courses, and a delicious cake made of whole wheat and honey, served with coffee or tea. The menu is in Spanish only.

There's another Vegetariano at Filomata 13, between 5 de Mayo and Madero, five blocks west of the Zócalo.

---

7   San Angel

Expensive

San Angel Inn, Diego Rivera 50, Col. San Angel. ☎ **616-2222** or **616-1652.**
   Cuisine: INTERNATIONAL. **Reservations:** Recommended. **Metro:** Línea 3, "Coyoacán."
   Prices: Appetizers $4–$10.50; main courses $8.50–$21.50.
   Open: Mon–Sat 1pm–1am, Sun 1–10pm.

Dining here is a chance to enjoy one of Mexico City's most tradi-tionally elegant dining establishments, created from an 18th-century Carmelite monastery. During your visit take time to stroll the col-onnaded arcades surrounding the interior garden. You can have drinks there seated in one of the groupings of chairs. Jacketed wait-ers roam the very refined interior, which features a blue and white decor with tablecloths matching the dinnerware. Although pasta, fish, and chicken are served, the specialties here are grilled beef dishes such as pepper steak, Sonoran T-bone, or steak brochette. (For a further description of the building see "Walking Tour 4—San Angel" in Chapter 7, "Strolling Around Mexico City.")

8 Specialty Dining

Tea

Auseba, Hamburgo 159B, between Florencia and Estocolmo.
☎ 511-3769.
Cuisine: CONTINENTAL. **Metro:** "Insurgentes."
Prices: Breakfast $2.75–$5.75; coffee or tea $1.50–$2.50; pastries $1–$3.75; light meals $4–$4.75.
Open: Mon–Sat 9am–10pm, Sun 11am–1pm.

One of the finest places for afternoon coffee or tea is Auseba, which serves pastries, light meals, and all kinds of coffee concoctions along with tea. The glass cases hold a delicious-looking display of cookies, meringues, bonbons, cakes, pies, and puddings, all prepared daily in the restaurant's own bakery. Paintings decorate one wall, and the little cloth-covered circular tables have modern black plastic chairs—eclectic, but comfortable.

Salon de Thé Duca d'Este, Hamburgo 164B, at Florencia.
☎ 525-6374.
Cuisine: CONTINENTAL. **Metro:** "Insurgentes."
Prices: Breakfast $3–$6.75; ice cream or pastry $2.25–$3.50; salads and soups $3.50–$6.
Open: Sun–Thurs 8am–11pm, Fri–Sat 8am–midnight.

This is another favorite of mine, opposite the above-mentioned Auseba. Small tea tables draped in apricot cloths look out onto the bustle of pedestrian traffic on Hamburgo and Florencia; but many of the customers are absorbed in gazing at the Duca d'Este's regrigerated display cases, which shelter many kinds of pastries, and fresh and candied fruits, ice creams, and other fare. There's a good selection of coffees, teas, and hot chocolates. You can have al light lunch or supper by ordering soup and salad.

Bakeries

Pastelería Ideal, 16 de Septiembre No. 14, 1¹/₂ blocks south of the Alameda, between Cárdenas and Gante. ☎ **585-8099.**
Cuisine: PASTRY. **Metro:** "Bellas Artes."
Prices: 50¢–$10.
Open: 7am–10pm daily.

This classy place has moderate prices and a constant stream of loyal customers. It's sure to charm you with its assortment of confections. Brown-bag your next breakfast from here—if you can resist that long.

Pastelería Madrid, 5 de Febrero No. 25, 2½ blocks south of the Zócalo, between República del Salvador and Uruguay. ☎ **521-3378.**

Cuisine: PASTRY. **Metro:** "Zócalo."

Prices: 50¢–$10.

Open: Daily 9am–10pm.

The walls of this enormous, well-lit bakery are lined with deep shelves filled with light, puffy, and absolutely fresh pastries, sweet rolls, danish, cookies, biscuits, fresh breads, jam-filled goodies, and custards. Here's how to make these treats yours: Pick up a circular aluminum tray and and a pair of tongs, pile your tray full, then entrust it to a young lady who deftly transfers the mountain of pastries to a paper bag, adding up the tab at the same time. Come for breakfast (coffee or tea, yogurt, and pastries). Here's a tip: Take your choices from the fullest tray, as those are the freshest.

Cantinas

La Ciudad de los Espejos, Mesones 123, at Pino Suárez. ☎ **522-2939** or **542-3570.**

Cuisine: MEXICAN. **Reservations:** Not required. **Metro:** "Pino Suárez."

Prices: National drinks $2–$10; appetizers $1.50–$5; main courses $7–$13; daily specials $3–$13.

Open: Mon–Sat 10am–11:30pm.

The corner on which this venerated cantina is situated looks unappealingly like skid row, with unsightly key-maker shops and a tacky quick-sandwich outlet. But inside, "The City of the Mirrors," as the name translates, is quite welcoming. It's plain in appearance compared to the Opera Bar or Salon Victoria, but it's about as authentic as a cantina gets. A wall of mirrors is back of the enormously long, wood look-alike, stand-up bar on the right as you enter. Cloth clad tables stretch the length of the restaurant and turn right to make an "L" shape along a wall with a mural of Rome burning. Waiters in white jackets, black slacks, and black bow ties scurry about attentively seeing to the patrons. Opened in the late 1920s, this is one of the city's most popular cantinas. Get there early though, for a seat before the 1:30 to 4:30pm lunch crowd. Daily specials might include cabrito (roasted kid) Segovia-style, or baked quail. Other specialties on the regular menu include such delicacies as beef brains, criadillas (bull testicles), paella Valenciana, osso buco, and cecina, thin-sliced grilled meat. If you want to just absorb the atmosphere before things get busy, try the quesadillas as an appetizer with guacamole salad.

★ **La Opera Bar,** 5 de Mayo No. 14, between Mata and Correo. ☎ **512-8959.**

Cuisine: INTERNATIONAL. **Reservations:** Recommended at lunch. **Metro:** "Bellas Artes."

Prices: Appetizers $5–$15.50; main courses $5–$15.50; mixed drinks $2–$6; beer $2.50; glass of wine $3.
Open: Mon–Sat 1pm–midnight.

La Opera Bar, three blocks east of the Alameda, is the most opulent of the city's cantinas. When you step into the place with its gilded baroque ceilings, slide into one of the dark wood booths with patches of beveled mirror and exquisite small oil paintings of pastoral scenes, or grab a table covered in linen and waiting with a basket of fresh bread. La Opera is the Mexican equivalent of a London club, although it has become so popular for dining that fewer and fewer men play dominoes. In fact, more and more the cavernous booths fill with couples enjoying romantic interludes. Tables of any kind are hard to find. The best bet is to arrive for lunch when it opens or go after 5pm when the throngs have diminished. The menu is sophisticated and extensive. While you wait for one of the jacketed waiters to bring your meal, look on the ceiling for the bullet hole that legend says Pancho Villa left when he galloped in on a horse.

Salón la Luz, Gante 23, corner of Carranza (2¹/₂ blocks south of the Alameda and south of Sanborn's Casa de Azulejos). ☎ **512-4246** or **512-2656.**
Cuisine: MEXICAN. **Reservations:** Not required. **Metro:** "Allende."
Prices: Main courses $8.50–$13.
Open: Mon–Sat 10am–11pm.

Since 1914 the Salón la Luz has been an institution in downtown Mexico City. Not only are women welcome but the whole family is accommodated. A trio playing traditional Mexican ballads entertains from 2 to 6pm and 7pm to closing. Inside it's cozy and inviting with bustling waiters and almost always full Formica-topped tables. The specialty here is a delicious carne cruda (steak tartare). If you'd like to try it and something else, order the combination plate. It's enough for two, and includes portions of carne cruda, ham, smoked pork, paté, and Chihuahua cheese. Come early when the food is freshest.

Salón Victoria, Lopez 43, corner of Marroqui. ☎ **512-4340.**
Cuisine: MEXICAN. **Reservations:** Recommended before 3pm for lunch. **Metro:** "Bellas Artes."
Prices: Appetizers $2.50–$9.50; main courses $7–$15.50.
Open: Daily 10am–10pm.

The newly remodeled Salón Victoria, located at the corner of a pedestrian walkway, is beginning to look like a classy English pub. With brass chandeliers and lamps and brass-framed prints, this is not quite the Salón Victoria of nearly 50 years ago—maybe it's better. Specialities here include paella Valenciana, manchamantales (translated literally "tablecloth stainer"—turkey dish with almost 20 ingredients), and goat head tacos. The latter are an acquired taste and if you want to try them, you must reserve an order in advance; the supply is limited and the Victoria hoards them for its best customers.

6

What to See & Do in Mexico City

Time usually runs out for tourists before they have exhausted all there is to do in this dynamic world capital. You'll find that in Mexico City even such routine activities as walking in the park can bring delightful surprises. Even a stroll through the city's markets presents the opportunity to admire and purchase exotic items. Mexico City's vibrancy is evident in its museums, which include some of the best in the world. And there is certainly variety here, from pre-Hispanic engravings to contemporary art. A downtown portion of the city comprising almost 700 blocks and 1,500 buildings has been designated the capital's **Centro Historico** (Historic Zone). (**Note:** A systematic restoration of historic buildings has been underway for several years and is only about a third complete. Buildings being reclaimed from years of neglect may be covered in scaffolding or closed during your visit, especially those in the Zócalo area.)

In the summer, always be prepared for rain, which comes daily. In winter carry a jacket or sweater: Stone museums are cold inside, and when the sun goes down, it becomes chilly.

For all the details on seeing the famed pre-Hispanic ruins at Teotihuacán, see Chapter 10, "Easy Excursions from Mexico City."

Suggested Itineraries

If You Have One Day

Arrive at the Museo Nacional de Antropología by 10am and follow the walking tour suggested in this book for the next two to four hours; this could easily become an all-day excursion, depending on your interest level. Have lunch in the museum, in nearby Polanco, or in the Zona Rosa. Return to your hotel for a rest (remember this is your first day at 7,240 ft.). In the evening take in a performance of the Ballet Folklorico de Mexico at either the Bellas Artes or Teatro de la Ciudad.

If You Have Two Days

Spend the first day as suggested here. Start the second day with an early breakfast. Then, head straight for the Pyramids of Teotihuacán, 30 miles northeast of the city proper (see Chapter 10, "Easy Excursions from Mexico City," for details). Not counting travel time, seeing the ruins takes between two and five hours, depending on whether or not you climb the pyramids and/or stop to read explanatory information and take photographs. Have a late lunch there or return to the city. In the early evening stroll the Zona Rosa and select an outdoor or indoor restaurant. The choices are innumerable.

If You Have Three Days

Spend days one and two as suggested here. Start your third day with a walking tour of the Zócalo, either using this book's tour or, if it's Sunday, following the free guided tour organized by the Mexico City Historic Center. You could combine it with the walking tour of the

Alameda, or selected Alameda highlights such as the Museo Franz Mayer and the Diego Rivera mural *Dream of a Sunday Afternoon in Alameda Park,* on the Parque Solidaridad beside the Alameda. Or, you could sign on for one of the day-long *Paseos Culturales* (cultural tours) sponsored by INAH, which are led by expert tour guides to historically significant areas outside the city.

If You Have Four Days

Spend your first three days as suggested here. Get an early start on the fourth day for touring the southern parts of the city. If it's Saturday, begin with the colorful Bazar Sábado (Saturday Bazaar) in San Angel. Otherwise, head for the suburb of Coyoacán, starting at the museum-home of Frida Kahlo, wife of Diego Rivera. Then walk a few blocks to the Museo de Leon Trotsky. Have lunch at one of the restaurants around the Plaza in Coyoacán, then take a taxi to the Anahuacalli (the Diego Rivera Museum). In the evening, listen to the mariachis around Garibaldi Square.

If You Have Five Days

If your fifth day is a Sunday don't miss La Lagunilla Market, especially if you love eclectic flea markets. The museums are free on Sunday and this would be a good day to see the most expensive ones; for example the Museo Nacional de Antropología and the Museo del Templo Mayor.

Alternatively, you might take one of the excursions suggested in Chapter 10. A day trip to Puebla, Tlaxcala, or Toluca would leave plenty of time for looking around either of those cities in time to return by late afternoon.

1 The Top Attractions

⭐ **Museo Nacional de Antropología,** Chapultepec Park. ☎ 553-6266.

Occupying 44,000 square feet, and with 21 exhibition rooms, Mexico's National Museum of Anthropology is regarded as one of the top museums in the world. First-floor rooms are devoted to the pre-Hispanic cultures of Mexico and include some of the most famous sculptures and artifacts gathered from archeological sites throughout the country. Among these treasures are the contents of King Pacal's tomb from Palenque; multi-ton stone Olmec heads; a giant sculpture of the rain god Tlaloc; a grotesque stone figure of Coatlíque, with a necklace of hands and hearts and a skirt of serpents; and the famous Aztec calendar. Second-floor rooms feature fascinating exhibits of contemporary rural cultures' crafts, culture, traditions, costumes, and everyday life. This museum is the single best introduction to Mexico. (**Note:** Occasionally some of the most famous pieces may be part of traveling exhibitions and therefore not on display. See also the walking tour of the museum in Chapter 7.)

Admission: $5.50; free Sun.

Open: Tues–Sat 9am–7pm, Sun 10am–6pm. **Metro:** Auditorio.

⭐ **Museo Franz Mayer,** Hidalgo 45, facing the Alameda.
☎ **518-2265.**

One of the capital's foremost museums, this museum opened in 1986 in a beautifully restored 16th-century building on the Plaza de la Santa Veracruz. The extraordinary 10,000 piece collection of antiquities, mostly from Mexico's 16th through 19th centuries, was amassed by one man, Franz Mayer. A German immigrant, he adopted Mexico in 1905 and grew rich there. Before his death in 1975 Mayer bequeathed his collection to the country and arranged for its permanent display through a trust with the Banco Nacional. The pieces, all utilitarian (as opposed to pure art objects), include inlaid and richly carved furniture; an enormous collection of Talavera pottery; gold and silver religious pieces; sculptures; tapestries; rare watches and clocks (the oldest is a 1680 lantern clock); wrought iron; old paintings from Europe and Mexico, and 770 El Quixote volumes, many of which are rare editions or typographically unique. There's so much that it may take two visits to absorb it all. (See also the walking tour of the Alameda in Chapter 7.)

Admission: $2.75 adults; 75¢ students; free Sunday. Guided tours, $1.50.

Open: Tues–Sun 10am–5pm. **Guided tours:** Tuesday through Saturday 10:30 and 11:30am and 12:30pm. **Metro:** Hidalgo or Bellas Artes.

⭐ **Museo del Templo Mayor (Great Temple),** off the Zócalo.
☎ **542-1717.**

Opened in 1987 at the site of the newly excavated Aztec Templo Mayor, the Templo Mayor museum has quickly become one of the city's top attractions. At the time of the Spanish Conquest the site was the center of religious life for the city of 300,000.

A small corner of the site had been exposed for years, but in 1978 a workman, digging on the east side of the Catedral Metropolitana (next to what is now the Palacio Nacional), unearthed an exquisite Aztec stone carving of the Aztec moon goddess Coyolxauhqui. Mexican archeologists followed up the discovery with major excavations, and what they uncovered were the interior remains of the Pyramid of Huitzilopochtli, also called the Templo Mayor, the most important religious structure in the Aztec capital. The excavated structures are actually the remains of the pyramids that were covered by the Great Temple.

The rooms and exhibits are organized by subject on many levels around a central open space. You'll see some marvelous displays of masks, figurines, tools, jewelry, and other artifacts, including the huge stone wheel of the moon goddess Coyolxauhqui—"she with bells painted upon her face"—on the second floor. The goddess ruled the night, so the Aztecs believed, but died at the dawning of every day, slain and dismembered by her brother Xiuhcoatl, the Serpent of Fire.

Look also for the striking jade-and-obsidian mask, and the full-size terra-cotta figures of the guerreros aguilas, or "eagle warriors." A

Frommer's Favorite Mexico City Experiences

Breakfast or Dinner at the Hotel Majestic Rooftop Restaurant Every visitor to Mexico City should start or end at least one day here under one of the colorful umbrellas overlooking the historic downtown and Zócalo.

The Ethnography Section of the Museo Nacional de Antropología Overlooked by many visitors, the Ethnography Section on the second floor is the perfect introduction to Mexican life away from the beaches, resorts, and cities. Fine, unusual weavings, pottery and handcrafts, furniture, huts, plows, and canoes are presented in the context of everyday life in the countryside. It's a must for those about to visit the interior of the country, for those who are curious about the villagers seen on the capital's streets, and for those who intend to venture off the beaten tourists' path during their journey.

Afternoon Tea at the Salon de Thé Duca d'Este In Mexico, visitors learn to take tea and coffee breaks as seriously as the Mexicans do. This cheerful Zona Rosa restaurant and pastry shop is perfect for sipping a frothy cappuccino and whiling away some time watching passersby through the huge windows facing the street.

The Ballet Folklorico de Mexico Among the best folkloric ballet groups in Mexico are those that perform in Mexico City, either at the Teatro Bellas Artes or at the Teatro de la Ciudad. At the Bellas Artes you'll get to see the famed Tiffany glass curtain, which is usually (but not always) shown before each performance. Performances are on Sunday morning and evening, and on Wednesday evening.

The Sunday Lagunilla Market The best flea market in Mexico, this one sprawls for blocks. My last visit found vendors selling santos, jewelry, antiques, pottery, miniatures, brass, glass, old locks and keys, a piece of Spanish armor, a 16th-century religious sculpture, an elkhorn ear ring, and many other things.

Shopping in the Zona Rosa and Polanco Dozens of fashionable shops line the streets of these attractive areas. Designer clothing, jewelry, and antiques are for sale, and there are many tempting restaurants in between shops.

The Bazar Sábado in San Angel On Saturdays, this exclusive colonial-era suburb of mansions near Parque San Jacinto is alive with hundreds of artists, antique sellers, and street vendors.

An Evening in the Zona Rosa The popular Zona Rosa sidewalk cafés and pedestrian streets are ideal for a night of hopping from place to place, without cover charges and taxis.

The Ruins of Teotihuacán There's nothing to compare with walking down the wide Avenue of the Dead, with the Pyramid of the Moon at one end and pyramidal structures on both sides. Imagine what it must have looked like when the walls were embellished with murals on brilliantly colored stucco.

IMPRESSIONS

My impression [of Diego Rivera] was of a large man with bulging sorrowful eyes, a man shy in manner, gentle in movement, and kindly in nature. I liked him from the first look at his homely face and the first touch of his large sensuous hand. With all his homeliness and his casual sloppiness—even with all his buttons buttoned and his brown shirt tucked in, he gave the impression of being doubtfully buttoned—he possessed an odd sort of attractiveness.
—Hudson Strode, *Now in Mexico* (1947)

cutaway model of the Templo Mayor shows the layers and Aztec methods of construction.

See also the walking tour of the Zócalo in Chapter 7.

Admission: $5.50; free Sun.

Open: Tues–Sat 9am–6pm. **Metro:** Zócalo.

★ **Palacio de Bellas Artes,** on the east side of the Alameda. ☎ **709-3111, ext.** 173.

This magnificent piece of architecture was built to feature performing arts from the opera to the ballet. The theater is very turn-of-the-century. Built during the Porfiriato, it is covered in Italian Carrara marble on the outside, but it's completely 1930s art-deco style inside. The theater has sunk some 12 feet into the soft belly of Lake Texcoco since construction was begun in 1900 (it was opened in 1934). The Bellas Artes is the work of several masters: Italian architect Adam Boari, who made the original plans; Antonio Munoz and Federico Mariscal, who modified Boari's plans considerably; and Mexican painter Gerardo Murillo ("Doctor Atl") who designed the fabulous art-nouveau glass curtain, which was constructed by Louis Comfort Tiffany in the Tiffany Studios of New York. The glass curtain, which is not always used, was made from nearly a million iridescent pieces of colored glass. It portrays the Valley of Mexico with its two great volcanoes.

On the third level of the theater are the famous murals by Rivera, Orozco, and Siqueiros. The controversial Rivera mural *Man in Control of his Universe* was commissioned in 1933 for Rockefeller Center in New York. Rivera completed the work there just as you will see it in Mexico City: A giant vacuum sucks up the riches of the earth to feed the factories of callous, card-playing, hard-drinking white capitalist bullies, while the noble workers of the earth, of all races, rally behind the red flag of socialism and its standard-bearer, Lenin. It should come as no surprise that the Rockefellers didn't appreciate the communist theme of their new purchase and had it destroyed. Rivera duplicated the mural in Mexico as *Man at the Crossing of the Ways.* The construction around the building, which may be evident when you visit the theater, is partly for stabilization of the building and partly to create an underground parking lot. For information on tickets and performances see Chapter 9, "Mexico City Nights."

Admission: Free.

Open: Daily 9am–9pm.

Did You Know?

- Over one million natives lived in the Valley of Mexico before the Conquest.

- Of the 200,000 inhabitants of the city of Tenochtitlán before the Conquest, only 66,000 were alive immediately after.

- The first 12 Franciscan friars arrived in Mexico in 1524 and walked barefoot 200 rugged and mountainous miles from Veracruz to Mexico City.

- The first mint in Mexico was established in 1535 in the Palacio Nacional in Mexico City. Gold was first coined there in 1679.

- The first recorded Aztec victim of smallpox was Cuitláhuac, Moctezuma's brother, who ruled only a short while before dying.

- The first wheat was brought to Mexico by Juan Garrido, one of Cortés's soldiers.

- Keeping a promise made by Cortés, the Mexican government paid pensions to the descendents of Moctezuma until 1933.

- More than a million Mexicans died during the revolutionary decade of 1910–1920.

- Most of the Aztec gold accumulated by the Spaniards was lost when the conquerors fled Tenochtitlán on the night known as *Noche Triste* (Sad Night).

- Mexico comes from the word *Mexica,* which means "place of the Mexicas."

★ Diego Rivera Murals

Diego Rivera (1886–1957), one of Mexico's most renowned muralists, left an indelible stamp on Mexico City's walls and, through his painted political themes, affected the way millions view Mexican history. See his stunning and provocative interpretations at the Palacio Nacional, the Bellas Artes, the National Preparatory School—which features Rivera's earliest efforts—the Department of Public Education, the National School of Agriculture at Chapingo, the National Institute of Cardiology and the Museo de la Alameda (formerly in the Hotel Del Prado). (See also the walking tours of the Zócalo and Alameda in Chapter 7.)

Be sure to see the Rivera murals in the Palacio Nacional. The quality of painting is readily evident and the content is easy to understand, if you know something of the history of Mexico. *Legend of Quetzalcoatl* depicts the famous legend of the flying serpent bringing a white man with a blond beard to the country. When Cortés arrived, many of the Aztecs remembered this legend and believed him to be Quetzalcoatl. Another mural, *American Intervention*, tells the tale of American invaders marching into Mexico City and the young Mexican cadets who died fighting them during the Mexican War. The most notable of Rivera's murals in the palace is *Great City of Tenochtitlán*, a pictorial study of the original metropolis in the Valley of Mexico. The city takes up only a small part of the mural, and the remainder is filled with what appears to be four million extras left over from a Hollywood epic. In fact, no matter what their themes, most of Rivera's murals incorporate ancient Mexican history, usually featuring Cortés and a cast of thousands.

Admission: Free.
Open: Daily 9am–5:30pm.

---

2 More Attractions

Near the Zócalo

 Catedral Metropolitana, facing the Zócalo. No phone.

The Metropolitan Cathedral, built on the foundations of an Aztec temple, took 240 years to complete (1573–1813). The result is an eclectic mix of architectural styles. The cathedral has undergone many changes over the centuries: The priceless and elaborate main altar carved in cypress by Jerónimo de Balbas around 1741 was demolished a little over a hundred years later and replaced with a crownlike neoclassic tabernacle. This too was removed in 1943 and opened the view to the *Retablo de los Reyes* (Altar to the Kings), also carved by de Balbas, which was behind the main altar. The carving of this altar took him seven years between 1718 and 1725. A native of Seville, de Balbas was one of the country's foremost wood carvers. His sons followed him in this vocation. The fabulous gilted *retablo* incorporates the first use of *estipite* (inverted and elongated pyramid-shaped pillars) in the New World, a style which then swept through colonial architecture. In 1967 a fire caused by an electrical short engulfed a major part of the interior of the cathedral and burned many of the priceless wood carvings attributed to de Balbas, and to other distinguished artisans as well. Replacement has been faithful to the originals. And over the years many of the retablo's rich adornments in silver and gold have disappeared. Still, much that is remarkable remains.

The immense building has 5 naves and 14 chapels. The first altar you'll see upon entering is called the Altar of Forgiveness—so named because this is where heretics, sentenced by the Holy Inquisition, were brought before execution. Behind it are the magnificent choir stalls with the sculpted three-dimensional saints of 17th-century artist Juan de Rojas. They were restored after the fire of 1967. Scaffolding inside and outside is the result of conservation efforts—the building and its neighbor, El Sagrario church, are sinking into the soft subsoil of the historic center.

Admission: Free.
Open: Daily 8am–10pm.

Catedral Metropolitana

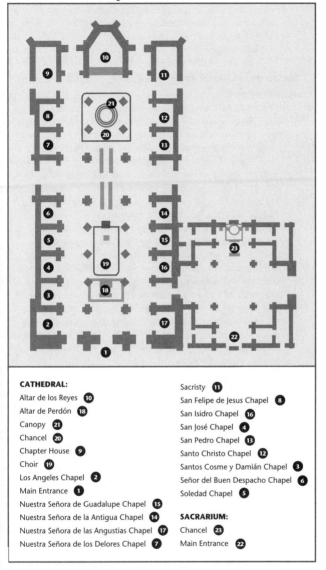

Museo Charrería, Isabel la Católica 108 at Izazaga. ☎ **709-4838** or **709-4793.**

Though a bit off the historic main road, this fascinating museum, devoted to the Mexican-style rodeo, is worth a detour. It's especially noteworthy if you have an interest in horses, horse gear, or rodeos. The Mexican version of the rodeo is much more elaborate than the rodeos of the U. S. Everything to outfit the most stylish *charro* (Mexican cowboy and cowgirl) is here, from chaps, spurs, and whips to hats and leather clothing.

Admission: Free.

Open: Mon–Fri 10am–6pm.

Museo de la Ciudad de Mexico, Pino Suárez 30. ☎ 542-0487 or 542-8356.

Before you enter, go to the corner of República del Salvador and look at the enormous stone serpent head, a corner support at the building's base. The stone was once part of an Aztec pyramid. Back at the entrance, a stone doorway opens to the courtyard of this mansion built in 1778 as the House of the Counts of Santiago de Calimaya. Originally the site was occupied by a house built in 1536 by the governor of Cuba, a relative of Cortés. A descendent of the governor, the Count of Calimaya (Juan Manuel Lorenzo Gutiérrez Altamirano Velasco y Flores), had the present building constructed for his home. Notice the cannon-shaped rain spouts along the roofline, which signified that it was the home of titled nobility. The family coat of arms is centered on the roofline above the central door. This classic building was converted into the Museum of the City of Mexico in 1964 and should be visited by anyone interested in the country's past. Dealing solely with the Valley of Mexico where the first people arrived in 8000 B.C., there are some fine maps and pictographic presentations of the initial settlements, outlines of social organization as it developed, and a huge mockup of Tenochtitlán, the city of the Aztecs. The conquest and destruction of Tenochtitlán by the Spaniards is suitably portrayed with a mural of Capdevila that appears to have been painted in fire.

Admission: Free.

Open: Mon–Sun 9:30am–6:30pm.

Museo de las Culturas, Moneda 13. ☎ 512-7452 or 510-1727.

Built as a part of the Palacio Nacional in the 1500s and once the home of La Casa de Moneda (the Mint) this building later housed the Museo Nacional de Antropología before that museum moved in 1964 to its current Chapultepec Park home. It now houses the Museum of Culture, and you'll find a fascinating assortment of exhibits here relating to other cultures, with especially good relics from Asia and Africa.

Admission: Free.

Open: Tues–Sat 9:30am–6pm, Sun 9:30am–4pm.

Near the Alameda

North, west, and south of the Alameda proper are other attractions worthy of note. For major highlights, see the walking tour of the Alameda in Chapter 7.

 Monumento a la Revolución & Museo Nacional de la Revolución, Avenida Juárez and La Fragua. ☎ 546-2115 or 566-1902.

The stocky art-deco Monument to the Revolution, set in the large Plaza de la República, has a curious and ironic history. It also houses an excellent but often overlooked museum. The government of Porfirio Díaz, the perennially "reelected" president of Mexico, began construction of what was intended as a new legislative chamber. But only the dome was raised by the time the Mexican Revolution (1910) put an end to his plans—not to mention his dictatorship. In the 1930s, after the turmoil of the revolution died down, the dome was finished off as a monument; the mortal remains of two revolutionary presidents, Francisco Madero and Venustiano Carranza, were entombed in two of its pillars and it was dedicated to the revolution. Later on, the bodies of presidents Plutarco Elías Calles and Lázaro Cárdenas were buried there, as was revolutionary leader Francisco ("Pancho") Villa.

Beneath the Monumento a la Revolución is the Museo Nacional de la Revolución. The tumultuous years from 1867 to 1917, when the present constitution was signed, are chronicled in excellent exhibits of documents and newspaper stories, photographs and drawings, clothing, costumes, uniforms, weapons, and furnishings. This museum is well worth the time if you're at all interested in the period or the Mexican Revolution.

Admission: Free.

Open: Tues–Sun 9am–5pm. **Directions:** From the Colón Monument on Reforma, walk one block north on either La Fragua or Ramirez and the monument looms up ahead.

Museo de San Carlos, Puente de Alvarado 50. ☎ **535-4848** or **592-3721.**

The San Carlos Museum shows works from students of the Academy of San Carlos. Most of the country's great painters—Diego Rivera among them—count it as their alma mater. The beautiful, converted mansion that houses the museum was built in the early 1800s for the Marqués de Buenavista by architect Manuel Tolsá.

Within the mansion's elliptical court are displays of 19th-century Mexican statuary and busts by Manuel Vilar and his pupils, and off to one side is a pretty garden court shaded by rubber trees.

The various rooms on the first and second floors hold some of Mexico's best paintings, by both Mexican and European artists. In Sala IV, for instance, you can view *Christ in Limbo* by Mostaert (ca. 1534–98), and also two paintings by Lucas Cranach the Elder: *Adam and Eve* and *Federico de Sajonia*. Upstairs, artistic treats include *La Coquea y el Jovenzuelo* by Fragonard and a portrait of Sir William Stanhope attributed to Sir Joshua Reynolds.

Admission: $2.75; free Sun.

Open: Tues–Sun 10am–6pm. **Directions:** Walk 5$^{1}/_{2}$ blocks west of the Alameda, and 2$^{1}/_{2}$ blocks west of the above-mentioned San Fernando Plaza at the corner of Arizpe.

 Museo de Zapato, Bolivar 27 near Madero. ☎ **512-7342.**

Opened in 1988, this private shoe museum is one of the most fascinating museums in the city. The thousands of shoes, all neatly displayed, are the collection of shoestore owner Don José Villamayor. The number and variety of shoes are amazing—shoes made of reeds, goatskin, palm, straw, silk, porcelain, bronze, and more. There are shoes from cultures all over the world and from several centuries. Among the boots are those worn by an astronaut on Apollo II.

Admission: Free.

Open: Mon–Fri 10am–6pm, Sat 10am–2pm.

⭐ **Museo Nacional de Arte,** corner of Tacuba and Condesa/Marconi. ☎ **521-7324** or **512-1684.**

The palace-like building that houses the National Museum of Art is another legacy of the years of the Eurocentric Porfirio Díaz. Originally built to house the government's offices of communications and public works, it was designed by Italian architect Silvio Contri and opened in 1904. It was completed in 1911 after Díaz fell from power, and the Museo Nacional de Arte took over the building in 1982. Most tourists don't take the time to see this museum, but it's contents are worthy of a visit. The interior of the building, with its frescoed ceilings, ornate banisters, glass chandeliers, and beveled glass windows, is magnificent. Against the elegant backdrop Mexico's artistic development from pre-Hispanic times almost to the present is portrayed, with representative works from major artists and important developmental periods.

Admission: $3.50; free Sun.

Open: Tues–Sun 10am–4:30pm.

⭐ **Museo Serfin.** Madero 33, near Bolivar. No phone.

Housed in a portion of a mansion constructed by the wealthy Taxco miner José de la Borda, this bank-operated museum is devoted to the textiles and clothing of Mexico's indigenous populations. Huipils, rebozos, quechquemetls, mens' homespun suits, women's wrap skirts, and waist-loomed belts and blouses are all on display. If you have no time for the ethnographic section of the Museo Nacional de Antropología, this would be a fine alternative. The clothing here is still worn today by the various peoples of Mexico. The museum is small but handsomely organized. The quality of the garments on the wall displays and on figures with Indian stature and features is truly exquisite. A full wall exhibit shows plants used to make natural dyes. Though dating back to the 18th century, the building has served many functions. For a long time it was the post office, then the "old post office," then a commercial establishment, and finally a movie house before its conversion to a museum.

Admission: Free.

Open: Tues–Sun 10am–5pm.

Plaza and Cemetery of San Fernando, Puente Alvarado and Vicente Guerrero.

At one end of the plaza is the 18th-century San Fernando Church and behind it a small cemetery used by a few of Mexico's elite families. It's the only 19th-century cemetery remaining in the city; President Benito Juárez was the last person buried here (on July 23, 1872).

His tomb is much like a Greek temple, with a sculpture representing the motherland cradling a beloved son. (Many of Mexico's more infamous characters are buried in the cemetery behind the original Basílica of Guadalupe.)

Admission: Free.

Open: Daily during daylight hours. **Directions:** Walk 2½ blocks west of the Alameda.

Plaza de las Tres Culturas, corner of Lázaro Cárdenas and Flores Magón. No phone.

Here three cultures converge—Aztec, Spanish, and contemporary. Surrounded by contemporary office and apartment buildings are large remains of the **Aztec district of Tlatelolco,** site of the last battle of the conquest of Mexico. Off to one side is the **Cathedral of Santiago Tlatelolco.** Tlatelolco was on the edge of **Lake Texcoco,** linked to the Aztec capital by a causeway. Bernal Díaz de Castillo, in his *True Story of the Conquest of New Spain,* described the roar from the dazzling market there. Later he described the incredible scene after the last battle of the Conquest in Tlatelolco on August 13, 1521—the dead bodies were piled so high that walking there was impossible. That final battle completed the Spanish Conquest of Mexico.

You may view the pyramidal remains of Tlatelolco from raised walkways over the site. The cathedral, off to one side, was built entirely of volcanic stone in the 16th century. The interior has been tastefully restored; little patches of fresco in stark-white plaster walls have been preserved, along with a few deep-blue, stained-glass windows and an unadorned stone altar. Sunday is a good day to combine a visit here with one to the Sunday Lagunilla Street market (See Chapter 8, "Mexico City Shopping," for details), which is within walking distance south across Reforma.

Admission: Free.

Open: Daily during daylight hours. **Directions:** It's about 2 miles north of the Alameda at Flores Magón just off Reforma, in Colonia Tlatelolco. To walk there from the Alameda, go north on Lázaro Cárdenas for six long blocks and then turn right on Rayón two blocks to the Lagunilla Market. Then turn left and follow the street the short distance to the traffic circle with the Cuitláhuac Monument—the Plaza is on the other side of the circle. **Metro:** Línea 3 to Tlatelolco; leave the terminal by the exit to Manuel González, and turn right on this street. Walk two blocks to Avenida Lázaro Cárdenas and turn right again. The plaza is about half a block south, on the left, just past the Clinico Hospital. The walk takes less than 15 minutes.

Sullivan Park/Jardín del Arte, Intersection of Insurgentes and Reforma.

Though not strictly "near the Alameda," you might want to continue your tour with a 10-minute walk southwest along Reforma to Sullivan Park, which on Sunday becomes Jardín del Arte (Garden of art). At the east end of this pretty park is the Monumento a la Maternidad (Monument to Motherhood); westward the park is filled with trees, shrubs, benches, fountains, and sculpture. On Sunday it's crowded with artists displaying their wares.

Admission: Free.

Open: Daily; artists exhibit on Sun.

In & Around Chapultepec Park

Located west of the Centro Historico and the Alameda, at the edge of both the fashionable Zona Rosa and Polanco areas, the nearly 3-square-mile Bosque de Chapultepec (Chapultepec Park) is one of the biggest city parks in the world. Besides accommodating picnickers upon worn-away grass under centuries-old trees, canoes on the lake, vendors of balloons, trinkets and food, the park features seven museums, a zoo (with the famed Russian Pandas), a garden for senior citizens only, a miniature train, a children's playground, an amusement park, the Auditorio Nacional, and Los Pinos, the home of the President of Mexico. The museums are worth the effort and include the Museo Rufino Tamayo; Museo Nacional de Antropología; Castillo de Chapultepec/Museo Nacional de Historia; Museo de Arte Moderno; El Papalote, Museo del Niño (Children's Museum); Museo Nacional de Historia Natural; and the Museo de Tecnología Moderna (Museum of Technology). (For details on the Museo Nacional de Antropología, see "The Top Attractions," above, as well as the walking tour in chapter 7.)

Chapultepec Park has become quite run down and is not the pleasant place it was in years past. Until there is a park renewal, the experience is less than it could be. Although you can get from place to place on foot, I recommend that, where possible, you enter and leave the park from a main entrance and head directly toward your sightseeing goal, rather than doing a lot of wandering through the park.

To reach the park, take any "Auditorio" or "Reforma/Chapultepec" bus on Reforma; they will drop you within a block of the Museo Rufino Tamayo and the Museo de Arte Moderno and within two blocks of the Museo Nacional de Antropología, all of which are situated off Reforma about half a mile past the Diana statue, near Chapultepec Park Zoo.

If you'd rather take the Metro, Línea 1 will take you to the Chapultepec station outside the park. Línea 7 will take you to Auditorio, which is even closer.

IMPRESSIONS

Carlotta gave [the Castillo de Chapultepec] a Louis XV bedroom; Don Porfirio . . . added a billiard table and card tables; Madero put in a bowling alley; Rubio a swimming pool; Cárdenas, so far, thinks it would be undemocratic to live there. But the bets are that he will succumb before long—and put in . . . Quien sabe? Perhaps a cock pit or a greyhound racetrack.

—Harry A. Franck, *Trailing Cortez through Mexico* (1935)

Chapultepec Park

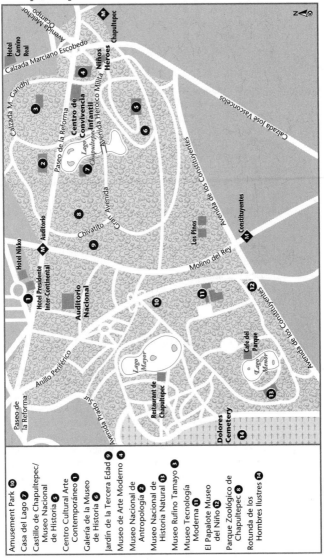

⭐ **Castillo de Chapultepec/Museo Nacional de Historia.**
☎ **553-6396** or **553-6224.**

The site of the Castillo (or Castle) of Chapultepec had been a fortress since the days of the Aztecs and the present palace was not built until the 1780s. At the time of the Mexican War, Chapultepec was the final defense before Mexico City—it was a plateau citadel. Santa Anna manned it with young people and the elderly in order to hold his best troops in reserve in case the citadel fell to U.S. troops, in which case the general planned to use his true troops to defend the city itself.

The castle offers a beautiful view of Mexico and it's reported that in the days of the French occupation during the 1860s, Empress Carlotta could sit up in bed and watch her husband, the Emperor Maximilian, proceeding down the Reforma on his way to work. Empress Carlotta, incidentally, designed the lovely garden surrounding the palace.

Until 1939 Chapultepec was still the official home of Mexico's presidents, and today it houses the Museo Nacional de Historia, which covers the period between the Conquest in 1521 to the end of the Mexican Revolution in 1917. Its large paintings, statues of Spanish leaders, and murals by Orozco, Siqueiros, O'Gorman, and others present a stunning vision of Mexico's often turbulent history. On the second floor are rooms displaying jewelry, colonial art objects, and impressive malachite vases. A bust of Cortés represents one of the few public admissions to his historic existence in Mexico City. It's an intriguing place through which to stroll, from the elaborate furnishings brought over from Europe by Maximilian and Carlotta, to the patios and fountains and the panorama of the city spread out below.

About 200 yards below The Castillo de Chapultepec is the **Galería de la Museo Nacional de Historia,** a circular glass building that spirals down the hillside. It's also known as the Museo Caracol ("the snail museum") because of its spiral shape, and as the Museo de la Lucha del Pueblo Mexican por su Libertad ("Museum of the Fight of the Mexican People for Their Liberty") because of its content. A condensed chronological history of Mexico for the years 1800 to 1917, the museum showcases portraits, reproductions of documents, and dramatic montages—in three dimensions—of famous scenes from Mexico's past. More recent years are also represented, with large photographs. Some of the scenes—such as the execution of Maximilian—are staged with a great sense of drama and imagination. The entrance begins with the earliest years and spirals down the hill and through the years of Mexico's growth toward independence. In many ways the museum is superior and more interesting than the Museo Nacional de Historia on the hill above.

Admission: $5.50 to the Castillo de Chapultepec; free on Sunday. Galería/Museo Caracol free. **Note:** Hold onto your ticket the entire time you're on the hill—you may be asked to show it.

Open: Tues–Sun (both castle and Galería/Museo Caracol) 9am–5pm, last ticket sold at 4pm.

 Centro Cultural Arte Contemporaneo, Campos Eliseos and Jorje Eliot. ☎ 282-0355.

This privately owned museum showcases a changing lineup of national and international art with some of the world's top artists. It's next to the Hotel Presidente Inter-Continental and opposite Chapultepec Park.

Admission: $1.60 for adults; children under 12 free; students with credentials half price; Sunday and Wednesday free for all.

Open: Tues–Sun 9am–5pm.

⭐ **Museo de Arte Moderno.** ☎ **553-6233** or **211-8729.**

The Museum of Modern Art is actually two buildings, set together in a statue-inhabited section of grassy park, with two entrances: one on Reforma, the other across from—and sort of behind—the Monumento a los Niños Héroes. The museum's interior is the perfect vehicle for showing works of art—simple with handsome parquet floors, marble and stone walls, wood-slatted ceiling, and circular windows.

The section at the Reforma entrance has four salons, two on each level, around a central dome of remarkable acoustic properties. The salons are attractive in their spaciousness, and give you the nice feeling that you're the only person in the museum—especially if you say something. Sala Antonieta Rivas Mercado has temporary exhibits, and Sala Carlos Pellecer commands a portion of the permanent collection on the second floor. Sala José Juan Tablada, on the first floor, is another temporary exhibition space. And Sala Xavier Villa Urrutia, also on the first floor, is a permanent exhibit for Mexican artists. The museum features both Mexican and foreign artists including such greats as Frida Kahlo, Diego Rivera, Orozco, Roberto Montenegro, Tamayo, Pedro Coronel, Magritte, Delvaux, Antonia Guerrero, Bissier, and Nay. In the smaller circular Galeria Fernando Gamboa, across the garden, near the Niños Heroes entrance to the museum, are more temporary exhibits.

Admission: $4; free on Sunday.

Open: Tues–Sun 10am–5:30pm.

Museo Nacional de Historia Natural. ☎ **566-2848** or **515-6304.**

On the far side of Chapultepec Park, not far from the President's home, this structure is notable from the outside for its series of 10 interconnecting domes. From a distance it looks like a cluster of brightly colored inverted bowls surrounded by foliage and flowers.

Inside the museum you'll see stuffed and preserved animals and birds, tableaux of different environments such as desert, seashore, and tropical forest, and arctic tundra with the appropriate wildlife. Other domes contain exhibits relating to geology, astronomy, biology, the origin of life, and such displays as a relief map of the world's mountains and an illuminated map of Mexico showing the topography of various mineral sites. The museum is fascinating for anyone with the slightest curiosity about nature, and is totally absorbing for youngsters.

Admission: 50¢; free Sun.

Open: Tues–Sun 10am–5pm. **Metro:** Chapultepec; enter the park from Avenida Constituyentes.

⭐ **Museo Rufino Tamayo.** ☎ **286-6599** or **286-3572.**

Oaxacan painter Rufino Tamayo not only contributed a great deal to modern Mexican painting but over the years the artist collected pre-Hispanic, Mexican, and foreign works of art; among them works by de Kooning, Warhol, Dali, and Magritte. The boldly modern museum is the perfect place to display these marvelous and attractive collections. Tamayo's pre-Hispanic collection is in a separate museum in the city of Oaxaca. In Mexico City you can see his paintings and his collection, unless they are temporarily displaced by a special exhibit. If you see an exhibit advertised (in the *Mexico City News,* for instance), don't miss it, for it's sure to be excellent. The Museo Rufino Tamayo is opposite Chapultepec Park proper, right off Reforma, just after crossing Calzada Escobedo and before the Museo Nacional de Antropología.

Admission: $4; free on Sunday.

Open: Usually Tues–Sun 10am–6pm. Free guided tours Sat–Sunday 10am–2pm.

Museo Tecnología Moderna (Museum of Technology).
☎ **516-0964** or **277-5779.**

The polyhedral dome outside this museum is the Planetarium, which has shows at 10am, noon, and 2pm daily. The museum is educational, to say the least, and it is always filled with students madly taking notes on scientific developments through the ages. Inside and outside are trains and planes, mockup factories, experiments of Morse and Edison, and various energy exhibits. When you're thoroughly exhausted, head for the basement, where there's a cafeteria for food or refrescos.

Admission: Free.

Open: Tues–Sun 9am–4:45pm.

⭐ **El Papalote, Museo del Niño (Children's Museum),**
Avenida de los Constituyentes, Chapultepec Park. ☎ **273-0774.**

This colorful, interactive children's museum opened in 1993 in three separate ultra-modern buildings. In Spanish, *Papalote* means "paper kite"; in Nahuatl, the word means "butterfly." The Building of the Pyramids dominates most of the exhibits. In the IMAX building there are films twice daily, changing exhibits, a restaurant, a gift shop, and an open-air theater. The hands-on exhibits teach children through participatory sections called "The Human Body"— brain, memory, senses, and nerves; "Communications," with use of computers and exposure to foreign languages while plugged into a globe of the earth and its countries; "Our World," covering cities, countries, nature, mechanics and more; "Con-Ciencia," (meaning "with science"), using magnets, light, energy, shadow, color, and including a manufactured rain forest complete with handmade animals, insects, and recreated biosphere; and "Expressions," where children indulge in art, music and theater. There's nothing here children can't touch, but they must be accompanied by adults.

Admission: $5 adults ($7.50 including IMAX show); $3.50 children ($5 including IMAX show).
Open: Tues–Fri 9am–6pm; Sat–Sun 9am–1pm, and 2–6pm.

Did You Know?

- The Aztec Calendar Stone, made of basaltic rock, weighs 24.5 tons.

- 1900 was the year of the first electric tram and first automobile in Mexico City.

- During the Porfiriato, *pulquerias* (where *pulque,* a fermented cactus juice, is sold) were prohibited from having windows, chairs, music, *and* women—all to no avail.

- President José Antonio Lopez de Santa Anna's amputated leg was disinterred from its burial site in Veracruz and reburied with grand processions and ceremony in Mexico City, but later an angry mob dug it up and dragged it through the streets.

- Tombs of Teotihuacán's rulers have not been discovered, and there's no record of what Teotihuacán residents looked like.

- Mexico's first stamp was issued in 1856 with the face of Miguel Hidalgo y Castilla.

- In 1882 the first train linked Mexico City and Toluca.

- The remains of Hernán Cortés, conqueror of Mexico, are in a vault in the chapel of the Hospital of Jesús Nazareño, the oldest functioning hospital in the Americas.

- Communist leader Leon Trotsky moved to Mexico City in 1938 and was assassinated there in 1940.

- More than 300,000 students attend the University Atonomia de Mexico (UNAM) in Mexico City. Founded in 1551, it is one of the oldest universities in the New World.

- In 1967 a fire inside the Catedral Metropolitana destroyed priceless 18th-century works.

- From 1973 to 1993 Mexico City's population swelled from 10 million to over 20 million inhabitants.

- One fourth of Mexico's 80 million inhabitants live in the Mexico City metropolitan area.

- Mexico's two "emperors" since the conquest were Augustín Iturbide (reign 1822–23), who lived in the Iturbide Palace on Avenida Madero, and Archduke Maximillian of Hapsburg who ruled from 1864 to 1867 and lived in The Castillo de Chapultepec. Both were executed by firing squads.

- Santa Anna, president of Mexico 11 times, died there poor and alone on June 21, 1876. His obituary appeared two weeks later.

Parque Zoológico de Chapultepec (Chapultepec Zoo).

A good way to see the animals here without much effort is to join the line of kids waiting to ride the miniature railway from the "train station" in the middle of the zoo. For a small fee you can ride in comfort around the whole zoo, catching tantalizing glimpses of monkeys, hippos, herons, polar bears, zebras, and many other creatures. To find the famed **Russian Pandas,** take the main zoo walkway to the right at the main circle. The pandas are behind glass, just past the caged panthers.

Admission: Free.

Open: Wed–Sun 9am–5pm.

Rotonda de los Hombres Ilustres, Dolores Cemetery, Chapultepec Park, Part Three.

The din of traffic recedes in the serene environment where Mexico's illustrious military, political, scientific, and artistic elite are buried. The rotunda is more like an outdoor museum of monuments than a cemetery. The stone markers are grouped in a double circle around an eternal flame; a stroll here will enliven a conversation about who's who in Mexican history. Among the famous men buried here are artists Diego Rivera, Alfredo Siquieros, José Clemente Orozco, and Gerardo Murillo (Dr. Atl); Presidents Sebastian Lerdo de Tejada, Valentin Gomez Farías, and Plutarco Calles; musicians Jaime Nuño (writer of the Mexican National Anthem), Juventino Rosas, and Augustin Lara; and outstanding citizens such as Carlos Pellicer. Stop in the entrance building and the guard will give you a map with a list of the illustrious dead buried here. The list includes biographical information.

Admission: Free.

Open: Daily 6am–6pm. **Directions:** Chapultepec Park; Dolores Cemetery, main entrance at Constituyentes and Av. Civil Dolores.

North of the City Center

Basílica of Our Lady of Guadalupe. No phone.

Within the northern city limits is the famous Basílica of Guadalupe. Tour groups often combine a trip to the Basílica with the Plaza de las Tres Culturas (see above) and the Pyramids of Teotihuacán (see Chapter 10), which makes for a rushed and exhausting day.

The Basílica of Our Lady of Guadalupe is on the site where a poor Indian named Juan Diego is reputed to have seen a vision, on December 9, 1531, of a beautiful lady in a blue mantle. The local bishop, Zumarraga, was reticent to confirm that Juan had indeed seen the Virgin Mary, and so he asked the peasant for some evidence. Juan saw the vision a second time, on December 12, and it became miraculously emblazoned on the peasant's cloak. The bishop immediately ordered the building of a church on the spot, and upon its completion the image was hung in the place of honor, framed in gold. Since that time millions upon millions of the devout and the curious have come to view the miraculous image that experts, it is said, are at a loss to explain. The blue-mantled Virgin of Guadalupe is the patron saint of Mexico.

So heavy was the flow of visitors—many of whom approached for hundreds of yards on their knees—that the old church that was already fragile was insufficient to handle the crowd, and an audacious new Basílica was built, designed by Pedro Ramírez Vazquez, the same architect who designed the breathtaking Museo Nacional de Antropología.

Walk behind the altar for a view of the miraculous cloak, which hangs behind bullet proof glass above the altar. Electric people movers going in two directions move the crowds a distance below the cloak. If you want to see it again, take the people mover going in the opposite direction; you can do it as many times as you wish.

To the right of the modernistic basilica is an old Basílica, actually the second one built to house the cloak—the original is higher up on the hill. Restoration of this Basílica has been ongoing for at least 10 years, but is moving more rapidly now. To the back of it is the entrance to the **Basílica Museum,** with a very good display of religious art in restored rooms. One of the side chapels, with a silver altar, is adjacent to the museum and nearing completion of restoration; it may be open by the time you are there.

Outside the museum is a garden commemorating the moment Juan Diego showed the cloak to the archbishop. There always seem to be numerous people gathered in these colorful confines to capture their visit on film. At the top of the hill, behind the Basílica, is a cemetery for Mexico's more infamous luminaries (Santa Anna among them). The steps up this hill are lined with flowers, shrubs, and waterfalls, and the climb, although tiring, is worthwhile for the view from the top.

If you visit Mexico City on December 12, you can witness the grand festival in honor of the Virgin of Guadalupe. The square in front of the Basílica fills up with the pious and the fiesta-minded. Prayers, dances, and a carnival atmosphere attract thousands of the devout. Many visitors combine a trip to the Basílica with one to the ruins of Teotihuacán—both are out of the city center and in the same direction.

Admission: Basílica, free; museum, $3.50.

Open: Basílica daily 8am–11pm; museum Tues–Sun 10am–5pm.
Metro: Línea 3 to the "Basílica" station; take the exit marked "Salida Av Montiel." A half-block or so north of the Metro station, turn right onto Avenida Montiel. The street is crowded with food and trinket vendors. After about 15 minutes' walking, you'll see the great church rising up ahead. Buses marked "La Villa" from the Metro will also let you off outside the shrine.

★ **Tenayuca and Santa Cecilia Pyramids,** Col. Tlalnepantla. No phone.

These two Toltec/Aztec ruins, six miles from the Zócalo, in the far northwest section of the city, are among the least visited ruins in the city—but perhaps two of the most interesting. Before the excavation at the Templo Mayor they were the only visible remains of Toltec/Aztec architecture in the city. Models of both, as they looked before the Spanish Conquest, are in the *Sala Mexica* of the Museo Nacional de Antropología. Tenayuca, with eight superimpositions, has one of the most visible examples of the pre-Hispanic tradition of constructing one building over another. Except for the stairways, what you see on the outside is the seventh superimposition, which is Aztec. Inside are Toltec temples, which are closer to the top; the lower ones are believed to be of Chichimec origin because they predated the Toltecs. Three sides of the pyramid are lined with stone serpents, one of the most unusual architectural embellishments in Mesoamerica. Remains of the two temples on top of the pyramid are gone, but they resembled those of the Templo Mayor, and were dedicated to Tlaloc, the rain god, and Huitzilopochtli, the primary god of the Aztecs. The stairs you climb to reach the top are on the north side of the structure, and are from the sixth superimposition.

Two miles from Tenayuca is the pyramid called Santa Cecilia, the only existing Aztec pyramid complete with temple on top, once dedicated to the god Huitzilopochtli. Archeologists discovered it beneath a later temple that had all but disappeared.

Directions to these two ruins are too convoluted to describe. A taxi driver should be able to get you there.

South of the City Center

The Polyforum Cultural Siqueiros, Insurgentes Sur and Filadelfia. ☎ 536-4524.

This gleaming arts center is quite controversial: some say it's bold and imaginative; others say it's a modern monstrosity with overpowering murals, low claustrophobic ceilings, and poor acoustics that echo the slightest sound. Whatever it is, the Polyforum does contain the world's largest mural (90,655 square feet), *The March of Humanity on Earth* and *Toward the Cosmos* collectively, by the famous Mexican muralist, David Alfaro Siqueiros.

Admission: free.

Open: Daily 10am–3pm, 4–7pm. **Directions:** Colectivos ("San Angel") and buses ("Indios Verdes-Tlalpan" or "Central Norte-Villa Olmpica") heading south along Insurgentes near the Zona Rosa both go to the Polyforum. The same buses goes to San Angel and the Bazar Sábado, the Ciudad Universitaria, the Pedregal, and the Cuicuilco Pyramid.

SAN ANGEL

⭐ **Anahuacalli (Diego Rivera Museum),** Calle Museo 150, Col. Tepetlapa. ☎ 677-2984.

Not to be confused with the Museo Estudio Diego Rivera near the San Angel Inn (see below), this is probably the most unusual museum in the city. Designed by Rivera before his death in 1957, it's devoted to his works as well as to his extensive collection of pre-Columbian art. The name means "House of Mexico," and it is constructed of pedregal (hard volcanic rock with which the area abounds) and resembles Mayan and Aztec architecture. The name *Anahuac* was the old name for the ancient Valley of Mexico.

In front of the museum is a reproduction of a Toltec ball court, and the entrance to the museum itself is via a coffin-shaped door. Light filters in through translucent onyx slabs and is supplemented by lights inside niches and wall cases containing the exhibits. Rivera collected nearly 60,000 pre-Columbian artifacts. The museum show-cases thousands of them, in 23 rooms in chronological order, stashed on the shelves, tucked away in corners, and peeking from behind glass cases.

Upstairs, a replica of Rivera's studio has been constructed, and there you'll find the original sketches for some of his murals, and two in-progress canvases. His first sketch (of a train) was done at the age of three, and there's a photo of it, plus a color photograph of him at work later in life in a pair of baggy pants and a blue denim jacket. Rivera studied in Europe for 15 years, and spent much of his life as a devoted Marxist. Yet he came through political scrapes and per-sonal tragedies with no apparent loss of creative energy, and a plaque in the museum proclaims him "A man of genius who is among the greatest painters of all time."

The Anahuacalli is located on the southern outskirts of the city in the suburb of San Pablo Tepetlapán south of the Museo Frida Kahlo.

Admission: Free.

Open: Tues–Sun 10am–2pm and 3–6pm. **Metro:** Take Línea 2 to the Tasqueña terminal. From the terminal, catch a bus ("Tasquena-Pena Pobre") west, which passes the museum. Another way to get there is by bus ("Zacatenco-Tlalpan") south along Balderas, or ("El Rosario-Xochimilco") south along Avenida Vasconcelos, Nuevo Leon, and Avenida Division del Norte. Hop off at the Calle del Museo stop.

Museo Centro Cultura Isidro Fabela (Casa del Risco), Plaza San Angel 15. ☎ **548-2329** or **548-5803.**

Formerly a mansion known as the Casa del Risco, this building was closed for years, reopening in 1992 as an art museum. Contempo-rary works are downstairs with a changing collection that often includes photographs. Upstairs is Isidro Fabela's international collection of paintings from the 16th to 18th centuries. The focal point of the house is the open courtyard, with its central fountain made of thousands of pieces of pottery (plates, saucers and cups), some broken and some whole. Many are shards of talavera pottery made in Puebla; others are from Holland, France, and England; and many are Chinese, having been brought to Mexico during the colonial-era sea trade between China and Mexico. Fabela bought the house in 1933; he was a governer of the state of Mexico in the 1940s.

Admission: Free.

Open: Tues–Sun 10am–5pm.

Museo Colonial del Carmen, Av. de la Revolución 4.
☎ **548-9849** or **548-2838.**

This former Carmelite convent, now filled with religious paintings and other ancient artifacts, also keeps a batch of mummified nuns in glass cases in the cellar. The museum, a maze of interlocking halls, corridors, stairways, chapels, and pretty flower-filled patios, is very pleasant to look around.

Admission: $1; free Sun.

Open: Tues–Sun 10am–4:45pm.

Museo de Arte Alvaro y Carmen T. Carillo Gil, corner of Desierto de los Leones and Revolución 1608. ☎ **550-4018** or **550-3983.**

Sometimes called the Museo de la Esquina (Museum on the Corner—it is at a major intersection on the Avenida de la Revolución), this modern gallery's collection of exhibit rooms include those dedicated to the works of Jose Clemente Orozco (1883–1942), Diego Rivera (1886–1957), David Alfaro Siqueiros (1896–1974), and rooms with works by a variety of Mexican painters.

Admission: $2; free Sun.

Open: Tues–Sun 9:30am–6pm.

⭐ **Museo Estudio Diego Rivera,** corner of Calle Diego Rivera and Avenida Altavista. ☎ **548-3032.**

It was here, in the studio designed and built by Juan O'Gorman in 1928, that Rivera drew sketches for his wonderful murals and painted smaller works. He died here in 1957. Now a museum, the Rivera studio holds some of the artist's personal effects and mementos, and there are changing exhibits relating to his life and work as well as other exhibits about Mexico City. It's opposite the Restaurant San Angel Inn, in San Angel.

Admission: $2.75; free Sun.

Open: Tues–Sun 10am–6pm.

COYOACÁN

⭐ **Museo Frida Kahlo,** Londres 247. ☎ **554-5999.**

Frida was born here on July 7, 1910, and occupied the house with Rivera from 1929 to 1954. The house is basically as she left it, and as you wander through the rooms you will get an overwhelming feeling for the life that they led. The couple's mementos are in every room, from the kitchen, where the names Diego and Frida are written on the walls, to the studio upstairs, where a wheelchair sits next to the easel with a partially completed painting surrounded by paint brushes, palettes, books, photographs, and other paraphernalia of the couple's art-centered lives.

The bookshelves are filled with books in many languages, nestled against a few of Rivera's files bearing such inscriptions as "Protest Rockefeller Vandalism," "Amigos Diego Personales," and "Varios Interesantes y Curiosos." Frida's paintings hang in every room, some of them dominated by the exposed human organs and dripping blood that apparently obsessed her in the final surgery-filled years of her life.

Frida and Diego collected pre-Columbian art, so many of the rooms contain jewelry and terra-cotta figurines from Teotihuacán and Tlatelolco. She even went to the extreme of having a mockup of a temple built in the garden where she could exhibit her numerous pots and statues. On the back side of the temple are several skulls from Chichén Itzá.

To learn more about the lives of this remarkable couple, I can recommend Bertram D. Wolfe's *Diego Rivera: His Life and Times* and Hayden Herrara's *Frida: A Biography of Frida Kahlo.* (See also "Famous Capitalinos" in Chapter 1 and the walking tour of Coyoacán in Chapter 7 for more on Diego and Frida.)

Admission: $4; no cameras allowed.

Open: Tues–Sun 10am–6pm. **Metro:** Coyoacán or Viveros stations; the museum is 10 blocks away.

★ **Museo Leon Trotsky,** Churubusco 410. ☎ 554-4482.

That Leon Trotsky, leading intellect of Soviet Communism, wound up in Mexico City is another of those curious quirks of Mexican history.

During Lenin's last days, when he was confined to bed, Stalin and Trotsky fought a silent battle for leadership of the Communist Party in the Soviet Union. Trotsky stuck to ideology, while Stalin took control of the party mechanism. Stalin won, and Trotsky was exiled, to continue his ideological struggle elsewhere. Invited by Diego Rivera, he settled here on the outskirts of Mexico City (this area was mostly fields then) to continue his work and his writing on political topics and communist ideology. His ideas clashed with those of Stalin in many respects, and Stalin, wanting no opposition or dissension in world communist ranks, set out to have Trotsky assassinated. A first attempt failed but it served to give warning to Trotsky and his household, and from then on the house became a veritable fortress, with riflemen's watchtowers on the corners of the walls, steel doors (Trotsky's bedroom was entered only by thick steel doors), and round-the-clock guards, several of whom were Americans who sympathized with Trotsky's philosophies. Finally a man thought to have been paid, cajoled, or blackmailed by Stalin directly or indirectly was able to get himself admitted to the house by posing as a friend of Trotsky's and of his political views. On August 20, 1940, he put a mountaineer's axe into the philosopher's head. He was, of course, caught, but Trotsky died of his wounds shortly thereafter.

Not long after Trotsky arrived, he and Diego Rivera had a falling out. When Trotsky was murdered both Rivera and Kahlo were suspects in the case for a short while.

The museum is divided into two parts. In the first section you pass through displays of newspaper clippings chronicling the life of Trotsky and his wife in Mexico and the assassination. Then you pass into the home, which is much more meager in its furnishings than you might expect for such a famous person—but not for a true communist, as Trotsky was.

If you saw the film *The Death of Trotsky* with Richard Burton you already have a good idea of what the house looks like, for although the movie was not made here the set was a very good replica of the house and gardens. You can visit Trotsky's wife Natalia's study, the communal dining room, Trotsky's study (with worksheets, newspaper clippings, books, and cylindrical wax dictating records still spread around), and his fortresslike bedroom. Closets still hold their personal clothing. Some of the walls still have the bullet holes left during the first attempt on his life. Trotsky's tomb, designed by Juan O'Gorman, is in the garden of the house. The house is between Gomez Farías and Morelos. If you walk on Viena, you'll recognize the house by the brick watchtowers on top of the high stone walls.

Admission: $4.

Open: Tues–Sun 10am–5pm.

Museo Nacional de Culturas Populares (National Museum of Popular Culture), Hidalgo 289, ☎ 554-3800 or 554-8882.

Through photographs and paintings, the museum displays contemporary Mexican life within the context of communities throughout the country. Because of the changing exhibits, each time you go will be a different experience. Often there's a performance or some other significant activity which complements the display. Call the museum or consult the English-Language newspaper, *The News,* for what's current.

Admission: Free.

Open: Tues–Sat 10am–5pm.

Museo Nacional de las Intervenciones (National Museum of Interventions), 20 de Agosto y General Anaya.
☎ 604-0699.

Technically this museum is in Churubusco, the neighboring suburb of Coyoacán, but it's only a few blocks from the Trotsky Museum. If your country had been invaded as many times as Mexico has, there would probably be a museum about it too. Housed in a beautiful old convent, the well-done displays chronicle each intervention, including the French invasions in 1838 and 1862, the War with the United States between 1846 and 1848 and the U.S. invasions of 1914 and 1916. This convent was the site of a battle between Americans and Mexicans on August 20, 1847. Visitors from France or the States, rather than being in for some America- or France-bashing, discover just the facts—and very well displayed. The building itself was the site of a battle between Mexican General Anaya with his troops and U.S. deserters on one side, and U.S. General Winfield Scott and his troops on the other (for more on the U.S. deserters, see stop 3, "Plaza San Jacinto," of the walking tour of San Angel in Chapter 7).

Admission: $4.

Open: Tues–Sun 9am–6pm.

CIUDAD UNIVERSITARIA (UNIVERSITY CITY)

This is one of the world's most flamboyant college campuses and, indeed, of one of the world's most flamboyant architectural sites. It's located on Avenida Insurgentes, about 11 miles south of the Alameda Central.

University City (it houses Mexico's National Autonomous University) was planned to be the last and grandest achievement of the regime of former president Miguel Aleman. The original university is said to date back to 1551, which would make it one of the oldest universities in the western hemisphere.

University City is an astonishing place and well worth seeing for its gigantic and brilliantly colored mosaics and murals. The most outstanding of these, by Juan O'Gorman, covers all four sides and 10 complete stories of the library building. Fittingly, the mosaic wall depicts the history of Mexican culture and covers a space in which $2^1/2$ million books can be stored. The two lower stories are glass-enclosed and are used as the library's reading rooms.

The administration building, closest to the road, is mostly travertine marble but also has an immense outer mural. This was executed by David Alfaro Siqueiros and depicts Mexican students returning the fruits of their labors to the nation. Diego Rivera contributed the sculpture-painting, adorning the world's largest stadium (capacity: 102,000) across the highway.

Wander at random around the campus, which accommodates 300,000 students. There is a cafeteria on the ground floor of the humanities building and this, especially in summer, is well patronized by American students attending classes. All the university cafeterias are open to the public, and charge very reasonable prices.

Upstairs in the humanities building, you will find various notice boards. They merit a few moments' study, as their signs sometimes offer low-priced excursions or rides back to the States on a cost-sharing basis.

South of the university's main campus, but north of the pyramid of Cuicuilco (see below) and east of Avenida Insurgentes Sur, is the Centro Cultural Universitario, a large arts-and-performance complex with several important venues.

Metro: The university has its own Metro station ("Universidad"), but it's more than a mile from the library, so you should seek out the "Copilco" station. **Bus:** Look for a colectivo or bus, with "Ciudad Universitaria," or simply "C.U.," in the window.

CUICUILCO RUINS

South of the university and its Centro Cultural, across the Periférico, almost where the Periférico and Insurgentes Sur (Highway 95) meet, this circular pyramid represents some of the earliest civilization in the Valley of Mexico. It predates Teotihuacán. Built in the Preclassic Period, around 1800 B.C., it was completely covered by a volcanic eruption (in A.D. 300), surviving only because it was protected by a strong outer wall.

Admission: $4.50.

Open: Daily 9am–5pm. **Metro:** Take the Metro as far as "Universidad," then a bus on Insurgentes. Get off after crossing the Periférico, then walk east.

THE PEDREGAL

Near the Ciudad Universitaria is Mexico's most luxurious housing development, the **Jardines del Pedregal de San Angel.** The word *pedregal* means lava, and that's precisely what makes up this enormous area. It stretches well beyond the university. In the Jardines del Pedregal, the only restriction placed upon homeowners is that they have enough money to buy at least 2,000 square meters of land and hire an architect to design their home. The result is that all the houses are exceptionally lavish, with swimming pools scooped out of the rock, split levels with indoor gardens, solid glass walls, and in one case, an all-glass sunroom on a narrow stilt above the house— like an airport's observation tower.

The pedregal, or lava, all came from the now-extinct volcano **Xitle,** whose eruption covered the Cuicuilco pyramid. Only in recent times has the pedregal been regarded as anything but a nuisance; at one time many of its caves hid bandits. Today all kinds of odd plants and shrubs grow from its nooks and crevices, and if you are interested in botany, you'll want to take a good look around. The main street is the north-south Avenida Paseo del Pedregal.

XOCHIMILCO

The Canals

Xochimilco (pronounced "so-chee-meel-co"), about 15 miles south of the historic center, is a survivor from the civilization of the Aztecs. Xochimilco means "flower cultivators." *Chinampas* (gardens/ cultivated fields) were built on a lake by filling them with fertile lake bottom mud and anchoring them in a shallow part of the lake, first with poles and then with tall, vertical *ahuejote* trees around the edges. The lake eventually filled in with chinampas and, contrary to popular thought, they don't float. They are narrow, rectangular-shaped islands, flanked on all sides by canals. In fact there are at least 50 miles of canals in Xochimilco.

If you've been to Xochimilco before and return now, you'll see a big difference. The long-announced revival and cleaning up of Xochimilco has finally happened. The rescue of the area has been effected by tending to four staples of Xochimilco—water, agriculture, archeology, and historic patrimony. There are two main parts to Xochimilco: the tourism-oriented area, in the historic center of town; and the ecology-oriented Parque Natural Xochimilco. The former is where you'll find the colorful boats that take loads of tourists through a portion of the canals. Lively music is a staple, some of it provided by mariachi and trio musicians for hire who board the boats. The area is flanked by historic buildings, restaurants, souvenir stands, curio sellers, and boat vendors who pester you to take one boat over another. The other section, north of the center of town, also has some colorful boats; these take tourists through the canals to see farming of the chinampas and the abundant bird life. Food and drink, however, are not allowed on boats in this section, though there are food, drink, and curio vendors where you board the boats. The chinampas have been used agriculturally for more than 500 years, and after almost 30 years of neglect are being reclaimed and put to use again as farmland. Descendents of the families that worked them in the past can be seen planting the fertile rectangular-shaped fields with flowers, broccoli, corn, cabbage, squash, and other vegetables. Among the more than 170 species of birds found here is the rare Martín pescador. A water treatment plant cleans the water in the canals and a man-made lake has been created to funnel fresh water into them and is stocked with carp for fishing. Fronting the lake is a huge modern visitor's center with a restaurant, book and gift shop, boat rentals (for the lake), and picnicking area. Beside it a botanical garden grows species of plants native to different areas around the city—Tlalpan, Texcoco, the Pedregal, Mixquic, and Xochimilco. The ecologically oriented section is calmly pastoral compared to the lively atmosphere of the more tourist-oriented area. Though the two are connected by canal, boats from one aren't allowed to go to the other.

On Sunday, Xochimilco (especially the tourist-oriented section) is jammed with foreign tourists and Mexican families with babies and picnic hampers; on weekdays, it's nearly deserted.

When you get to the town of Xochimilco, you'll find a busy market in operation, specializing in rugs, ethnic clothing, and brightly decorated pottery. As you enter Xochimilco proper you will see many places to board boats. Should you miss them, however, turn along Madero and follow signs that say "Los Embarcaderos" (the piers). If you can resist the inevitable curio salesmen and shills, you will eventually arrive at the docks.

Admission to Xochimilco's gardens is free; boat rides cost $17 (boats can be shared by up to 10 people, reducing cost to roughly $1.75 per person). The gardens are open daily dawn to dusk. To get here, take the Metro to the "Tasqueña" stop, then the *tren ligero* (light train) which stops at the outskirts of Xochimilco. From there take a taxi to the main plaza of Xochimilco. Buses run all the way across the city from north to south to end up at Xochimilco, but they take longer than the Metro. Of the buses coming from the center, the most convenient are "La Villa-Xochimilco," which you catch going south on Correo Mayor and Pino Suárez near the Zócalo; or near Chapultepec on Avenida Vasconcelos, Avenida Nuevo Leon, and Avenida Division del Norte.

The Village of Xochimilco

Xochimilco (pop. 300,000), a colonial-era gem with its bricked streets and light traffic, seems like a small town despite its sizeable population. Leave the hubbub of the colorful canals behind and take an hour or so to stroll around the town. Restaurants are at the edge of the canal and shopping area, and historically significant churches are within easy walking distance of the main square.

Among these, facing the main square (at the corner of Pino and Hidalgo), is the 16th-century **Convent of San Bernardino de Siena,** with its flower petals carved in stone—a signature of the Indians who did most of the work—and 16th-century retable (a church altar fixture), one of the country's three such retables miraculously preserved for more than 400 years. (Another is at Huejotzingo, near Puebla; see Chapter 10 for details.) The last Indian governor of Xochimilco, Apoxquiyohuatzin, is buried here. Inside and to the right, the skull over the font is from a pre-Hispanic skull rack signifying an Indian/Christian mixture of the concept of life and death. Eight lateral retables date from the 16th to the 18th centuries. The fabulous gold gilted main altar, also from the 16th century, is like an open book of sculpture and religious paintings. A profusion of cherubim decorate columns and borders. Some of the altar paintings are attributed to Baltasar Echave Orio the Elder. Over the altar, above the figure of Christ, is San Bernardino, with the *caciques* (local authorities) dressed in clothing with Indian elements and without shoes. Five blocks away at the corner of Sabino and J. O. de Dominguez is the **Iglesia de San Juan Tlaltentli.** Quetzalcoatl is symbolized by a snail and Aztec face on the walls. The enormous ahuehuete tree across the street is hundreds of years old. From February through October the tree is bristling with nesting cranes.

A mile and a half south of the central plaza at the crossroads of Avenida Tenochtitlán and Calle La Planta in the town of Santa Cruz Acalpixcan is the **Archeological Museum of Xochimilco.** The building dates from 1904 when it was the pump house for the springs. It houses artifacts from the area, many of them found when residents built their homes—10,000-year-old mammoth bones, and figures dating from the Teotihuacán period—figures of Tlaloc (god of water and life); Ehecatl (god of the wind); Xipe Totec (god of renewal and of plants); and Huehueteotl (god of fire); polychromed pottery; carved abalone; and tombs showing funerary practices of 23 Teotihuacán inhabitants. One of the most unique pieces is a clay figure of a child holding a bouquet of flowers. The museum (☎ **675-0168** or **675-0426**), is open Tuesday through Sunday from 10am to 5pm and admission is free.

Across the road, but not within walking distance, is the **archeological zone/Centro Ceremonial Azteca Cualama,** consisting of a series of petroglyphs meandering up a rocky hill. Steps go up the incline. On top is a large clearing that is still used for ceremonial dancing on March 21, for Fiesta de la Primavera Tlacaxipeualiztli, and on October 12, at noon, for the Fiesta del Pueblo Altepeilhuitl. There's no admission.

On the same road about two miles away is the village of Santiago Tulyehualco and the **amaranth factory/Tehutl-Amaranto** (☎ **842-0752** and **842-2778**). Amaranth was the sacred crop of the Aztecs, a plant yielding tiny whitish lysine-heavy round seeds that can be toasted or ground, and nutritious leaves that look like spinach. (Lysine is an essential amino acid that's sometimes absent in plant protein). Because the Aztecs used amaranth in their rituals, the

Xochimilco

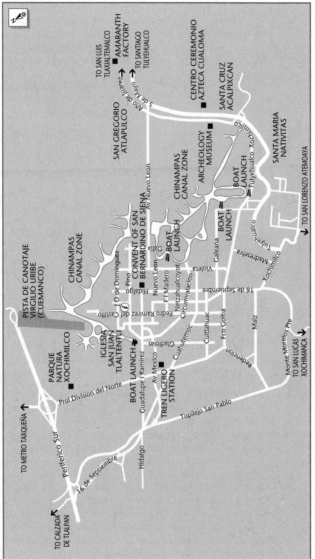

Spaniards forbade its cultivation, but as we see they weren't entirely successful. As you enter the front door, amaranth plants are on the left. Ask permission to see the process in back, where seeds are separated, grated, toasted, and packaged. To the right of the entrance is a store selling amaranth products, which include amaranth mixed with powdered chocolate for a hot drink, flour, cereal, pasta for soup, cookies, and granola. During the Days of the Dead amaranth skulls are sold at street markets nationwide. Amaranth is grown commercially in Puebla and Morelos states and locally on family plots. Green and black olives and olive oil are also sold, made from trees grown in the area. Each February the village hosts an **Olive and Amaranth fair.** The factory is open daily from 7am to 8pm.

Xochimilco celebrates with at least 422 festivals annually, the most famous of which is for the **Niñopa,** a figure of the Christ child that since 1875 is believed to possess miraculous powers. The figure is venerated on January 6 (Three Kings Day), February 2 (changing of the Niñopa's custodian), December 16–24 (posadas for the Niñopa), and April 30 (Day of the Child). Caring for the Niñopa is a coveted privilege that lasts a year, and the schedule of approved caretakers is filled through the year 2031.

Other significant festivals and commemorative occasions include the Olive and Alegria Fair (varying date, January 30–February 14) in Santaigo Tulyehualco. During the Days of the Dead (November 1–2), families decorate graves and perform cemetary vigils. The Day of Guadalupe (December 12) is especially celebrated in the barrio (neighborhood) of La Guadalupita Xochitenco. The *Feria de la Flor Más Bella del Ejido* (varying date, March 28 through April 4) is a flower fair when the most beautiful girl with Indian features and costume is selected. For more information and exact dates, contact the Xochimilco Tourist Office (Subdirección de Turismo), Pino No. 36 (☎ **676-0810,** fax 676-0879), two blocks from the main square. It's open Monday through Saturday from 9am to 7pm.

3 Organized Tours

Generally speaking, I can't recommend any commercial tours since so many readers have complained that these tours slight sightseeing in favor of shopping (where tour guides get a commission on your purchases), or the tour is rushed, or the factual information is more like a fairy tale. If you meet someone who has recently taken a guided tour and liked it, go with the same company.

The most frequently offered tours are a four-hour city tour that includes such sites as the Catedral Metropolitana, the Palacio Nacional, and Chapultepec Park and Castle; a four- to six-hour tour of the Basílica of Guadalupe and the nearby pyramids in the Teotihuacán archeological zone; and the Sunday tour that begins with the Ballet Folklorico, moves on to the floating gardens of Xochimilco, and may or may not incorporate lunch and the afternoon bullfights. Almost as popular are the one-day and overnight tours to Puebla and Tlaxcala, and to Cuernavaca, Taxco, and Acapulco. There are also several popular night-club tours which include the *mariachis* in Garibaldi Square.

Paseo Por El Centro (☎ **709-1899** or **709-5589**), is the city-operated open-window, rubber-wheeled trolly that takes visitors on an hour-long tour of the Centro Historico. The tour starts and ends on the plaza opposite the Museo de la Ciudad at the corner of

Pino Suárez and El Salvador. Unfortunately, because of traffic and time, the tour only superficially covers a few high spots—the Museo de la Ciudad, Zócalo, Colegio San Idelfonso, Plaza Santo Domingo, Plaza de la Santa Veracruz, the Post Office, Palacio de Bellas Artes, and Palacio de Iturbide—though it passes many more historic buildings. However, if you're unfamiliar with the city, it's a good way to orient yourself for a return to some of the buildings on your own. The cost of $5 per person seems a bit steep, considering the tour's limits and lack of depth. Tours in Spanish leave Tuesday through Sunday every half hour from 10am to 5pm. Tours in English are the same days at 11am, and in French at 1pm.

An alternative to an organized tour would be to hire the services of a **licensed, English speaking guide.** Many of these official tour guides drive taxis (the non-metered, deluxe type) that are parked in front of better hotels. The price of a day of touring will depend on the itinerary you organize, but the tour will be to your specifications and it's generally worth the price. Size up the level of the guide's English first and ask to see his official Secretary of Tourism license with his photo on it. After you've outlined where you'd like to go, negotiate the price and settle on it in advance.

I can highly recommend the services of my friend for many years, **Guillermo Arias** (☎ 5/397-2838), a licensed English speaking guide who can take you anywhere inside or outside the city. Write him at Acacias 82, Viveros de la Loma, 54080 Estado de México. That address is just north of the city center, but he can meet you anywhere. Besides touring, he and his brother Julian are also adept at getting business executives to appointments around the city, and can confirm appointments and flights.

A couple of non-commercial **cultural tours** may be worth taking if your Spanish is good, since most tours don't offer English speaking guides. Among these are free guided tours sponsored by the **Mexico City Historical Center,** Donceles and República de Chile (☎ **510-2541** or **518-1100** ext. 1499), which is housed in the 18th-century home of Don Manuel de Heras y Soto, one of the notables who signed Mexico's Act of National Independence in 1821. Groups meet each Sunday at 11am at a central gathering place for that day's tour, which varies from Sunday to Sunday. Tours are free and might explore a historic street in the downtown area, cafes and theaters, cemeteries, or colonial churches of Xochimilco, etc. Most tours, which last about two hours, are in Spanish, and as many as 300 people may be divided among 10 guides. However, visitors with other language requirements may inquire in advance for a guide who speaks their language.

It's almost impossible to reach the center by phone (it's always busy). So, to obtain a list of upcoming tours and group departure locations, you'll have to visit the office. Office hours are Monday through Friday 9am to 3pm and 4 to 9pm. The office is in the far back of the building on the right and up a spiral staircase.

Some of the most interesting and unusual tours are **Paseos Culturales del INAH,** organized and led by specialists from the

Instituto Nacional de Antropologiá y Historia (INAH), Frontera 53, Tizapán, San Angel 01100, México, D.F. (☎ 5/550-9676 or 550-8631; fax 5/550-3503). Tours are in Spanish and include day trips in and around the city and longer trips that last several days to elsewhere in the country. INAH produces a small catalog of tour descriptions covering tours February through June and July through January. A recent catalogue described day trips to a pulque hacienda in Tembleque, State of Mexico, the nearby pyramid sites of Tenayuca and Santa Cecilia, the convents of Mexico City, and restoration projects in the city. Longer trips that are still fairly close to the city included the missions of Fray Junipero Serra in the Sierra Gorda area of Querétaro, baroque architecture of Tlaxcala, the colonial-era mining area of Pachuca, Real del Monte and Huasca in the state of Hidalgo, and colonial architecture in Huejotzingo and Calpan. Other trips go farther afield into Oaxaca, Veracruz, Tabasco, Michoacán, and Guerrero states. Each is led by a specialist such as a curator, conservationist, architect, anthropologist, ethnohistorian etc. Unless otherwise notified, tours meet at Cordoba 45, Col. Roma. Prices start at $12 for city trips and go up depending on the logistics.

4 Spectator Sports

Jai Alai

Pronounced "hi-lie," this game is played at the Fronton de Mexico, Plaza de la República (☎ 546-5369 or 546-3240). Jai alai must be the fastest game in the world, and is exciting to watch even without prior knowledge of how it is played. It doesn't much matter when you arrive, as there are several games on each night's schedule. As you walk into the fronton, the ticket office is to your left: There you pay and pick up a program, then take a seat.

Jai alai players wear small baskets on their right arms, with which they catch and sling at fantastic speeds a hard but springy ball against the wall to the right of where you're sitting. In the best game, four players, two with blue armbands and two with red ones, are competing with each other in a fashion similar to tennis, but even more similar to squash. The member of one team hurls the ball against the wall, and the other team has to return it. The whole thing is done at an incredible speed and how they manage to see, much less catch, a ball traveling at 100 miles per hour—or faster—is marvelous.

The most fun is in the betting; you'd be amazed at how much more exciting a game seems when you have money riding on the result. Wait until the program announces a game of 30 points (partido a treinta tantos) and watch the bookies. These colorful gentlemen, wearing burgundy vests, carry little pads of betting slips edged in red (rojo) or blue (azul), and when the game begins, they'll be offering only a slight edge on one team or another. Bets are placed inside of slashed tennis balls and thrown to bookies during the game. When the scoring starts, however, the odds will change. If you're as good a mathematician as most jai alai aficionados, you'll be able to bet on both sides at different points of the game—and still finish ahead. **Note:** This has become a game for elite spectators: For men a coat and tie is required. Women must be similarly elegant. Admission is $18.

The box office opens at 6:30pm and games are held year-round on Tuesday through Sunday at 5pm. To get to the Jai alai fronton, head for the northeast corner of the Plaza de la República (at the corner of Calle Ramos Arizpe, a few blocks along Juárez west of Reforma). Any bus going west along Juárez will take you to the Juárez-Reforma intersection, and it's a short walk from there. Or you can take the Metro to the "Revolución" station, and walk three blocks down Arriaga (south) to the plaza.

Bullfights

This spectator sport, long identified with Mexico, can be experienced at the Plaza de Torros Monumental, 3 miles south of the city center. It's among the largest bullrings in the world. It seats 64,000 people and on Sunday during the professional season (usually December through April) most seats are taken. On other Sundays through the year the arena is given over to the beginners or *novilleros;* most of them are as bad as the beginners in any other sport. Six fights make up a *corrida,* which begins precisely at 4pm and is one of the few things in Mexico that always begins on time.

When you arrive you'll see dozens of men and women selling nuts, hats, and all kinds of whatnots. Look for a woman or *muchacha* selling chewing gum and waving small "programs." If you buy the chewing gum, she'll give you (free) the one-page sheet that lists the names of the day's toreros. Unless you want to pay more, take your place in the line at one of the windows marked "Sol General." The seat will be in the sun and it will be high up. But the sun isn't too strong (it sets quickly, anyway), and you won't see many other tourists that way. Seats in *la sombra* (shade) are more expensive, of course. Tickets cost between $3 and $26. Fights start at 4pm, but get there well in advance for a good seat.

Usually, there are six separate bulls to be killed (two by each matador) in a corrida, but I'd suggest that you leave just before the last bull—to avoid the crowds. Outside, around two sides of the bullring is a scene of frantic activity. Hundreds of tiny stalls have masses of food frying, cold beer stacked high, and radios blaring with a commentary on the action inside the ring.

The bullring is 3 miles south of town on Insurgentes. Any big hotel or tour agency will be happy to book you onto a tour with transportation to the ring. To get there on your own, however, you can take the Metro to the "San Antonio" station on Línea 7. You can also take a colectivo. The number of colectivos that normally roam Insurgentes is supplemented by Sunday afternoon taxis headed for the plaza, and they'll often pick up extra passengers going their way. Or you can catch the buses marked "Plaza Mexico" that travel down Insurgentes on Sunday afternoon.

Horse Racing

Horse races take place at the Hipodromo de las Americas, (☎ 557-4100), Mexico City's racetrack. It's as extraordinarily beautiful as many of the city's other popular spots. Approached by way of a tree-lined boulevard and containing a small lake on which an occasional swan or heron basks, the stadium has stands built on a hillside for a good view of the track.

You may enter through a *specia* (free) tourist gate, paying only the applicable tax. The normal price of admission is through purchase of a program. Without a program, you won't have much idea what's going on. Two or more people may enter on one program, but each must pay the program tax.

Once past the admissions gate, head for the stands and grab a seat. If you're willing to spend the extra loot, you can climb one level higher and sit at a table where the view is excellent and a minimum amount must be consumed in either food or drink.

You can bet either to win (*primera*), to place (*segunda*), or to show (*tercera*). All windows have signs in both English and Spanish. On certain races, marked on the program with bold letters, you can win a substantial sum by picking the horses that will come in first and second and placing a bet on your selections. In some races, there is an alternative way of betting called the quiniela. This operates on a similar principle, except that your choices for first and second can come in second and first.

The track operates on Tuesday (in winter only), and Thursday at 3pm, Friday, Saturday, and Sunday at 2:30pm for 11 months of the year; it is closed only for part of September and October.

To get there take a colectivo marked "Hipodromo" along Reforma, which takes you through Chapultepec to the Anillo Periférico (also called Avenida Manuel Avila Camacho). The track is just off this main entry, near the intersection with Calzada Legaria. You can also take the Metro to "Toreo Quatro Caminos" (Línea 2); then then walk up out of the Metro station, cross over to the bus yard, which is immediately adjacent. Go to traffic island 2, the center stall, and look for buses marked "Hipodromo." Get off when you see the ring and a sign. It's a short walk from there.

Charros

Charros, Mexican-style rodeo, is held at Chapultepec park and at the Fiesta de Charros, 500 Constituyentes. This is a Sunday event in both places. The rodeos start around noon with a grand promenade of riders, display of the flag and singing of the Mexican National Anthem. Colorful and lively, these games of horsemanship are participated in by both men and women, each richly dressed in charro costumes. Often several *charro* groups will be competing and the crowds go wild, cheering and throwing their hats in the air. Usually there's at least one band and often more, which adds to the festive thrill. Admission is usually free.

Strolling Around Mexico City

You CAN EXPLORE THIS CITY BY TOUR BUS, BUT THE BEST WAY IS ON FOOT. The everyday sights and sounds of daily life in the capital may be just as interesting as any specific tourist attractions. As you walk about the area around the Zócalo you'll have a chance to examine at leisure the remarkable architectural details that fill the city. The walking tours included here cover the top attractions of Mexico City in four easily walkable sections of the city, and one fabulous museum as well. Some of the tours take only a few hours' time, but the major tours can be divided up: You may wish to walk part of a tour one day, and save the rest for another time—depending of course, on how much time you want to spend at the various attractions. **Special Note:** Because of the ongoing renovation of historic buildings around the Zócalo and Alameda, some buildings mentioned on those tours may be closed temporarily.

Walking Tour 1
The Zócalo/Centro Historico

Start   Zócalo.

Finish   Burial vault of Hernán Cortés at the Hospital de Jesús Nazareño.

Time   1 or 2 days, depending on the length of time you spend at each stop.

Best time   Sunday, when museums are free and when vehicular traffic is relatively scarce, or the week before or after September 15 (Mexican Independence Day), or around Christmas when the Zócalo and surrounding streets are festooned in ribbons and lights.

Worst time   Monday, when the museums are closed.

1.   **The Zócalo.** Every Spanish colonial city in North America was laid out according to a textbook plan, with a plaza at the center surrounded by a church, government buildings, and military headquarters. As capital of New Spain, Mexico City's Zócalo is one of the grandest, and is graced on all sides by stately 17th- and 18th-century buildings. The look of these buildings has changed dramatically over the centuries, resulting in the architecture of today.

   Zócalo actually means "pedestal," or "plinth." A grand monument to Mexico's independence was planned and the pedestal was actually built, but the project was never completed. Nevertheless, the pedestal became a landmark for visitors, and soon everyone was calling the square after "the Zócalo," even though the zócalo itself was later removed. Because of this one, central plazas throughout Mexico are often dubbed "zocalo." This one is officially named Plaza de la Constitución. It covers almost 10 acres and is bounded on the north by 5 de Mayo, Pino Suárez on the east, 16

Walking Tour—The Zócalo

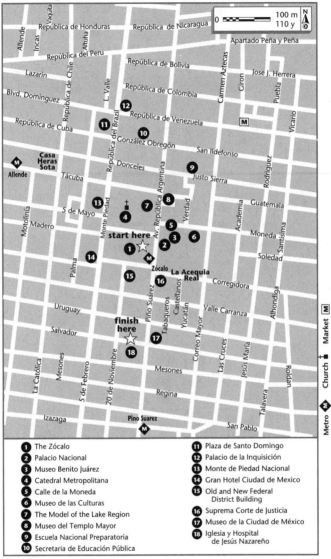

1. The Zócalo
2. Palacio Nacional
3. Museo Benito Juárez
4. Catedral Metropolitana
5. Calle de la Moneda
6. Museo de las Culturas
7. The Model of the Lake Region
8. Museo del Templo Mayor
9. Escuela Nacional Preparatoria
10. Secretaría de Educación Pública
11. Plaza de Santo Domingo
12. Palacio de la Inquisición
13. Monte de Piedad Nacional
14. Gran Hotel Ciudad de Mexico
15. Old and New Federal District Building
16. Suprema Corte de Justicia
17. Museo de la Ciudad de México
18. Iglesia y Hospital de Jesús Nazareño

de Septiembre on the south, and Monte de Piedad on the west. Unfortunately for our walk through the city's past, many of the streets entering the Zócalo have been widened and straightened (to link it with the Alameda) by destroying historic and architecturally significant and striking colonial-era buildings.

The Zócalo proper has been the central marketplace, a transportation center for horse-drawn buggies, electric trolleys, and a gorgeous, tree-filled, manicured park. Today it's often the center of political protests, mounted by groups as disparate as striking taxi drivers and dissatisfied farmers from Veracruz and Puebla. And it's the center of celebration, the biggest of which is Independence Day, when the whole plaza is jammed with people awaiting the traditional pronouncement given by the president of Mexico from the balcony above the center door.

Occupying the entire east side of the Zócalo is the majestic, red tezontle stone:

2. Palacio Nacional, begun in 1692 on the site of Moctezuma's "new" palace, which became the site of Hernán Cortés's home and the residence of colonial viceroys. It has changed much in 300 years, taking on its present form in the late 1920s when the top floor was added. The complex of countless rooms and wide stone stairways, and numerous courtyards adorned with carved brass balconies, is also where the president of Mexico works. But to most visitors it's better known for the fabulous **Diego Rivera murals** on the second floor, which depict the history of Mexico. Just 30 minutes here with an English-speaking guide will provide good background for understanding Mexico's history. Costs are negotiable with each guide, but in general start around $12.

Enter by the central door. Over it hangs the church bell rung by Padre Miguel Hidalgo to summon his parishioners from the town of Dolores Hidalgo for his famous *Grito* in 1810—his words became the catalyst to Mexico's independence from Spain. Each September 15, Independence Day in Mexico, the president of Mexico steps out onto the balcony above the palacio's door to shout out "Mexicanos, Viva México!" an echo of Hidalgo's cry before the thousands that await in the Zócalo.

Take the stairs to the Rivera murals, which were painted over a 25-year period. (See also the listing for Rivera's murals in "The Top Attractions" in Chapter 6.)

Inside the corridors of the Palacio Nacional at the northern end is the comparatively little-known:

3. Museo Benito Juárez (☎ 522-5646). To the north inside the palace, past the statue of Benito Juárez then up the stairs to the left, is the Juárez Museum and the well-preserved apartments where the former president of Mexico died. It's usually bustling with schoolchildren studying the handwritten letters and papers kept in glass cases around the room. Other cases hold tablecloths, silverware, medals, shirts, watches, a briefcase, and symbolic keys to the city—all personal effects of the much-beloved former president. There's a beautiful library here and anyone may study the books.

The last room at the rear is Juárez's bedroom, which gives one the eerie feeling that the former president might walk in at any moment; his dressing gown is laid out on the four-poster bed, and a chamber pot peeks from under the bed. The museum is supposedly open Monday through Friday 9am to 7pm, but hours may be more erratic than that. Admission is free.

Before heading north, you may want to take a look at *La Acequia Real* (the Royal Canal) on the south side of the building at the corner of Corregidora. It was the most important canal in colonial times, carrying commerce from the southern outskirts of the city. A portion of it was recently restored.

From the Palacio Nacional, go to the northern edge of the Zócalo and the:

4. Catedral Metropolitana (Metropolitan Cathedral). This religious sanctuary in the heart of the city has a steady stream of visitors, most staying only long enough to pray before a revered saint or special chapel. With elaborate and delicate wood, stone, and metal ornamentation, it's something of a miracle that so much has survived the many protests that get played out on the Zócalo "stage." The scaffolding you see inside and out are part of ongoing stabilization—the cathedral is slowly sinking into the soft subsoil. (For more on the cathedral, see listing in Chapter 7.)

In the same predicament is the much older looking church next to the cathedral, El Sagrario, another tour de force of Mexican baroque architecture built in the mid-18th century.

Outside, to the west of the cathedral, is a gathering place for carpenters, plasterers, plumbers, painters, and electricians who have no shops. Each craftsperson displays the tools of his trade, sometimes with pictures of his work.

From the Cathedral Metropolitano go out the front door, turn left towards the Palacio Nacional, and continue straight ahead across Seminario to the pedestrians-only street left of the Palacio Nacional, the:

5. Calle de la Moneda (Street of the Treasury or Mint). According to the city historian Guillermo Tovar de Teresa, this is probably the best preserved 16th-century street in the city. It's lined with aged buildings constructed of *tezontle,* the local volcanic rock. On the left, at the corner of Calle Verdad, is the Edificio Arzobispal, the former archbishop's palace. True to Spanish tradition, the chief ecclesiastical official's power base was built smack on top of the Aztec's Temple of Tezcatlipoca, the multifaceted god who gave life and governed a host of lesser gods. It was on this site that Juan Diego revealed for the first time to the archbishop the cloak with the figure of the Virgin of Guadalupe. The building from which the street takes its name is at No. 13, on the right about halfway down, and it houses the:

6. **Museo de las Culturas,** Moneda 13. Here, in a portion of the Palacio Nacional which dates from the 16th century, are art and artifacts showing the development of humankind throughout the world. See the listing in Chapter 6 under "More Attractions" for details.

Refueling Stop

If you are ready for a break, backtrack across the Zócalo to the **Hotel Majestic** rooftop restaurant. From the 7th floor indoor/outdoor rooftop, there's a wonderful view of the Zócalo. On a clear day you can even see the Ixta and Popo volcanoes. It's great to begin your Zócalo tour here, to stop here midday, or to pay a late visit to the bar, which adjoins the restaurant (there's a live singer nightly). Hours are 7:30am to 10:30pm; any time of day is good for sitting outside to enjoy the Zócalo or inside to experience the bustle of patrons and other tourists. Or for a quick respite, try **Los Metates,** next to the entrance of the Hotel Majestic. It's small, but service is fast.

Back across the Zócalo to the corner of Moneda, with the cathedral on your left, you'll notice pigeons perched at ground level on:

7. **The Model of the Lake Region.** This model shows what the area around today's Zócalo might have looked like when Cortés entered the city for the first time. The two cities of Tenochtitlán (the area where you are standing) and Tlatelolco (roughly the area around the Plaza de las Tres Culturas—see below) were surrounded by the waters of Lake Texcoco and linked by raised causeways and canals. The model's fountain fills the canal-like "streets" with water just as they did in the heyday of the Aztec capital.

Continuing on Seminario a half block on the right are remnants of pre-Conquest Mexico at the:

8. **Museo del Templo Mayor** (☎ **542-1717** or **542-0606**). No other museum shows the variety and splendor of the Aztec Empire the way this one does. All

6,000 pieces came from the relatively small plot of excavated ruins just in front of the museum, the **Templo Mayor Archeological Site.** (See also the listing under "The Top Attractions" in Chapter 6.)

Strolling along the walkways built over the site, you pass a water-collection conduit constructed during the presidency of Porfirio Díaz, as well as far earlier constructions. Building dates are on explanatory plaques (in Spanish), which explain the time frames in which construction took place. Shelters cover the ruins to protect traces of original paintwork, carving, and ongoing excavations. Note especially the Tzompantli, or Altar of Skulls, a common Aztec and Mayan ritual sculpture.

To enter the Museo del Templo Mayor, which opened in 1987, take the walkway to a large building at the back portion of the site, which contains the artifacts from on-site excavations.

Inside the door, a model of Tenochtitlán gives a good idea of the scale of the vast city of the Aztecs.

Here's a quick guide to the exhibit rooms. Sala 1, "Antecedentes," has exhibits about the early days of Tenochtitlán. Sala 2, "Guerra y Sacrificio," examines the details of the Aztec ritual practice of war and human sacrifice. Sala 3, "Tributo y Comercio," deals with Aztec government and its alliances and commerce with tributary states. Sala 4, "Huizilopochtli," treats this most important of Aztec gods, a triumphant warrior, the son of Coatlíque, who bore him without losing her virginity. Huizilopochtli, the "hummingbird god," was the one who demanded that human sacrifices be made to sustain him. In Sala 5, "Tlaloc," there are exhibits explaining the role of the Aztec rain god in daily and religious life. Sala 6, "Faunas," deals with the wild and domesticated animals common in the Aztec Empire at the time when the capital flourished. Sala 7, "Religion," explains Aztec religious beliefs, which are amazingly complex and sometimes quite confusing because they are so different from the familiar religions of Europe and the Middle East. Sala 8, "Caida de Tenochtitlán," recounts the fall of the great city and its last emperors, Moctezuma and Cuauhtémoc, to Hernan Cortés and his conquistadores.

When you're finished at the museum, exit and return to the entrance on Seminario opposite the cathedral. The street changes to República de Argentina in front of the archeological site. Continuing north a half block, to the corner of Argentina and Donceles, turn right and a half block on the left is the:

9. **Escuela Nacional Preparatoria,** an 18th-century building of red tezontle stone with murals by three Mexican greats: Rivera, Orozco, and Siqueiros. Today the building is a school, but it's been under restoration for some time.

Continuing north on Argentina, crossing Calle Gonzalez Obregón, turn left and on the right will be the entrance to the:

10. **Secretaría de Educación Pública,** decorated with a great series of over 200 Diego Rivera murals, painted in 1923 and 1924. Other artists did a panel here and there, but it's the Rivera murals that are superb. The building is usually open Monday through Friday from 8am to 3pm. Renovations may be complete by the time you are there.

From the front door of the Secretaría turn right a half block to the corner of República de Brasil and across the street on the right is the:

11. **Plaza de Santo Domingo,** with a wonderful slice of Mexican life. It's a fascinating plaza with arcades on one side, a Dominican church on the other, all dominated by a statue of the *corregidora* (magistrate's wife) of Querétaro, Josefa Ortiz de Domínguez. The plaza is best known for the scribes who compose and type letters for clients unable to do so for themselves. Years ago it was full of professional public writers clacking away on ancient typewriters. A few still ply their trade on ancient electric typewriters. There's also a proliferation of small print shops producing calling cards and invitations of all kinds. Emperor Cuauhtémoc's palace occupied this land and later Dominicans built their monastery there.

Across the street at the corner of Venezuela and Brasil is the:

12. **Palacio de la Inquisición** (Palace of the Inquisition), built in 1732. For more than 200 years (1571–1820) accused Mexican heretics and other religious "criminals" were strangled and/or burned at the stake. For almost a hundred years this was the building where they were held prisoner and their fates were decided. The last accused heretic to be executed was José María Morelos, hero of Mexican independence. Today it houses several rooms devoted to the very interesting **Museum of the History of Mexican Medicine,** with displays of modern and pre-Hispanic medicine. Informational signs are in Spanish only. To the left of the palace as you enter is a small bookstore and historical library of art, medicine, and culture. Outside the bookstore is a small restaurant with light refreshments. The building and museum are open daily from 10am to 6pm.

Refueling Stop

From the front door of the Palacio de la Inquisición, veer right (don't make a hard right around the corner) one block on Dominguez; on the right will be the **Hostería de Santo Domingo** (☎ 510-1434), established in 1860 and reportedly the oldest restaurant in Mexico City. Meals and drinks are a little expensive, but it's lively at mid-day and the service and atmosphere are delightful. Open daily from 9am to 11pm.

From the Hostería de Santo Domingo double back to the corner of Dominguez and Brasil and turn right in the direction of the Zócalo, walking 2¹/₂ blocks. On the right is the:

13. Monte de Piedad Nacional, or national pawn shop (☎ 597-3455), at the corner of Monte de Piedad and 5 de Mayo. Who ever heard of touring a pawn shop? In Mexico City it's done all the time, in what could be described as the world's largest and most elegant Good Will/Morgan Memorial thrift store. Electric power tools, jewelry, antique furniture, heavy machine tools, sofa beds, and a bewildering array of other things from trash to treasure are all on display. Buying is not required, but taking a look is recommended. The building is on the site of Moctezuma's "old" Axayácatl palace—his "new" palace occupied the site of the present Palacio Nacional. This is where the captive Emperor Moctezuma was killed. The site was later occupied by an enormous viceregal palace constructed by Cortés. The present building was built by Pedro Romero de Terreros, the Count of Regla, an 18th-century silver magnate from Pachuca, so that Mexican people might obtain low-interest loans. It's open Monday through Saturday from 10am to 2pm and from 5 to 7pm.

Continue south on Monte Piedad, with the Majestic Hotel on your right and the Zócalo on your left, to the next corner, 16 de Septiembre, and turn right a few steps to the:

14. Gran Hotel Ciudad de Mexico. Originally El Centro Mercantil (department store), built by Frenchman Sebastian Robert and completed in 1899, in 1966 this building was converted to a hotel. The hotel has one of the most splendid interiors of any downtown building. Step inside to see the lavish lobby, topped with a breathtaking stained-glass canopy designed by Jacques Graber in 1908. Gilded open elevators flank the lobby on both sides and live canaries sing away in brass cages.

Backtrack a half block east on 16 de Septiembre toward the Zócalo and across 5 de Febrero (Monte Piedad), and on the right are the:

15. arcades of the 16th-century **Old Federal District Building** and the **New Federal District Building,** which dates from 1935 but looks like the older building. Both are on the south side of the Zócalo. Continuing east across the next street, Pino Suárez, with the Palacio Nacional on the left, on the right is the:

16. **Suprema Corte de Justicia,** built in the mid-1930s. Inside, on the main staircase and its landings, are José Clemente Orozco murals expressing the theme of justice, which he was given the liberty to interpret. Two and a half blocks farther south on Pino Suárez, on the left, at the corner of Repúblic del Salvador is the:

17. **Museo de la Ciudad de México,** which is not only a splendid example of opulent housing in the 18th century but a fine museum chronicling the city's eventful history (see also the listing in Chapter 6 under "More Attractions.")

   At the corner of Suárez and Salvador is the:

18. **Iglesia y Hospital de Jesús Nazareño,** founded by Hernán Cortés soon after the conquest. A stone cenotaph outside marks it as the spot where Cortés and Moctezuma reportedly met for the first time. Cortés died in Spain in 1547 and his remains are in a vault inside the chapel, which is entered by a side door on República del Salvador. Vaults on the opposite wall store the remains of Cortés's relatives. Notice the Orozco mural *The Apocalypse* on the choir ceiling. The chapel is open Monday through Saturday from 7am to 8pm and on Sunday 7am to 1pm and 5pm to 8pm.

Walking Tour 2
Near the Alameda

Start   Torre Latino America (Metro: "Bellas Artes").

Finish   Museo de Artes e Industrías Populares.

Time   1 or 2 days, depending on the time spent at each location.

Best Time   Saturday, when museums and shops are open, and around Christmas and Independence Day (Sept. 15), when the area is festooned in holiday color.

Worst time   Monday, when museums are closed.

Today the tree-filled Alameda Central is a magnet for pedestrians, cotton candy vendors, lovers, organ grinders—everyone in the park enjoying a respite from their day. Long ago, the site of the Alameda was an Aztec marketplace. When the conquistadores took over in the mid-16th century, heretics were burned at the stake there under the Spanish Inquisition. In 1592 the governor of New Spain, Viceroy Luis de Velasco, converted it to a public park.

Walking Tour—Near the Alameda

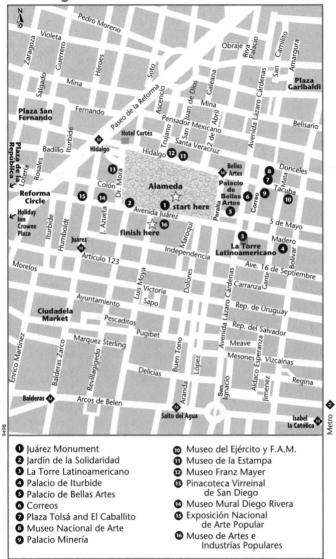

1 Juárez Monument
2 Jardín de la Solidaridad
3 La Torre Latinoamericano
4 Palacio de Iturbide
5 Palacio de Bellas Artes
6 Correos
7 Plaza Tolsá and El Caballito
8 Museo Nacional de Arte
9 Palacio Minería

10 Museo del Ejército y F.A.M.
11 Museo de la Estampa
12 Museo Franz Mayer
13 Pinacoteca Virreinal de San Diego
14 Museo Mural Diego Rivera
15 Exposición Nacional de Arte Popular
16 Museo de Artes e Industrías Populares

As you wander around the Alameda Central, you're bound to notice the:

1. **Juárez Monument,** sometimes called the **Hemiciclo** (hemicycle, half-circle), facing Avenida Juárez.
   Enthroned as the hero he was, Juárez assumes his proper place here in the pantheon of Mexican patriots. Most of

the other statuary in the park was done by European
sculptors (mostly French) in the late 19th and early 20th
centuries.

On the west side of the Alameda, along Avenida
Juárez where the old Hotel Regis once stood, is the:

2. Jardín de la Solidaridad, or Solidarity Garden, built
in 1986 in remembrance of those who died during the
terrible earthquake of 1985.

Opposite the southeastern edge of the Alameda at
the corner of Juárez and Lázaro Cárdenas is:

3. La Torre Latino Americana (or the Latin American
Tower, ☎ **510-2545** or **521-7751**). On the 42nd floor
of this skyscraper soaring above the intersection of Juárez
and Cardenas, you can see the route of your walking
tour from the observation deck, as well as fabulous views
of the whole city. Buy a ticket for the deck (which is
open daily from 9am to 11pm) at the booth as you
approach the elevators—admission is $4.50 for adults,
$3.75 for children. Tokens for the telescope up top are
on sale here too. You then take an elevator to the 37th
floor, cross the hall, and take another elevator to the
42nd floor. An employee will ask for your ticket as you
get off.

The view is magnificent, with mountains surrounding the capital on all sides, but those to the north are the
nearest and Avenida Lázaro Cárdenas seems to head
straight for them. To the north just below is the white
marble Palacio de Bellas Artes; to the west is the green
patch of the Alameda. Further west is the Monumento a
la Revolución, just beyond the intersection of Juárez and
Reforma. You can't see Reforma too well because it's
hidden by the buildings that line it, but the green swath
of Chapultepec Park and its palace on the hilltop are
easy to spot. To the east is the Zócalo, dominated by the
Catedral Metropolitana. To the south is an area densely
packed with homes, factories, and tall apartment
buildings.

From the front door of the tower, turn right to the
corner, right (west) on Madero (the street name changes
from Juárez), and walk a block and a half past the Iglesia
de San Francisco to the magnificent:

4. Palacio de Iturbide, at Madero 17. This ornate stone
palace, with huge hand-carved wooden doors and a
wildly baroque 40-foot-high carved stone archway, was
built in the 1780s for the Marqués de Jaral de Berrio,
but by 1821 belonged to Don Agustín de Iturbide, who
later became the self-proclaimed Agustín I, Emperor of
Mexico (1822–23). His reign lasted only a matter of
months, for although he was a partisan of Mexican
independence, his political outlook was basically royalist

and conservative, and the future of Mexico lay in the liberal social reforms advocated by the great revolutionaries Hidalgo and Morelos. Iturbide was exiled, and later, upon unauthorized return, was executed in Padillo, Tamualipas, and buried there. Years later his contribution to Mexican independence was recognized and his body was reburied in the Catedral Metropolitana (See "Walking Tour 1—The Zócalo"), where it remains today.

Banamex, present owner of the building, restored the palace in 1972 and the result is beautiful. Enter a courtyard with three tiers of balconies: The ground floor is a banking office and has a temporary art exhibition area; the upper floors have executive offices. Period paintings and statues grace walls and corners, and the second-floor chapel has been beautifully restored. Banamex produces a brief-but-free printed guide to the building. Ask the guard for one and come in and have a look anytime Monday through Friday from 9am to 6pm. While you are here you may want to stop in next door at the American Book Store or take a look at the exterior of the Casa Borda (which belonged to the silver baron from Taxco), on the same side of the street at the corner of Madero and Allende, across from the bookstore.

Now cross the street to the opposite side of Madero and double back on Madero toward the Alameda.

Refueling Stop

On the way back from the Iturbide Palace toward the Alameda, whether or not it's time for a break, you must stop in—however briefly—at a downtown institution: **The Casa de Azulejos** ("House of Tiles"; ☎ **518-6676**). You can't miss it—the building is all decked out in gorgeous blue-and-white tiles. One of Mexico City's most precious colonial gems and popular meeting places, the building dates from the end of the 16th century, built for the Count of the Valley of Orizaba. As the most popular story goes, during the count's defiant youth, his father proclaimed "You will never build a house of tiles"—a tiled house was a sign of success at the time, and the father was sure his son would amount to nothing. So when success came, the young count covered his house in tiles, which are a fine example of Puebla craftspeople's work. Today the tile-covered house is a branch of the Sanborn's restaurant/newsstand/gift shop chain. You can stroll through to admire the interior and have a refreshing drink or a full meal. Pause to see the Orozco mural *Omniscience* on the landing way leading to the second floor (where the bathrooms are). It's open daily from 7am to midnight.

Continuing back toward the Alameda, turn right at the next corner—the busy Avenida Lázaro Cárdenas. Cross it to the beautiful, white marble:

5. **Palacio de Bellas Artes,** at the east end of the Alameda. Pronounced "Bey-ahs Arr-tess," the building is a supreme achievement of art-deco lyricism, which, aside from being a concert hall, also houses permanent and traveling art shows. (See also the listing in Chapter 6 under "The Top Attractions.")

   Go back across Cárdenas. The huge building at the corner of Guardiola and Cardenas is the:

6. **Correos,** or post office. The beautiful white stone building, built between 1902 and 1907, was designed by Italian architect Adamo Boari, who also contributed to the Bellas Artes.

   From the Correos building front door go right (north) barely a half block, to the corner of Tacuba, and turn right again. On the left is the:

7. **Plaza Tolsá and El Caballito,** a huge equestrian statue in front of the Museo Nacional de Arte. The gallant statue of King Carlos IV of Spain atop a highstepping horse was crafted by the Mexican sculptor Manuel Tolsá. Mexicans call the statue El Caballito ("The Little Horse"), and the name reveals a lot: They prefer not to mention Carlos, who was king shortly before Mexico's independence movement from Spain began in 1810. However, the statue is actually one of the largest and most finely crafted equestrian statues in the world. Erected first in the Zócalo, it was later moved (1852) to a traffic circle in the Paseo de la Reforma. A few years ago El Caballito was moved to this more dignified and appropriate position in front of the museum and opposite the handsome Palacio Minería (see below) also designed by Tolsá.

   Just behind the statue is the entrance to one of the city's best but seldom visited museums, the:

8. **Museo Nacional de Arte.** Wander through the immense rooms with polished wooden floors as you view the wealth of paintings showing from the beginning of the development of Mexican art, but primarily covering the period from 1810 to 1950. There's a large collection of paintings by José María Velasco, father of Mexican landscape painting.

   The beautiful building across the street from the Museo Nacional de Arte is the:

9. **Palacio Minería,** built in the 19th century, one of architect Manuel Tolsá's finest works. Formerly the

school of mining, today it's used for concerts and
cultural events. (see listing in Chapter 9, "Mexico City
Nights"). If it's open, step inside for a look at the several
patios and fabulous stone work.

Refueling Stop

Next to the museum (out the front door and to the left)
is **La Mansión,** an indoor/outdoor restaurant with
colorful umbrellas and a good place to recharge. It's
open Monday through Saturday from 1 to 8pm.

Cross the street and backtrack east on Tacuba half a
block to the corner of Mata and you'll find the:

10. **Museo del Ejército y F.A.M.,** Calle de Tacuba and
Filomeno Mata 6 (☎ **512-7586** or **512-3215**), one of
the city's newest museums. Ejército means "army," and
delicately and artistically displayed inside these beautiful
high-ceilinged, serene rooms are select instruments used
in warfare—from coats of armor and swords to modern
weapons. Blood and suffering seem like they could never
have been a part of anything so tastefully designed and
presented.

Follow Tacuba back across Cárdenas; walk one and a
half blocks. Opposite the north side of the Alameda near
the corner of Hidalgo and Trujano is the:

11. **Museo de la Estampa,** Hidalgo 39 (☎ **521-2244**)
next door to the Museo Franz Mayer. *Estampa* means
engraving or printing, and the museum is devoted to
understanding and preserving the graphic arts. Housed
in a beautifully restored 16th-century building, the
museum has permanent displays on the second floor and
changing exhibits on the first floor. Displays include
those from pre-Hispanic times when clay seals were used
for designs on fabrics, ceramics, and other surfaces. But
the most famous works there are probably those of José
Guadalupe Posada, Mexico's famous printmaker, who
poked fun at death and politicians through his skeleton
figure drawings. If your interest in this subject is deep,
ask to see the video programs on graphic techniques—
woodcuts, lithography, etching etc. The museum is open
Tuesday through Sunday, 10am to 6pm. Admission is
$2.75; free on Sunday.

From here, go west a few steps across the plaza to the
entrance of the:

12. **Museo Franz Mayer,** Hidalgo 45. German immigrant
Franz Mayer spent a lifetime collecting rare furniture
and other decorative pieces dating from the 16th to the
19th centuries. When he died in 1975 he bequeathed
them to the Mexican people with a trust fund for their
care and display. The resulting museum is one of the

best in the city. The opulence of the colonial era is seen here through the objects that decorated homes during those 300 years. (See also the listing in Chapter 6 under "The Top Attractions.")

Refueling Stop

If a break is in order at this point, try a light snack at the **Cafeteria of the Museo Franz Mayer.** You may relax at its marble-topped tables in a pleasant courtyard. It's open the same days and hours as the museum. Or take in another ancient religious structure: Continue one block farther west of the Museo Franz Mayer on Hidalgo at the corner of Reforma and there you'll find the **Hotel de Cortés,** an 18th-century building that's been both an insane asylum and a hospice for Augustinian monks, now converted to a hotel. Step inside the red tezontle-stone edifice to the open courtyard, dripping with pink bougainvillea and outfitted in umbrella-clad tables. The restaurant serves rather high-priced Mexican and international dishes. Drinks, however, are inexpensive. It's open daily 7am to 10:30pm. (See "Mexico City Nights" for details on the Friday night Mexican Fiesta.)

From the Hotel de Cortes, cross Hidalgo toward the park and just at the corner on your right opposite the Alameda, passing the Centro Cultural José Martí, is the:

13. Pinacoteca Virreinal de San Diego, Dr. Mora 7 (☎ **510-2793** or **512-2079**). This former church is now a gallery of paintings, mostly from the 16th and 17th centuries, and mostly ecclesiastical in theme. Highlights are apparent immediately: In the wing to the right of where the altar would have been is a room with a gorgeous blue-and-gilt ceiling and gleaming rosettes, along with a striking 1959 mural by Federico Cantu, one of the few modern works on display. Upstairs in a cloister are many small paintings by Hipolito de Rioja (who worked in the second half of the 17th century), Baltazar de Echave Ibia (1610–40), and others. By the way, the tremendous painting on the cloister wall called *Glorificacion de la Inmaculada,* by Francisco Antonio Vallejo (1756–83), should be viewed from upstairs— the lighting is better. The Pinacoteca is open Tuesday through Sunday from 9am to 5pm. Admission is $1. Turn right out the front door, and right again on Colón down a short street facing the Plaza de la Soledaridad to the entrance to:

14. Museo Mural Diego Rivera (☎ **510-2329**), housing Diego Rivera's famous mural *Dream of a Sunday*

Afternoon in Alameda Park. Painted on a wall of the Hotel del Prado in 1947, the hotel was demolished in the 1985 earthquake, but the precious mural, perhaps the best known of Rivera's works, was saved and transferred to this location in 1986. The huge picture, 50 feet long and 13 feet high, chronicles the history of the park from the time of Córtes onward. Among the historical figures who have made their mark in the history of Mexico are these, portrayed more or less from left to right, but not in chronological order: Cortés; a heretic suffering under the Spanish Inquisition; Sor Juana Inez de la Cruz, a brilliant and progressive woman who became a nun to help those in need; Benito Juárez, putting forth the laws of Mexico's great *Reforma*; the hapless Gen. Antonio López de Santa Anna, handing the keys to Mexico to the invading American Gen. Winfield Scott; Emperor Maximilian and Empress Carlota; Jose Martí, the Cuban revolutionary; Death, with the plumed serpent (Quetzalcoatl) entwined about his neck; Gen. Porfirio Díaz, great with age and medals, asleep; a police officer keeping the Alameda free of "riff-raff" by ordering a poor family out of the elitist's park; and Francisco Madero, the martyred democractic president who caused the downfall of Díaz, whose betrayal and alleged murder by Gen. Victoriano Huerta (pictured at the right) resulted in years of civil turmoil in Mexico. The museum is open Tuesday through Sunday from 10am to 2pm and from 3 to 6pm; admission is $3, free for all on Sunday.

Folk art enthusiasts will delight in two excellent government-operated craft shops. For the first one turn right out the front door of the Museo de la Alameda; at the corner turn left one block, then right on Juárez and on the right is the:

15. **Exposición Nacional de Arte Popular,** Juárez 89 (☎ **518-3058**) described in more detail in a listing in Chapter 8, "Mexico City Shopping." The ground floor of this 18th-century mansion is packed with crafts from all over Mexico. It's open daily from 10am to 6pm.

Another even larger crafts shop is reached by backtracking on Juárez for 2¹/₂ blocks. Turn left two and a half blocks and on the right is the:

16. **Museo de Artes e Industrías Populares,** at Juárez 44 (☎ **521-6679**). The building, once the Corpus Christi Convent, was built during the 18th century. The upstairs museum portion has reopened and you can see it Tuesday through Friday between 9am and 6pm. The museum entrance is in the rear of the building. The showrooms are filled with good quality regional crafts. The store is open daily from 9am to 6pm.

Refueling Stop

A good place to finish a tour of the Alameda area is the
Fonda Santa Anita, Humboldt 48 (☎ **518-4609**).
Serving good traditional Mexican food and gaily
decorated with colorful banners and painted chairs,
this is a good place to kick back and review the day.
It's open Monday through Friday from noon to 10pm
and Saturday and Sunday from 1:30 to 9pm. Or walk
back across the Alameda to the **Palacio de Bellas Artes
lobby restaurant**—open daily from 9am to 8pm—
and the excellent adjacent **bookstore.**

Walking Tour 3
Museo Nacional de Antropología

Start   Sala (Room) 1.
Finish   Sala (Room) 22.
Time   At least 2 or 3 hours, even if you're a dedicated museum-rusher.
Best Times   Early any weekday and Sunday, when it's free.
Worst Times   Monday, when the museum is closed, or a national holiday, when it will be very crowded.

The Museo Nacional de Antropología (National Museum of Anthro-pology; ☎ **553-6243** or **553-6381**) is breathtaking in its splendor, with a massive patio half-sheltered by a tremendous stone umbrella designed by José Chávez Morado. It's open Tuesday through Satur-day from 9am to 7pm, on Sunday from 10am until 6pm. Admis-sion is $5.50 (free on Sunday). Free tours are available on request Tuesday through Saturday from 10am to 5pm in English, French, and Spanish for a minimum of five people.

There are three sections in the museum. First is the entrance hall to the museum proper with a checkroom and museum bookstore on the left. The bookstore has a superior collection of guidebooks with subjects covering a full range of Mexican attractions from cultural to culinary.

Inside the museum proper is an open courtyard with beautifully designed spacious rooms running around three sides on two levels. The ground-floor rooms are theoretically the most significant, and they are the most popular among studious visitors, devoted as they are to history and prehistoric subjects all the way up to the most re-cently explored archeological digs. These rooms include dioramas of the way Mexico City looked when the Spaniards first arrived, and reproductions of part of a pyramid at Teotihuacán. The Aztec Calendar Stone "wheel" takes a proud place here.

Save some of your time and energy, though, for the livelier and more readily understandable ethnographic rooms upstairs. This por-tion is a "living museum" devoted to the way people throughout

Walking Tour—
Museo Nacional de Antropología

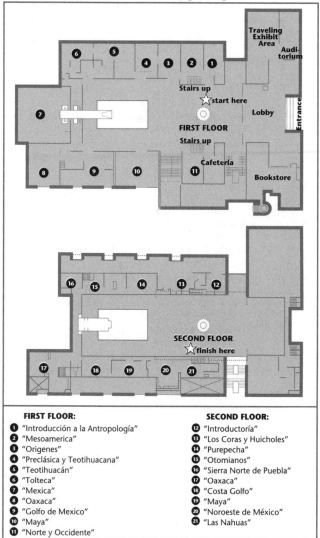

Traveling Exhibit Area

Auditorium

6 **5**

4 **3** **2** **1**

Stairs up

⭐ start here

7

Lobby

Entrance

FIRST FLOOR

Stairs up

Cafetería

8 **9** **10**

11

Bookstore

16 **15** **14** **13** **12**

SECOND FLOOR
⭐ finish here

17 **18** **19** **20** **21**

FIRST FLOOR:
1 "Introducción a la Antropología"
2 "Mesoamerica"
3 "Origenes"
4 "Preclásica y Teotihuacana"
5 "Teotihuacán"
6 "Tolteca"
7 "Mexica"
8 "Oaxaca"
9 "Golfo de Mexico"
10 "Maya"
11 "Norte y Occidente"

SECOND FLOOR:
12 "Introductoría"
13 "Los Coras y Huicholes"
14 "Purepecha"
15 "Otomianos"
16 "Sierra Norte de Puebla"
17 "Oaxaca"
18 "Costa Golfo"
19 "Maya"
20 "Noroeste de México"
21 "Las Nahuas"

Mexico live today, complete with straw-covered huts, tape recordings of songs and dances, crafts, clothing, and lifelike models of village activities. To me, both floors are equally interesting, one dealing with the past and the other dealing with the living past, so to speak, because so much Mexican village life retains vestiges of pre-Hispanic customs.

There is a lovely restaurant in the museum with moderate prices, air-conditioning, and cheerful patio tables.

Note: The museum is mostly wheelchair accessible; however, assistance will be needed in places. Signs are in Spanish only.

After you pass by the ticket taker into the courtyard, here are the museum's highlights, room (*sala*) by room beginning on your right:

1. **"Introducción a la Antropología."** The entrance mural by Z. Gonzalez Camarena depicts women of various nations. Exhibits deal with the various peoples of the world, their progress and development, and how these subjects are studied by anthropologists.

2. **"Mesoamerica."** Here you see the cultural interrelation of the Mesoamerican people even though they are dispersed over a widespread landscape, which is demonstrated by a large color map showing locations of the great cultures. A timeline puts them in chronological perspective. A mural in the Mesoamerican room, by Raul Anguiano, shows the Maya cosmogony: 13 heavens are held up by a giant ceiba tree; nine hells are beneath. The mural is directly above an exhibit of burial customs. You'll see other fascinating displays of pottery, jewelry, skeletal remains, painting, sculpture, and architecture.

    The next sign you'll see, "Salas de Etnografa en la Planta Alta," means "Ethnographic Rooms on the Upper Floor." There's a stairway here so you can reach those rooms. But for now, continue around the right side of the courtyard on the main level to:

3. **"Origenes."** The Room of Origins traces the history of the earliest men and women in the Americas with specific emphasis on their remains in Mexico. Don't miss the *mamut 2* (mammoth 2) of Santa Isabel Iztapan discovered in 1954 northwest of Mexico City. Of considerable interest is the miniature display of diverse architectural styles evidenced in Mexico's pyramids.

4. **"Preclásica y Teotihuacána."** Exhibits here are of preclassic times (2000 B.C.–A.D. 300) just before the Mesoamerican cultures reached their zenith. Religion, agriculture, hieroglyphic writing, numbering, and art were in use. One display shows a reconstructed archeological site found during archeological digs at Tlatilco (1300–800 B.C.) including pottery, figures and skeletal remains. Tlatilco was known for its appliqué technique: the use of clay pieces for figure making, with many formed in the shapes of animals, birds, frogs, and squash. Among the most interesting displays are clay figures that effectively show the appearance of people in those times—including pottery pieces attributed to the Olmecs.

5. **"Teotihuacán."** First, view the model of this important site, which flourished just outside Mexico City between

100 B.C. and A.D. 700. Outside on the back patio at eye level is another mockup view of the site. This room is a great preparation before seeing the ruins in person—something you must do. Chronologically displayed pottery gives a clear picture of the development of this utilitarian art at Teotihuacán. Other exhibits show tools for building, sculptures, fresco painting, jewelry making, and weaving. There's a reproduction of the mural *Paradise of the God Tlaloc* and visitors are dwarfed beside the lifesize replica of a portion of the temple of Quetzalcoatl.

6. **"Tolteca."** Toltec, Chichimec, and Cholulan cultures are preserved here, but the exhibit begins with Xochicalco, a site between Cuernavaca and Taxco that was both a crossroads of many cultures and perhaps a bridge culture between Teotihuacán and the development of the Toltecs at Tula north of Mexico City. Xochicalco building and pottery show a cross-cultural mix with the Maya, Teotihuacán, and the Toltecs. One of the huge Atlantean-men statues from the Temple of Tlahuizcalpantecutli, at Tula, is in the hall along with other great monoliths and pottery. Toltec artistic elements influenced many groups that followed them. They were the developers of serpentine columns, chac mools, Atlantan figures, the eagle motif, and pilasters of war figures. A model shows what the site of Tula looked like, and another shows how it may have been constructed. A model of the pyramidal site at Cholula, by volume the largest pyramid in the world, shows its three super-impositions (buildings one on top of another). Cholulan pottery was especially accomplished, so don't miss the displays of it here.

7. **"Mexica."** At the far end of the courtyard, lettering on the lintel reads "Cem Anahuac Tenochca Tlalpan," and beneath it is the entrance to one of the most important rooms in the museum. *Mexica* is what the Aztecs called themselves. This room is an excellent one to see before visiting the Aztec Templo Mayor site and museum near the Zócalo in the Centro Historico of Mexico City. Among the carved stones are: the Aztec Calendar Stone, which bears symbols for all the ages of humankind (as the Aztecs saw them); the Piedra de Tizoc; Xiuhcoatl, the fire-serpent; a Tzompantli, or wall of skulls; the terrifying monolith of Coatlíque, goddess of earth and death with two serpents' heads coming from her neck, a necklace of hands and hearts, and a skirt of serpents; and the stone head of the moon goddess, Coyolxauhqui, with bells on her cheeks, sun disks in her earlobes, and a nose ring.

Amid all this ominous dark volcanic rock, the iridescent feathered headdress of Moctezuma blazes, as impressive today (a copy) as it must have been when the Aztec emperor proceeded regally through the streets of Tenochtitlán. Near the glass case holding the headdress is a large model of Moctezuma's fabulously rich capital city; a mural echoes the city's grandeur as well. One of my favorite displays is the enormous diorama of the thriving market at Tlatelolco, which brings to life the description of it by Bernal Díaz de Castillo. (Remains of Tlatelolco are north of the Zócalo in the Plaza de las Tres Culturas.)

8. **"Oaxaca."** After the "Mexica" room comes that of Oaxaca, with its Zapotec, Mixtec, and Olmec influences, and priceless artifacts from the Monte Alban excavations. The huge display of pottery is arranged chronologically to show its evolution, and a deerskin Mixtec codice exemplifies picture writing. The Mixtecs were accomplished metalworkers, gemsmiths, and wood carvers, and you'll see fine examples of their work. A huge mural shows how the mountaintop ruins of Monte Alban looked at its apogee. Take time to admire the reproduction of Tomb No. 105 from Monte Alban. Go down the stairs to a reproduction of Tomb No. 104, complete with wall frescoes and burial figure surrounded with offerings.

9. **"Golfo de Mexico."** Divided into four sections, the Gulf of Mexico hall covers the rich cultures of the Huastecs from the northern part of Veracruz and Tamaulipas, the Remojadas and Totonacs, who occupied the middle portion of the region, and the Olmecs of southern Veracruz and northern Tabasco states, whose influence was enormous. Certainly the most visible highlight here is an enormous, multi-ton, basaltic rock head, though one of the finest is the graceful and beautifully sculpted "Wrestler." Both are of Olmec origin; the Olmecs were master stone carvers. The Huastecs were known for their exquisite polychromed pottery with anthropomorphic and zoomorphic forms; the pottery display does justice to the culture. But the tall, slender, stone-carved figure of the "Huasteca Adolescent," with a baby on its back, is one of Mesoameraca's most graceful stone artworks. There are models of the archeological sites at El Tajín near Papantla and Zempoala near the city of Veracruz as well.

10. **"Maya."** Don't miss this room! The exhibits here are wonderful. Displays here include a fine collection of well-preserved, beautiful Maya carvings, not just from Mexican territory, but from other parts of Mesoamerica (Central America) as well.

Models of ancient cities include Copan (Honduras), Yaxchilan (Chiapas), Tulum (Quintana Roo), and Uaxactun (Guatemala). Downstairs is a model of the fabulous tomb discovered in the Temple of the Inscriptions at Palenque, complete with a rich jade mask for the deceased monarch. Outside the exhibit room is a full-scale replica of a temple at Hochob (Campeche), and another of the Temple of Paintings at Bonampak, plus replicas of stele from Quirigua (Guatemala). Notice in all these examples especially the finesse of the carving. In the Tablero de la Cruz Enramada, from Palenque, note the fine work in the glyphs.

11. **"Norte y Occidente."** These rooms deal with the "culture of the desert" from northern and western Mexico. If you're familiar with the culture of the Indians of the southwestern United States, you'll notice similarities here. Many of the artifacts are from the Casas Grandes pueblo in the state of Chihuahua, where the people lived in adobe pueblos and made pottery very much like the peoples of New Mexico and Arizona.

The occidental (western) exhibits echo the great civilization of the Valley of Mexico, mostly from sites such as Tzintzuntzan (Michoacán), Ixtlan (Nayarit), Ixtepete (Jalisco), and Chupicuaro (Guanajuato), but also including San Miguel de Allende and San Luis Potosí. The chac mool from Ihuatzio, for instance, looks like a bad copy, or a stylized rendering, of the great chac mools of Tula and Chichén Itzá. There's also a model of a *yacata,* or vast, stepped ceremonial platform, as found at many sites in the western zone.

Refueling Stop

After the Maya room, descend a wide staircase to reach the reasonably priced **Cafeteria Museo.** Beer, mixed drinks, and soft drinks are served, as well as breakfast, soups, salads, and sandwiches or more substantial main courses. It's open Tuesday through Saturday 9am to 7pm and Sunday 9am to 6pm.

From here goto the end of the patio next to the "Sala de Origenes" to the stairs leading up to the splendid displays of daily life in the Ethnographic Section. Begin in the first room on the right:

12. **"Introductoría."** Murals, maps, photographs, textiles, jewelry, and other objects present a perspective on Mexico's daily life from pre-Hispanic times to the present.

13. **"Los Coras y Huicholes."** Devoted to inhabitants of the West Coast states of Nayarit and Jalisco, in this

room you'll see lifelike figures, clad in traditionally embroidered clothing, seated on *equipal* (leather) stools before an authentic indigenous hut. Note particularly the pottery and *morales* (woven bags), all of which are in use in villages today.

14. **"Purepecha."** The Purepecha, more generally known as Tarascans, live in the state of Michoacán and carry on crafts learned centuries ago under the influence of the first bishop of Pátzcuaro, Vasco de Quiroga. The main calling card of this display is the enormously long dugout canoe at the entrance. You'll see guitars from Paracho, copper objects from Santa Clara del Cobre, and fine dinnerware from potters around Lake Pátzcuaro. Occasionally on display is the exquisite black and white, reversable *serape* trimmed with stylized designs of quetzal birds and produced by weavers from Angahuan, a village near the Paricutín volcano.

15. **"Otomianos."** Otomi Indians speak several languages within the Otomangue language group. They live in the states of Hidalgo, Mexico (which almost surrounds Mexico City), San Luis Potosí, and Querétaro. The Otomianos include Nahua, Azteca, Mazahua, and Matlatzinca, all of which are descendents of the Toltec. Here you see figures weaving ixtle fibers of the maguey plant. There are products made for everyday use and trade such as baskets, belts, jars, blouses and serapes.

16. **"Sierra de Puebla."** The northern part of the state of Puebla is one of the country's most interesting, yet is seldom visited by tourists. Note the villagers of San Pablito pounding bark into paper, the unfinished pink and black *quechquémitl* (women's shoulder cape) on an unusual loom that rounds corners, and the finely embroidered blouses with flower and animal designs.

17. **"Oaxaca."** The southern state of Oaxaca is one of the most interesting in the country, due in part to the numerous varieties of colorful *huipils* (loose tunics) worn by women from different indigenous groups. A full-size hut is on display, complete with furnishings, weaving looms, pottery and an oxcart outside. Another section shows different styles of huts used along the coast of Oaxaca, and men and boys weaving palm.

18. **"Costa Golfo."** This region is comprised of indigenous groups of Huastecas, Totonacas, and Nahuas. Huastec Indians speak a language related to Maya. Inside a hut, women wearing embroidered blouses and ribbons twisted through their braided hair are surrounded by pottery and frozen in the action of decorating and forming clay by hand.

19. **"Maya."** The land of the Maya comprises the states of Tabasco, Chiapas, Yucatán, Campeche, and Quintana

Roo; of these the most colorful is Chiapas. Besides the costumes and pottery, there are musical instruments and furnished huts. A market scene from the Chiapas highlands shows men and women in regional attire— heavy wool tunics and colorful loomed and richly brocaded huipils. In another scene a woman from the Yucatán weaves henequen fiber on a stick loom.

20. **"Noroeste de Mexico."** Seri, Tarahumara, and Yaqui Indians live in northwestern Mexico in the states of Sonora, Chihuahua, Sinaloa, and Baja California. You'll see among the unusual items beautiful basketry, which is quite similar to some in the southwestern United States. A painting shows how the Seri women decorate their faces.

21. **"Las Nahuas."** The last room is devoted to this Indian group of modern Mexico. They live in central Veracruz, Hidalgo, Guerrero, Morelia, Durango, Tlaxcala, Jalisco, and the State of Mexico. The display shows them in various rounds of their daily life, which is based on the corn culture. A written narrative states that this group is in a precarious situation due to poor health care, unemployment, illiteracy, injustice, and oppression.

Walking Tour 4
San Angel

Start   Museo Colonial del Carmen.

Finish   San Angel Inn.

Time   3 to 6 hours.

Best Times   Saturday, to visit the Saturday-only Bazar Sábado.

Worst Times   Monday, when the museums are closed.

San Angel is a fashionable suburb of cobblestone streets with several worthwhile museums. The nearest Metro station is "M.A. Quevedo." From downtown, take a colectivo ("San Angel") or bus ("Indios Verdes-Tlalpan" or "Central Norte-Villa Olímpica") south along Insurgentes near the Zona Rosa. Ask to get off at La Paz. There's a pretty park here—the Plaza del Carmen—to the east, and on the west side of Insurgentes is a Sanborn's store and restaurant, good for a quick, moderately priced meal.

Walk west, up the hill on La Paz, and in a block you'll come to Avenida de la Revolución. To the left (south) is the dark colonial stone bulk of the:

1. **Museo Colonial del Carmen,** Avenida de la Revolucion 4 (☎ **548-9849** or **548-2838**). A former Carmelite convent, this museum is open Tuesday through Sunday from 10am to 4:45pm and admission is $1; free on Sunday. (See listing in Chapter 6 for details.)

From the Museo Colonial del Carmen follow Revolución to the right (north) three long blocks to the:

2. Museo de Arte Alvaro y Carmen T. Carrillo Gil, Revolución 1608, corner of Desierto de los Leones (☎ **548-7467**). Jose Clemente Orozco, Diego Rivera, and David Alfaro Siqueiros are among the painters whose works are featured at this museum. (See listing in Chapter 6 for more information.) It's open Tuesday through Sunday from 9:30am to 6pm. Admission is $2; free on Sunday.

From the Gil museum head up the hill through the Plaza del Carmen on Madera or Armaragua to the:

3. Plaza San Jacinto. On Saturday it's filled with artists and their paintings. Many of the old buildings surrounding the Plaza San Jacinto have fine courtyards where crafts are sold. While you're there look for the plaque honoring the St. Patrick's Battalion. When the United States invaded Mexico in 1846 this group of Irish Catholic immigrants was persuaded to take up the Mexican cause by a Mexican Catholic priest. So they deserted U.S. General Zachary Taylor and joined the Mexicans in the War with Mexico. Some of them were executed on the Plaza San Jacinto as traitors. They are considered heroes in Mexico. Up the street and to the right is the:

4. Bazar Sábado (Saturday Bazaar). Two stories of shops are jammed into this beautiful colonial building. But this isn't just another curio market—rather, the ordinary is mingled with the extraordinary. Some of Mexico's best designers have shops here, or started out here, so there's ample opportunity to find just the right decorative object, along with crafts and textiles. The crowds inside can be incredible, especially if it's a holiday weekend, but be sure to take a turn through the building, whether or not you intend to buy. It's open on Saturday only from 10am to 7pm.

Outside, in a plaza off to one side, is another area where you are just as likely to see Zapotec Indians from Oaxaca weaving huipils, or Indians from the paper-making village of San Pablito, or vendors selling masks and wooden fish from the state of Guerrero, as you are to see a contemporary artist with an easel. Prices are fixed inside the bazaar, but out here, feel free to haggle.

5. Museo Centro Cultura Isidro Fabela, Plaza San Angel 15. The former Casa del Risco is open Tuesday through Sunday from 10am to 5pm and admission is free. (See listing in Chapter 6 for more information.) Restrooms are upstairs.

Walking Tour–San Angel

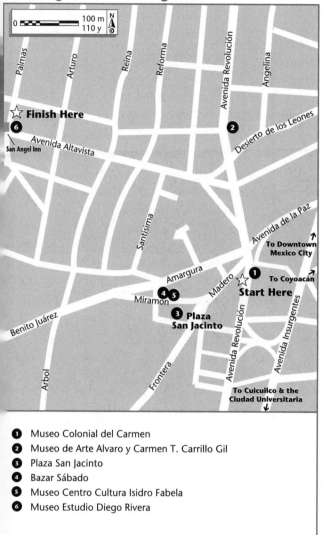

① Museo Colonial del Carmen
② Museo de Arte Alvaro y Carmen T. Carrillo Gil
③ Plaza San Jacinto
④ Bazar Sábado
⑤ Museo Centro Cultura Isidro Fabela
⑥ Museo Estudio Diego Rivera

Refueling Stop

The **Sanborn's** on Insurgentes is a good bet. You can
also try the buffet (expensive) in the courtyard of the
Bazar Sábado, and outdoor restaurants line the streets
leading to the Bazar.

From the front door of the Fabela Museum, turn right and right again at the corner, cross Amargura, jog left then right again at the next corner and walk to Avenida Altavista. Turn left and walk four long blocks to the:

6. **Museo Estudio Diego Rivera,** corner of Calle Diego Rivera and Avenida Altavista. Like the Frida Kahlo home (See the Coyoacán tour below), with easels and personal effects all around, here you feel engulfed in the life of this famous artist.

Don't confuse Rivera's studio with his museum, the Anahuacalli, which is in a different section (San Pablo Tepetlapan) south of the suburb of Coyoacan. (For more on the painter, see "Famous Capitalinos" in Chapter 1; on this museum, see listing in Chapter 6.)

Refueling Stop

Whether or not it's break time, don't leave the area without at least looking around the **San Angel Inn** (☎ **616-2222**), corner of Palmas and Altavista, across the street from the Museo Estudio Diego Rivera. This famous 18th-century Carmelite monastery, a national monument, is one of the city's most fashionable places to dine. It's had many uses: retreat of the Spanish viceroys; pulque and cattle hacienda; home of Fanny Calderon de la Barca (wife of the first Spanish Ambassador to Mexico); quarters for Santa Anna's troops; site of the summit between Pancho Villa and Emiliano Zapata at which they divided their territories into north and south during the Mexican Revolution. Among dignitaries who have dined here are Prince Philip of England, Princess Beatriz of Holland, President Nixon, Lady Bird Johnson, Robert Kennedy, Neil Armstrong, U.N. secretary general U. Thant, and Hollywood stars Rock Hudson, Gina Lolobrigida, and Brigitte Bardot. You can order a drink under the *portales* (arcades) facing the inn's plant-filled courtyard, or dine inside in the plush dining rooms. The full luncheon will run $20 to $40, but many items are much less.

Walking Tour 5
Coyoacán

Start   Museo Nacional de Culturas Populares.
Finish   Nuseo Nacional de las Intervenciones.
Time   Half a day.
Best Time   Tuesday through Sunday, when museums are open; the

Walking Tour–Coyoacán

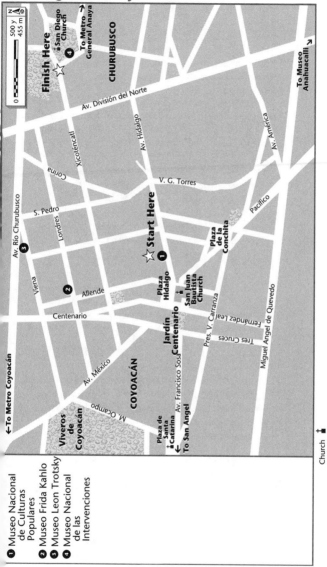

Start Here ①

Finish Here

To Metro General Anaya →

↑ San Diego Church ④

CHURUBUSCO

Av. División del Norte

Xicoténcatl

Corina

Av. Hidalgo

V. G. Torres

To Museo Anahuacalli ↗

Av. América

Pacífico

S. Pedro

Londres

Av. Río Churubusco ③

Viena

Allende ②

Plaza de la Conchita

Centenario

Plaza Hidalgo

↑ San Juan Bautista Church

Jardín Centenario

Pres. V. Carranza

Fernández Leal

Tres Cruces

Miguel Angel de Quevedo

Av. México

← To Metro Coyoacán

COYOACÁN

Av. Francisco Sosa

M. Ocampo

Viveros de Coyoacán

Plaza de Santa Catarina ✝

To San Angel ↓

N

500 y
455 m

Church ✝

❶ Museo Nacional de Culturas Populares
❷ Museo Frida Kahlo
❸ Museo Leon Trotsky
❹ Museo Nacional de las Intervenciones

Museo Nacional de Culturas Populares is closed on Sunday.
Worst Time   Monday, when museums are closed.

Coyoacán is a pretty, and wealthy, suburb with many colonial-era houses and cobbled streets. At the center are two large, graceful plazas—the Plaza Hidalgo and Jardín Centenario, and the Church of San Juan Bautista (1583). Once the capital of the Tepanec kingdom, Coyoacán was later conquered by the Aztecs, then by Córtes, who lived here during the building of Mexico City.

From downtown, the Metro, Línea 3, can take you to the "Coyoacán" or "Viveros" stations, within walking distance of Coyoacan's museums. Or buses named "Iztacala-Coyoacan" will get you from the center to this suburb.

Coming from San Angel, catch the "Alcantarilla-Col. Agrarista" heading east along the Camino al Desierto de los Leones or Avenida Altavista, near the San Angel Inn. When the bus gets to the corner of Avenida Mexico and Xicotencatl in Coyoacan, disembark. Or—simpler, quicker, and easier—take a cab for the 15-minute ride. Sosa, a pretty street, is the main artery into Coyoacán from San Angel.

1. **Museo Nacional de Culturas Populares** (National Museum of Popular Cultures), Hidalgo 289. Housed in a beautiful old mansion, the changing exhibits include photographs and paintings and occasional musical or theatrical performance. It's closed on Sunday.

Refueling Stop

Coyoacán's beautiful central Plaza Hidalgo, surrounded by sienna-colored colonial buildings, invites lingering. Numerous restaurants are scattered around the central squares, among them **La Guadalupana,** at the corner of Higuera and Caballocalco, which is good for a snack or a full meal.

Six very long blocks north on Allende is the:
2. **Museo Frida Kahlo,** at Londres 247. The birthplace of Frida Kahlo, wife of Diego Rivera, was also their home for several decades. It offers a view of the life and times of that famous couple, since the home is much as Frida left it. (For more on Kahlo, see "Famous Capitalinos" in Chapter 1; the listing in Chapter 6 gives details on the museum.)

From the Frida Kahlo Museum, turn right out the front door, then right on Allende two blocks to Viena; turn right and walk 2¹/₂ blocks then left again a half block to Churubusco; left again is the entrance to the:
3. **Museo Leon Trotsky,** Churubusco 410, between Gómez Farías and Morelos. Walk on Viena, until you see the house on the left with brick watchtowers on top of the high stone walls. After walking through the section devoted to newspaper articles and letters about the Trotskys, you enter the home, which is surrounded by walls and gardens. (See also listing in Chapter 6.)

From the Trotsky Museum turn right and walk to the intersection of Viena and Churubusco; cross the busy Division del Norte and turn at the next available street, jogging right at the first street and left at the next one to the:

4. **Museo Nacional de las Intervenciones** (National Museum of Interventions, ☎ **604-0699**), 20 de Agosto y General Anaya. Technically this museum is in Churubusco, the neighbor suburb of Coyoacán. A visit here will explain Mexico's strong feelings about the United States and the dubious use of its military clout. This convent was the site of a battle between Americans and Mexicans on August 20, 1847.

Once you've seen Coyoacán, find your way to Avenida Mexico-Coyoacán, and follow it northwest to the Metro station. If you're heading west to San Angel go to Calle Cuauhtéhmoc and catch a "San Angel" bus.

The Anahuacalli (Museo Diego Rivera) is a short distance south of Coyoacán. See listing in Chapter 6 for details.

Mexico City Shopping

NO MATTER WHAT YOU HAVE IN MIND, YOU'LL FIND IT IN THE CAPITAL OF Mexico. From designer clothing, antiques, fine art, and decorative accessories to exquisite native crafts—it's all here. Here's the rundown on the best places to shop, from small, selective crafts stores and exclusive clothing boutiques, to vast general markets.

1 The Shopping Scene

The best areas for browsing and shopping are on Avenida Juárez facing the Alameda; Avenida Madero and the parallel streets to it; the Zona Rosa; and fashionable Polanco. Dozens of cashmere cloth stores line Isabel la Católica in the historic district between 16 de Septiembre and Madero. Jewelry stores line Madero and the portals facing the Palacio Nacional.

Shipping purchases back to the States via the Mexican postal service isn't recommended. It's generally best to buy only what you can carry or check as luggage on your flight home.

2 Shopping A to Z

Antiques

Connoisseur Art Gallery, Amberes 33. ☎ **208-6454.**

Fax 208-3780.

Opened in 1993, this elegant gallery, which in quality is more like a fine, small museum, specializes in antiques from the 15th to the 18th centuries. As an example, when I browsed, I encountered a 19th-century baptismal font; a Ching Dynasty porcelain bowl; and a 19th-century baroque altar. The connoisseur is open Monday through Friday from 11am to 7pm and Saturday from 11am to 2pm. It's at the corner of Hamburgo.

Plaza del Angel, Centro de Antiguidades, Londres 161.

No phone.

Weekdays stores in this Zona Rosa minimall showcase antiques. On Saturdays, it becomes a flea market. On that day, the public walkways are lined with dealers who set up temporary "shop" (often just a rug—perhaps a Persian one) displaying wares—jewelry, antique furniture, old coins, retablos, santos, masks, glass, books, brass—you name it. It's an upscale mini Lagunilla market and great for browsing. The plaza is located between Florencia and Amberes. Open Monday through Friday from 10am to 7pm, Saturday from 10am to 3pm.

Crafts

⭐ **Exposición Nacional de Arte Popular (Fonart),**
Juárez 89. ☎ **521-6681.**

This government-operated store is usually crowded with crafts. There are papier-mache figurines, textiles, earthenware, colorfully painted candelabras, indigenous clothing, hand-carved wooden masks, straw goods, beads, bangles, and glass. It is operated by the Fondo Nacional para el Fomento de las Artes, a government organization that helps village craftspeople. The store is open daily from 10am to 6pm. **Metro:** Hidalgo or Juárez.

⭐ **Fonart,** Londres 136 A. ☎ **525-2026.**
Another branch of the government-operated store is in the heart of the Zona Rosa. Though situated in small, narrow, upstairs quarters, it is absolutely packed with folk art, much of it not duplicated at the larger store on Juárez. Open Monday through Saturday from 10am to 7pm.

Michoacán, Londres 117. ☎ **514-2025.**
This Zona Rosa store features crafts from the state of Michoacán, northwest of Mexico City. The state has a rich craft heritage and is known for several patterns of dinnerware, textiles, wood carving, straw ornaments, and pottery. It's open Monday through Friday from 10am to 2pm and 3 to 7pm and Saturday from 11am to 6pm.

⭐ **Museo Nacional de Artes e Industrias Populares,** Juárez 44. ☎ **521-6679.**
The museum and store, located across the street from the Benito Juárez statue in Alameda Park, has an enormous selection of high-quality Mexican crafts from all over for sale. Because the prices are fixed here, you can get an idea of quality's relation to cost for later use in market bargaining. Upstairs (the entrance is in back) is a museum. It's open daily from 9am to 6pm; the museum is open Monday through Friday from 9am to 6pm.

Victor's Artes Populares Mexicanas, Madero 10, second floor, Room 305. ☎ **512-1263.**
Victor's, near the Alameda, is a shop for serious buyers and art collectors. Victor's is owned by the Fosado family, who have been in the folk art business for more than 60 years. They buy most of their crafts from Indian villages near and far, and supply various exhibits with native craftworks. It's open theoretically Monday through Friday from 12:30 to 7pm. See also "Markets" below. **Metro:** Bellas Artes.

Fashion

Aca Joe, Amberes 19. ☎ **525-2718.**
This Zona Rosa branch of the popular clothing store features the trendy, casual attire for which it is famous all over the country. Sweaters, jeans, khaki shorts, shirts, jackets, and more are invitingly displayed. Open Monday through Saturday from 10:30am to 8pm and Sunday from 2 to 8pm.

Ambras, Mazaryk 320, Col. Polanco. ☎ **281-3161.**
Opposite the restaurant Chez Wok at Eugenio Sue, in the Polanco area, Ambras is a store of fine clothing featuring the work of Italian

and French designers. There's clothing for both sexes from day and evening wear to accessories such as scarves, overcoats, jackets, jewelry, perfume, and sunglasses. Open Monday through Saturday from 11am to 8pm.

Artesanías Patricia, Londres 139, Col. Juárez. ☎ **525-7192** or **525-9333.**

Artesanías Patricia, in the Zona Rosa, specializes in fine quality embroidered dresses from Oaxaca. The selection is huge and well-chosen. It's catercorner from the Hotel Calinda Geneve and opposite Fonart. Open Monday through Saturday from 10am to 7pm.

Fiesta Della Moda, Tennyson 177 at Mazaryk. ☎ **415-6160.**

The quality of fine evening and day wear will attract women to this exclusive little Polanco shop. Besides French designer suits, dresses, and evening gowns, it proffers Spanish designer leather boots and shoes, jewelry, and trendy sunglasses. Open Monday through Saturday from 11am to 7:30pm.

Flavio Gatto, Hamburgo 159. ☎ **525-8261.**

This Zona Rosa store features fine Italian shoes for men and women plus purses, jackets, and coats. It's next to Auseba restaurant and open Monday through Saturday from 11:30am to 8:30pm.

Gucci, Hamburgo 136. ☎ **207-9997.**

If you can't get enough Gucci in your own country, then you have another chance here in the Zona Rosa. The long showcase window tempts passersby with elaborate displays of Gucci products. Open Monday through Saturday from 9:30am to 8pm and Sunday from 11am to 8pm.

Michel Domit, Mazarek 360. ☎ **281-1939** or **281-2195.**

Another Polanco area store, this one caters to the well dressed man with suits, dress shirts, and ties as well as shoes. Open Monday through Friday from 10am to 7:30pm, Saturday from 10am to 8pm, and Sunday from 11am to 7:30pm.

Mondi Collections, Mazaryk 336. ☎ **281-4931.**

Mondi, in Polanco, is a small shop of well-selected women's wear featuring coats, suits, slacks, jackets, blouses, and hats. Open Monday through Saturday from 11am to 8pm.

Nautica, Mazaryk 336. ☎ **281-4158.**

Men needing something for a resort or the golf course will find it in this fine casual clothing store in Polanco. There's a good selection of sweaters, jackets, slacks, knit and cotton shirts, and belts—well, a complete casual ensemble. It's open Monday through Saturday from 11am to 8pm.

Regina Romero, Mazaryk at Julio Verne. ☎ **281-0461.**

For the woman looking to add a little something to the dressy wardrobe, this fashionable store offers women's fine suits, belts, bags, shoes and jewelry. Open Monday through Saturday from 10am to 8pm.

Robert's, Juárez 10. ☎ 521-2518.

Opposite the Alameda and Bellas Artes, this men's clothing store has the basics for well-dressed business or casual attire. There are shirts, ties, socks, jackets and suits, and burmuda shorts—everything except shoes. Open Monday through Saturday from 10am to 8pm.

Telas Escalera, Genova 65B. ☎ 511-8308.

Batik cloth and clothing with Mexican designs is the specialty here. Plus, there's a selection of Talavera pottery made in Puebla, Tlaxcala, Guanajuato, and by Dolores Hidalgo. You'll find it at the corner of Londres in the Zona Rosa. Open Monday through Saturday from 10am to 7pm.

Glass

★ **Avalos Brothers,** Carretones 5. ☎ 522-5311. Fax 522-6420.

Ever since Camilo Avalos Razo founded the business in 1889, blown glass has been issuing forth from this same location in the old section of town. You can watch men and women scurry around with molten glass in various stages of shaping. A showroom to the left of the entrance contains shelves full of glass objects—pitchers, vases, plates, glasses, flowers, cream and sugar containers, etc., in various colors. The Carretones glass objects were the subject of an exhibition at the Palacio de Bellas Artes in 1960. Few tourists seem to find their way here, but it's always been popular with locals for selection and price. It's located one block from Izazaga/San Pablo at Tapacio and Carretones. To find it walk south of the Zócalo on Jesús María, cross Izazaga, and turn left. Walk two blocks straight to Topacio. Turn right on Topacio, and left at the next block, which is Carretones. The factory is immediately on the right. Open Monday through Friday from 10:30am to 3pm and Saturday from 10:30am to 2pm.

Jewelry

There are dozens of jewelry stores and optical shops on Madero from Motolinia to the Zócalo, in the portals facing the National Palace, and the Monte de Piedad Nacional (National Pawn Shop), also opposite the National Palace, has an enormous jewelry selection.

Bazar del Centro, Isabel la Catolica 30. No phone.

Located between the Alameda and the Zócalo, this colonial era building was the palace of the Counts of Miravale. Now it houses shops selling jewelry, precious stones, and silver. Open Monday through Friday from 10am to 7pm, Saturday from 10am to 3pm.

★ **Los Castillo,** Amberes 41. ☎ 511-6198 or 511-8396.

This Zona Rosa branch of the famous Taxco silversmith family houses some of the best of their work—pieces you won't see at their shop in Taxco. Handsome silver jewelry, decorative bowls made of porcelain fused with silver, napkin rings, and furniture with silver and porcelain tops can all be found here. Open Monday through Friday from 10am to 7pm, Saturday from 10am to 3pm.

★ **Tane,** Amberes 70. ☎ **207-8202** or **510-9429.**

Tucked in the Zona Rosa, this is the original store of one of the top silver designers in Mexico, with branches only in the best hotels and shopping centers. The quantity and quality of silver work is enormous, from jewelry to platters, pitchers, dinner plates, cutlery, frames, candlestick holders, and even china by Limoge. Open Monday through Friday from 10am to 7pm, Saturday from 11am to 2:30pm.

Records & Tapes

Mercado de Discos, Eje Central/Cárdenas 10. ☎ **521-5853.**

This may not be the most upscale-looking place, but the selection of national and international records and tapes is immense. Located between Madero and 16 de Septiembre, only two blocks from the Palacio de Bellas Artes. Open Monday through Saturday from 10am to 8pm.

Rugs

Temoaya Tapetes Mexicanos S. A., Hamburgo 235, Col. Juárez. ☎ **533-6420** or **533-3851.** Fax 511-0069.

If you aren't planning a trip to Temoaya (outside of Toluca) but you want to see the rugs, this is the place. A full selection of the Persian-style rugs made in Temoaya (Chapter 10 "Easy Excursions" for a full description), are found at this outlet of the rugmaker's cooperative. These sought-after works of art are made using hooked rug techniques taught by Iranian rugmakers, and design motifs from the indigenous peoples of Mexico. Color combinations can make the same design appear to be completely different. If you don't find just the rug for you in the showroom, you can select colors and designs to your liking from their catalog and have one made to order. Completion takes several months and they don't ship. A 6-by-9-foot rug costs around $800. Manager Isaac Garci Dueñas y Rodriguez has a good command of the design motifs and their meaning. Open Monday through Friday from 10am to 6pm and Saturday from 10am to 2pm.

Sculpture

Sergio Bustamante, Amberes 13. ☎ **525-9059.**

One of Mexico's best known contemporary sculptors and artists, Señor Bustamante's Zona Rosa store has a broad selection of his surrealistic and very collectible work. Each piece is signed. Showcases in the front of the store hold his gold jewelry designs, many of them miniatures of his sculptures. There's another Bustamante outlet in the lobby of the Hotel Nikko. The store is between Hamburgo and Reforma. Open Monday through Friday from 10am to 7:30pm and Saturday from 10am to 7pm.

Stamps

Filatelia Vackimes, Reforma 418. ☎ **207-6329.**

If you are a stamp collector you'll want to pay this store a visit. Stamps from all over the world are here including most of the stamps ever printed in Mexico. Ask about the store's catalog. The phone is usually out of order. Open Monday through Friday from 10am to 7pm and Saturday from 10am to 3pm.

Sweets

Dulcera de Celaya, Motolina 36. ☎ **518-4548.**

Dulcera de Celaya, between Madero and 16 de Septiembre, is a beautiful old confectioner's shop founded in 1874. In its 19th-century windows you'll see a mouth-watering selection of the sweets for which the city of Celaya is famous: candied fruits of all varieties, jars of sweetened goat milk, sugar-coated almonds, fudge, pecan candies. Even if your diet doesn't allow you to buy, you should at least take a look at the lovely shop. Open: Mon–Sat, 7am to 8pm.

3 Markets

Bazar Sábado, San Angel.

The Bazar Sábado in San Angel is held on Saturday, as its name indicates, in a colonial-era suburb of cobbled streets, mansions, and parks a few miles south of the city. This is the only day the actual bazar building (a fine two-story mansion built around an interior courtyard) is open. The bazar showcases dozens of permanent stalls with high-quality decorative art. Outside, on the adjacent plazas, hundreds of easel artists display their paintings, and members of indigenous craftspeople from Puebla and elsewhere bring their folk art—baskets, masks, pottery, textiles, etc. Leisurely diners fill restaurants (some of them in mansions) lining the streets. Plan to spend all of Saturday touring the attractions on the southern outskirts of the city. (See also the walking tour of San Angel in Chapter 7.)

Buenavista Central Crafts Market, Aldama 187. ☎ **529-1254.**

Across from Estacion Buenavista (Buenavista Railroad Station) is the Central Crafts Market, a very tourist-oriented, commercial concern with a lot of floor space and an uninspired collection of crafts at rather high prices. They offer customers free soft drinks at a small snack bar in the shop. The Central Crafts Market employs agents who prowl the length of Avenida Juárez and other tourist-frequented areas to tout the excellence of the market's wares. Offering "free tourist information" or "free guide service," they are friendly and helpful, but their goal is to persuade you to visit the market. It's open Monday through Saturday from 9am to 6pm and Sunday from 9am to 2pm.

Centro Artesanal (Mercado de Curiosidades), corner of Ayuntamiento and Dolores.

This is a rather modern building set back off a plaza at this corner. It's composed of a number of stalls on two levels selling everything from leather to tiles. They have some lovely silver jewelry and, as in most non-fixed-price stores, the asking price is high but the bargained result is often very reasonable. **Metro:** Salto del Agua.

Lagunilla Market (Thieves Market), a few blocks north of the Plaza de Garibaldi.

This is another market well worth visiting. The best day is Sunday when the Lagunilla becomes a colorful outdoor market filling the streets for blocks. Vendors sell everything from axes to antiques. Be alert to the danger of pickpockets. The two enclosed sections are open all week and are separated by a short street, Calle Juan Alvarez. They have different specialties; one is noted for clothes, rebozos, and blankets to the north, and tools, pottery, and household goods, such as attractive copper hanging lamps, to the south. This is also the area for old and rare books, many at a ridiculously low cost, if you're willing to hunt and bargain. Most, however, are in Spanish. **Metro:** Allende.

Mercado De Artesanías ("La Ciudadela"), Plaza de la Ciudadela.

An interesting market—large, clean, and with numerous stalls, it rambles on forever just off Balderas and Ayuntamiento in the Plaza de la Ciudadela. Here you'll find crafts from all over Mexico including a good selection of the highly collectable large Huichol Indian yarn "paintings." The quality is good here, and bargaining skills are a must. It's open daily from 11am or noon to 8pm. **Metro:** Juárez.

Mercado Insurgentes, on Londres between Florencia and Amberes.

Mercado Insurgentes is a full-fledged crafts market tucked in the Zona Rosa. Because of its Zona Rosa address, you might expect exhorbitant prices, but vendors in the maze of stalls are eager to bargain and good buys are not hard to come by.

Merced Market, Circunvalación between General Anaya and Adolfo Gurrión.

This is the biggest market in the city and among the most fascinating in the country, with an intense activity and energy level akin to the Abastos market in Oaxaca and the Friday Ocotlán market south of there. Several years ago the city tried to move this market because of the traffic congestion around the market and because its semipermanent street-vendor sprawl had almost reached the steps of the Palacio Nacional. The effort was fruitless because the Merced has been functioning successfully here for centuries, although there's a limit to street vendors now. Officially, the Merced consists of several modern buildings, but shops line tidy-but-people-filled streets all the way to the Zócalo. Near the market, street vendors hawk their wares as well. The first building is mainly for fruits and vegetables; the others contain just about everything you would find if a department store joined forces with a discount warehouse—a good place to shop— especially for housewares such as hand-held lemon, lime, and orange juicers of all sizes; tinware; colorful spoons; decorative oil cloth; etc. The main market is east of the Zócalo on Circunvalación between

General Anaya and Adolfo Gurrión. To get here from the Zócalo take Corregidor, the street to the right of the Palacio Nacional, and follow it five blocks to Circunvalación and turn right. Walk for two long blocks and you'll see the entrance to the market on the left. It's also interesting to meander past all the shops on other streets as you zigzag your way to the market. Or take the Metro from the Zócalo to the Merced stop right outside the market. To return to the Zócalo or anywhere else within the city, take the Metro (Línea 1) from the Merced station, which is just outside the enclosed market. You can change at Pino Suárez (first stop) to take you to the Zócalo.

9

Mexico City Nights

IF YOU HAVE ANY ENERGY LEFT AFTER SIGHTSEEING AT THIS HIGH ALTITUDE, the capital of Mexico offers up quite a variety of nighttime entertainment. From mariachi and reggae to opera, from regional folkloric dancing to classic ballet, from dinner shows to drinking establishments, the choices are numerous. And for the most part, you can enjoy them in Mexico City at a price that is less than what you would spend for nightlife in another of the world's major cities. On the other hand, if you're willing to let *la vida Mexicana* put on its own fascinating show for you, the bill will be much less. People watching, cafe sitting, music, even a dozen mariachi bands all playing at once, can be yours for next to nothing.

For current information on entertainment at all of the establishments listed here, the best source is the Sunday edition of *The News,* which has a full schedule of events. A limited number of events are printed on days other than Sunday. *Donde,* a free magazine found in hotels, is another good source for locating nightlife, but it doesn't list changing entertainment or current exhibits. For major attractions tickets can usually be obtained through **Ticketmaster** (☎ **325-9000**).

Lobby bars tend to have live entertainment of the low-key type in the late afternoon and on into the evening. Discos are alive and well in Mexico, with flashy light shows and megadecible music. Throbbing discos and dinner dance establishments tend to get going around 9 or 10:30pm and last until at least 3am. Most dance clubs operate only Thursday through Saturday. Fiesta nights give visitors a chance to dine on typical Mexican food and see Mexico's wonderful regional dancing, which seems always to be a treat no matter how many times you've seen it.

Much of the city's nightlife takes place around the **Zona Rosa,** a traditional place to stroll, imbibe, and eat at several places, if you want—appetizers one place, dinner at another, and dessert somewhere else, winding up at a nearby disco or dancing establishment, hotel lobby bar, or cozy coffeehouse. Outdoor cafes on **Copenhague Street** are in the thick of the Zona Rosa scene. With one or two exceptions, however, it has become more expensive than it is worthwhile. Another tradition is Garibaldi Square, where mariachis tune up and wait to be hired. Restaurants and drinking establishments there feature mariachis in a typical Mexican atmosphere. It's a slice of Mexican life that every traveler must experience at least once.

1   The Performing Arts

Auditorio Nacional, Chapultepec Park, on Reforma. ☎ **520-3502.**
The National Auditorium, in Chapultepec Park, is usually a theater for symphonies, international ballet, opera, and theater companies.
   Tickets: Vary depending on the performance.
   Metro: Auditorio.

Palacio de Bellas Artes, Lázaro Cárdenas, on the east side of the Alameda. ☎ **709-3111,** ext. 173.

Besides hosting traveling ballet and opera companies from around the world, performances of Mexico's famed Ballet Folklórico de Mexico are held here several times weekly. (See also the Alameda walking tour in Chapter 7.)

The Ballet Folklórico is a celebration of pre- and post-Hispanic dancing in Mexico. A typical program will include Aztec ritual dances, agricultural dances from Jalisco, a Veracruz-style fiesta, and a Christmas celebration—all melded together with mariachis, marimba players, singers, and dancers.

Because many other events are held in the Bellas Artes—visits by foreign opera companies, for instance—there are times when the Ballet Folklórico is moved. Usually, it reappears in the Auditorio Nacional in Chapultepec Park. Check at the Bellas Artes box office. There are two companies—three, if you count the one usually on tour. The show is popular and tickets are bought up rapidly (especially by a tour agency at twice the cost). The box office is on the ground floor of the Bellas Artes, main entrance. **Note:** The theater tends to be very cold so you may want to bring a sweater.

Major Concert & Performance Halls

Auditorio Nacional, Chapultepec Park (☎ **202-3502**).

Casa del Lago, Chapultepec Park (☎ **553-6318** or **553-6362**).

El Granero, Chapultepec Park (☎ **280-8771**, ext 411 or **290-7844**).

Foro Shakespeare, Zamora 7. Col. Condesa (☎ **553-5242**).

Palacio de Bellas Artes, Lázaro Cárdenas, Col. Centro (☎ **709-3111**, extension 173).

Palacio de Minería, Tacuba 5, Col. Centro (☎ **521-4022** or **521-4021**).

Sala Netzahualcoyotl, Centro Cultural Universitario, Insurgentes Sur 3000 (☎ **655-1344,** ext. 7055).

Sala Silvestre Revueltas (formerly Sala Ollin Yolixtli), Centro Cultural Universitario, Insurgentes Sur 3000 (☎ **606-8848** or **655-3611**).

Teatro Blanquita, Lázaro Cárdenas, Col. Centro 14 (☎ **512-8264** or **510-1581**).

Teatro de la Ciudad, Donceles 36, Col. Centro (☎ **521-2355**).

Teatro de los Insurgentes, Insurgentes Sur 1587, Col. San José Insurgentes (☎ **660-2429**).

Teatro Fabregas, Serapio Rendón, Col. San Rafael (☎ **566-1644** or **566-1645**).

Teatro Santa Catarina, Plaza De Santa Catarina, Col. Coyoacán (☎ **658-0560**).

Tickets: $25.50–$35.50.

Open: Box office, Mon–Sat 11am–7pm, Sun 8:30–9am; Ballet Folklórico performances, Sun 9:30am and 9pm; Wed 9pm. **Metro:** Bellas Artes.

Teatro de la Cuidad, Donceles 36. ☎ 521-2355.

An alternative to the Ballet Folklórico de Mexico is the Ballet Folklórico Nacional Aztlán, in the beautiful turn-of-the-century Teatro de la Cuidad, a block northeast of the Palacio de Bellas Artes between Xicotencatl and Allende. Performances here are as good as the better-known ones in the Bellas Artes, but tickets are a lot cheaper and much easier to obtain. Other major performances of ballet, concerts, etc., also appear here.

Tickets: $9 to the Ballet Folklórico; call about other performances.

Open: Shows Sun 9:30am, 2:30pm; Tues 8:30pm. **Metro:** Bellas Artes.

Centro Cultural Universitario (University Cultural Center—University of Mexico Campus), Insurgentes Sur 3000. ☎ 665-2580.

The Centro Cultural is part of the University of Mexico, but located south of the university proper and north of the Periférico, in the southern limits of the city (see listing for Ciudad Universitario in Chapter 6). The most popular hall here is the Netzahualcoyotl Concert Hall (☎ 655-1344). The other is the Sala Silvestre Revueltas (☎ 606-8848). Also in this area are the Sala Miguel Covarrubias movie theater; the Salas Julio Bracho and Carlos Chávez; the Justo Sierra Auditorium; the Teatro Juan Ruiz de Alarcon; and the Foro Experimental Sor Juana Ines de la Cruz.

Palacio de Minería, Tacuba 5. ☎ 521-4022 or 521-4023.

The handsome 19th-century neo-Colonial Palacio de Minería, near the Alameda, was formerly the school of mining. (See also the Alameda walking tour in Chapter 7.) Today it's used by chamber orchestras and for other small cultural and entertainment events.

Theater

Theater productions, as you may expect, will be in Spanish. Most are written by Mexican and European authors, but occasionally you can find adaptions of U.S. theater hits, especially musicals. Theaters listed below seem to have regular attractions, but there are many more theaters in the city where live performances can be enjoyed.

El Granero (The Granary), Chapultepec Park. ☎ 280-8771, ext. 411 or 280-7844.

Performances are usually in Spanish, but check local listings. El Granero is behind the National Auditorium, which faces Reforma across from the Hotel Presidente Inter-Contintal. **Metro:** Auditorio.

Teatro Blanquita, Lazaro Cárdenas 14, ☎ **512-8264.**

For some of the country's best popular musical performances as well as comedy and vaudeville shows, check out what's on at the Teatro Blanquita, north of the Latin American Tower. **Metro:** Bellas Artes.

Teatro Fabregas, Serapio Rendón, Col. San Rafael. ☎ **566-1644.**

This theater, in the Alameda area, has plays and musicals all year. **Metro:** Bellas Artes.

2   The Club & Music Scene

Mariachis

At some time or other, everybody—Mexicans and "turistas" alike—goes to see and hear the mariachi players. The mariachis are strolling musicians who wear distinctive costumes that make them look like Mexican cowboys dressed up for a special occasion. Their costumes—tight spangled trousers, fancy jackets, and big floppy bow ties—date back to the French occupation of Mexico in the mid-19th century, as indeed, does their name. *Mariachi* is believed to be the Mexican mispronunciation of the French word for marriage, which is where the musicians were often on call for their services.

In Mexico City, the mariachis make their headquarters around the **Plaza de Garibaldi,** which is a 10-minute stroll north of the Palacio de Bellas Artes up Avenida Lázaro Cárdenas, at Avenida República de Honduras. You will pass dozens of stores and a couple of burlesque houses.

In the Plaza de Garibaldi itself, mariachi players are everywhere. At every corner, guitars are stacked together like rifles in an army training camp. Young musicians strut proudly in their flashy outfits, on the lookout for señoritas to impress. They play when they feel like it, when there's a good chance to gather in some tips, or when someone orders a song—the going rate seems to be around $5 or $10 per song. The best time to hear music in the square itself is after 9 or 10pm, especially on Sunday.

In any of the eating and drinking establishments around the plaza you can enjoy the mariachi music that swirls through the air. **Tlaquepaque,** across the square, is a well-known tourist-oriented restaurant where you can dine as mariachis stroll by. But remember—if you give a bandleader the sign, you're the one who pays for the song, just like outside in the square.

IMPRESSIONS

You may become as drunk as you wish to in a cantina and, even with the doors open, talk as loud and as long as you are able, for cantinas were made to get drunk and talk loud in.
—Charles Flandrau, *Viva Mexico* (1908)

Another popular place on the square is **Plaza Santa Cecilia,** Amargura 30 (☎ 526-2455 or 529-1102). Monday through Saturday shows are at 9 and 10:30pm, midnight, and 1:30am, for $12.

Pulquería Hermana Hortensia, Amargura 4 (☎ 529-7828), is perhaps the most adventurous spot for newcomers to Mexico City. It's on the Plaza de Garibaldi near the northeast corner at Amargura and República de Honduras. Unlike most pulque bars, La Hermana Hortensia is a *pulquera familiar* (a "family" bar, that is, you can bring your wife—but not your kids). Pulque (that's "pool-keh") is a thick and flavorsome drink made by fermenting the juice of a maguey (century) plant. Discovered by the ancient Toltecs and shared with the Aztecs, pulque was a sacred drink forbidden to the common people for centuries. One of the effects of the Spanish Conquest was to liberate pulque for the masses. Was this good or bad? Ask your neighbor in La Hermana Hortensia as you quaff the thick brew. Pulque packs a wallop, although it's not nearly so strong as those other maguey-based drinks, tequila and mezcal. By the way, the pulque here can be ordered with nuts blended in for a different flavor.

Don't get the idea that you'll see only your countryfolk in the Plaza de Garibaldi, for it is indeed a Mexican phenomenon. As evening falls, lots of people from the neighborhood come to stroll or sit. (See also listing for Jorongo Bar, below).

Trio Music

El Chato La Posta, Londres 25. Col. Juárez. ☎ 546-1199 or 705-1457.

This popular bar features great trio music and botanas (snacks) with the drinks. Several different groups entertain.

Admission: $30.

Open: Thurs–Sat 10:30–3am.

Jorongo Bar, Hotel María Isabel Sheraton, Reforma 325. ☎ 207-3933.

For wonderful Mexican trio music in plush surroundings, make your way to Jorongo Bar at the María Isabel-Sheraton Hotel, facing the Angel Monument. The reputation for this bar's trio/mariachi music has been good for decades—it's an institution.

Admission: $13 cover charge; drinks $3.50–$6.

Open: 7pm–2am.

Jazz

Maquiavelo, Hotel Krystal, Liverpool 155. ☎ 211-0092 or 211-3460.

This little-known nightclub, in the heart of the Zona Rosa, changes from an informal bar during the day to a jazz center in the evenings.

Admission: $13 for live jazz, 5pm–midnight.

Open: 1pm–midnight.

Salsa, Merengue & Reggae

Allegro, Cuauhtémoc 87, Col. Roma. ☎ **525-8064** or **525-8082.**

Lots of fun and lively music here, with the sounds of the Caribbean and Latin America. It's near the Zona Rosa between Colima and Durango.

Admission: $14.50.

Open: Thurs–Sat 10pm–3am.

Antillanos, Pimental 78, Col. San Rafael. ☎ **592-0439** or **591-0914.**

Known for its salsa music, you'll hear good bands and have space to dance as well. Antillanos is north of the Zona Rosa and Sullivan Park in the quadrant bounded by Sullivan, San Cosme, Insurgentes Norte, and Melchor Ocampo.

Admission: Varies.

Open: Thurs–Sat 10pm–3am.

Dinner Shows & Mexican Fiestas

El Patio, Atenas 9, Col. Juárez. ☎ **566-1743.**

Some of Mexico's most famous singers and entertainers perform in a lengthy after-dinner show. El Patio is at the far eastern edge of the Zona Rosa.

Admission: Call for current charge.

Open: Tues–Sat 10pm–3am.

Hotel de Cortes, Avenida Hidalgo 85. ☎ **518-2182.**

Unless it rains, there's a Mexican Fiesta every Saturday on the open patio of this colonial-era convent-turned-hotel on the Alameda. (See also the walking tour of the Alameda in Chapter 7.) The price of admission includes drinks, dinner, and the show.

Admission: $17–$25.50.

Open: Sat 8–10pm.

La Veranda, Hotel María Isabel Sheraton, Reforma 325, at Río Tiber, ☎ **207-3933.**

The elaborate Fiesta Mexicana dinner and show here has also been a staple of Mexico City entertainment for years, featuring a good dinner and a lively display of Mexican regional dancers in colorful attire.

Admission: $25.50–$34.

Open: Mon–Fri 7–10pm.

Nightclubs & Discos

Chez'Ar, at the Hotel Aristos, Reforma 276, at Copenhague. ☎ **211-0112.**

The French specialty restaurant of the Hotel Aristos features ballroom and swing dancing nightly. You can come for just the dancing if you like. Coat and tie preferred.

Admission: $13–$21.50

Open: Mon–Sat 7am–1pm and 6pm–2:30am.

La Cucaracha, Hamburgo 77, Col. Juárez. ☎ 207-2059.

This is a dance club and restaurant very popular among a young crowd. If you enter the disco you pay the cover.

Admission: $8.50.

Open: Daily 6pm–2am.

Dynasty Disco, Hotel Nikko, Campos Elíseos 204, Polanco. ☎ 280-1111.

This up-scale dance venue is in one of the capital's top hotels. Besides the disco there are two live shows nightly of mariachi or trio music which last about 45 minutes each, all for the price of admission. Drinks, of course, are extra.

Admission: Mon–Thurs $6 and Fri, Sat, Sun $10.

Open: Mon–Thurs 9pm–1:30am; Fri–Sun 9pm–3am.

Hotel Fiesta Americana Reforma, Colón Circle. ☎ 705-1515.

This enormous, fashionable hotel offers one of the best lineups of low-key, late-night entertainment. First there's the **Caballo Negro** Monday through Saturday at 8pm and 1am. The shows change but often feature singers and comics. In **Las Sillas** there are two shows Tuesday through Saturday at 10pm and 3am featuring trios singing the best of Mexican ballads. **Barbarela** has a dance floor but there's also entertainment. It's open Wednesday through Saturday with shows at 10pm and 3am. However, double check for current times, cover charges, and entertainers.

Hotel Majestic, Madero 73. ☎ 521-8600.

The popular rooftop bar of this hotel overlooks the Zócalo and the Catedral Metropolitana. A variety of good singers (usually) entertain, and there could be a trio crooning romantic Mexican favorites.

Admission: Free.

Open: Daily noon–1am; entertainment 7pm–1am.

Lipstick Disco, Aristos Hotel, Reforma 276, at Copenhague. ☎ 211-0112.

For a lively place try this Zona Rosa disco, in Aristos on Reforma just down from Copenhague, the popular streetside dining area.

Admission: $21.50 for men with an open bar; women free.

Open: Thurs–Sat 8pm–2:30am or so.

Mekano, Genova 44, Col. Juárez. ☎ 208-9611 or 208-9551.

For the really hip—this Zona Rosa dance club will give you a workout.

Admission: Women free, men $34.

Open: Thurs–Sat 9pm–3am.

Lobby Bars

Caviar Bar, Hotel Marquís Reforma, Reforma 465, Col. Cuauhtémoc, ☎ 211-3600.

While guests enjoy light meals and drinks in the lobby Caviar Bar of this stylish hotel, a string quartet plays in the evening hours. Totally elegant and wonderfully soothing.

The Glass Box, Hotel Emporio, Reforma 124. ☎ **566-7766.**

Beveled glass windows surround the Glass Box, the classy bar of the Hotel Emporio. Entertainment includes Mexican comedians and singers offering a variety of music styles.

Tickets: Cover charge varies.

Open: Mon–Sat 9pm–1am.

Hotel Camino Real, Mariano Escobedo 700, Col. Nueva Anzures. ☎ **203-2121.**

You'll be surrounded by people enjoying the piano music at this very popular lobby bar. Order a drink and kick back for a relaxing respite.

Admission: Free.

Open: Daily noon–1am.

Hotel Galeria Plaza, Hamburgo 195, at Varsovia. ☎ **211-0014.**

Ever since this luxury hotel opened in the early 1980s it's been known for its inviting Lobby Bar entertainment. The type of music varies but often includes jazz.

Admission: Free.

Open: 11am–1am; live music 7pm–1am.

La Mancha Piano Bar, Aristos Hotel, Reforma 276, at Copenhague. ☎ **211-0112.**

Call first to make sure of the hours and type of entertainment. Usually there's live music from 1pm to midnight and three shows nightly.

Tickets: $13, with an $11.50 drink minimum.

Open: Thurs–Sat 1pm–3am; shows 9pm, 11pm, 1am.

---

3 More Entertainment

Movies

You'll find many current first-run hits playing in Mexico City, usually in the original-language version with Spanish or English subtitles, and usually under the same title (although the title will be translated into Spanish).

The best national and international movies are shown at several primary places: **Cineteca Nacional,** Calzada Mexico-Coyoacán 389, at the southern end of Avenida Cuauhtémoc (☎ **688-3272**), which shows quality foreign films and often retrospective series; several theaters in the **Centro Cultural Universitario** (☎ **665-2580**); **Casa del Lago** in Chapultepec Park (☎ **553-6318** or **553-6362**); and the **Cinematografo del Chopo,** Dr. Atl 37, Col. Santa María la Ribera.

The best place to check for current cinematic offerings is in the Friday and Sunday entertainment section of Mexico City's English-language paper, *The News.*

10

Easy Excursions from Mexico City

M EXICO CITY IS SURROUNDED BY SUBURBAN AREAS THAT ARE AS fascinating as the city itself, and all of them are within the reach of a short bus ride. This chapter focuses on the main attractions of these places. The ruins of Teotihuacán, the Viceregal Museum at Tepotzotlán, and the cities of Toluca and Pachuca are suitable for day trips short enough to have you back in town by evening. Tlaxcala and Puebla are also good choices for day trips but you may find these cities' attractions worthy of more than one day. Valle de Bravo and Ixtapan de la Sal, known for their golf courses and spas, are only about two hours from Mexico City but are best thought of as two- or three-day getaways.

1   The Pyramids of San Juan Teotihuacán

30 miles NE of Mexico City

GETTING THERE & DEPARTING • By Bus   Buses leave every half hour (from 5am to 10pm) every day of the week from the Terminal Central de Autobuses del Norte, and the trip takes one hour. When you reach the Terminal Norte, look for the **Autobuses Sahagun** sign located at the far northwest end all the way down to the sign "8 Espera."

Since entrances to the archeological zone were changing when this book was written, be sure to ask the driver where you should wait for returning buses, how frequently buses run, and especially the time of the last bus back.

• By Car   Driving to San Juan Teotihuacán on either the toll Highway 85D or free Highway 132D will take about an hour. Head north on Insurgentes to get out of the city. Highway 132D passes through picturesque villages and the like, but it is excruciatingly slow, due to the surfeit of trucks and buses; Highway 85D, the toll road, is duller but faster.

Teotihuacán is one of Mexico's most remarkable ruins, and you shouldn't miss it. The name means "place where gods were born." Occupation of the area of Teotihuacán began around 500 B.C. but it wasn't until 100 B.C. that construction of the Pyramid of the Sun at Teotihuacán was begun. It corresponds to the time when the Classical Greeks were building their great monuments on the other side of the world, and with the beginning of cultures in Mexico's Yucatán Peninsula, Oaxaca, and Puebla. Teotihuacán was the dominant city in Mesoamerica during the Classical Period, covering 8 square miles with its magnificent pyramids, palaces, and houses. At its zenith around A.D. 500 there were at least 200,000 inhabitants, more than in contemporary Rome. Through trade and other contact, its influence was felt in other parts of Mexico and as far south as Mexico's Yucatán peninsula and Guatemala. But little is known about the city's inhabitants, what language they spoke, what they looked like, where they came from, or why they abandoned the place in A.D. 700. It is known that at the beginning of the first century A.D. the Xitle volcano erupted near Cuicuilco (south of Mexico City) and destroyed

Excursions from
Mexico City

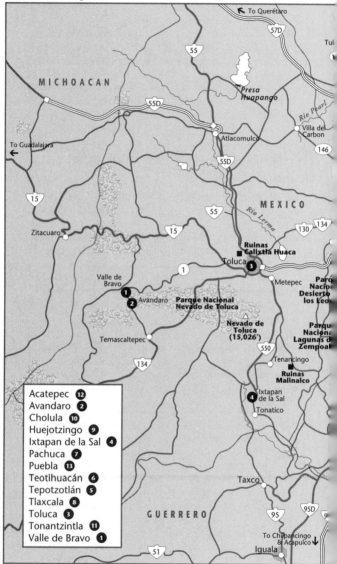

that city, which was the most dominant city of the time. Those inhabitants migrated to Teotihuacán—perhaps overwhelming the city's resources. Scholars believe that Teotihuacán's decline was gradual, perhaps over a 250-year period, due in part to overpopulation and depletion of natural resources. In the end it appears that the people

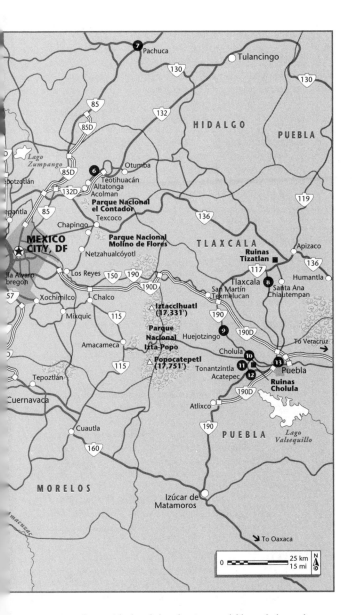

were poorly nourished and that the city was deliberately burned. Ongoing excavations have revealed something of the culture. According to archeoastronomer John B. Carlson, the cult of Venus that determined wars and human sacrifices elsewhere in Mesoamerica was prominent at Teotihuacán as well. Ceremonial rituals were timed with the appearance of Venus as the morning and evening star. The symbol of Venus at Teotihuacán (as at Cacaxtla 50 miles away, near Tlaxcala), appears as a star or half star with a full or half circle. Carlson also suggests the possibility that Teotihuacán was conquered by people from Cacaxtla, because name glyphs of conquered peoples at Cacaxtla show Teotihuacán-like pyramids. Numerous tombs with human remains (many of them either sacrificial inhabitants of the city or perhaps war captives), and objects of jewelry, pottery, and daily life have been uncovered along the foundations of buildings. It appears that the primary deity at Teotihuacán was a female "Great Goddess," for lack of any other known name. Today what remains are the rough stone structures of the three pyramids and sacrificial altars, and some of the grand houses, all of which were once covered in stucco and painted with brilliant frescoes (mainly in red). The Toltecs, who rose to power after the decline of Teotihuacán, were fascinated with Teotihuacán and incorporated Teotihuacán symbols into their own cultural motifs. The Aztecs, who came after the Toltecs, were likewise fascinated with the Toltecs and the ruins of Teotihuacán, and adopted many of *their* symbols and motifs. (For more information on Teotihuacán and it's influence in Mesoamerica see also the "History" and "Archeology" section in Chapter 1, "Introducing Mexico City.")

Orientation

As this book went to press, a number of changes were in the works at Teotihuacán. Parking lots and souvenir stands were being moved to the outer edges of the roadway around the site. A small train was to be installed to take visitors from the entry booths to various stops within the site. The museum and cultural center were to be in a new location. The map included in this book reflects these changes, which may or may not have been moved or built by the time you arrive.

Do keep in mind these important points: You will be doing a great deal of walking, and perhaps some climbing, at an altitude of more than 7,000 feet. Take it slowly; bring sunblock and a hat; be prepared for the summer rainy season, when it rains almost every afternoon.

A good place to start is at the **museum.** Findings during recent digs are on display, including several tombs with skeletons wearing necklaces of human and simulated jawbones, and newly discovered sculpture.

THE LAYOUT

The grand buildings of Teotihuacán were laid out on a cosmic plan. The front wall of the **Pyramid of the Sun** is exactly square to (facing) the point on the horizon where the sun sets twice annually. So if a line were drawn from the apex of the pyramid to the sun at noon on the day when the sun reaches its highest point, the line would in theory be perfectly vertical. The rest of the ceremonial buildings were laid out at right angles to the Pyramid of the Sun.

Teotihuacán

The main thoroughfare, called by archeologists the **Avenue of the Dead,** runs roughly north-south. The **Pyramid of the Moon** is at the northern end, and the **Ciudadela** is on the southern part of the thoroughfare. Actually, the great street was several miles long in its heyday, but only a mile or so has been uncovered and restored.

The Teotihuacán Archeological Site

THE CIUDADELA

The Ciudadela, or Citadel, was named by the Spaniards. Actually, this immense sunken square was not a fortress at all, although the impressive walls make it look like one. It was the grand foundation for the Feathered Serpent Pyramid—the Temple of Quetzalcoatl. Scholars aren't certain that the Teotihuacán culture embraced the Quetzalcoatl deity so well known in the Toltec, Aztec, and Maya cultures. The feathered serpent is featured in the Ciudadela, but whether it was worshiped as Quetzalcoatl or a similar god isn't yet known. Once you've admired the great scale of the Ciudadela, go down the steps into the massive court and head for the ruined temple, in the middle.

The Temple of Quetzalcoatl was covered over by an even larger structure, a pyramid. As you walk toward the center of the Ciudadela's court, you'll be approaching the pyramid. The Feathered Serpent Pyramid will be on your left. Walk around to the right of it, and soon you'll see the reconstructed temple close behind the pyramid. There's a narrow passage between the two structures, and traffic is supposed to be one way—which is why I directed you to the right.

Early temples were often covered over by later ones in Mexico and Central America. The Pyramid of the Sun may have been built up in this way. Archeologists have tunneled deep inside the Feathered Serpent Pyramid and found several ceremonially buried human remains, interred with precise detail and position, but as yet no person of royalty has been unearthed. Drawings of how the building once looked show that every level was covered with faces of a feathered serpent. As for the Temple of Quetzalcoatl, you'll notice at once the large, fine, carved serpents' heads jutting out from collars of feathers carved in the stone walls. Other feathered serpents are carved in relief low on the walls. You can get a good idea of the glory of Mexico's ancient cities from this temple.

AVENUE OF THE DEAD

The Avenue of the Dead got its strange and forbidding name from the Aztecs, who mistook the little temples that line both sides of the avenue for tombs of kings or priests.

As you stroll north along the Avenue of the Dead toward the Pyramid of the Moon, look on the right for a bit of wall sheltered by a modern corrugated roof. Beneath the shelter, the wall still bears a painting of a jaguar. From this fragment, you might be able to build a picture of the breathtaking spectacle that must have met the eye when all the paintings along the avenue were intact.

PYRAMID OF THE SUN

The Pyramid of the Sun is located on the east side of the Avenue of the Dead. As pyramids go, this is the third largest in the world. The Great Pyramid of Cholula, near Puebla, is the largest structure ever built. Second-largest is the Pyramid of Cheops on the outskirts of Cairo, Egypt. Teotihuacán's Pyramid of the Sun is, at the base, 730 feet per side—almost as large as Cheops. But at 210 feet high, the Pyramid of the Sun is only about half as high as its Egyptian rival. No matter. It's still the biggest restored pyramid in the Western Hemisphere, and an awesome sight. Although the Pyramid of the Sun was not built as a great king's tomb, it does have secret tunnels and chambers beneath it, but they aren't open to the public.

The first structure of the pyramid was probably built a century before Christ, and the temple that used to crown the pyramid was finished about 400 years later (A.D. 300). By the time the pyramid was discovered and restoration was begun (early in our century), the temple had completely disappeared, and the pyramid was just a mass of rubble covered with bushes and trees.

If you're game, trudge up the 248 steps to the top. The view is marvelous—if the smog's not too thick.

PYRAMID OF THE MOON

The Pyramid of the Moon faces an interesting plaza at the northern end of the avenue. The plaza is surrounded by little temples, and by the Palace of Quetzal-Mariposa (or Quetzal-Butterfly), on the left (west) side. You get about the same range of view from the top of the Pyramid of the Moon as you do from its larger neighbor, because the moon pyramid is built on higher ground. The perspective straight down the Avenue of the Dead is magnificent.

PALACE OF QUETZAL-MARIPOSA

The Palace of Quetzal-Mariposa lay in ruins until the 1960s, when restoration work began. Today it echoes wonderfully with its former glory, as figures of Quetzal-Mariposa (a mythical exotic bird-butterfly) appear painted on walls or carved in the pillars of the inner court.

Behind the Palace of Quetzal-Mariposa is the Palace of the Jaguars, complete with murals showing a lively jaguar musical combo, and some frescoes. It's open daily from 8am to 5pm. Admission is $5 Monday through Friday and free to all on Sunday; there's a $7 fee for permission to use a video camera.

Where to Dine

You may want to pack a lunch to take to the ruins; a box lunch will save you a long walk to any of the restaurants. Almost any hotel or restaurant in Mexico City can prepare it for you. Vendors at the ruins also sell drinks and snacks.

Among the possibilities at the ruins are several dozen tidy little **cookshops** tended by bright and energetic senoritas. Walk out to the traffic circle and turn left; you'll find them along the road. Pick a place that appeals to you, take a look at what's cooking, and ask prices in advance. Many of them put out little signs advertising their specialty of *mixiotes,* a wonderful regional dish, usually of chicken, potatoes, carrots, and a light white sauce (not spicy) all wrapped and cooked in a thin parchment paper made from the maguey leaf. It's delicious and differs from mixiotes elsewhere, which are usually made with beef, pork, or lamb in a red sauce. A full lunch costs from $3.50 to $5. Cold soft drinks and beer are served.

EXPENSIVE

La Gruta. ☎ 595/6-0127 or 6-0104.

Cuisine: MEXICAN. **Directions:** Ask for the most direct way from where you exit.
Prices: Main courses $7.50–$16.
Open: Daily 11am–7pm.

La Gruta is a huge, delightfully cool natural grotto filled with nattily attired waiters and the sound of clinking glasses. Soft drinks and beer are served until the full bar opens. You have the option of ordering a five-course fixed-price lunch or choosing your own combination—perhaps a hamburger and a soft drink.

Hotel-Restaurant Villa Arqueologica, outside the southern end of the site. ☎ 595/6-0244 or 6-0909.

Cuisine: FRENCH/MEXICAN. **Directions:** Ask directions from wherever you exit; it's just outside the pyramid grounds fence.

Prices: Fixed price lunch or dinner $21.50.
Open: Daily 7:30am–11pm.

A good spot for lunch (in a fairly elegant dining room) or a post-prandial coffee (perhaps on the patio overlooking the swimming pool). The hotel part of the Villa Arqueologica is the very comfortable Club Mediterranee hotel, within view of the ruins, just as the Chichén Itzá, Cobá, Uxmal, and Cholula. Cactuses line the driveway, and red tiles and white stucco give the place a country ambience. The hotel has a library, tennis court, pool, and souvenir shop, as well as comfortable modern guest rooms.

2 Puebla

80 miles E of Mexico City

GETTING THERE & DEPARTING • By Bus   Buses to Puebla leave from Mexico City's TAPO station. The trip from Mexico City to Puebla takes about two hours by bus. You arrive at the CAPU bus station in Puebla, which is a distance from the center of town. City buses ("CAPU") travel between the bus station in Puebla and the downtown area.

From Mexico City, **Pullman Plus** has deluxe service to and from the capital every half hour. **ADO** (Autobuses del Oriente) buses depart from the capital every 10 minutes from 7am to midnight daily. **Autobuses Unidos** provides convenient second-class service from Mexico City to Puebla every 15 minutes **Autobuses Estrella Roja** provides similar second-class services to Mexico City (every 10 minutes, 24 hours daily). If you're going on to Tlaxcala or Pachuca from Puebla, **Flecha Azul** (☎ 49-7128), or **ERCO** (☎ 49-7177), have the most direct service. **Autobuses Surianos** (☎ 49-9055) goes directly to Huamantla every 10 minutes as does **ATAH** (☎ 49-7011).

• By Car   There are two roads to Puebla from the capital: Highway 190—an old, winding drive that you'll travel with great frustration, following convoys of lumbering trucks (with no chance to pass them); and Highway 150D, a new toll road that is faster.

ESSENTIALS • Information   The **State Tourist Office** (☎ 46-1285) is at Av. 5 Oriente no. 3, next to the cathedral and the Biblioteca Palifoxiana; the office is open Monday through Friday from 8am to 8:30pm, Saturday from 9am to 8:30pm, and Sunday from 9am to 2pm—closed holidays. The **City Tourist Office** faces the main plaza at Portal Hidalgo 14 (☎ 32-0357), on the same side of the plaza as the Royalty Hotel. It's open daily from 9am to 9pm. On Saturday and Sunday this office sponsors **free bus tours** from 10am to 6pm. Buses pass every half hour in front of the office on the zócalo and have 34 stops on their route around the city. Tourists can get on and off at their leisure and the cost is $1.50.

Puebla (altitude 7,040 ft.; population 1,250,000), founded around 1531, has preserved much of the wealth and architecture created

Puebla

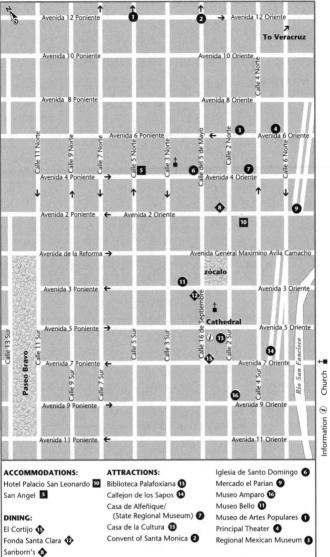

ACCOMMODATIONS:
Hotel Palacio San Leonardo 10
San Angel 5

DINING:
El Cortijo 15
Fonda Santa Clara 12
Sanborn's 8

ATTRACTIONS:
Biblioteca Palafoxiana 13
Callejon de los Sapos 14
Casa de Alfeñique/
 (State Regional Museum) 7
Casa de la Cultura 13
Convent of Santa Monica 2

Iglesia de Santo Domingo 6
Mercado el Parian 9
Museo Amparo 16
Museo Bello 11
Museo de Artes Populares 1
Principal Theater 4
Regional Mexican Museum 3

during its first centuries. The area around Puebla was already a center for pottery making before the Conquest, and afterward *talavera*
pottery makers from Toledo, Spain, blended their talents with those
of the native population to create a wonderful pottery and tile tradition that is very visible today. You'll see the craft in many church
domes and building facades covered in tile, on display in museums,

and in talavera factories here. This is a great place for pottery and tile purchases. Christianity flourished until 1767, when an anti-Catholic movement closed many churches and convents. Some 99 churches survive, along with many grand monasteries, convents, and a magnificent bishop's palace next to the cathedral.

What to See & Do

IN TOWN

The heart of town is the shady **zócalo,** known as the **Plaza de la Constitución,** a beautiful place with a central fountain and painted iron benches. On one side is the **Cathedral,** completed in 1649, and Calle 3 Oriente and the other sides are flanked by the *portales* (arcades) of colonial-era buildings, which today house restaurants, hotels, and shops. Most of the museums, shops, and hotels mentioned here are within walking distance of the zócalo.

Just across the street from the cathedral, on the corner of Avenida 5 Oriente and Calle 16 de Septiembre, is the old **Archbishop's Palace,** which now houses the **Casa de la Cultura** and the **Biblioteca Palafoxiana** (library). This library (on the second floor), which is the oldest one in the Americas (also the most beautiful), was built in 1646 by Juan de Palafoxe y Mendoza, then archbishop and founder of the College of Saints Peter and Paul. It bespeaks the glory of this period with its elegant tile floor, hand-carved wood walls and ceiling, inlaid tables, and gilded wooden statues. Bookcases are filled with 17th-century books and manuscripts in Spanish, Creole, French, and English.

The **Iglesia de Santo Domingo** on Calle 5 de Mayo between Avenidas 4 and 6 Oriente, originally part of a monastery, was finished in 1611. The **Capilla del Rosario** (chapel) inside it is a fantastic symphony of gilt and beautiful stone dedicated to the Virgin of the Rosary and built in 1690.

Opened in 1991, the **Museo Amparo,** Calle 2 Sur No. 708 (☎ 46-4200) is among the top archeological museums in the country, and it's housed in a colonial-era building dating from 1534. There are seven *salas* on the first floor and five on the second floor. Sala "Arte Rupestre" shows examples of cave paintings throughout the world. In the Sala "Codice del Tiempo" a wonderful wall-size timeline places important cultures and world events from 2500 B.C. to A.D. 1500. Other first-floor salas include information on the discovery of corn and its importance to Mexican culture, on art production techniques, and on the function of art in society. Upstairs is a fabulous collection of pre-Hispanic art covering the pre- to post-classic periods. Some of the clay figures from Nayarit are especially amazing. Signs are in Spanish and English. No cameras are permitted. It's at the corner of Calle 2 Sur. Admission costs $3; students $1.50; Monday free. It's open Wednesday through Monday (closed Tuesday) from 10am to 6pm.

The **Museo Bello** (also called the Museum of Art), near the corner of Calle 3 Sur and Avenida 3 Poniente (☎ 41-4296), holds some of the finest 17th-, 18th-, and 19th-century art in Mexico—French porcelain, beautiful hand-carved furniture, several very fine organs, and numerous paintings. The mandatory guided tour (in English or Spanish) is included in the admission cost of $3. It's open Tuesday through Sunday from 10am to 4:30pm.

The exterior architectural decoration of the **Casa de Alfeñique (State Regional Museum),** at Calle 4 Oriente (☎ **41-9475**), resembles an elaborate wedding cake—in fact, the name means "sugar-cake house." There's a good collection of pre-Hispanic artifacts and pottery, exhibits of regional crafts, colonial-era furniture, and a sizeable collection of *china poblana* costumes (the national costume of Mexico). The museum is $3^1/_2$ blocks northwest of the zócalo, between Calles 7 and 6 Norte. Admission is $1 for adults and 50¢ for children. It's open Tuesday through Sunday from 10am to 4:30pm.

When the convents in Puebla were closed in 1767, the **Convent of Santa Monica,** Av. 18 Poniente No. 103 (☎ **32-0178**), operated secretly, using entrances through private homes, which hid the convent from public view. It was "rediscovered" in 1935 and is a museum kept as it was found. It's at the corner of Avenida 18 Poniente and Calle 3 Sur. Admission is $2.50 and it's open Tuesday through Sunday from 10am to 4:30pm.

The **Santa Rosa Convent** was the largest convent in Puebla and belonged to the Dominican order. Today it houses the **Museo de Artes Populares,** Calle 3 Norte at Avenida 12 Poniente (☎ **46-4526**). On the first floor is the cavernous and beautifully tiled kitchen—where many native Mexican dishes were created—and the gift shop selling Puebla crafts. The second floor showcases the state's native groups and their arts, including 6-foot earthenware candelabras, regional costumes, minute scenes made of straw and clay, and hand-tooled leather. Tours last 20 minutes and the last one starts at 4:30pm. The museum is eight blocks northwest of the zócalo. Admission is $1 and it's open Tuesday through Sunday from 10am to 4:30pm.

AN EXCURSION TO CHOLULA

Six miles northwest of Puebla, the town of Cholula (population 45,000) is one of the holiest places in Mexico, noted for having the largest pyramid by volume, its staggering number of churches, and the two notable Indian baroque churches nearby. Nearby also is Huejotzingo, with its 16th-century church and one of the best pre-Lenten *carnavals* in Mexico.

To get to Cholula from Puebla, take one of the small white vans marked "Cholula" at the corner of Avenida 10 Poniente and Calle 11 Norte, or on Avenida 6 Norte at the corner of Calle 13 Norte. A taxi from Puebla costs $5 to $7.

On the outskirts of the city, within walking distance of the main plaza, the **Tepanapa Pyramid**—the largest pyramid in the world—looks like a mud and weed covered hill with a church on top; you can see the church from the main plaza. A small portion of the pyramid is restored. Archeologists have tunneled through it, so vestiges of its interior superimpositions are exposed. Excavations on the outside are ongoing. This town was a religious pilgrimage site for centuries before the Spaniards arrived. Quetzalcoatl, the famed man-god depicted as a feathered serpent, is thought to have lived here in exile for a time after he was forced to leave his city of Tula, capital of the Toltecs, in A.D. 900. The small museum, to the left of the entrance, has a model of what this pyramid looked like. It's open daily from 10:30am to 5pm; admission is $3 Monday through Saturday and free on Sunday and holidays.

If you go to Cholula, you must visit the two Indian baroque churches of ★ **Santa María Tonantzintla** and ★ **San Francisco Acatepec.** The churches are called "Indian baroque" because the Indians used pre-Hispanic ideas to present Christian concepts. Thus a saint is swaddled in stylized quetzal bird feathers once used to depict the god Quetzalcoatl, or clownlike faces protrude from a headdress of corn leaves as if to honor the corn god. The interior of the Tonantzintla church is covered floor to ceiling in fabulous gilded and polychromed faces, cherubs, and foliage—an unforgettable sight. While less fantastic on the inside, the facade of the Acatepec church is a tile fantasy. These memorable examples of Indian baroque architecture are decorated with beautifully colored Puebla tiles and wood carved by local artisans.

To get here from Cholula, take one of the buses marked "Chupito," which go by the entrance to the ruins. Both churches close between 1 and 3pm and are often closed at other hours as well; the caretaker is usually not far away, so ask around for him and chances are he'll appear.

Nine miles northwest of Cholula is **Huejotzingo,** Puebla (altitude 7,550 ft.; population 30,000). The stellar attraction here is the **Franciscan monastery,** opposite the town plaza. Built between 1529 and 1570, and very plain on the outside, it has one of three remaining 16th-century Renaissance altar pieces in Mexico. (Another is at Xochimilco—see Chapter 6, "What to See & Do in Mexico City"). Designed by the Flemish painter Simón Pereyns, the altar has five gilded wood levels ornamented with 10 paintings, and more than a dozen saints. The cross mounted on a pedestal in the courtyard dates from the 1500s as well. The monastery building next door has a few excellent friezes in black and white painted by Fray Antonio de Rola in 1558.

There's an open-air market in the plaza on Saturday in Huejotzingo, and sparkling (alcoholic) cider, a local specialty, is bottled and sold at many stores nearby. The monastery is open Tuesday through Sunday from 10am to 4:30pm; there is a small admission fee.

One of the most colorful **carnaval celebrations** takes place here the Tuesday before Ash Wednesday—firecrackers pop and roar as a cast of thousands parades around in brilliantly colored costumes; the carnaval market is at least 10 blocks square.

To get there from Cholula take a taxi from the central plaza for around $5.

SHOPPING

If you're in the market for a set of **talavera dinnerware,** or colorful **hand-painted tiles,** this is the city. Numerous workshops produce the famous pottery, which is very expensive. Among them is the **Casa Rugerio,** Av. 18 Poniente No. 111 at Calle 3 Norte (☎ **41-3843**), a family-owned shop that's been in business for generations. There's a small sales showroom in front and visitors can tour the small production area in back. Orders for complete sets of dinnerware can take two to five years for delivery, and you must make a down payment. The shop is closed on holidays. **Uriarte Talavera,** Calle 4 Poniente No. 911 (☎ **32-1598**), is one of the most established potters in Puebla. A sophisticated showroom displays a full range of pottery designs. Some are for sale there and others are floor models. Ask to see the museum-showroom upstairs. It's open Monday through Friday from 9am to 6:30pm, Saturday from 10:30am to 6:30pm, and Sunday from 11am to 3pm.

The **Centro Talavera Poblana,** Calle 6 Oriente No. 11 (☎ **42-0848**), offers a wide range of talavera ware from producers in Puebla as well as Tlaxcala. The showroom is huge and prices are fixed. They have full sets with between 6 and 12 place settings ready to take with you. It's between Calle 2 Norte and Calle 5 de Mayo. Open daily from 9:30am to 8pm.

The state-operated **Casa de Artesanías** is on Avenida 5 Oriente between Calle 16 de Septiembre and Calle 2 Sur. Crafts made in the state fill the room and include fine pottery from Acatlán and Izucar de Matamoros. Pottery from these two villages southwest of Puebla is nothing like the talavera pottery so readily seen in Puebla. It's open Monday through Saturday from 10am to 6pm. **Arte Popular DIF,** at Portal Hidalgo 14 (☎ **2-1017**), faces the zócalo. Sponsored by the arm of the government that helps children and families, this showroom focuses on folk art produced in Puebla. The selection is smaller than at the Casa de Artesanías, and the selection is similar. It's open daily from 10am to 8pm.

Where to Stay

INEXPENSIVE

Hotel Palacio San Leonardo, Av. 2 Oriente No. 211, Puebla, Pue. 72000. ☎ **22/46-0555.** 75 rms (all with bath). TV TEL
Rates: $28 single; $35.50 double.

The Palacio San Leonardo's lobby is entered by massive wooden doors, and there's a crystal chandelier hanging from the stained-glass ceiling. However, the second you step into the elevator you leave the 18th century behind: the freshly painted and well-maintained rooms have carpeting and modern furnishings. Try to get a room on the sixth floor with a great view of the church domes and the surrounding mountains. There is a nice restaurant to the right of the lobby entry doors, and on the roof a tiny swimming pool and a terrace. The hotel is 2¹/₂ blocks north of the zócalo, between Calles 2 and 4 Norte.

San Angel, Av. 4 Poniente No. 504, Puebla, Pue. 72000. ☎ and fax **22/32-3845.** 37 rms (all with bath). TEL TV

Rates (including breakfast): $42.50 single; $52.50 double.

This cheery little hotel, which opened in 1993, is a welcome addition to Puebla's downtown scene. Converted from a large 19th-century three-story townhouse (with an elevator), it's centered around a bright covered interior patio. The hotel's inviting little restaurant occupies the central patio where guests take the complimentary breakfast or other meals. The carpeted rooms are exceedingly cheerful, with matching bedspreads and drapes and reading lights over the beds. Bathrooms are small, but the sink is conveniently outside the toilet and shower area. It's near the corner of Calle 5 Norte.

Where to Dine

Puebla is known throughout Mexico for the famous *mole poblano, tinga,* and *mixiotes. Dulces* (sweets) shops are scattered about town with display windows brimming over with marzipan crafted into various shapes and designs, candied figs, guava paste, and *camotes,* which are little cylinders of a fruity, sweet-potato paste wrapped in waxed paper.

INEXPENSIVE

⭐ **El Cortijo,** Calle 16 de Septiembre No. 506. ☎ **42-0503.**
Cuisine: MEXICAN.
Prices: Appetizers $3–$4; main courses $6.50–$15; comida corrida $9.
Open: Daily 10am–7pm. (comida corrida served 1–3pm.)

With large wooden doors and a charming patio that's always crowded, you'll find the atmosphere is comfortable and the food tasty. Dishes range from pork chops to a delicious jumbo shrimp or paella. The cubierto (or comida corrida) starts with a fruit cocktail, then a choice of two soups, a mid-course of perhaps paella or spaghetti, then the main course, which might include a choice of pork leg, mole, fish, or chicken. This is a good place for that large afternoon meal and a bottle of wine. The restaurant is 2¹/₂ blocks south of the zócalo between Calle 16 de Septiembre and Calle 2 Sur.

⭐ **Fonda Santa Clara,** Av. 3 Poniente. No. 307. ☎ **42-2659.**
Cuisine: REGIONAL.
Prices: Appetizers $2–$6; lunch $7–$10; dinner $3–$7.
Open: Tues–Sat noon–9:30pm, Sun 11am–9:30pm.

One of the city's most popular and traditional restaurants, serving regional food, the Fonda Santa Clara is busy but cozy. The menu includes local dishes such as pollo mole poblano, mixiotes, and tinga. There are seasonal specialties as well, such as fried grasshoppers in October and November, maguey worms in April and May, chiles enogada July through September, and huitlacoche in June. The dinner menu is light with such specials as tacos, tamales, pozole, mole de panza (mole with stomach meat), and atole. The restaurant is 1½ blocks west of the zócalo, opposite the Museo Bello.

Sanborn's, Av. 2 Oriente No. 6. ☎ **42-9436.**

> **Cuisine:** INTERNATIONAL.
> **Prices:** Breakfast $2–$4.50; main courses $3.50–$10.
> **Open:** Sun–Fri 7:30am–11pm, Sat 7:30am–midnight.

Despite the modern facade, this local restaurant is set up just like those in Mexico City, with sales counters for magazines, cameras, jewelery, and gifts. The nice dining room is in a fine colonial courtyard, with tables set out around a stone fountain. The atmosphere is cool and quiet. Avoid the tenderloin tips and order the chicken with chilaquiles, or a hamburger and fries, instead. Sanborn's is 1½ blocks north of the zócalo, between Avenidas 2 and 4 Oriente.

3 Tlaxcala

75 miles E of Mexico City; 35 miles NE of Puebla

GETTING THERE & DEPARTING • By Bus   Buses to Puebla leave from Mexico City's T.A.P.O. station. If you're going on to Tlaxcala from Puebla, **Flecha Azul** (☎ **49-7128**) or **ERCO** (☎ **49-7177**) provide the most direct service. **Autobuses Surianos** (☎ **49-9055**) goes directly to Huamantla every 10 minutes, as does **ATAH** (☎ **49-7011**).

ESSENTIALS • Information   The **Oficina del Turismo del Estado** (state tourism office) is in the former Palacio Legislativo, one block from the zócalo at the corner of Juárez and Lardizábal (☎ **246/ 2-5037** or **2-0027,** fax 246/2-5309). It's open Monday through Friday from 9am to 7pm.

Only 35 miles northeast of Puebla and 80 miles east of Mexico City, Tlaxcala (population 75,000) is capital of a like-named state, smallest in Mexico with only one million people. It is a pretty colonial-era city with several unique claims to fame.

Tlaxcalan warriors, who allied themselves with Cortes against the Aztecs, were essential in Cortés's defeat of the Aztecs. Tlaxcalan chiefs were the first to be baptized by the Spaniards, and for their crucial role in the Conquest the kings of Tlaxcala were allowed to remain as kings reporting directly to the king of Spain—not the viceroy of New Spain. Tlaxcalans were the first to have an official shield, the first to ride horses, and the first to walk on the streets with Spanish weapons.

What to See & Do

IN TOWN

The baptismal font used for Tlaxcalan chiefs is found in the **Monastery of San Francisco** (two blocks from the main plaza), noted for its elaborately inlaid Moorish ceiling below the choir loft. A painting inside the Chapel of the Third Order shows the baptism of the chiefs. Less than a mile from town center, the famed **Ocotlán**

Sanctuary was constructed in 1541. Baroque inside and out, the elaborate interior decorations of carved figures and curling gilded wood date from the 1700s. The **Government Palace,** on the handsome tree-shaded central zócalo, is painted inside by local artist Desiderio Hernández Xochitiotzin. Vivid murals show Tlaxcalan history.

Tlaxcala's main attraction, however, is Cacaxtla (pronounced kah-*kahsh*-tlah), a unique pre-Hispanic hilltop site 12 miles southwest of the city of Tlaxcala.

CACAXTLA ARCHEOLOGICAL SITE

Unearthed in 1975, scholars were startled by the discovery of vivid murals in red, blue, black, yellow, and white, which showed Maya warriors (from the Mexican Yucatán peninsula 500 miles south). Since then more murals, more history, and at least eight eras of construction have been uncovered. Presently scholars attribute the influence of the site to a little-known group, the Olmec-Xicalanca, from Mexico's Gulf Coast. Among the translations of its name, "merchant's backback" seems most revealing. Like Casas Grandes north of Chihuahua City and Xochicalco (also with distinctive Maya influence) between Cuernavaca and Taxco, Cacaxtla apparently was an important crossroads for merchants, astronomers, and others in the Mesoamerican world. Its apogee, between A.D. 650 and A.D. 900, corresponds with the abandonment of Teotihuacán (near Mexico City), the beginning of Casas Grandes culture, and, in the final phase, the decline of the Maya in Yucatán, emergence of the Toltec culture at Tula, and spread of Toltec influence to Yucatán. How, or even if, those events affected Cacaxtla isn't known yet. Apparently the mural is a victory scene with warrior figures clothed magnificently in jaguar skins and seemingly victorious over figures dressed in feathers who were to be sacrificial victims. Some of the victims are even painted on the floor, where they endure the ultimate humiliation of being walked on by the victors. Numerous symbols of Venus (half a star with five points) found painted at the site have led archeoastronomy scholar John Carlson to link warmaking with the culture's need for captives to be sacrificed at the appearance of Venus; human sacrifice at the star's appearance was thought to assure fertility of crops. These symbols—blood, toads, and turtles (all water symbols), sacrifice, and Venus, together with other symbols of corn stalks and cacao (chocolate) trees (symbolizing fertility)—were all meant to appease the gods and thus assure a productive cycle of rains, crops, and trade. The latest mural discoveries show a wall of corn and cacao trees leading to a merchant whose trade pack is laden with these symbolic crops. The murals flank a grand acropolis with unusual architectural motifs. The grand plaza and murals are now protected by a giant steel roof. **Important notes:** It's about a mile from the parking lot to the top of the hillside entrance to the site. Be careful of weak and crudely made wooden steps, which become slippery with the accumulation of dust. Since neither a flash nor a tripod are allowed, the site is difficult to photograph from the inside because of dust and low light

Tlaxcala

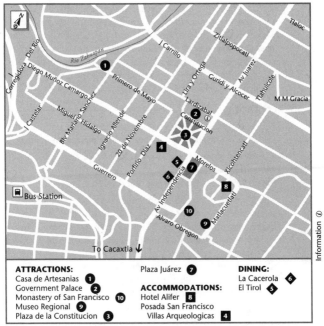

Information ⓘ

ATTRACTIONS:
Casa de Artesanias ❶
Government Palace ❷
Monastery of San Francisco ❿
Museo Regional ❾
Plaza de la Constitucion ❸

Plaza Juárez ❼

ACCOMMODATIONS:
Hotel Alifer ⑧
Posada San Francisco
Villas Arqueologicas ④

DINING:
La Cacerola ◆6
El Tirol ◆5

caused by shading from the giant roof. It's open Tuesday through
Sunday from 9am to 5pm; admission is $4.50 and $7 per camera,
either still or video; free on Sunday and Mexican holidays.

To get to the ruins from Tlaxcala take a combi (collective minivan)
or city bus to the village of San Miguel Milagro (nearest the ruins).
From there, walk or take a taxi to the ruins. If you're driving from
Tlaxcala, take the road south to Tetlatlahuaca and the turn (right)
there to Nativitas, where there are signs to Cacaxtla. From Puebla
take Highway 119 north to the crossroads near Zacualpan and turn
left passing Tetlatlahuaca; turn right when you see signs to Nativitas
and Cacaxtla.

A SIDE TRIP TO HUAMANTLA

Located 30 miles southeast of Tlaxcala, this small village is noted for
its commemoration of the **Assumption of the Virgin on August
12.** On the evening preceding the event, the streets are decorated in
murals made of flower petals and colored sawdust, all of which
are destroyed when a figure of the virgin is carried through downtown streets. The following weekend a running of the bulls takes place
through the downtown streets. Just as colorful and fascinating is the
**Museo Nacional del Titere Rosete Aranda (Rosete Aranda Na-
tional Puppet Museum),** a rare collection of handmade puppets
from the Aranda family, who lived in Huamantla. As early as 1835
the family toured the state and went to the capital with their puppet
plays—poking fun at politics and history, and performing dances,
parades, cockfights, bullfights, and circus acts, complete with

marching bands playing instruments—all with puppets. The idea for the character of Cantinflas (a Mexican comedian played by Mario Moreno), came from an Aranda puppet called Vale Coyote. The museum also houses puppets from around the world and from several centuries. The museum is near the main plaza; ask for directions to it from there. Admission is $3 and the museum is open Tuesday through Sunday from 10am to 4pm.

Where to Stay

Besides these listed below, Tlaxcala has several restaurants and budget hotels in town near the zócalo and along the road to Apizaco.

Hotel Alifer, Morelos 11. Tlaxcala, Tlax. 90000. ☎ 246/2-5678. 18 rms. TEL TV

Rates: $25.50 single; $34 double. **Parking:** Free.

The Alifer is only two blocks from the Plaza Constitución, but the second block is a steep one guaranteed to get your blood circulating by the time you reach the top. The clean rooms have a Spanish colonial decor including a black-and-red color theme. Each is carpeted and comes with one or two double beds or a double and a twin, and tile and marble baths with showers. To get there from the Plaza Constitución, stand with your back to the Posada San Francisco, walk to the right two blocks, and the hotel is at the top of the hill. The parking lot is next to the lobby entrance.

Posada San Francisco Villas Arqueologicas, Plaza de la Constitución 17, Tlaxcala, Tlax. 90000. ☎ 256/2-6402 or 2-6022. Toll free **800/258-2633** in the U.S. or toll free **91-800/9-0170** in Mexico. Fax 256/2-6818. 62 rms, 6 suites. TEL TV

Rates: $83.50 single; $102 double; $142 suite. **Parking:** free.

Opened in 1992 on Tlaxcala's zócalo, the San Francisco occupies a turn-of-the-century building known locally as the Casa de las Piedras (House of Stones). It's the most beautiful hotel in the city, and is operated by Club Med as one of the Villas Arqueologicas. Two stories of rooms are set around a beautiful swimming pool and patio beyond the central entrance patio, which was part of the original structure. Each room is handsomely furnished in a peach and blue color theme, with whitewashed furniture, remote-control TV, heaters, and marble baths with combination tub/shower. The hotel has two restaurants covering all three meals. The parking lot is entered one street behind the hotel's front entrance, which faces the zócalo.

Where to Eat

Typical local foods to try include *sopa Tlaxcalteca, pollo Calpulalpan,* rabbit, mixiotes, and the famed Tlaxcala bread made in nearby villages and transported to festivals throughout the country.

La Cacerola, Av. Independencia 9. ☎ 2-7467.

Cuisine: INTERNATIONAL/REGIONAL.
Prices: Breakfast dishes $2–$6; main courses $7–$8.50.
Open: Daily 9am–10pm.

Pachuca

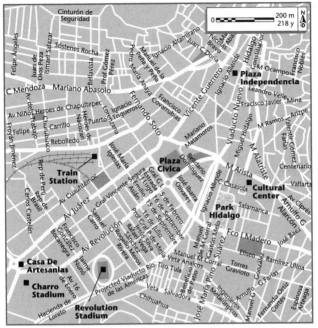

Facing the Plaza Xicohtencatl just off the zócalo, this cozy restaurant is one of the most popular in the city. Linen-clad tables and samples of Tlaxcala-made talavera-style pottery line subtly lighted shelves around the dining room. Besides steaks, seafood, and chicken main courses with a continental flare, this is a good place to try some of the regional specialties such as escamoles (ant eggs, in season from May through July), rabbit in chile sauce, sopa Tlaxcalteca, quail in prune sauce, and chicken or lamb mixiotes.

El Tirol, Av. Independencia 7. ☎ **2-1770.**

Cuisine: MEXICAN/REGIONAL.
Prices: Breakfast dishes $1.50–$5; main courses $4–$10.
Open: Daily 8am–11pm.

Day or night, El Tirol is a popular hangout for working folk and tourists alike. Facing the Plaza Xicohtencatl, a half block from the zócalo, cloth-covered tables are set on three spacious split levels. The menu includes some of Mexico's usual specialties such as chilaquiles, quesadillas, and enchiladas, as well as local dishes such as pipian verde and pollo calulalpan. There's a lengthy drink menu. The breakfast menu offers the usual plus some surprises such as banana split and peaches in rompope or cream.

4 Pachuca

50 miles NE of Mexico City

GETTING THERE & DEPARTING • By Bus Buses to Pachuca depart frequently from the Terminal del Norte in Mexico City and the trip takes about an hour and a half. The terminal isn't far from town but it's too far to walk. Buses going to town are marked "Centro" and pass in front of the terminal.

• By Car From the Pyramids of Teotihuacán take the connecting road just north of San Martín de las Pirámides to Hwy 85 north to Pachuca. Or you can backtrack south on 132D to Hwy 85 north to Pachuca. From the pyramids the trip takes less than an hour.

Pachuca (altitude 8,000 ft.; population 180,000) is an attractive old town swept by cooling breezes. In the hills around the town, silver has been mined for at least five centuries, and is still produced in large quantities. It is well worth the effort to climb one of the narrow, precipitous streets up the hillside, from which there is an excellent view of the irregular surrounding terrain.

What to See & Do

Pachuca has a small, clean market through which it is pleasant to stroll. One section appears to specialize in making funeral wreaths with dozens of different white flowers woven into the greenery. There are many bake shops with appetizing cookies and pastries on show.

The **Regional History Museum** in the Hidalgo Cultural Center is located in what used to be the **Convent of San Francisco** on Bartolome de Medina Plaza, about five blocks south of the main square (ask for directions). The former convent, considered to be the most important and original building in Pachuca, is an architectural gem itself. Built in 1596, it has seen a progression of uses: first a mission base, it has since been a mining school, city hospital, penitentiary, and is now home to the National Photographic Archives and Hidalgo State historical memorabilia, as well as the Hidalgo Cultural Center. Take the time to stop in at this promising first-of-its-kind regional museum and browse through the historical and cultural past of this area. Open from 9am to noon and 3 to 5pm. Admission is $2.

Where to Stay & Dine

If you're looking for a meal or a bed for a night, home in on the **Plaza Independencia.** There are several other plazas in town, each unique. You won't miss this one if you look for the massive clock and bell tower. The remainder of the plaza is bare concrete, but it's surrounded by several visible moderately priced hotels and restaurants.

5 Tepotzotlán

27 miles N of Mexico City

GETTING THERE • By Metro and Bus You can make the trip in a morning or an afternoon by taking the Metro (Línea 7) to the

"Tacuba" (not "Tacubaya"!) station, walking over Aquiles Serdan on the pedestrian bridge, and then catching a bus (a one-hour trip) to Tepotzotlán. The bus back to Mexico City usually passes right through the main square, but you should ask exactly where to catch it for the return trip.

• **By Car** If you drive, go west on Paseo de la Reforma, and shortly after you pass the Auditorio Municipal (on your left) in Chapultepec Park, turn right (north) onto the Anillo Periférico. This soon becomes the Avenida Manuel Avila Camacho, which in turn becomes Hwy. 57D, the toll road to Queretaro. About $22^1/_2$ miles out of the city, look for the turn to Tepotzotlán, which is about $1^1/_2$ miles west of the highway.

The colonial town of Tepotzotlán has one main attraction—the **Church of San Francisco Xavier/Museo Nacional del Virreinato,** Plaza Hidalgo 99 (☎ **987-0332**). The facade of the church (built in 1682), on the main square, is one of the three finest examples of *churrigueresque* (Mexican baroque) decoration in Mexico, the other two being the Santa Prisca in Taxco and La Valenciana in Guanajuato. The grand extravagance of the facade is echoed inside the church, which is richly decorated with carved altarpieces and paintings. Ten altars in the exaggerated baroque churrigueresque style bear paintings by Miguel Cabrera, and 22 canvases by Cristobal de Villalpando outline the life of San Ignacio de Loyola. Attached to the convent section, to the right of the church entrance, is the Museo Nacional del Virrienato (National Museum of the Viceregal Era), once the Novitiate of the Company of Jesus (1585). It houses some of the country's most important religious treasures. Here you'll find dozens of rooms with a rich collection of paintings, ceremonial church objects, vestments, pottery, and carvings. Across from the church is a market around which are several nice restaurants.

The museum and church are open Tuesday through Sunday from 10am to 5pm. Admission is $4.50.

6 Toluca

45 miles W of Mexico City

GETTING THERE • By Bus Take the Metro to the "Observatorio" station, and look for the Terminal Poniente bus station. Reserved-seat buses ("Toluca-Directo") of various companies depart every 5 or 10 minutes on the hour-long trip. ETN, at the far end of the concourse, offers deluxe service to Toluca and is well worth the little extra in cost over standard buses. The buses discharge passengers at the central bus station in back of the famed Friday market. Both are on Isidro Fabela near the intersection of Tollocan.

• **By Car** From Mexico City follow the Paseo de la Reforma west until it merges with *Carretera a Toluca* which is Highway 15.

ESSENTIALS • Information The helpful **state tourist office** is in the central city in the Edificio Plaza Toluca, second floor, at Lerdo

Poniente 101 (☎ 721/14-1342 or fax 13-3142). Hours are 9am to 3pm and 4 to 9:30pm Monday through Friday. They have a wide variety of booklets with maps outlining the state's regions, as well as Toluca maps and museum information. The booklet "State of Mexico Tourist Atlas," in English or Spanish, has excellent maps and information on the whole state and is available at the tourist office.

The capital of the state of Mexico, Toluca (population 250,000) is—at 8,760 feet—the highest city in Mexico. The hour-long trip there from Mexico City offers spectacular scenic views. Toluca's main attractions include the famed Friday market, the colonial heart of the city, and it's fine collection of museums.

What to See & Do

THE MARKET

The gigantic **Mercado Juárez,** at the edge of town just off Paseo Tollocan and the highway to Mexico City, has both market buildings and open-air grounds. Shops in the buildings are open all week but on Friday natives from surrounding villages crowd the marketplace with their chattering chickens, serapes, pottery, clothing, fruits, vegetables, beautiful locally made baskets and more. It's gigantic and frantic and the hubbub is taxing: an hour or two should do it, even for the die-hard market lover. Follow that by a trip to **CASART,** the large, modern, and air-conditioned state-operated crafts store on Tollocan (the highway from Mexico City) a long block from the market. It's open daily from 10am to 7pm. Then catch a bus marked "Centro" for downtown.

THE HISTORIC CENTER

This area in the heart of Toluca is bordered by Avenidas Hidalgo, Juárez, and Sebastian Lerdo de Tejada. Here you'll see the housing for the heart of state government in stately buildings framing the square—the Palace of Justice, Chamber of Deputies, Government Palace, and Municipal Palace, Cosmovitral Botanico, and the cathedral, which was established by the Franciscans in the mid-1800s. In this area too are several excellent fine art museums housed in historic buildings.

IMPRESSIONS

A kind of liquefaction of Indian talk, in Otomi, Aztec, and Matlalaltzinga, mingling with the Spanish, created a strange droning noise [in the Toluca market]. A jackass brayed, a fettered turkeycock gobbled, an offended dog yelped, a church bell clanged stridently. On the narrow sidewalks, merchandise was spread so haphazardly that in order to pass, pedestrians had to press against the wall or leap the display. We negotiated an islandlike exhibit of cans of sewing-machine oil, suckling pigs, squash flowers, and old empty bottles.
—Hudson Strode, *Now in Mexico* (1947)

Toluca

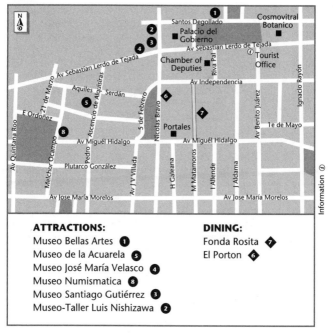

ATTRACTIONS:
Museo Bellas Artes ❶
Museo de la Acuarela ❺
Museo José María Velasco ❹
Museo Numismatica ❽
Museo Santiago Gutiérrez ❸
Museo-Taller Luis Nishizawa ❷

DINING:
Fonda Rosita ❼
El Porton ❻

The famous arcades (*portales*) of Toluca, one block east, are a popular meeting, shopping, and dining place. From the Days of the Dead (November 1 and 2) through Christmas they're filled with temporary vendors selling the candy for which the state is famous.

Located in the city's historic center, off the Plaza de los Martires, on the corner between the Chamber of Deputies and the Government Palace, is the **Cosmovitral Botánico,** at the corner of Juárez and Lerdo (☎ 721/14-6785). The Cosmovitral is an indoor botanical garden within the walls of a 19th-century art-nouveau building. It's one of the city's greatest creations, and formerly housed the Friday market. The upper half of the building is emblazoned with 54 bold stained-glass panels telling the story of humanity in relation to the cosmos. The stained glass, however, is only the frame for the gardens showing plants native to the state of Mexico and other countries. The gardens are open Tuesday through Sunday from 9am to 5pm; admission costs $2.

It's only fitting that the man known as Mexico's foremost 19th-century landscape painter should have a museum honoring him in his home state—the **Museo José María Velasco,** Lerdo de Tejada 400, corner of N. Bravo. (☎ 13-2814). Velasco's vast landscapes show enormous Mexican valleys, usually with a volcano in the background. Viewers of his work are allowed to feel as though they are standing on the same mountaintop as the painter. Some of his works are also in the Museo Nacional de Arte in Mexico City. The Velasco museum is opposite the main plaza, across the street from the Palacio del Gobierno, and a block from the Cosmovitral Botanico. It's open Tuesday through Sunday from 10am to 6pm; admission is free.

In a grand mansion connected to, and next door to, the Velasco museum, is the **Museo Santiago Gutiérrez,** Nicolas Bravo Norte 303 (☎ **13-2814**). It pays homage to another of the state's famous painters. Gutiérrez and Velasco were friends and both studied at the San Carlos Museum. Gutiérrez was the country's foremost portrait, figure, and *costumbrista* artist of the 19th century. Costumbrista paintings present Mexican themes showing figures clad in Mexican attire. Gutiérrez traveled and studied widely, founding the Academia de Artes de Bogotá, Colombia, during his years there. The Museo Gutiérrez in Toluca houses the largest collection of his works, one of which was included in the spectacular "Thirty Centuries of Mexican Art" exhibit that toured the United States in 1990. It's open Tuesday through Sunday from 10am to 6pm. Admission is free.

You may never have heard of the master painter Luis Nishizawa, but you won't forget his work, which is housed on two floors of an 18th-century mansion—the **Museo–Taller Luis Nishizawa,** Nicolas Bravo Norte 305 (☎ **13-2647**). It's just up the block from the Velasco and Gutiérrez museums. His oil portraits and skilled use of color are unforgettable. Born to a Japanese father and Mexican mother, he moved with his parents from Toluca to Mexico City in 1925. At age 24 he entered the San Carlos Academy and within three years was given the title of Master of Plastic Arts. In his long career he has won hundreds of awards. Now in his 70s, he divides his time between Mexico City and teaching classes at the museum on Saturday. The stained glass ceiling over the patio is a Nishizawa creation. It's open Tuesday through Sunday from 10am to 6pm.

Housed in a recently restored, early 19th-century mansion, the new **Museo de la Acuarela,** Pedro Ascencio at Nigromante (☎ **14-7304**), is devoted entirely to watercolor paintings. Featured here are either the works of state-born artists, or paintings about the state by artists from around the world. Because the large state of Mexico almost surrounds the Federal District, the subject matter—from archeological sites to landscapes and village streets—is vast. It's only 1½ blocks west of the central square. To find it from the northwest corner of the main plaza (where Bravo meets Independencia), turn left onto Independencia (which becomes Serdan) and walk straight one block, then left on Pedro Ascencio de Alqisiras; the museum is on the right about a half block down. It's open Tuesday through Sunday from 10am to 6pm. Admission is free.

Housed in a grand turn-of-the-century stone mansion, the new **Museo de Numismatica,** Av. Hidalgo Poniente 506 (☎ **13-1927**), features Mexican currency from pre-Hispanic times through the Revolution to the present. To find it from the southwest corner of the main plaza, walk west on Hidalgo crossing 5 de Febrero and Pedro Ascencio de Alquisiras. It's in the middle of the next block on the right. If you're coming from the Museo de la Acuarela, turn right out the front door and walk two blocks to the corner of Hidalgo. Turn right; it's on the right. The museum is open Tuesday through Saturday from 10am to 6pm and Sunday from 10am to 4pm; admission is free.

THE CENTRO CULTURAL MEXEQUENSE

In 1987 the Centro Cultural Mexequense (☎ 72/12-4113 or 12-4738), opened on the sprawling grounds of the former Hacienda de la Pila, in a southeastern suburb of the city. The ambitious and beautiful museum incorporates four cultural outfits and a library that were once scattered throughout Toluca. The various buildings form a one-story "U" shape around an enormous central yard where orchestras and dancers sometimes entertain. To get there take "Líneas 2 de Marzo" bus, either from the bus station by the market or as it comes through the central plaza, approximately every 15 minutes.

The center and all its museums are open Tuesday through Sunday from 9am to 5pm; the restaurant is closed on Sunday. The $6.50 admission price includes all the buildings and museums at the Centro. Admission is paid at the kiosk in the parking lot, not in the museum. There's no admission fee on Sunday.

At the **Popular Arts Museum,** on the right in the original hacienda building, you'll see polychromed clay "trees of life" from the artisans of Metepec, regional costumes, Persian-like tapestries from Temoaya, leather-covered chests from San Mateo Atenco, embroidery from Ameyalco, a great display of charro attire, and much more. A cozy restaurant (inexpensive), bookstore, and shop are in this building as well.

Opposite the Popular Arts exhibit and next to the library is the **Museum of Modern Art,** offering a close-up view of paintings by Rufino Tamayo, Juan O'Gorman, Jose Chávez Morado, Orozco, and Diego Rivera, all of whom (except Tamayo) were better known for their murals. The works are quite good and you'll likely discover other lesser-known artists whose efforts rival their better-known contemporaries.

In the middle, between the Popular Arts and Modern Art museums, is the **Museum of Anthropology.** Objects from the state's 10 most important archeological sites include beautiful pottery and mural fragments from Teotihuacán, the famous wood drum from Malinalco, showing carved jaguars and eagles, and fascinating memorabilia from colonial days to the present.

Where to Eat

Fonda Rosita, Portal Madero, Plaza Fray Andrés de Castro.
☎ 5-1394.
Cuisine: MEXICAN.
Prices: Appetizers $2–$3; main courses $6–$13.
Open: Daily 1–8pm.

Inside the *portales* (arcades) of the historic city center on the Plaza Fray Andrés Castro is this bustling place, known for its high quality

Mexican food. The sopa medula (bone-marrow soup) and baked pork loin are especially good.

El Porton, Paseo Tollocan 1031. ☎ **17-9690.**

Cuisine: MEXICAN.

Prices: Soups $2–$3.50; tacos $2–$3.50; plate-lunch special $5.50–$7.

Open: Daily 8am–11pm.

This gleaming restaurant, one block south of the market, is geared toward tourists who don't speak Spanish. The menu has color photos of all their specialties, making it easy to point and pick from among the soups, tacos, platter meals, and daily specials. The service is friendly and swift.

7 Ixtapan de la Sal

75 miles SW of Mexico City

GETTING THERE & DEPARTING • By Bus   From Mexico City's Terminal Poniente, **Omnibus Azteca de Oro** and **Tres Estrella del Oro** buses leave for Ixtapan de la Sal every few minutes. Get one that's taking the toll road, which cuts the travel time from $2^1/2$ hours to about $1^1/2$ hours. To return, buses marked **"Mexico Directo"** leave every 10 minutes and usually stop in Toluca (but confirm that yours does if that's your destination). Buses from here also go to Cuernavaca and Taxco every 40 minutes.

• By Car   To get here from Mexico City by car take Highway 15 to Toluca. In Toluca Highway 15 becomes Paseo Tollucan. Follow Tollucan south until you see signs pointing left to Ixtapan de la Sal. After the turn, continue straight for around 10 miles. Just before the town of Tenango del Valle you have a choice of the free road to Ixtapan de la Sal or the toll road. The free road winds through the mountains and takes an hour and a half. The two-lane toll road has fewer mountain curves, costs $2.50, and takes around an hour—it's worth it. The toll road stops about 10 miles before Ixtapan where you resume a curvy mountainous drive.

An hour and a half (via the toll road) southwest of Mexico City, hotels in the whitewashed town of Ixtapan de la Sal (not to be confused with Ixtapa on the Pacific coast), cater to pleasures based on thermal water baths and other sybaritic delights such as massages, facials, and mud baths. The **Balneario Ixtapan,** next to the Hotel Spa Ixtapan, is the town's public spa and bathhouse, where you can take private thermal water baths, have a massage, facial, hair treatment, paraffin wrap, pedicure, and manicure, all of which cost between $10 and $20 each. It's open daily from 8am to 6pm. Hotels in Ixtapan de la Sal are packed on weekends and Mexican holidays. There's little to do but relax in the town. Cuernavaca, Taxco, and Toluca are all easy side trips.

Ixtapan de la Sal

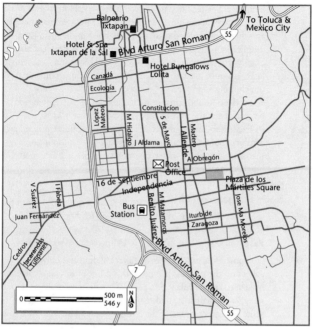

Where to Stay & Eat

EXPENSIVE

⭐ **Hotel Spa Ixtapan,** *Bulevar San Roman s/n, Ixtapan de la Sal, Estado de Mexico 51900.* ☎ **724/3-0021,** *or toll free* **800/638-7950** *or* **800/223-9832** *in the U.S. 200 rms, 50 villas.* MINIBAR TEL TV

Rates (including 3 daily meals): 7-day spa plan $926.50 single, $772 per person double; 4-day, 5-night spa packages available; $100–$132 single or double per night non-spa plan. Parking: Free.

Set on several manicured and flower-filled acres, the town's only first-class hotel is also one of the country's best spa hotels, with more than 40 years of service. When you compare its comfort, weight loss programs, good food, and relaxing pace to other spas, you'll see how the excellent value accounts for its continued popularity. A typical day starts with an hour's hike into the surrounding hills, followed by an hour of aerobics or yoga, water exercise, then a personalized treatment schedule which includes massages, facials, and hair treatments; herbal wraps and salt-glow loofa scrubs; saunas, steam baths, and whirlpool tubs; and perhaps a tennis or golf lesson. A reflexologist is also available. Programs are separate for men and women, but dining is combined for the two. The spa week goes from Monday through Friday, with Sunday arrival preferred. On Saturday morning spa participants are treated to a final hairdo, pedicure, and manicure. Spa facilities are closed on Sunday. Hotel guests not on the spa program can use the spa facilities on a per-treatment pay plan, and there's no daily admission charge. Food in the main (non-spa) dining room (also included in the room price) is excellent and graciously served. Rooms have cable TV with U.S. channels. Rooms are large, comfortable, and stylishly furnished. Bring your own workout clothing and robe.

Services: Round-trip transportation from Mexico City airport can be arranged at the time of your reservation; cost is $136.

Facilities: Challenging nine-hole golf course, fully equipped gym, aerobics room, three indoor whirlpools, two outdoor pools (one thermal and one fresh-water) two tennis courts, spa dining room, and hotel dining room. Horseback riding is available.

INEXPENSIVE

Hotel Bungalows Lolita, Blv. Arturo A. San Roman 33, Ixtapan de la Sal, Edo. de Mexico 51900. ☎ **724/3-0169.** Fax 724/3-0230. 36 rms.

Rates (including 3 meals): $42.50–$51 per adult. **Parking:** Free.

Composed of a two-story main hotel building and individual bungalows on the grounds behind it, this is one of several comfortable little hotels in the village. On a small scale, it offers massages, facials, reflexology, pedicures, and manicures. The public bath house is a short walk away. Some of the bungalows are quite large with three bedrooms and two baths, a living room, and a dining room. There's a swimming pool and the large restaurant is open daily. You'll see the sign for the hotel when you enter town on Bulevar San Roman.

8   Valle de Bravo & Avandaro

95 miles SW of Mexico City

GETTING THERE & DEPARTING • By Bus   From Mexico City's Terminal Poniente, buses leave every 20 minutes on the **Mexico–Toluca–Zinacantepec** bus lines. The same line has first-class buses hourly and the trip takes around three hours.

• By Car   The quickest route from Mexico City by car is via Highway 15 to Toluca. In Toluca Highway 15 becomes Paseo Tollucan. Follow Tollucan south until you see signs pointing left to Highway 134 and Valle de Bravo, Francisco de los Ranchos, and Temascaltepec. After the turn, continue on Highway 134 until Francisco de los Ranchos, where you bear right, following signs to Valle de Bravo. The drive takes $1^1/2$ to 2 hours.

One of Mexico's hidden retreats, Valle de Bravo (altitude 6,070 feet) has aptly been called the Switzerland of Mexico. Ringed by pine forested mountains, and built beside a beautiful manmade lake, Valle de Bravo is a 16th-century village with cobblestone streets and colonial structures built around a pretty town plaza. Like San Miguel de Allende and Taxco, it's a National Monument village; new

Valle de Bravo & Avandaro

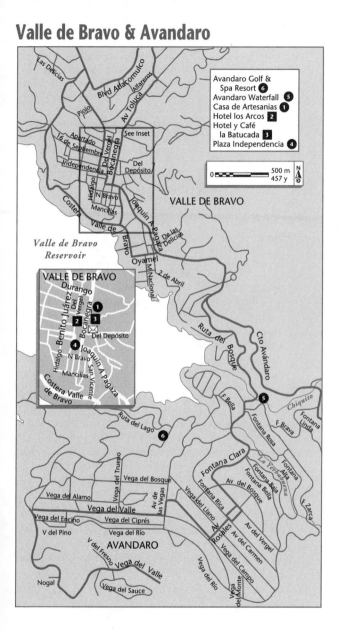

Avandaro Golf & Spa Resort **6**
Avandaro Waterfall **5**
Casa de Artesanias **1**
Hotel los Arcos **2**
Hotel y Café la Batucada **3**
Plaza Independencia **4**

construction must conform to the colonial style of the original village. Its neighbor Avandaro, 4 miles away, is a weekend retreat for well-to-do Capitalinos who have built palatial estates in this alpine setting. The cobbled streets, small restaurants, hotels, and shops of Valle de Bravo are full on weekends. Some shops and restaurants may be closed weekdays. The crafts market, three blocks from the main square, is open daily from 10am to 5pm, and colorfully dressed Mazahua Indians sell their handmade tapestries daily around the town plaza. Fishing for bass and water skiing are two lake activities. Possible excursions from here include one to the nesting grounds of the monarch butterfly between November and February. A day at the Toluca museums would be time well spent. Besides the summer rainy season, it can be very rainy and chilly from September through December.

Where to Stay & Dine

Besides the restaurants at the hotels listed here, there are several fine restaurants on or near Valle de Bravo's central square.

EXPENSIVE

Avandaro Golf and Spa Resort, Fracc. Avándaro, Valle de Bravo, Edo. de Mexico. ☎ **726/2-0626** or toll free **800/ALL SPAS** or **800/448-8355.** Fax 726/2-0627. 40 rms, 60 suites. A/C MINIBAR TV

Rates: $72–$85 single or double cabaña; $132–$212.50 single or double deluxe room. Seven-day spa or golf package, per person $1,445–$2,210 single; $1,190–$1,870 double.

Nestled on 296 acres in a neighborhood of large estates, beside lushly forested mountains and a gorgeous rolling 18-hole golf course, this resort has one of the prettiest settings in the country. It's a member of the Small Luxury Hotels of Mexico. Rooms come in two categories: large, beautifully furnished deluxe suites; and cabañas, which are small and need updating. Both have fireplaces and terraces or balconies overlooking the grounds. Only the deluxe suites can be booked through the toll-free numbers mentioned above; cabañas must be booked directly with the hotel. A variety of spa and golf packages are available. Some packages include a $25 daily meal credit, but meals per person could easily run $50 a day. The golf course is excellent. Green fees, which are usually included in golf packages, cost $60 to $72, depending on the time of week. The ultra-modern spa compares to the best in the United States, with a well-trained staff and a full range of services. Spa packages usually include the $20 daily spa admission and several treatments. On a per treatment basis costs run $20 to $50 for a massage and $20 to $40 for a facial. Two restaurants serve all meals. A pool overlooks the golf course. Daily, staff-led walks go past the estates and into the surrounding hills beside the lake.

Services: Massages, wraps, facials, aerobics, exercise classes, numerous special treatments for cellulite, facial lines, etc. Spa attire is provided. Transportation can be arranged from Mexico City.

Facilities: Sauna and steam rooms, hot and cold whirlpools, state-of-the-art weight-training equipment, 25-meter junior-olympic-size pool, seven tennis courts, 18-hole golf course.

Hotel y Café la Batucada, Bocanegra 207, Valle de Bravo, Edo. de Mexico 51200. ☎ **726/2-0480.** 8 rms. TV

Rates: $110–$130 single or double; $140 suite single or double.

Just a block from the Valle de Bravo's main square, this hotel, opened in 1993, occupies a 19th-century town house built around a handsome garden courtyard. Rooms are all different, decorated in antiques, paintings, and local photographs. Room 8 is the smallest. Room 7 is a suite overlooking Bocanegra. Even for Valle de Bravo, these prices are a bit steep. Inquire about discounts.

INEXPENSIVE

Hotel los Arcos, Bocanegra 310, Valle de Bravo, Edo. de Mexico 51200. ☎ **726/2-0042.** Fax 726/2-2878. 25 rms.

Rates: $47–$56 single or double Sun–Thurs; $78–$88 single or double Fri–Sat.

Also close to the main square, the Hotel los Arcos has two stories on one side and three stories on the other, all built around a swimming pool, and facing views of the village and mountains. Rooms 13, 14, and 15 have a fireplace, which is something to consider in winter here. Some rooms have balconies and most have glass walls with views. Eleven rooms have television and the highest rates are for these rooms. The restaurant is open on weekends.

Appendix

A   Telephones & Mail

USING THE TELEPHONES

Area codes and city exchanges are being changed all over the country. If you have difficulty reaching a number, ask an operator for assistance. Mexico does not have helpful recordings to inform you of changes or new numbers.

Most **public pay phones** in the country have been converted to Ladatel phones, many of which are both coin and card operated. Those that accept coins accept the old 100 peso coins, but at some point may begin accepting New Peso coins. Instructions on the phones tell you how to use them. Local calls generally cost the peso equivalent of 75¢ per minute, at which time you'll hear three odd sounding beeps, and then you'll be cut off unless you deposit more coins. Ladatel cards come in denominations of 10, 20, and 30 New Pesos. If you're planning to make many calls, purchase the 30 New Peso card; it takes no time at all to use up a 10 peso card (about $3.35). They're sold at pharmacies, bookstores, and grocery stores near Ladatel phones. You insert the card, dial your number, and start talking, all the while watching a digital counter tick away your money.

Next is the *caseta de larga distancia* (long-distance telephone office), found all over Mexico. Most bus stations, and airports now have specially staffed rooms exclusively for making long-distance calls and sending faxes. Often they are efficient and inexpensive, providing the client with a computer printout of the time and charges. In other places, often pharmacies, the clerk will place the call for you, then you step into a private booth to take the call. Whether it's a special long distance office or a pharmacy, there's usually a service charge of around $3.50 to make the call, which you pay in addition to any call costs if you didn't call collect.

For **long-distance calls** you can access an English-speaking ATT operator by pushing the star button twice then 09. If that fails, try dialing 09 for an international operator. To call the United States or Canada tell the operator that you want a collect call (Una llamada por cobrar) or station-to-station (telefono a telefono), or person-to-person (persona a persona). Collect calls are the least expensive of all, but sometimes caseta offices won't make them, so you'll have to pay on the spot.

To make a long-distance call from Mexico to another country, first dial 95 for the United States and Canada, or 98 for anywhere else in the world. Then, dial the area code and the number you are calling.

To call long distance (abbreviated "lada") within Mexico, dial 91, the area code, then the number. Mexico's area codes (claves) may be one, two, or three numbers and are usually listed in the front of telephone directories. In this book the area code is listed under "Fast Facts" for each town. (Area codes, however, are changing throughout the country.)

To place a phone call to Mexico from your home country: Dial the international service (011), the Mexico's country code (52), then the Mexican area code (for Cancún, for example, that would be 98), then the local number. Keep in mind that calls to Mexico are quite expensive, even if dialed direct from your home phone.

Better hotels, which have more sophisticated tracking equipment, may charge for each local call made from your room. Budget or moderately priced hotels often don't charge, since they can't keep track. To avoid check-out shock, it's best to ask in advance if you'll be charged for local calls. These cost between 50¢ and $1 per call. In addition, if you make a long-distance call from your hotel room, there is usually a hefty service charge added to the cost of the call.

POSTAL GLOSSARY

Airmail	Correo Aereo
Customs	Aduana
General Delivery	Lista de Correos
Insurance (insured mail)	Seguros
Mailbox	Buzón
Money Order	Giro Postale
Parcel	Paquete
Post Office	Oficina de Correos
Post Office Box (abbreviation)	Apdo. Postal
Postal Service	Correos
Registered Mail	Registrado
Rubber Stamp	Sello
Special Delivery, Express	Entrega Inmediata
Stamp	Estampilla or Timbre

B   Basic Vocabulary

Most Mexicans are very patient with foreigners who try to speak their language; it helps a lot to know a few basic phrases.

I've included a list of certain simple phrases for expressing basic needs, followed by some common menu items.

English-Spanish Phrases

ENGLISH	SPANISH	PRONUNCIATION
Good day	**Buenos días**	bway-nohss dee-ahss
How are you?	**¿Cómo está usted?**	koh-moh ess-tah oo-sted
Very well	**Muy bien**	mwee byen
Thank you	**Gracias**	grah-see-ahss
You're welcome	**De nada**	day nah-dah
Goodbye	**Adios**	ah-dyohss
Please	**Por favor**	pohr fah-bohr
Yes	**Sí**	see
No	**No**	noh
Excuse me	**Perdóneme**	pehr-doh-ney-may
Give me	**Déme**	day-may
Where is . . . ?	**¿Dónde está . . . ?**	dohn-day ess-tah
the station	**la estación**	la ess-tah-see-own
a hotel	**un hotel**	oon oh-tel
a gas station	**una gasolinera**	oon-nuh gah-so-lee-nay-rah
a restaurant	**un restaurante**	oon res-tow-rahn-tay
the toilet	**el baño**	el bahn-yoh
a good doctor	**un(a) buen(a) médico(a)**	oon bwayn may-dee-co
the road to	**el camino a . . .**	el cah-mee-noh ah
the beach	**la playa**	lah plie-ah
To the right	**A la derecha**	ah lah day-ray-chuh
To the left	**A la izquierda**	ah lah ees-ky-ehr-dah
Straight ahead	**Derecho**	day-ray-cho
I would like	**Quisiera**	keyh-see-air-ah
I want	**Quiero**	kyehr-oh
to eat	**comer**	ko-mayr
a room	**una habitación** or **un cuarto**	oon-nuh ha-bee-tah-see-own
Do you have?	**¿Tiene usted?**	tyah-nay oos-ted
a book	**un libro**	oon lee-bro
a dictionary	**un diccionario**	oon deek-see-own-ar-eo
How much is it?	**¿Cúanto cuesta?**	kwahn-to kwess-tah
When?	**¿Cúando?**	kwahn-doh
What?	**¿Qúe?**	kay
There is (Is there?)	**¿Hay . . .**	eye
Yesterday	**Ayer**	ah-yer
Today	**Hoy**	oy

Tomorrow	**Mañana**	mahn-yawn-ah
Good	**Bueno**	bway-no
Bad	**Malo**	mah-lo
Better (best)	**(Lo) Mejor**	(loh) meh-hor
More	**Más**	mahs
Less	**Menos**	may-noss
No Smoking	**Se prohibe fumar**	seh pro-hee-beh foo-mahr
Postcard	**Tarjeta postal**	tahr-hay-ta pohs-tahl
Insect repellent	**Rapellante**	rah-pey-yahn-te
	contra insectos	cohn-trah een sehk-tos

MORE USEFUL PHRASES

Do you speak English?
¿Habla usted inglés?

Is there anyone here who speaks English?
¿Hay alguien aquí quien hable inglés?

I speak a little Spanish.
Hablo un poco de español.

I don't understand Spanish very well.
No entiendo muy bien el español.

I like the food.
Me gusta la comida.

What time is it?
¿Qué hora es?

May I see the menu?
¿Puedo ver el menú?

The check please.
La cuenta por favor.

What do I owe you.
¿Cúanto le debo?

What did you say?
¿Mande? (colloquial expression for American "Eh?")

I want (to see) a room.
Quiero (ver) un cuarto (una habitación).

for two persons
para dos personas

with (without) bath.
con (sin) baño

We are staying here only one night.
Nos quedamos aquí solamente una noche.

one week.
una semana.

We are leaving tomorrow.
Partimos mañana.

Do you accept traveler's checks?
¿Acepta usted cheques de viajero?

Is there a laundromat near here?
¿Hay una lavandería cerca de aquí?

Please send these clothes to the laundry.
Hágame el favor de mandar esta ropa a la lavandería.

Numbers

1	**uno**	(ooh-noh)
2	**dos**	(dohs)
3	**tres**	(trayss)
4	**cuatro**	(kwah-troh)
5	**cinco**	(seen-koh)
6	**seis**	(sayss)
7	**siete**	(syeh-tay)
8	**ocho**	(oh-choh)
9	**nueve**	(nway-bay)
10	**diez**	(dee-ess)
11	**once**	(ohn-say)
12	**doce**	(doh-say)
13	**trece**	(tray-say)
14	**catorce**	(kah-tor-say)
15	**quince**	(keen-say)
16	**dieciseis**	(de-ess-ee-sayss)
17	**diecisiete**	(de-ess-ee-see-ay-tay)
18	**dieciocho**	(dee-ess-ee-oh-choh)
19	**diecinueve**	(dee-ess-ee-nway-bay)
20	**veinte**	(bayn-tay)
30	**treinta**	(trayn-tah)
40	**cuarenta**	(kwah-ren-tah)
50	**cincuenta**	(seen-kwen-tah)
60	**sesenta**	(say-sen-tah)
70	**setenta**	(say-ten-tah)
80	**ochenta**	(oh-chen-tah)
90	**noventa**	(noh-ben-tah)
100	**cien**	(see-en); **ciento** (adj.)
200	**doscientos**	(dos-se-en-tos)
500	**quinientos**	(keen-ee-ehn-tos)
1000	**mil**	(meal)

Bus Terms

Bus **Autobús**
Bus or Truck **Camión**
Lane **Carril**
Nonstop **Directo**
Baggage (claim area) **Equipajes**
Intercity **Foraneo**
Luggage storage area **Guarda equipaje**
Gates **Puerta**

Arrivals **Llegadas**
Originates at this station **Local**
Originates elsewhere; stops if seats available **De Paso**
First (class) **Primera**
Second class **Segunda**
Nonstop **Sin Escala**
Baggage Claim Area **Recibo de Equipajes**
Waiting Room **Sala de Espera**
Toilets **Sanitarios; baños**
Ticket Window **Taquilla**

C Menu Savvy

BREAKFAST (DESAYUNO)

jugo de naranja orange juice
café con crema coffee with cream
pan tostada toast
mermelada jam
leche milk
té tea
huevos eggs
huevos cocidos hard-boiled eggs
huevos poches poached eggs
huevos fritos fried eggs
huevos pasados al agua soft-boiled eggs
huevos revueltos scrambled eggs
tocino bacon
jamón ham

LUNCH AND DINNER

antojitos Mexican snacks
caldo broth
sopa soup
sopa clara consomme
sopa de lentejas lentil soup
sopa de chicharos pea soup
sopa de arroz dry rice (not soup!)
caldo de pollo chicken broth
menudo tripe soup
salchichas sausages
taco filled tortilla
torta sandwich
tamales rusos cabbage rolls

SEAFOOD (MARISCOS)

almejas clams
anchoas anchovies
arenques herring
atún tuna
calamares squid
camarones shrimp

caracoles snails
corvina bass
huachinango red snapper
jaiba crab
langosta lobster
lenguado sole
lobino black bass
mojarra perch
ostiones oysters
pescado fish
pez espada swordfish
robalo sea bass/snook
salmón salmon
salmón ahumado smoked salmon
sardinas sardines
solo pike
trucha arco iris rainbow trout

MEATS (CARNES)

ahumado smoked
alambre shish kebab
albóndigas meatballs
aves poultry
bistec steak
cabeza de ternera calf's head
cabrito kid (goat)
callos tripe
carne meat
carne fría cold cuts
cerdo pork
chiles rellenos stuffed peppers
chicharrones pigskin cracklings
chorizo spicy sausage
chuleta chop
chuleta de carnero mutton chop
chuletas de cordero lamb chops
chuletas de puerco pork chops
conejo rabbit
cordero lamb
costillas de cerdo spareribs
faisán pheasant
filete de ternera filet of veal
filete milanesa breaded veal chops
ganso goose
hígado liver
jamón ham
lengua tongue
lomo loin
paloma pigeon
pato duck

pavo turkey
pechuga chicken breast
perdiz partridge
pierna leg
pollo chicken
res beef
riñones kidneys
ternera veal
tocino bacon
venado venison

VEGETABLES (LEGUMBRES)

aguacate avocado
aceitunas olives
arroz rice
betabeles beets
cebolla onions
champinones mushrooms
chicharos peas
col cabbage
coliflor cauliflower
ejotes string beans
elote (also maiz) corn (maize)
entremeses hors d'oeuvres
esparragos asparagus
espinaca spinach
frijoles beans
hongos mushrooms
jicama potato/turnip-like vegetable
lechuga lettuce
lentejas lentils
papas potatoes
pepino cucumber
rábano radish
tomate tomato
verduras greens, vegetables
zanahorias carrots

SALADS (ENSALADAS)

ensalada de apio celery salad
ensalada de frutas fruit salad
ensalada mixta mixed salad
ensalada de pepinos cucumber salad
guacamole avocado salad
ensalada de lechuga lettuce salad

FRUITS (FRUTAS)

banana banana
chavacano apricot
ciruela prune
coco coconut

durazno peache
frambuesa raspberry
fresas con crema strawberries with cream
fruta cocida stewed fruit
granada pomegranate
guanabana green pear-like fruit
guayaba guava
higos figs
lima lime
limón lemon
mamey sweet orange fruit
mango mango
manzana apple
naranja orange
pera pear
piña pineapple
plátano plantain
tuna prickly pear fruit
uva grape
zapote sweet brown fruit

DESSERTS (POSTRES)

arroz con leche rice pudding
brunelos de fruta fruit tart
coctel de aguacate avocado cocktail
coctel de frutas fruit cocktail
compota stewed fruit
fruta fruit
flan custard
galletas crackers or cookies
helado ice cream
nieve sherbet
pastel cake or pastry
queso cheese
torta cake

BEVERAGES (BEBIDAS)

agua water
aqua mineral mineral water
brandy brandy
café coffee
cafe con crema coffee with cream
café de olla coffee with cinnamon and sugar
café negro black coffee
cerveza beer
gaseosa soft drink
ginebra gin
hielo ice
jerez sherry
jugo de naranja orange juice

jugo de tomate tomato juice
jugo de toronja grapefruit juice
leche milk
licores liqueurs
licuado fruited water or milk
manzanita apple juice
refrescos fruit drinks
ron rum
sidra cider
sifón soda
té tea
vaso de leche glass of milk
vino blanco white wine
vino tinto red wine

CONDIMENTS & CUTLERY

aceite oil
azúcar sugar
bolillo roll
copa goblet
cilantro coriander
cuchara spoon
cuchillo knife
mantequilla butter
manteca lard
mostaza mustard
pan bread
pimienta pepper
sal salt
sopa soup
taza cup
tenedor fork
tostada toast
vinagre vinegar
vaso glass

PREPARATIONS

asado roasted
cocido cooked
bien cocido well done
poco cocido rare
milanesa Italian breaded
empanado breaded
frito fried
al mojo de ajo garlic and butter
a la parrilla grilled
al horno baked
Tampiqueño long strip of thinly sliced meat
Veracruzana tomato, garlic, and onion topped

D Menu Glossary

Achiote Small red seed of the annatto tree.

Achiote preparada A prepared paste found in Yucatán markets made of ground achiote, wheat and corn flour, cumin, cinnamon, salt, onion, garlic, oregano. Mixed with juice of a sour orange or vinegar and put on broiled or charcoaled fish (tikin-chick) and chicken.

Agua fresca Fruit-flavored water, usually watermelon, canteloupe, chia seed with lemon, hibiscus flour, or ground melon seed mixture.

Antojito A Mexican snack, usually masa-based with a variety of toppings such as sausage, cheese, beans, onions; also refers to tostadas, sopes, and garnachas.

Atole A thick, lightly sweet, warm drink made with finely ground rice or corn and usually flavored with vanilla; often found mornings and evenings at markets.

Birria Lamb or goat meat cooked in a tomato broth, spiced with garlic, chiles, cumin, ginger, oregano, cloves, cinnamon, and thyme and garnished with onions, cilantro, and fresh lime juice to taste; a specialty of Jalisco state.

Botana A light snack—an antojito.

Buñelos Round, thin, deep-fried crispy fritters dipped in sugar or dribbled with honey.

Burrito A large flour tortilla stuffed with beans or sometimes potatoes and onions.

Cabrito Grilled kid; a Northern Mexican delicacy.

Cajeta Carmeled cow or goat milk, often used in dessert crêpes.

Carnitas Pork that's been deep-cooked (not fried) in lard, then steamed and served with corn tortillas for tacos.

Ceviche Fresh raw seafood marinated in fresh lime juice and garnished with chopped tomatoes, onions, chiles, and sometimes cilantro and served with crispy, fried whole corn tortillas.

Churro Tube-shaped, bread-like fritter, dipped in sugar and sometimes filled with cajeta or chocolate.

Cilantro An herb grown from the coriander seed chopped and used in salsas and soups.

Chiles rellenos Poblano peppers usually stuffed with cheese, rolled in a batter and baked; but other stuffings may include ground beef spiced with raisins.

Chorizo A spicy red pork sausage, flavored with different chiles and sometimes with achiote or cumin and other spices.

Choyote Vegetable pear or merleton, a type of spiny squash boiled and served as an accompaniment to meat dishes.

Cochinita pibil Pig wrapped in banana leaves, flavored with pibil sauce and pit-baked; common in Yucatán.

Corunda A triangular tamal wrapped in a corn leaf, a Michoacan specialty.

Enchilada Tortilla dipped in a sauce and usually filled with chicken or white cheese and sometimes topped with tomato sauce and sour cream (enchiladas Suizas—Swiss enchiladas) or covered in a green sauce (enchiladas verdes) or topped with onions, sour cream, and guacamole (enchiladas Potosiños).

Epazote Leaf of the wormseed plant, used in black beans and with cheese in quesadillas.

Escabeche A lightly pickled sauce used in Yucatecan chicken stew.

Frijoles charros Beans flavored with beer, a Northern Mexican specialty.

Frijoles refritos Pinto beans mashed and cooked with lard.

Guacamole Mashed avocado, plain or mixed with onions and other spices.

Garnachas A thickish small circle of fried masa with pinched sides, topped with pork or chicken, onions, and avocado or sometimes chopped potatoes, and tomatoes, typical as a botana in Veracruz and Yucatán.

Gorditas Thickish fried-corn tortillas, slit and stuffed with choice of cheese, beans, beef, chicken, with or without lettuce, tomato, and onion garnish.

Gusanos de maguey Maguey worms, considered a delicacy, and delicious when charbroiled to a crisp and served with corn tortillas for tacos.

Horchata Refreshing drink made of ground rice or melon seeds, ground almonds, and lightly sweetened.

Huevos motulenos Eggs atop a tortilla, garnished with beans, peas, ham, sausage, and grated cheese, a Yucatecan specialty.

Huevos mexicanos Scrambled eggs with onions, hot peppers, and tomatoes.

Huevos rancheros Fried egg on top of a fried corn tortilla covered in a tomato sauce.

Huitlacoche Sometimes spelled "cuitlacoche," mushroom-flavored black fungus that appears on corn in the rainy season; considered a delicacy.

Manchamantel Translated means "tablecloth stainer," a stew of chicken or pork with chiles, tomatoes, pineapple, bananas, and jícama.

Machaca Shredded dried beef scrambled with eggs or as salad topping; a specialty of Northern Mexico.

Masa Ground corn soaked in lime used as basis for tamales, corn tortillas, and soups.

Mixiote Lamb baked in a chile sauce or chicken with carrots and potatoes both baked in parchment paper made from the maguey leaf.

Mole Pronounced "moh-lay," a sauce made with 20 ingredientes including chocolate, peppers, ground tortillas, sesame seeds, cinnamon, tomatoes, onion, garlic, peanuts, pumpkin seeds, cloves and tomatillos; developed by colonial nuns in Puebla, usually served over chicken or turkey; especially served in Puebla, State of Mexico, and Oaxaca with sauces varying from red, to black and brown.

Molletes A bolillo cut in half and topped with refried beans and cheese, then broiled; popular at breakfast.

Pan dulce Lightly sweetened bread in many configurations usually served at breakfast or bought at any bakery.

Pan de muerto Sweet or plain bread made around the Days of the Dead (Nov. 1–2), in the form of mummies, dolls, or round with bone designs.

Papadzules Tortillas are stuffed with hard-boiled eggs and seeds (cucumber or sunflower) in a tomato sauce.

Pavo relleno negro Stuffed turkey Yucatán-style, filled with chopped pork and beef, cooked in a rich, dark sauce.

Pibil Pit-baked pork or chicken in a sauce of tomato, onion, mild red pepper, cilantro, and vinegar.

Pipian Sauce made with ground pumpkin seeds, nuts, and mild peppers.

Poc-chuc Slices of pork with onion marinated in a tangy sour orange sauce and charcoal broiled; a Yucatecan specialty.

Pollo calpulalpan Chicken cooked in pulque, a specialty of Tlaxcala.

Pozole A soup made with hominy and pork or chicken, in either a tomato-based broth Jalisco-style, or a white broth Nayarit-style, or green chile sauce Guerrero-style, and topped with choice of chopped white onion, lettuce or cabbage, radishes, oregano, red pepper, and cilantro.

Pulque Drink made of fermented sap of the maguey plant; best in state of Hidalgo and around Mexico City.

Quesadilla Four tortilla stuffed with melted white cheese and lightly fried or warmed.

Rompope Delicious Mexican eggnog, invented in Puebla, made with eggs, vanilla, sugar, and rum.

Salsa mexicana Sauce of fresh chopped tomatoes, white onions, and cilantro with a bit of oil; on tables all over Mexico.

Salsa verde A cooked sauce using the green tomatillo and pureed with mildly hot peppers, onions, garlic, and cilantro; on tables countrywide.

Sopa de calabaza Soup made of chopped squash or pumpkin blossoms.

Sopa de lima A tangy soup made with chicken broth and accented with fresh lime; popular in Yucatán.

Sopa de medula bone marrow soup.

Sopa tlalpeña A hearty soup made with chunks of chicken, chopped carrots, zucchini, corn, onions, garlic, and cilantro.

Sopa tlaxcalteca A hearty tomato-based soup filled with cooked nopal cactus, cheese, cream, and avocado with crispy tortilla strips floating on top.

Sopa tortilla A traditional chicken broth–based soup, seasoned with chiles, tomatoes, onion, and garlic, bobbing with crisp fried strips of corn tortillas.

Sopa tarascan A rib sticking pinto bean–based soup, flavored with onions, garlic, tomatoes, chiles, and chicken broth and garnished with sour cream, white cheese, avocado chunks, and fried tortilla strips; a specialty of Michoacán state.

Sopa seca Not a soup at all, but a seasoned rice which translated means "dry soup."

Sope Pronounced "soh-pay," a botana similar to a garnacha, except spread with refried beans and topped with crumbled cheese and onions.

Tacos al pastor Thin slices of flavored pork roasted on a revolving cylinder dripping with onion slices and juice of fresh pineapple slice.

Tamal Incorrectly called tamale (tamal singular, tamales plural), meat or sweet filling rolled with fresh masa then wrapped in a corn husk, a corn or banana leaf and steamed; many varieties and sizes throughout the country.

Tepache Drink made of fermented pineapple peelings and brown sugar.

Tikin xic Also seen on menus as "tikin chick," char-broiled fish brushed with achiote sauce.

Tinga A stew made with pork tenderloin, sausage, onions, garlic, tomatoes, chiles, and potatoes; popular on menus in Puebla and Hidalgo states.

Torta sandwich, usually on bolillo bread, usually with sliced avocado, onions, tomatoes, with a choice of meat and often cheese.

Torta ahogado A specialty of Lake Chapala is made with scooped out roll, filled with beans and beef strips, and seasoned with either a tomato or chile sauce.

Tostadas Crispy fried corn tortillas topped with meat, onions, lettuce, tomatoes, cheese, avocados, and sometimes sour cream.

Venado Venison (deer) served perhaps as pipian de venado, steamed in banana leaves and served with a sauce of ground squash seeds.

Queso relleno "Stuffed cheese" is a mild yellow cheese stuffed with minced meat and spices, a Yucatecan specialty.

Xtabentun (pronounced "Shtah-ben-toon") a Yucatán liquor made of fermented honey, and flavored with anise. It comes seco (dry) or crema (sweet).

Zacahuil Pork leg tamal, packed in thick masa, wrapped in banana leaves and pit baked; sometimes pot-made with tomato and masa; specialty of mid to upper Veracruz.

E Metric Measures

LENGTH

1 millimeter (mm)	=	0.04 inches (or less than $^1/_{16}$ in.)
1 centimeter (cm)	=	0.39 inches (or under $^1/_2$ in.)
1 meter (m)	=	39 inches (or about 1.1 yd.)
1 kilometer	=	0.62 miles (or about $^2/_3$ of a mile)

To convert kilometers to miles, multiply the number of kilometers by 0.62. Also use to convert kilometers per hour (kmph) to miles per hour (mph).

To convert miles to kilometers, multiply the number of miles by 1.61. Also use to convert from mph to kmph.

CAPACITY

1 liter	=	33.92 fluid ounces	=	2.1 pints
	=	1.06 quarts	=	0.26 U.S. gallons
1 Imperial gallon	=	1.2 U.S. gallons		

To convert liters to U.S. gallons, multiply the number of liters by 0.26.

To convert U.S. gallons to liters, multiply the number of gallons by 3.79.

To convert Imperial gallons to U.S. gallons, multiply the number of Imperial gallons by 1.2.

To convert U.S. gallons to Imperial gallons, multiply the number of U.S. gallons by 0.83.

WEIGHT

1 gram (g)	=	0.035 ounces (or about a paperclip's weight)
1 kilogram (kg)	=	35.2 ounces
1 metric ton	=	2,205 pounds (1.1 short ton)

To convert kilograms to pounds, multiply the number of kilograms by 2.2.

To convert pounds to kilograms, multiply the number of pounds by 0.45.

AREA

1 hectare (a)	=	2.47 acres		
1 square kilometer (km^2)	=	247 acres	=	0.39 square miles

To convert hectares to acres, multiply the number of hectares by 2.47.

INDEX

287

ACCOMMODATIONS

RESTAURANTS

Now Save Money On All Your Travels By Joining FROMMER'S™ TRAVEL BOOK CLUB The World's Best Travel Guides At Membership Prices!

Frommer's Travel Book Club is your ticket to successful travel! Open up a world of travel information and simplify your travel planning when you join ranks with thousands of value-conscious travelers who are members of the Frommer's *Travel Book Club*. Join today and you'll be entitled to all the privileges that come from belonging to the club that offers you travel guides for less to more than 100 destinations worldwide. **Annual membership is only $25.00 (U.S.) or $35.00 (Canada/Foreign).**

The Advantages of Membership:

1. Your choice of **three free** books (any **two** Frommer's Comprehensive Guides, Frommer's $-A-Day Guides, Frommer's Walking Tours or Frommer's Family Guides—plus **one** Frommer's City Guide, Frommer's City $-A-Day Guide or Frommer's Touring Guide).

2. Your own subscription to the **TRIPS & TRAVEL** quarterly newsletter.

3. You're entitled to a **30% discount** on your order of any additional books offered by the club.

4. You're offered (at a small additional fee) our **Domestic Trip-Routing Kits.**

Our **Trips & Travel** quarterly newsletter offers practical information on the best buys in travel, the "hottest" vacation spots, the latest travel trends, world-class events and much, much more.

Our **Domestic Trip-Routing Kits** are available for any North American destination. We'll send you a detailed map highlighting the best route to take to your destination—you can request direct or scenic routes.

Here's all you have to do to join:

Send in your membership fee of $25.00 ($35.00 Canada/Foreign) with your name and address on the form below along with your selections as part of your membership package to the address listed below. Remember to check off your three free books.

If you would like to order additional books, please select the books you would like and send a check for the total amount (please add sales tax in the states noted below), plus $2.00 per book for shipping and handling ($3.00 Canada/Foreign) to the address listed below.

FROMMER'S TRAVEL BOOK CLUB
P.O. Box 473
Mt. Morris, IL 61054-0473
(815) 734-1104

[ ] **YES!** I want to take advantage of this opportunity to join Frommer's Travel Book Club.

[ ] My check is enclosed. Dollar amount enclosed_____ *
(all payments in U.S. funds only)

Name _____

Address _____

City _____ State _____ Zip _____

Phone ( ) _____ (In case we have a question regarding your order).

All orders must be prepaid.

To ensure that all orders are processed efficiently, please apply sales tax in the following areas: CA, CT, FL, IL, IN, NJ, NY, PA, TN, WA and CANADA.

*With membership, shipping & handling will be paid by Frommer's Travel Book Club for the three FREE books you select as part of your membership. Please add $2.00 per book for shipping & handling for any additional books purchased ($3.00 Canada/Foreign).

Allow 4-6 weeks for delivery for all items. Prices of books, membership fee, and publication dates are subject to change without notice. All orders are subject to acceptance and availability.

Please send me the books checked below:

FROMMER'S COMPREHENSIVE GUIDES

*(Guides listing facilities from budget to deluxe,
with emphasis on the medium-priced)*

	Retail Price	Code		Retail Price	Code
☐ Acapulco/Ixtapa/Taxco, 2nd Edition	$13.95	C157	☐ Jamaica/Barbados, 2nd Edition	$15.00	C149
☐ Alaska '94-'95	$17.00	C131	☐ Japan '94-'95	$19.00	C144
☐ Arizona '95 (Avail. 3/95)	$14.95	C166	☐ Maui, 1st Edition	$14.00	C153
☐ Australia '94-'95	$18.00	C147	☐ Nepal, 2nd Edition	$18.00	C126
☐ Austria, 6th Edition	$16.95	C162	☐ New England '95	$16.95	C165
☐ Bahamas '94-'95	$17.00	C121	☐ New Mexico, 3rd Edition (Avail. 3/95)	$14.95	C167
☐ Belgium/Holland/ Luxembourg '93-'94	$18.00	C106	☐ New York State '94-'95	$19.00	C133
☐ Bermuda '94-'95	$15.00	C122	☐ Northwest, 5th Edition	$17.00	C140
☐ Brazil, 3rd Edition	$20.00	C111	☐ Portugal '94-'95	$17.00	C141
☐ California '95	$16.95	C164	☐ Puerto Rico '95-'96	$14.00	C151
☐ Canada '94-'95	$19.00	C145	☐ Puerto Vallarta/ Manzanillo/Guadalajara '94-'95	$14.00	C135
☐ Caribbean '95	$18.00	C148			
☐ Carolinas/Georgia, 2nd Edition	$17.00	C128	☐ Scandinavia, 16th Edition (Avail. 3/95)	$19.95	C169
☐ Colorado, 2nd Edition	$16.00	C143	☐ Scotland '94-'95	$17.00	C146
☐ Costa Rica '95	$13.95	C161	☐ South Pacific '94-'95	$20.00	C138
☐ Cruises '95-'96	$19.00	C150	☐ Spain, 16th Edition	$16.95	C163
☐ Delaware/Maryland '94-'95	$15.00	C136	☐ Switzerland/ Liechtenstein '94-'95	$19.00	C139
☐ England '95	$17.95	C159	☐ Thailand, 2nd Edition	$17.95	C154
☐ Florida '95	$18.00	C152	☐ U.S.A., 4th Edition	$18.95	C156
☐ France '94-'95	$20.00	C132	☐ Virgin Islands '94-'95	$13.00	C127
☐ Germany '95	$18.95	C158	☐ Virginia '94-'95	$14.00	C142
☐ Ireland, 1st Edition (Avail. 3/95)	$16.95	C168	☐ Yucatan, 2nd Edition	$13.95	C155
☐ Italy '95	$18.95	C160			

FROMMER'S $-A-DAY GUIDES

(Guides to low-cost tourist accommodations and facilities)

	Retail Price	Code		Retail Price	Code
☐ Australia on $45 '95-'96	$18.00	D122	☐ Israel on $45, 15th Edition	$16.95	D130
☐ Costa Rica/Guatemala/ Belize on $35, 3rd Edition	$15.95	D126	☐ Mexico on $45 '95	$16.95	D125
			☐ New York on $70 '94-'95	$16.00	D121
☐ Eastern Europe on $30, 5th Edition	$16.95	D129	☐ New Zealand on $45 '93-'94	$18.00	D103
☐ England on $60 '95	$17.95	D128			
☐ Europe on $50 '95	$17.95	D127	☐ South America on $40, 16th Edition	$18.95	D123
☐ Greece on $45 '93-'94	$19.00	D100			
☐ Hawaii on $75 '95	$16.95	D124	☐ Washington, D.C. on $50 '94-'95	$17.00	D120
☐ Ireland on $45 '94-'95	$17.00	D118			

FROMMER'S WALKING TOURS

*(Companion guides that point out the places
and pleasures that make a city unique)*

	Retail Price	Code		Retail Price	Code
☐ Berlin	$12.00	W100	☐ New York	$12.00	W102
☐ Chicago	$12.00	W107	☐ Paris	$12.00	W103
☐ England's Favorite Cities	$12.00	W108	☐ San Francisco	$12.00	W104
☐ London	$12.00	W101	☐ Washington, D.C.	$12.00	W105
☐ Montreal/Quebec City	$12.00	W106			

SPECIAL EDITIONS

	Retail Price	Code		Retail Price	Code
☐ Bed & Breakfast Southwest	$16.00	P100	☐ National Park Guide, 29th Edition	$17.00	P106
☐ Bed & Breakfast Great American Cities	$16.00	P104	☐ Where to Stay U.S.A., 11th Edition	$15.00	P102
☐ Caribbean Hideaways	$16.00	P103			

FROMMER'S TOURING GUIDES

*(Color-illustrated guides that include walking tours,
cultural and historic sites, and practical information)*

	Retail Price	Code		Retail Price	Code
☐ Amsterdam	$11.00	T001	☐ New York	$11.00	T008
☐ Barcelona	$14.00	T015	☐ Rome	$11.00	T010
☐ Brazil	$11.00	T003	☐ Tokyo	$15.00	T016
☐ Hong Kong/Singapore/ Macau	$11.00	T006	☐ Turkey	$11.00	T013
☐ London	$13.00	T007	☐ Venice	$ 9.00	T014

*Please note: If the availability of a book is several months away, we may
have back issues of guides to that particular destination.
Call customer service at (815) 734-1104.*

FROMMER'S CITY $-A-DAY GUIDES

	Retail Price	Code		Retail Price	Code
☐ Berlin on $40 '94-'95	$12.00	D111	☐ Madrid on $50 '94-'95	$13.00	D119
☐ London on $45 '94-'95	$12.00	D114	☐ Paris on $50 '94-'95	$12.00	D117

FROMMER'S FAMILY GUIDES

*(Guides listing information on kid-friendly
hotels, restaurants, activities and attractions)*

	Retail Price	Code		Retail Price	Code
☐ California with Kids	$18.00	F100	☐ San Francisco with Kids	$17.00	F104
☐ Los Angeles with Kids	$17.00	F103	☐ Washington, D.C. with Kids	$17.00	F102
☐ New York City with Kids	$18.00	F101			

FROMMER'S CITY GUIDES

*(Pocket-size guides to sightseeing and tourist
accommodations and facilities in all price ranges)*

	Retail Price	Code		Retail Price	Code
☐ Amsterdam '93-'94	$13.00	S110	☐ Montreal/Quebec City '95	$11.95	S166
☐ Athens, 10th Edition (Avail. 3/95)	$12.95	S174	☐ Nashville/Memphis, 1st Edition	$13.00	S141
☐ Atlanta '95	$12.95	S161	☐ New Orleans '95	$12.95	S148
☐ Atlantic City/Cape May, 5th Edition	$13.00	S130	☐ New York '95	$12.95	S152
☐ Bangkok, 2nd Edition	$12.95	S147	☐ Orlando '95	$13.00	S145
☐ Barcelona '93-'94	$13.00	S115	☐ Paris '95	$12.95	S150
☐ Berlin, 3rd Edition	$12.95	S162	☐ Philadelphia, 8th Edition	$12.95	S167
☐ Boston '95	$12.95	S160	☐ Prague '94-'95	$13.00	S143
☐ Budapest, 1st Edition	$13.00	S139	☐ Rome, 10th Edition	$12.95	S168
☐ Chicago '95	$12.95	S169	☐ St. Louis/Kansas City, 2nd Edition	$13.00	S127
☐ Denver/Boulder/Colorado Springs, 3rd Edition	$12.95	S154	☐ San Diego '95	$12.95	S158
☐ Dublin, 2nd Edition	$12.95	S157	☐ San Francisco '95	$12.95	S155
☐ Hong Kong '94-'95	$13.00	S140	☐ Santa Fe/Taos/ Albuquerque '95 (Avail. 2/95)	$12.95	S172
☐ Honolulu/Oahu '95	$12.95	S151	☐ Seattle/Portland '94-'95	$13.00	S137
☐ Las Vegas '95	$12.95	S163	☐ Sydney, 4th Edition	$12.95	S171
☐ London '95	$12.95	S156	☐ Tampa/St. Petersburg, 3rd Edition	$13.00	S146
☐ Los Angeles '95	$12.95	S164	☐ Tokyo '94-'95	$13.00	S144
☐ Madrid/Costa del Sol, 2nd Edition	$12.95	S165	☐ Toronto '95 (Avail. 3/95)	$12.95	S173
☐ Mexico City, 1st Edition	$12.95	S170	☐ Vancouver/Victoria '94-'95	$13.00	S142
☐ Miami '95-'96	$12.95	S149	☐ Washington, D.C. '95	$12.95	S153
☐ Minneapolis/St. Paul, 4th Edition	$12.95	S159			